An Enlarged Europe

Regions in Competition?

Regional Policy and Development series

Retreat from the Regions
Corporate Change and the Closure of Factories
Stephen Fothergill and Nigel Guy
ISBN 1 85302 101 6 hb
ISBN 1 85302 100 8 pb
Regional Policy and Development 1

Spatial Policy in a Divided Nation
Edited by Richard T. Harrison and Mark Hart
ISBN 1 85302 076 1
Regional Policy and Development 2

Regional Development in the 1990s
The British Isles in Transition
Edited by Peter Townroe and Ron Martin
ISBN 1 85302 139 3
Regional Policy and Development 4

Sustainable Cities
Graham Haughton and Colin Hunter
ISBN 1 85302 234 9
Regional Policy and Development 7

The Regional Dimension of Transformation in Central Europe
Grzegorz Gorzelak
ISBN 1 85302 301 9
Regional Policy and Development 10

The Regional Imperative
Regional Planning and Governance in Britain,
Europe and the United States
Urlan A. Wannop
ISBN 1 85302 292 6
Regional Policy and Development 9

An Enlarged Europe

Regions in Competition?

Edited by Sally Hardy, Mark Hart,
Louis Albrechts and Anastasios Katos

Regional Studies Association

Jessica Kingsley Publishers
London and Bristol, Pennsylvania

Regional Studies Association
London

First published in the United Kingdom in 1995 by
Jessica Kingsley Publishers Ltd
116 Pentonville Road
London N1 9JB, England
and
1900 Frost Road, Suite 101
Bristol, PA 19007, U S A

and Regional Studies Assocation (Registered Charity 252269)

Copyright © 1995 Regional Studies Association and Jessica Kingsley Publishers

Library of Congress Cataloging in Publication Data
A CIP catalogue record for this book is available from the Library of Congress

British Library Cataloguing in Publication Data
A CIP catalogue record for this book is available from the British Library

ISBN 1-85302-188-1

Printed and Bound in Great Britain by
Cromwell Press, Melksham, Wiltshire

Contents

List of Tables

List of Figures

Acknowledgements

This collection of papers originates from the Greek Halkidiki conference organised under the auspices of the Regional Studies Association's European Urban and Regional Research Network (EURRN) held in September 1991. An enormous debt is owed to all those who enabled the success of that event. In particular, we would like to thank for their financial support the European Commission (under the ACE programme), the British Council in Thessaloniki and the Bank of Macedonia. Furthermore, invaluable administrative support was provided by ICBS and the University of Macedonia in Thessaloniki as well as the Department of Applied Economics at the University of Ulster in Northern Ireland. However, we would like to say a personal thank-you to Rigas Tzelepoglou (President of ICBS), his assistant Margaret Stanino and Tasos Katos (one of the co-editors of this volume) for providing a constant source of encouragement in the period leading up to the conference. The time spent at the Porto Carras complex in Halkidiki was made all the more memorable by the very generous welcome extended to the delegates by the Carras family.

The production of an edited volume is never an easy task and we would like to take this opportunity to thank all of those involved. The multitude of editorial changes and the production of the final copy was handled with a great deal of skill by the three secretaries in the Department of Applied Economics: Beverly Coulter, Sharon McCullough and Pamela King. Finally, the diagrams were all redrawn by Ian Alexander at the University of Ulster in his usual professional manner.

Part One

Introduction

CHAPTER 1

Economic Change in the Regions of Europe

Mark Hart and Sally Hardy

Background

The decade of the 1990s was seen by many observers as an important watershed in the history of the European Union (EU). The push towards greater European integration with the launch of the Single European Market (SEM) programme in 1985 provided the stimulus for a wide-ranging debate throughout the member states of the EC concerning the ways in which the internal and external relationships of the Community would be radically altered in the final years of the 20th century. With the 'delivery date' set for the creation of the SEM at the end of 1992 there was general agreement that the resultant changes would have a profound impact on the 12 nation states of the EU and their peoples.

However, there was considerably less consensus on the exact nature of these impacts in terms of their sectoral and spatial scale, and also the pace with which they would begin to take effect. Consequently, the inexorable move towards '1992' was regularly punctuated with the latest predictions on the 'winners' and 'losers' from the creation of the Single Market. The constant overlapping of economic, political and social debates added further to the confusion concerning the outcomes of the SEM. In essence, the inability to disentangle fact from fiction heightened the general awareness of the SEM and as a result January 1993 was regarded as being the most significant date in the history of the EU since the signing of the Treaty of Rome in 1957.

As the debates raged over the potential impacts of the SEM events elsewhere in Europe further marked the 1990s as a major pivotal decade. The remarkable political and economic collapse and subsequent transformation of the former communist nations of East and Central Europe, and in particular the former Soviet Union, has unquestionably presented the Western world with one of the greatest challenges of the 1990s. These largely unforeseen events, and the pace with which they have occurred, have taken most observers completely by surprise. Thus, as the EU moved towards the creation of the SEM the rapidly changing context further East threw into disarray many of the predicted scenarios associated with greater integration. The unification of both Germanies and the more general westward orientation of the East European countries has created tensions in the 'European Economic Space' which demand an immediate response.

Another pressure on the developments of the EU of twelve is its enlargement by the demands of some EFTA countries to gain entry. In total four countries entered into negotiations to join the EU (Austria, Finland, Norway and Sweden). At the time of writing the negotiations with the four countries have been completed and, with the exception of Norway, were ratified by national referenda in 1994.

Against this backdrop of rapid and radical change, which will clearly have a profound effect upon the future internal and external relationships of the EU, a particular concern emerged regarding the spatial impact of the various processes associated with these changes. To what extent would the long-standing pattern of regional disparities within the EU be ameliorated with the move towards greater European integration, as signalled by the creation of the SEM and the admission of additional member states? Many commentators and experts (e.g. Cecchini 1988, Delors 1989) paid either scant attention to the spatial effects or simply assumed that the trickle-down effects of European economic growth associated with the creation of the SEM would lead automatically to regional convergence. However, more recently an increasing number of studies have emphasised the complexity of the regional impact of the SEM. Indeed, a theme issue of *Regional Studies*, the house journal of the Regional Studies Association, was devoted to the theme of 1992 and regional development (Bachtler and Clement 1992). The common message to emerge from these studies is that there is an even greater need for a better targeted and resourced regional policy in the wake of 1992 than ever before.

In contrast to this relatively ordered and self-inflicted integration process within the EU the radical, and as some would argue catastrophic, restructuring of the East European economies will potentially have a significant, if as yet largely unknown, effect upon the spatial order in the EU and the broader 'European Economic Space'. At a very basic level tensions are beginning to manifest themselves in the greater competition between the economic regions of Europe as they each seek to restructure and increase their potential for economic growth. The capacity of a larger and unified European market to provide such a level of growth remains a moot point in the mid-1990s.

Thus, the regional effects of both West and East European integration processes are occupying the minds of researchers and policy-makers alike as they attempt to understand and counteract the trends towards greater regional divergence. There is an urgent need to develop an overall strategy for the transition process in order to efficiently allocate the associated resource requirements.

As a consequence of these events in Europe the Regional Studies Association, under the auspices of its European Urban and Regional Research Network (EURRN), organised a major international conference at Porto Carras in Halkidiki, Northern Greece, towards the end of 1991 to consider the theme of 'An Enlarged Europe: Regions in Competition?' This volume is a result of that conference and contains many of the contributions presented at the conference in addition to three specially commissioned chapters to address some of the broader issues in the integration process.

Structure of the Book

It should be stated at the outset that the emphasis in the vast majority of the contributions to this volume is primarily on the economic agenda associated with European integration and regional development. That is not to say that the social and political agendas associated with the SEM, enlargement and the restructuring of the East European economies are any less important, but simply a recognition of one of the major areas of interest within the research community in the early 1990s.

The book is organised into four parts. Part One contains three chapters each reflecting the three aspects of the European integration process outlined above. The first, by Hall and Van der Wee, provides an overview of the performance of the Community's regions and discusses the characteristics of EU regional policies and their potential for readjustment in the 1990s. This is followed by two general essays on the rapidly changing spatial structures in Europe. Albrechts considers a range of likely outcomes resulting from the shifts in orientation of cities and regions across Europe, while Horváth focuses specifically on the economic reforms in Central and Eastern Europe and their implications for the EU.

Part Two contains a number of contributions which reflect upon various regional aspects of the EU in the post-1992 period. Quévit opens the discussion with a detailed account of the regional impact of the achievement of the SEM and draws attention to the particular problems of the less-favoured regions in achieving substantial benefits from the integration process.

Newlands provides an important contribution to the debate on the increasingly popular demand for regional government throughout the EU by considering in some detail the precise economic role that regional governments can, or should be permitted to, develop. As he correctly points out, there has been almost a dearth in the literature on the theoretical arguments concerning the possible economic functions of regional governments. Hart and Roberts continue the focus on the nature of regional government by reviewing the implications of the SEM for local and regional authorities and how they might successfully respond to such a rapidly changing environment.

Danson reminds us that the regional impact of the SEM should not solely be constrained to a consideration of differential economic performance, but should include analysis of the spatial effects of the social dimension contained within the Social Chapter. Using the traditional, industrialised peripheral regions as examples, and in particular his work on the East End of Glasgow, he demonstrates how the policies and programmes of the Social Chapter may impact upon these areas compared to other more prosperous regions in the EU.

There follow two chapters on perhaps one of the most talked about dimensions of the SEM – the process of European financial integration. Leyshon and Thrift provide a wide-ranging and detailed review and analysis of the move towards European Monetary Union (EMU) and the search for monetary stability. An important aspect of this discussion is the assessment of the likely regional impacts of EMU. Begg augments this analysis by concentrating on the sectoral effects of the completion of the SEM, and in particular the fortunes of the financial services sector and its regional distribution.

The final three chapters in Part Two focus on aspects of public policy within the EU. MacKay addresses the implication of European integration on the future scale and orientation of regional support in the light of continued, and perhaps widening, regional divergence. Barnett and Borooah focus their attention on the Structural Funds and the question of additionality. They critically discuss the procedures adopted by the Commission to assess whether expenditure is truly additional. Finally, Fothergill looks at RECHAR, one of the EU's special programmes, and evaluates its adequacy in dealing with the problems facing the coal areas throughout the EU.

Part Three contains four chapters and concentrates on an assessment of the transformation process in the East European countries. The first two chapters look in detail at the former Soviet Union and provide an interesting assessment of how free-market ideologies may be hindering the development of an appropriate response to the severe regional disparities which exist. Ozornoy provides a more overtly political economy approach in documenting the pattern of spatial inequality in the Gorbachev era, while Dmitrieva concentrates on analysing in some detail the exact nature of the regional industrial structure within the former Soviet Union. Hungary is the focus of the chapter by De Souza and Korompai as they seek to assess the regional impact of a country undergoing rapid transformation. The emphasis in all these contributions is the apparent downgrading of the regional dimension by the various governments in the early stages of the reform process. The final chapter in this section, by Nikas, assesses the potential impact on labour mobility between Eastern and Western Europe of the reform of the former East European economies.

The final section of the book examines in more detail the specific problems of the peripheral regions and nations of the EU as they undergo the process of adjustment in the period after the completion of the SEM. The examples chosen are Northern Greece, Portugal and Ireland and together they provide important perspectives on the nature of the restructuring processes taking place and the desired public policy response of both national and EU governments.

Bachtler, in the concluding chapter of the book, draws together the analysis and arguments of all the contributors and sets out in some detail the policy agenda confronting the EU in the decade of the 1990s. In particular, he attempts to 'translate' the various approaches and results of the previous chapters into a synthesis that can be readily understood by policy-makers seeking to grapple with the appropriate responses to European integration in its widest sense.

References

Bachtler, J. and Clement, K. (1992) '1992 and Regional Development' *Regional Studies 26*, 4, 305–306.

Cecchini, P. (1988) *The European Challenge: 1992, The Benefits of the Single European Market.* Aldershot, Hants: Wildwood House.

Delors, J. (1989) 'Regional implications of economic and monetary integration.' Report on Economic and Monetary Union in the European Community, collection of papers submitted to Committee for the Study of Economic and Monetary Union, CEC, Brussels.

CHAPTER 2

The Regions in an Enlarged Europe

Ronnie Hall and Mik van der Wee[1]

Introduction

The European Community is set on a course towards greater integration during the 1990s. This will be a process of great significance for the regions, especially if it binds the Member States into a single currency area by the end of the decade as foreseen under the Maastricht Treaty. In recognition of these challenges the European Community plans to transfer nearly 160 billion ecu (1992 prices) to the weaker Member States and regions over the period 1994 to 1999. These resources represent a considerable vote of confidence in a regional policy which has only effectively existed at the Community level since 1989.

This chapter begins with a brief consideration of what these regional policies are and how the regions which they benefit have performed since their introduction. The chapter considers the challenges ahead for the next period, in particular those arising as a result of the process of 'deepening' – especially the move towards a single currency – and as a result of the process of 'widening' as the Community prepares to admit the first new members since 1986 while entering into close cooperation with its neighbours in the former centrally-planned economies of Central and Eastern Europe.

Regional Policy at the Community Level

Regional policies conceived and implemented at supranational level for the European Community date from the decisions in 1988 which led to the reform of

---

1   The views expressed in this chapter are not necessarily those of the European Commission.

the Structural Funds. The 1988 reforms were the beginning of a genuine Community regional policy since interventions in this field prior to then were essentially actions by the Community in support of nationally-determined regional policy objectives. There was no such thing as a Community vision of what constituted Community regional problems.

All of this changed in 1988. The results of this change are well known and have been written up extensively elsewhere (see for example, European Commission 1989, 1990). In brief, under the reforms three regional development priorities ('objectives') were identified to be tackled at the Community level. The objectives reflected a typological approach to regional problems. Each problem-type had its own set of criteria determining eligibility and its own set of priorities for the actions to promote regional growth and development.[2] These regional objectives were designed to assist:

1. Regions whose development is lagging behind (Objective 1). The standard condition of eligibility for Objective 1 was that a region had to have a GDP per head less than 75% of the Community average.

2. Traditional industrial regions undergoing restructuring (Objective 2). Eligibility was determined mainly according to quantitative labour market criteria: unemployment rate, rate of industrial employment, industrial job losses.

3. Rural problem areas (Objective 5b). These were determined according to a mixture of quantitative and qualitative criteria, mostly relating to relative dependence on a declining agricultural sector.

In all, some 125 million people were covered by these regional objectives with just over half of them – 70 million – living in areas eligible for Objective 1 which were allocated nearly 65% of the total resources of 70 billion ecu (1992 prices) available for the planning period 1989–93.

The immediate reason for the introduction of the 1988 reforms was the agreement by the Member States which led to the amendment of the Treaty of Rome by the Single European Act in 1986. This paved the way for the completion of the Single Market removing barriers to the free movement of people, goods, services and capital across the Member States' national frontiers. The specific aim of the reforms was to enhance the competitiveness of the weaker regions so that they too could share in the anticipated benefits of the frontier-free market.

The Single Market and the Regions

The view that the freedoms embodied in the Single Market would unleash a new wave of economic activity and growth was, in fact, by no means universally shared by economists and, as Molle (1992) has argued, the political decision to proceed

---

2   Regulation (EC) no. 2052/88, Articles 8 and 9; Regulation (EC) no. 4253/88, Article 4.

with the programme flew in the face of much of the economic advice circulating at the time. How, then, has the Community's economy, and more specifically how have its regions, performed in the light of the progressive introduction of the measures associated with the Single Market and accompanying policies to improve the competitiveness of the regions?

The Commission's own estimations of the effects of the Single Market Programme, *ex ante*, foresaw the raising of Community GDP by 4 to 5% over the medium-term, and the creation of nearly two million new jobs. Unfortunately, it is still too early for a definitive *ex post* assessment of the macroeconomic effects of the Single Market Programme. In fact, it is difficult to choose a base year from which to consider the impact of the Single Market because there is evidence that even before the Single Act was agreed businesses were already adopting strategies in anticipation (Cegos-Idet 1989). For purposes of illustration, however, the following analysis considers how the Member States and regions have performed in the second half of the 1980s compared with the first half. The data support the view that there was indeed a considerable improvement in certain key respects. Thus GDP in the Community as a whole expanded by 16% in volume terms in the five-year period from 1985–1989 (inclusive) compared with 6% in the previous five-year period. Employment meanwhile expanded by nearly 7% in the second half of the 1980s compared with a fall of nearly 2% over the previous five years.[3]

There can be no simple relationship between this improvement and the effects of the Single Market. The changes of the 1980s have much to do with the effects of the business cycle and the gradual emergence of the Community's economy from world recession at the beginning of the decade, a recovery which was prolonged by the investment boom following German unification. Nevertheless, the survey evidence coming from producers themselves in the Member States suggests that the Single Market programme was on balance having a positive impact on business confidence. In one such survey, taking in 9000 enterprise managers throughout the Community, only one in six believed that the dangers of an increasingly competitive market place overshadowed the opportunities (Ifo 1990). Further evidence also comes from the foreign direct investment flows to the Community, much of which appears to have been motivated by the desire to sell to, and produce in, the world's largest marketplace. Between 1985 and 1989, the inflow of such investment to the EC increased five-fold from 5.1 billion to 27.6 billion ecu per year. By comparison over the same period EC investments abroad merely doubled, from 15.1 billion to 32.9 billion ecu per year (Eurostat 1992).

Regarding the distribution of the benefits of more rapid economic growth between Member States and between regions, the recent statistical evidence on the performance of the weakest parts of the Community is relatively encouraging. At

---

3   These data are derived from the Annual Economic Reports of the European Commission.

the level of the Member States, the evidence suggests that the four weakest countries – Spain, Portugal, Greece and Ireland – together grew in line with the Community average over the five-year period 1980–84. In the next five-year period to 1989, however, they achieved growth considerably ahead of the rest of the Community, recording a volume increase of 21%. As a result, the four less-developed countries have converged on the GDP per head obtaining else-where. In particular, there has been a marked improvement in GDP per head in Spain (which has been an important net recipient of direct investment from other Member States), Portugal and Ireland since the mid-1980s relative to the rest of the Community.[4] The same is not true, however, of Greece where GDP per head has been diverging from that of the rest of the Community.

In the period since 1989, the European economy has gone into recession with growth falling from 2.8% in 1990 to 1.4% in 1991 and to 1.1% in 1992. This has affected all of the Community's Member States although the four less developed countries have been able to maintain growth equal to or above the average. Greece in 1992 attained a growth rate (1.5%) which was above the Community average for the first time since 1985.

In relation to employment, the four weakest Member States experienced a drop of over 4% in the first half of the 1980s but a 10% increase in the second half.[5] Whilst some of the weakest regions of the Community in terms of GDP per head are also those with the highest unemployment rates (especially Ireland, the Spanish regions and the Mezzogiorno in Italy), and therefore those with the greatest needs in terms of employment creation, they are also in need of growth in productivity to increase the underlying competitiveness of their economic base. These conflict-ing needs in the weaker regions appear to have been resolved in the second half of the 1980s by rapid growth (in most cases) outstripping productivity growth and permitting employment to rise.

These latter years also represent the period when the Structural Funds began to impact on the weakest regions. Here, studies of the European Commission (1992a) estimate that the contribution of the Structural Funds to the performance of the weaker regions was to increase annual growth rate in Portugal by 0.7% per annum and by 0.5% per annum in Greece (while for other Objective 1 regions the increase is of the order of 0.3%).

The data for Member States allow a relatively up-to-date assessment of economic performance. At the level of individual regions of the Community, the time-series data are subject to a lag of two years and cover the period up to 1990. Nevertheless, these data are useful for an appreciation of the differences in performance between regions in the Member States (see Table 2.1).

---

4   Annual Economic Reports of the European Commission.
5   Annual Economic Reports of the European Commission.

Table 2.1 GDP (in purchasing-power standards)
EC-12 = 100 (excluding ex-GDR)

	1985	1988	1989	1990	88/90 average
Greece	51	49	49	47	48
Spain					
Galicia	55	56	57	58	57
Asturias	73	71	73	74	73
Catilla y León	67	67	69	69	68
Catilla-la-Mancha	57	62	63	64	63
Extremadura	48	47	48	48	48
Comunidad Valecniana	73	74	75	76	75
Andalucía	54	56	56	57	56
Murcia	63	70	71	71	71
Ceuta y Melilla	65	60	61	61	61
Canarias	68	74	75	75	75
Total Objective 1	61	63	64	64	64
France					
Corse	82	81	82	82	82
Départements d' Outre-Mer	–	44 (1986)	–	–	–
Total Objective 1	–	–	–	–	–
Ireland	62	62	65	68	65
Italy					
Campania	70	66	66	66	66
Abruzzi	89	88	88	88	88
Molise	78	79	79	79	79
Puglia	71	73	73	72	73
Basilicata	66	62	62	62	62
Calabria	62	57	57	56	57
Sicilia	69	68	68	68	68
Sardegna	76	75	75	74	75
Total Objective 1	70	69	69	69	69
Portugal	51	54	55	56	55
United Kingdom					
Northern Ireland	78	77	77	74	76
Objective 1 average (excluding French overseas departments)	62	62	62	63	62
Other regions average	110	110	110	110	110

Of particular interest is the performance of the Objective 1 regions which are those most challenged by the competitive pressures released under the Single Market Programme, while as indicated they have been subject since 1989 to substantial Community programmes of assistance to improve their economic competitiveness. It is possible to divide the Objective 1 regions into three groups according to their performance relative to the Community as a whole. The first group comprises those most favourably placed, i.e. growing faster than the Community average between 1985 and 1990; these comprise most, but not all, of the Spanish Objective 1 regions, Ireland and Portugal. A second group comprises those which have experienced a decline in GDP per head relative to the Community average over the period and includes Greece, Ceuta y Melilla (Spain), four (or half) of the Italian Objective 1 regions and Northern Ireland (UK). The third group are those which could be said to have experienced little or no change over the period *vis-à-vis* the rest of the Community: Extremadura (Spain), Corsica (France) and the remaining Italian Objective 1 regions.

Unfortunately, it has to be admitted that we are some way from a full understanding of the reasons underlying the differences in performance between the regions. From economic theory we know a great deal about the necessary conditions for economic development in the regions, but we seem to know less about the sufficient conditions. Thus, conventional economic theory tends to point to deficiencies in human capital endowments or underequipment in modern infrastructures such as transport, telecommunications and energy as important determinants of regional development over the longer term. However, even the most ambitious policy of education and training and infrastructural investment to bridge the gaps in the weaker regions cannot ensure more rapid economic growth. According to Biehl (1986) '...the conditions for the successful use of infrastructure as an instrument for development purposes must be considered carefully'. Perhaps what is lacking from the traditional approach is a fuller understanding of the regional development process in terms of the way in which resources become mobilised. By its nature, this might suggest a multidisciplinary approach – which appeared to go out of fashion in the 1980s – using not only the insights of economics but also those of the other social sciences. Alternatively, we may be forced to conclude that the problem is simply one whereby the specificities of individual regional problems limit the scope for a viable general theory of regional development.

The implicit recognition of the mobilisation factor in Community regional development programmes could be said to be represented by the partnership arrangements whereby regional and local actors are given a key role in the decision-making and management associated with the development programmes. With the additional emphasis in Community policies on the principle of subsidiarity, the partnerships between the Community and the regional and local level will feature prominently for the next period while the institutional provision under the Maastricht Treaty for a Committee of the Regions will strengthen the bottom-up approach to regional development. This political faith in a devolved approach to regional development remains largely unbacked by a systematic intellectual conception of the role of social groups and institutions in the regional development process. In that sense, the policy agenda and the academic research agenda may be out of phase analogous to the situation which prevailed on the issue of the Single Market as described by Molle.

Regional Prospects and Policy 1994–1999

The context for the Community's regional and other policies over the rest of the decade is that of the moves towards greater integration. Specifically, in December 1991 the Community's governments signed the Maastricht Treaty, seeking to broaden and in some cases to deepen the range of issues which could be subject to shared decision-making. Of particular significance for regional policy, the new Treaty recognised the need for cohesion as a basic condition for further economic and social progress. Cohesion would no longer be viewed as an accompanying measure to the completion of the internal market, as in the past, but as an integral component of the Community's political, economic and social development.

It was the role of the European Commission to translate the ambitions of the Maastricht Treaty into concrete proposals for action in the course of the 1990s. Faced with the ongoing challenges presented by the Single Market, and the new challenges of full economic and monetary union and the adoption of a single currency by the end of the decade at the latest, the Commission's proposals – the Delors II package (European Commission 1992b) called for a significant increase in resources especially for structural actions to promote economic and social cohesion.

In the event, the Delors II recommendations for the level of resources for policies to promote cohesion found widespread acceptance in the Member States even without the framework of the Maastricht Treaty, which remained unratified when the Member States took their decision on future financing.[6] In consequence, the Community will have at its disposal over 21 billion ecu for structural policies in 1993 rising by 41% to nearly 30 billion ecu in 1999 (see Table 2.2).

The new financial perspectives effectively remove an important element of uncertainty over the development of the Community for the rest of this decade. In terms of regional policy, they provide the essential basis upon which to determine the beneficiaries and, eventually, the financial allocations. As agreed by the Council of Ministers in Edinburgh the principal objectives of regional policy will remain the same but with an increasing concentration of resources on the weakest regions. By 1999, the share of the Structural Funds (including the

---

6   For the new Cohesion Fund, destined for Member States with GNP per head less than 90%
    of the Community average, in the absence of the legal basis created by the Maastricht Treaty,
    a temporary instrument has had to be created.

Cohesion Fund) going to the four weakest Member States will rise to nearly 70% of the total available (from slightly less than 65% during the period 1989–1993 inclusive).

Table 2.2 Community Resources 1993–1999 (ecu bn, 1992 prices)

	1993		1996		1999	
	ecu	*%*	*ecu*	*%*	*ecu*	*%*
Agriculture	35.2	50.9	36.4	48.4	38.4	45.7
Structural actions	21.3	30.8	25.0	33.2	30.0	35.7
(Cohesion fund	*1.5*	*2.2*	*2.3*	*3.1*	*2.6*	*3.1)*
(Structural funds	*19.8*	*28.6*	*22.7*	*30.2*	*27.4*	*32.6)*
Internal policies	3.9	5.6	4.5	6.0	5.1	6.1
External action	4.0	5.8	4.6	6.1	5.6	6.7
Other	4.8	6.9	4.8	6.4	5.0	5.9
Total commitments*	69.2	100	75.2	100	84.1	100
Total payment appropriations	65.9		71.3		80.1	
% Community GNP (EUR (12))	1.2		1.21		1.26	

* Total commitments relate to the legal obligation undertaken by the Community even if the total payment appropriations are not undertaken in the period indicated.

In accordance with the subsidiarity principle, it is for the Member States to propose the development priorities for their regions for the next period beginning in January 1994. It is the role of the Commission to ensure that the resources are used effectively to promote catching up in the weaker regions so that real economic convergence accompanies the nominal convergence which would be required for successful European Monetary Union (EMU) as prescribed under the Maastricht Treaty. Real convergence needs to be understood in terms of eliminating differences in competitivity and not simply in terms of reducing gaps in standards of living, although the latter will be important if EMU is to achieve widespread acceptance among the Community's population.

In the absence of independent budgetary and monetary policies under EMU, such a strengthening of the competitive position of the weaker Member States and regions is essential to build up their resistance to economic shocks. This is especially important in view of the lower propensity to migrate of Community citizens compared with their counterparts in, for example, the USA. Fluctuations in demand in the economies of the Member States and regions are less likely to provoke migration of labour which help to restore regional equilibria (Delors 1989). This may change over time although whether migration on a significant scale is to be welcomed is another matter since it would probably lead to greater congestion in some of the Community's traditionally prosperous regions and the under-utilisation of social overhead capital in the regions losing population.

There is therefore a heavy responsibility falling on the ensuing generation of economic development strategies ('Community Support Frameworks') to ensure that a firm foundation is provided for catching up to be achieved. In making the best use of the increased resources, attention will need to be given to those regions which on the evidence presented above seem to be falling further behind the rest of the Community (as well as to the very specific problems of the economies in transition in the new German Länder). It is clear that the situation of this group of regions calls for further reflection on the causes of poor regional economic performance.

The Commission's particular contribution to this reflection is to bring to bear the kind of information and experience to the preparation of the next generation of development programmes which regions have most difficulty in obtaining for themselves. In other words, the Commission is well placed to provide information on developments at the transregional level. In this way, regions can set their ambitions in a comparative perspective, providing targets for their efforts to improve their infrastructures, human resource endowments, etc. both in terms of the levels achieved elsewhere and, just as important, the input cost of their delivery.

The Commission also has an important role to play in a number of other areas, beyond those directly associated with the regional development programmes to be co-financed by the Community, which have at the same time a crucial bearing on the effort to promote real convergence. For example, there are the issues relating to national regional policy through which resources are transferred within Member States. In the richer Member States these resources are of considerably greater significance than those under the Community's budget. For example, the level of such aids per capita in Germany, Italy (Centre and North), the United Kingdom and France is five times that in Portugal, Greece, Ireland, and the less-favoured areas of Spain (Marques 1992).

There are also general transfers arising in the pursuit of particular sectoral objectives – such as the promotion of research and development – which have a differential impact on the regions which is not well documented at the national level. Taking into account all aids, national expenditures in the Community between 1988 and 1990 averaged an estimated 89 billion ecu (about 2% of total Community GDP) with some 36 billion ecu going to the manufacturing sector. Such policies at the national level have a clear impact on cohesion and yet we are still some way from a clear understanding of the effects on the regions of all of the various forms of transfer – the 'net' regional policy.

State aids at national level are an obvious example of a field which has a bearing on efforts to promote economic and social cohesion at the Community level. The cohesion dimension is therefore an important consideration in Community competition policies. But there are many other common policies – internal as well as external – where it is crucial that the effects on regional prospects are taken into account.

The Community's other internal policies concern such fields as RTD, and agriculture (the latter still absorbing as much as 50% of the Community budget in 1993 although falling to 46% in 1999 – see Table 2.2). All such policies have regional effects. These can sometimes be positive for the weaker regions, but equally they can be negative. Consider, for purposes of illustration, the Community's RTD policy. For many years, the Community has supported the R&D efforts of European companies to help them in the critically important task of becoming more competitive on world markets. But most of the R&D establishments are located in the central and more developed regions. As a result, the major share of resources provided under these RTD programmes goes to the richer regions. For example, of the 4500 participants in the EC programmes in this field over the period 1988–1990 few were located in southern Europe (especially Portugal and Greece). Almost uniquely among the lagging regions was the high share of such programmes in Ireland. In general, however, it seems inevitable that the RTD policy of the Community would tend to contribute to maintaining the divisions in RTD capacity between the regions and, in all probability, to a widening of the knowledge gap between the developed and less developed areas. This is clearly in conflict with the objective of cohesion. For this reason it is important that the possible negative regional effects of the Community's other policies are reduced to a minimum or, more positively, that these policies are designed in a way which benefits the weaker regions as well. In the RTD field, for example, there might be an emphasis on the regional diffusion of technical innovation.

A second set of challenges to the Community's regions derives from the international context and the Community's policies in the external field. In particular, there are the consequences of the process of enlargement of the Community and what might be regarded as its interim phases: the formation of the European Economic Area (EEA) and the Europe Agreements with the other countries of Central and Eastern Europe. A further issue concerns the conclusions of the Uruguay Round of the General Agreement on Tariffs and Trade (GATT).

In relation to GATT, at the time of writing it is too early to speculate on the likely outcome of negotiations, although the consequences of failure are well recognised. In particular, some of the areas figuring in disputes between the USA and the Community agricultural subsidies and steel production could have damaging consequences for many of the weaker regions. Reduced opportunities for agricultural trade would add to the problems of rural economies already attempting to adjust to the reduction of Community food surpluses. The imposition of tariffs on Community steel would hit further an industry which is already attempting to reduce capacity and which on some estimates may need to shed 50–100,000 jobs (*The Economist* 1993), with severe consequences for many traditional regions undergoing restructuring. The need for an orderly growth in world trade through a new agreement is all the more important in a world economy in recession.

In relation to the admission of new members, the Edinburgh agreement could probably be regarded as a watershed in the Community's development in regard to the dual objectives of 'deepening' (increasing the integration and solidarity of the existing Member States) and 'widening' (enlargement). This agreement combined with the ratification of the Maastricht Treaty would represent a major step towards deepening. The focus of attention can then move to widening the Community to accommodate the growing number of candidate governments requesting membership.

What would be the dimensions of an enlarged European Community? At the time of writing, the applications for membership which are most advanced are those of Sweden, Austria and Finland with other EFTA countries – Norway and Switzerland – following behind. For Sweden, Austria and Finland the deadline is 1995 although experience of previous successful negotiations indicates that the period can vary considerably (for Spain and Portugal: 6/7 years; for Greece: around 18 months).[7] Looking beyond these countries, many others in Central and Eastern Europe seem firmly committed to membership of the Community at least by the end of the decade. These countries view the 'Europe Agreements' which they have concluded with the Community as an interim step towards this goal. A tentative assessment of the cumulative effect on Community population and its economic capacity of adhesion of only four of these countries (and bearing in mind that there are others such as Bulgaria, Romania, the Baltic States, Slovenia and so on), together with the EFTA candidates and three countries of the Eastern Mediterranean, are set out in Table 2.3.

Table 2.3 Enlargement Scenario for the European Community
EC (12) = 100 (excluding the ex-GDR)

	Population (millions)	Cumulative population (millions)	GDP/head EUR (12) = 100
EUR (12) pre-German unification	328	328	100
ex-GDR	16	344	97
EFTA (a)	30	374	99
Eastern Mediterranean (b)	56	430	91
Visegrad countries (c)	66	496	86

Notes: (a) Sweden, Austria, Finland, Norway, Switzerland
       (b) Turkey, Cyprus, Malta
       (c) Poland, Hungary, Czech and Slovak republics

7   In the event, accession negotiations with Norway, Sweden, Finland and Austria were successfully concluded at the beginning of 1994 and are now subject to referenda in the second half of the year. Switzerland did not participate in the negotiations having earlier decided not to join the wider European single market known as the European Economic Area which embraces the Twelve plus the other EFTA countries.

From Table 2.3 it can be seen that a Community enlarged to include the EFTA countries would return the average per capita GDP to that which prevailed before the de facto enlargement which followed German unification. In effect, the contribution to raising per capita GDP by the relatively prosperous EFTA countries would offset the reduction which followed the inclusion of 16 million East Germans.

Thereafter, data problems mean that the situation becomes more difficult to assess. A meaningful comparison depends on the availability of GDP per head data in purchasing power standards. Such data pose particular methodological problems in relation to Central and Eastern European countries since estimating the real value of the goods they produce is complicated by quality factors. For this reason it is probably best to proceed on the basis of assumptions. In Table 2.3, for illustrative purposes the GDP per head of the four Visegrad countries has been assumed to be 50% of the present Community average in purchasing power standards. Data in purchasing power parities, directly comparable to those of the EC, have been produced for the EFTA countries while first estimates are now available for the ex-GDR. For Turkey, estimates by the OECD for GDP per head in purchasing power parities suggest a figure (for 1988) some 40% of the Community average while Cyprus and Malta (with a combined population of just over 1 million) have been assimilated to Greece (50% of the Community average GDP per head).

Based on these estimates, a Community of 23 Member States tomorrow would have a GDP per head averaging some 14 percentage points below its level today. Even over a longer timespan and assuming more rapid economic growth in the non-EFTA countries, it is probable that a significantly enlarged Community would have important consequences for policies to increase economic and social cohesion, admitting as it would large areas and populations with comparatively low standards of living.

Even in the case of the EFTA countries, initial expectations that adhesion would be of little consequence for regional policies seem unlikely to be borne out. This is particularly true for the Nordic countries where economic restructuring is taking its toll on the regions, typified by the eastern border regions of Finland which have suffered considerably from the economic effects of reform in the former Soviet Union with which it shares a common frontier. While the EFTA countries would undoubtedly be net contributors to the Community's budget overall, there will be additional demands on the Structural Funds.

The problems of the regions in the countries of Central and Eastern Europe are of a different order of magnitude again. Nevertheless, the Community – quite rightly – has decided that as far as the countries of Central and Eastern Europe are concerned the issue is not only an economic one. In its submission to the European Council in Edinburgh, the Commission drew attention to the many other issues at stake including the security dimension where the opportunity exists to integrate these countries into a coherent security structure with Western Europe.

At present the Community, in its capacity as coordinator of the G24 group of countries, is participating in food aid programmes for Central and Eastern Europe although its long-term approach to relationships with those countries, as with the developing world, can be summarised under the slogan 'trade, not aid'. Probably the best way to contribute to economic reform in Eastern Europe is to liberalise trade relations. This would enable these countries to export their products – rather than their population – and to earn much-needed hard currencies. The same also applies to the developing countries in the Third World. Such an approach would also benefit the Community's economy. By enabling Eastern Europe to export their products, these countries will also be able to buy Community products. Such an arrangement would then be beneficial for all parties involved.

However, from a regional point of view, this arrangement may be less attractive. There is a risk that Central and Eastern Europe and the Third World countries would be mainly interested in buying products with a relatively high scientific or technological content, products and services which are produced mainly in the developed regions. It is clear therefore that the arrangement would benefit mainly the richer parts of the Community. In return, the Community would be expected to open its markets for imports of agricultural produce and low-tech, labour-intensive products such as textiles, clothing and footwear. The distribution of the benefits of trade could therefore be somewhat asymmetric to the possible disadvantage of the poorest regions, such as Portugal and Greece, which are heavily specialised in these areas.

The possible risks of future enlargement serve to underline the importance of the Edinburgh agreement for the Community's weaker regions. In effect it must be seen as providing the means to equip the poorer parts of the Community to strengthen their economic competitiveness and to develop the capacity to diversify into sectors and segments which will allow them to trade on the basis of an unfettered comparative advantage with economies in transition in Central and Eastern Europe. In that sense, the rest of the 1990s can be viewed as an important breathing-space during which the Community's weaker regions will have an unrepeatable opportunity to lay the basis for sustainable economic growth in the enlarged and increasingly competitive European marketplace of the next century.

References

Biehl, D. (1986) *The Contribution of infrastructure to Regional Development.* Study financed by the European Commission.

Cegos-Idet (1989) *Les conséquences régionales de l'ouverture des marchés publics; le cas des secteurs des télécommunications, du gros matériel électrique et du matériel ferroviaire.* Study financed by the European Community.

Commission of the European Communities (1989) *Guide to the Reform of the Community's Structural Funds.* Luxembourg: CEC.

Commission of the European Communities (1990) *The Regions in the 1990s: the Fourth Periodic Report on the Situation and Development of the Regions of the European Community.* COM(90)609. Luxembourg: CEC.

Commission of the European Communities (1992a) *Community Structural Policies: Assessment and Outlook.* COM(92) 84 final. Luxembourg: CEC.

Commission of the European Communities (1992b) *From the Single Act to Maastricht and Beyond: The Means to Match our Ambitions.* COM(92)2000. Luxembourg: CEC.

Delors, J. (1989) 'Regional Implications of Economic and Monetary Integration.' In Committee for the Study of Economic and Monetary Union (eds) *Report on Economic and Monetary Union in the European Community.* Luxembourg: Office for Official Publications of the EC.

The Economist (1993) *'The End of Europe's Iron Age'.* March 6th.

Eurostat (1992) *European Community Direct Investment 1985–1989.* Theme 6(D).

Ifo (1990) *An Empirical Assessment of Factors Shaping Regional Competitiveness in Problem Regions.* Study financed by the European Commission.

Marques, A. (1992) 'Community Competition Policy and Economic and Social Cohesion'. *Regional Studies 26*, 4, 404–407.

Molle, W. (1992) *Costs and benefits of economic integration in the Community; from empirical economics to social reality.* Paper presented to Centre for European Policy Studies Conference, Brussels 22nd June.

CHAPTER 3

Shifts in Europe and Their Impact on the European Spatial Structure

Louis Albrechts

Introduction

We are living in a fascinating time of fundamental refurbishing of the world system. This refurbishing, at present, goes together with a spectacular restructuring of economic, political, ideological and social relations. One of the world regions experiencing important changes is undoubtedly Europe:

- On the one side the collapse of state-controlled economic systems in Eastern Europe.
- On the other side the constitution of a unified European economy (Europe 1992).

These recent developments are nothing but the most obvious expression of the fundamental restructuring of the world economy.

Between the 1940s and the 1980s the United States regarded itself as the custodian of the international economic (and political) system. It is now shedding its patriarchal role, as the burdens of external and internal deficits have been coupled with lagging productivity and weakening technological leadership (Hufbauer 1990). This development is underlined by the division of the world in new hegemonic blocks (North America, Europe, South East Asia).

The end of the cold war brings into sharp focus the shifting balance between military and economic power. As national security alliances recede (NATO) or collapse (Warsaw Pact), new economic alliances gather strength. Japan is forging special economic ties with China and its other Asian neighbours; the United States is creating a North American free trade area that could extend from Canada to

Mexico; and the European Community is moving to complete its internal market – the Europe 1992 process – and to establish stronger links with the nations of the European Free Trade Association (EFTA) and Eastern Europe (MacLaury 1990).

The changes that are currently occurring in both East and West, though dramatic in quality, are logical outcomes of lengthy structural processes of change. Such a statement does not imply that the changes will, without question, proceed along a predictable course. It does, however, imply that there is real momentum behind these changes and, furthermore, that even if the particular programmes currently being pursued, or the particular group of leaders currently in charge should for one reason or another falter, the underlying pressures that gave birth to them will remain (Ludlow 1990). This has been proved by the recent events in Russia.

The completion of the Single Market is a major step towards the gradual integration of the EU. It has an immense symbolic value (Illeris 1991) and it is considered as an immense challenge (European Commission 1991); others – from outside this fortress Europe, and those from the inside fearing for a centralistic and technocratic Europe – look at it with a lot of suspicion.

Eastern Europe is regarded as a historic opportunity to spread democratic values and free markets. Historically transitions in society from one system to another have been relatively gradual and evolutionary. Major shifts (from agrarian to industrial society, from subsistence to market economy) took centuries, or at least several generations. Eastern Europe and the former USSR face a historical task of unprecedented difficulty in moving from a command economy to a market economy in a very short timespan. In these circumstances the threat of a breakdown and a disruption of society becomes, as recent events obviously prove, especially acute (see Kollontai 1992).

These dual developments in Eastern Europe and within the EU are likely to produce effects on the European spatial structure.

Changing Forms of Spatial–Regional Organisation

Beginning in the 1960s, the organisation of economic activity entered a period of pronounced transformation. This transformation expressed itself in the altered structure of the global and national frameworks and also assumed forms specific to particular regions. Familiar facets of the transformation are the dismantling of once powerful industrial centres abandoning entire areas while new high-tech industries and advanced service activities mushroomed in other areas. Perhaps less familiar was the rapid industrialisation of the financial industry in the 1980s, which has incorporated a multiplicity of financial centres into a worldwide network of transactions. Advances in computer technology and telecommunications have facilitated simultaneous world-wide dispersal and participation in global markets (Sassen 1991). Yet labour market and less tangible factors, such as the need to maintain awareness of new product developments through face-to-face contact, exert strong agglomerative pressures and the world's financial and business services remain heavily concentrated in a handful of global metropolitan centres (Thrift and Leyshon 1988, Tickel 1990).

The more people, goods, capital, services and information freely move across space, the more local and regional governments are having to recognise that local and regional development have an international dimension. A knowledge of the international forces which cause, influence or determine the process of internationalisation is thus essential for politicians and planners working at local, regional or national levels of government. In the future the development of policies at local and regional level will have to acknowledge and work in harmony with developments at the European level.

The notion of economic restructuring contains three dimensions: a quantitative dimension, typified by the loss of manufactured jobs and the growth of services; a qualitative one, suggested by the greater incidence of both low-wage, low-skill jobs and high-level professional jobs in service industries, a decline in wages and unionisation rates in manufacturing jobs, and a feminisation of the job supply; and a spatial dimension, most commonly associated with the geographical redistribution of manufacturing jobs at the national and international scale (Sassen 1990, Bluestone and Harrison 1982, Massey and Meegan 1982, Massey 1984).

In the 1980s the state in the West became more ideologically conservative and more subservient to the needs and demands of capital, turning away from the simultaneous pursuit of both economic growth and welfare (Beauregard 1989). As the mode of regulation by the state changes from Keynesian interventions to monetarist disintervention then more has to be achieved by the purer operation of market forces regarding the question of development. Ends and goals are increasingly provided by the market. Furthermore, the world-wide changing forms of spatial–regional organisation constitute a general frame of reference against which specific developments (European integration, changes in Eastern Europe, spatial impacts) have to be projected.

European Integration

In March 1957, six nations signed the historic Treaty of Rome setting in motion the economic and political integration of Western Europe. The infant European Community was launched in the context of an international system dominated by East–West rivalry and characterised in the West by United States hegemony. The United States retained much influence in macroeconomic and monetary issues, in foreign and security questions and trade issues. Much of the most important policy formulation took place in bilateral discussions (Bonn and Washington, Rome and Washington, Paris and Washington...). These bilateral relations exceeded in significance any multilateral groupings of a purely European character for a very long time. In the course of the 1960s and early 1970s this system began to dissolve (Ludlow 1990).

The European Community had from the beginning an overriding priority to unite countries previously at war and in so doing lay the basis of a European union. The actual agenda of the new Community was, however, essentially concerned with more routine policy issues: trade, agriculture, transport, coal and steel. The Treaty of Rome envisaged the ultimate goal of an integrated market for the free movement of goods, services, capital and people. These are known as the 'four freedoms'. The acceleration of the process of economic integration culminated in the adoption of the Single European Act. With its adoption, the Community set itself two major objectives: on the one hand, the Heads of Government of the twelve Member States committed themselves to complete the internal market by the end of 1992; on the other hand they recognised the need to strengthen action to reduce regional disparities within the European Community. Both objectives are closely interrelated. The proponents (Cecchini 1990) of the 1992 programme maintain that the removal of the remaining barriers to trade between Member States would make for a considerable improvement in the economic performance of the Community as a whole. At the same time it has to be recognised that there is no certainty about the geographical distribution of the costs and benefits which the completion of the Single Market is expected to bring. The danger therefore exists that Europe 1992 will benefit mainly the economically stronger regions, and this at the expense of the less developed areas of the European Community. The inclusion in the Single Act of a chapter on economic and social cohesion should be viewed in this context, i.e. as the other side of the internal market coin and as a commitment by the Community to strengthen its actions in support of the weaker regions.

The uniting of Europe has led to considerable changes. There is a tendency to reduce the position of the traditional dominant nations and to strengthen the importance of individual regions. Whilst nations might now lobby in Brussels on behalf of their regions, in the future the regions will probably be doing the lobbying themselves.

The Gulf war, the pulling down of the Berlin Wall, the breaking up of the Eastern block and the former Soviet Union, the tragic ongoing (civil) war in the former Yugoslavia clearly expose the weakness of the European Community. The Community remains too much an economic community without political and military competence. After the reunification Germany became the dominant power in Europe. Consequently, France, fearing that Germany would become a Super Power, intended to anchor Germany once and for all in the European Community. Furthermore, the movement towards a European single currency would restrain the omnipotence of the German mark.

These issues – together with the fact that a growing number of former Eastern Block countries began knocking at the European Community door – composed the agenda of two intergovernmental conferences in early January 1991: one on the EMU (European Monetary Union) and one on the EPU (European Political Union). In December 1991 the conclusions were moulded in the Treaty of Maastricht. The initial Danish 'No' to the Treaty and the extremely tight majority of 'Yes' in France provoked a shock wave in the Union. It showed an alienation of citizens of the member countries from Europe and created the possibility at one stage of a 'multispeed' Europe, with Germany, France and the Benelux countries forming an integrated core with a single currency and seamless borders.

Changes in Eastern Europe

The process that began in Eastern Europe in 1989 is of unprecedented historical proportion. The political collapse of communist regimes occurred against a background of structural economic crisis. With this collapse the image of Eastern Europe as monolith fell apart and the enormous cultural diversity began to re-emerge – the former Yugoslavia as its recent violent history proves, was constituted of seven or eight countries which eye one another with frustration, envy and resentment (Glenny 1990). The disintegration of the former USSR provides a further example of these trends on an even greater scale.

The economies of Eastern Europe range from the highly industrialised regions of Bohemia, Moravia and former East Germany to the Third World conditions of Romania, Kosovo and Albania. Some areas can boast powerful democratic traditions while others have known only dictatorship and violence (Glenny 1990). The fall of the communist regime was unexpectedly aided by Soviet *perestroika* which in turn had been primarily caused by the economic stagnation affecting the Soviet Union since the late 1970s. Although remarkable differences exist between the various countries involved, the introduction of the market economy is generally considered in the East as the solution to overcome the general crisis of Soviet-type economic systems.

Kollontai (1992) argues that

> a very important, but mostly ignored problem is that of attaining legitimacy for the market. When the overall objective of moving towards a market economy was adopted most people did not understand the essence of the issues involved. Now they are slowly beginning to comprehend, that the main questions are not simply these of attaining greater freedom and democracy, but also those of a major powershift, of a fundamental change of the whole structure of society, of a total reconstruction of its institutional framework, value systems, human relations. A decisive factor is the privatization process, its forms, methods and the resulting social structures, the degree and scope of marginalization that it will engender. (p.6)

The market works in all industrialised countries throughout the West. Yet, in each country it has its own pattern of operation. There are indeed quite different types of market mechanisms in the West; differences lie in the institutional set-up, the mode of government intervention, the type of social compromises, the regulatory mechanisms of the economy and the capital–labour relations. Strictly speaking, the market economy does not exist, as each country is characterised by its own market regulatory structures. Different national establishments formulate different trade and market policies affecting corporate strategies, technical development and international competition in different ways. Apparently similar structures and institutions may play completely different roles (Chavance 1991). Only if this point is fully understood can Eastern Europe move slowly towards an appropriate market system tailored to its very specific needs.

The unplanned conversion of State-planned economies into market economies has turned out to be much more difficult than many politicians and economic planners anticipated (Kuklinkski 1992). The growing loss of governance, as a result of the dismantling of the old system, is undermining not only the capacities for change but even the normal functioning of the economy and the state (Kollontai 1992). The adaptation process is extremely slow and cumbersome. People are clearly scared of the two main evils associated with the transformation to a market economy: inflation and unemployment.

The existing and newly created economic, spatial and environmental problems (Eastern Europe offers an endless list of ecological nightmares) exceed the absorptive management capacities of the many newly created national, regional and local governments (Ache and Kunzmann 1991, Glenny 1990).

The recent developments in the former Soviet Union make it extremely clear that attempts to control crisis by instituting a process of democratic change and economic reform 'from above' have encountered growing opposition from more conservative layers of the bureaucracy and the nomenclature as well as from newly politicised and trade-unionised sections of the working class determined to prevent a further erosion of living standards and social rights threatened in the name of *perestroika* (see Blackburn 1991).

Besides strengthening their democratic political institution, most Eastern European countries must meet three interrelated challenges, that is, stabilise their economies, implement economic restructuring and effect market institutional change (Chavance 1991). Therefore, there is a strong need for transitional mechanisms: financial transition, structural transition and institutional transition. All these transitions have a different speed and must be seen as multistage movements (Kollontai 1992). They need coordination at every stage.

Production and internal markets for most consumer goods in the former Soviet Union are shrinking drastically because of a lack of proper interaction between market and regulatory mechanisms.[1] The consumption pattern changed dramati-

---

1 Communication by Kollontai at the first World-Wide Conference on Planning Science, Palermo, September 8th–12th, 1992.

cally: food takes 70–75% of the budget, housing 15–20%. So almost nothing is left for other goods leading to a virtual collapse of some domestic markets.

Under the traditional system, central authorities could use instruments of macroeconomic control which were linked to a mesoeconomic and microeconomic regulation of activities. This was the cornerstone of central planning whereby macroeconomic objectives were broken down along the hierarchy into detailed microeconomic orders. The risk exists that the old macroeconomic control mechanisms will become too weak before they have been replaced by the new ones and before people have become familiar with them (Chavance 1991).

A frequent mistake is the belief that a radical and brutal deregulation (the shock therapy) and flexibilisation of the old system will allow the spontaneous formation of the self-regulating market, that prices resulting from a free interplay of demand and supply will take care of eliminating shortages and of necessary adjustments (on the labour market for sectoral restructuring, for comparative international advantage...), and eventually that the restoration of equilibrium – often a painful intermediate period – will be relatively quick (Chavance 1991).

Spatial Impacts

The Ebiras study[2] indicates that the completion of the Single European Market in itself will not turn present economic or spatial patterns and tendencies in the European Community regions upside down (see also Illeris 1991). The role of the European business community in the project Europe 1992 should not be underestimated. Indeed, although at first scepticism was rampant, large industrial corporations and enterprises, insurance companies and banks, transportation companies, media enterprises and developers soon convinced themselves that the internal market programme would provide the framework for economic expansion. They had early prepared to profit from a growing European-wide market, by establishing or buying subsidiaries in other European countries, by merging or forming international networks and by recruiting internationally experienced staff for their headquarters. The removal of physical and fiscal barriers will only facilitate their international businesses. European stock markets boomed. As Agnelli, the Italian industrialist and chairman of Fiat, wrote:

> ironically, it was politicians who in 1957 first conceived the idea of a common market often over objections from the business community. Now the situation has been reversed, it is the entrepreneurs and corporations who

---

2   EBIRAS Project. Research project – Spatial Impacts of the Single European Market on the Federal Republic of Germany – commissioned on behalf of the Bundesminister für Raumordnung, Bauwesen und Städtebau, Bonn (German Ministry of Planning, Housing and Urban Development). Eight country reports have been prepared for this research project (Belgium, Sweden, USA, Spain, Portugal, UK, France, the Netherlands).

are keeping the pressure on politicians to transcend considerations of local and national interest.

Ache and Kunzmann (1991) assume that in the medium term synergetic forces of the Single European Market project will positively or negatively strengthen and/or accelerate existing trends in selected regions of the European Community. The removal of internal frontiers within the Community is likely to have its most powerful spatial effects on border areas. They will have to adjust to new roles and to think and act complementarily within the wider European space compared with their traditional position on the periphery of the Member States, with a legacy of national and local administrative practice which still inhibits cross-border coop-eration. Through networking, border areas are able to enhance beneficial inter-connections and to exploit potential complementarities among cities and regions, improve flows of information, develop best practice, pool financial resources and share development costs of innovative projects (European Commission 1991, Kunzmann and Wegener 1991). These areas can expand their hinterland and increase their trade, if regional/local decision-makers take up the new challenge. It is for these areas that the need for consultation and cooperation in (physical) planning and development is greatest (European Commission 1991).

1992 strengthened the competition among European regions. Efficient and attractive residential and work environments will become extremely important. Indeed, the quality of the environment and services are essential to a region's competitive position as demonstrated in an in-depth survey carried out among some 9000 firms in regions throughout the Community (Institut für Wirt-schaftsforschung 1990; see also Healy and Baker 1990, van der Berg, Klaassen and van der Meer 1990).

Some results from Healy and Baker (1990) are shown in Table 3.1.

The question asked was how important to your company is (each factor) – is it absolutely essential, important but not essential, not very important or not at all important? 'Absolutely essential' responses only are included here.

Ifo (1990) and a conference in Dublin with over 100 senior business people (cited in *Europe 2000*) found that among the most important factors influencing location decisions are:

- rapid and efficient transport and communications systems
- the availability of a well-qualified workforce
- access to local educational institutions and research bodies
- the presence of high-quality business services, as firms increasingly contract out services they would previously have undertaken for themselves
- the quality of the social and cultural environment, including sporting and leisure facilities.

Table 3.1 Essential factors for locating business (Healy and Baker 1990)

	% All (base 506)
Easy access to markets, customers or clients	60
The quality of telecommunications	59
Transport infrastructure	57
Cost and availability of staff	35
The climate government creates for business through tax policies and the availability of financial incentives	30
Availability of office space	27
Value for money of office space	22
Language spoken	17
The quality of life for employees	14

Source: Healy and Baker Research Services Ltd

A number of studies (Massey 1984, Massey and Meegan 1982, Sassen 1990, 1991, Kunzmann and Wegener 1991) point out the growing division of labour between cities and regions. These trends will have an important influence on the development of the urban system in Europe in the 1990s:

- *Spatial polarisation*
  The internationalisation and integration of the European economy, the emerging high-speed transport infrastructure, the Channel Tunnel, and the ongoing transformation of economic activities through technological shifts in the production (kanban, just-in-time...) and distribution systems (combined transport, trucking, hub and spoke) increase the relative advantage of cities in the European core over cities at the European periphery. Striking examples in this respect are the fruity images of the European urban system by Brunet (1989) – the Blue Banana – and by Kunzmann and Wegener (1991) – the European grape.

- *Functional specialisation*
  More and more cities in Europe have become specialised centres for particular industries, be it for special types of manufacturing (e.g. car production, electronics: Eindhoven), for specialised services (e.g. financing: London, Frankfurt) for political decisions (Brussels) or which are linked to historical endogenous potentials (e.g. tourism: Venice). With growing specialisation, the city develops a unique 'label' or image, and this helps to attract further specialised economic activities and skilled labour force, which in turn stimulates the expansion of the particular specialised functions. The Harris weighted score based upon the Healy and Baker (1990) survey ranks London, Paris, Frankfurt and Brussels as the best cities to locate a business in 1990.

The last decade of the twentieth century will not stop the dominant trends. On the European as well as the national level, the prosperous, successful cities will continue to flourish economically and culturally while the large number of small and medium-sized cities will struggle to attract more public and private capital and investment for promoting their economic development. The urban system in Europe will continue to be effected by technological and structural economic change, which is likely to be enforced and accelerated by the Single European Market.

The dominance of larger cities in Europe will further increase as they offer attractive jobs for skilled workers and provide the high-quality services and cultural and leisure facilities the post-modern society wishes to have within easy reach.

The emerging European high-speed rail network complemented by the Channel Tunnel (see Wegener and Spiekerman 1991) and the existing rail networks linking the medium-sized cities to the larger metropolitan areas will reinforce the dominance of larger cities. With this increasing importance of the accessibility to the large cities in the core of Europe, cities at the periphery of the continent will face increasing difficulties.

Gateway cities (cities with large international airports, cities bordering Eastern Europe or North Africa) will experience increasing pressure by immigration flows from Eastern Europe, Africa and the Middle East. This is exemplified by the dramatic experiences with migrants in Italy and Germany. The decision to move the German capital from Bonn to Berlin will provoke a major migration stream to this city.

According to Amin, Malmberg and Maskell (1991) and also Begg (1989) the shape of post-1992 Europe seems less likely to be cast in terms of a network of interdependent local production complexes than to adopt the more familiar form of widening regional inequalities with growth concentrating in the established metropolitan core areas such as London and Paris, at the expense of the de-industrialised peripheral regions such as Northern England, the Mezzogiorno, Greece, etc.

The expansion of the spatial division of labour from the core to the periphery in the 1960s, both within and between nations, is likely to be repeated in the new European configuration (because of the low wages in Eastern Europe and the continuous search of multinational firms for new markets). Most likely growth will concentrate in major cities (Budapest, Prague, Moscow etc.) because of the availability of skilled workers and a minimum of infrastructure.

The discussion on Europe 1992 and Eastern Europe puts an overwhelming emphasis on (regional) development and growth. The same is true for a large part of the theoretical discourse. This leads to a neglect or an absence of explicit attention to distributive issues. Social redistribution programmes remain indispensable to cope with historico-structural problems (Albrechts and Swyngedouw 1989). So there is a responsibility to put these issues back on the political agenda.

Conclusion

European leaders had accorded first priority to the core 1992 programme to ensure firstly a deep internal integration and only then respond to new opportunities offered by close ties with non-member States. The democratic revolution that swept Eastern Europe recently – especially the reunification of Germany, the disintegration of the former USSR, the ongoing fighting in former Yugoslavia – and the threat of a multispeed Europe now threaten this vision and will profoundly affect the Europe 1992 process.

The opening towards Eastern Europe could in the long term far exceed the importance of 1992. Indeed, the greatest challenge of the next decade will be to overcome the wide gap in economic prosperity between the regions in Western and Eastern Europe. Local and regional labour markets in Eastern Europe offer few opportunities: their infrastructure is obsolete, their environmental conditions are desolate, their housing stock is far below West European standards and local/regional governments are almost incapable of managing their own development. The Community could provide in this respect some initial guidance as to how the former centrally planned economies might ensure that they evolve models for their future development which avoid the pitfalls which have been experienced in the development of the regions of Western Europe and even provide concrete help to organise the complex and difficult process of restructuring and modernising regions. Indeed, support to these countries and their people should incorporate an analysis of the different options available including the possible institutional and systemic alternatives.

A test for the European Community will be whether it is prepared (and economically able) to extend social and economic solidarity to the peoples of Eastern Europe and the former Soviet Union as they build a democratic order and tackle the problems of post-Communism in a capitalist world. The West has refused any substantial help on the issue of debt cancellation. For many Eastern Europeans the horizon looks gloomy and the promise of mass unemployment is unsettling much of the area. But in the long term only Western capital, especially that from America and Japan, can resuscitate one of Europe's most seriously disabled economies. Eastern Europe desperately needs an economic revival (Glenny 1990).

At this moment the preferred arrangement offered to the Central European countries takes the form of an association which denies them any representation in the Community Institutions. Wider membership would entail a generous programme of socioeconomic and ecological rehabilitation to guarantee economic development, ecological protection, democratic institutions and a fair distribution of welfare throughout Europe (see Blackburn 1991). A Lomé-style Convention for Eastern Europe should be avoided. In the meantime non-member countries should think of all kinds of associations to push for their interests to be recognised in the Community. In this respect, Austria, the Czech Republic and Hungary could think of a 'neo-Habsburgist' trans-Danubian Association.

References

Ache, P. and Kunzmann, K. (1991) 'Towards a new national planning concept for Germany?' Paper presented at the Joint ACSP-AESOP Congress, Oxford, 8–12 July.

Albrechts, L. and Swyngedouw, E. (1989) 'The challenges for regional policy under a flexible regime of accumulation.' In L. Albrechts, F. Moulaert, P. Roberts, E. Swyngedouw (eds) *Regional Policy at the Crossroads. European perspectives.* London: Jessica Kingsley Publishers.

Amin, A., Malmberg, A. and Maskell, P. (1991) 'Structural change and the geography of production in Europe.' Paper presented at European Science Foundation, Workshop on Urban and Regional Restructuring in Europe, Lisbon.

Beauregard, R.A. (1989) 'Between modernity and postmodernity: the ambigious position of U.S. planning.' *Environment and Planning: Society and Space 7,* 381–395.

Begg, I. (1989) 'European integration and regional policy.' *Oxford Review of Economic Policy 5,* 90–104.

Blackburn, R. (1991) 'The European Community and the challenge of the new Europe.' In M. Kaldor (ed) *Europe from below. An East–West dialogue.* London: Verso.

Bluestone, B. and Harrison, B. (1982) *The deindustrialization of America.* New York: Basic Books.

Brunet, R. (1989) *Les Villes Européennes,* La Documentation Française, Reclus, Datar.

Cecchini, P. (1990) *Alles op alles voor Europa: de uitdaging 1992.* Brussel: Borsen.

Chavance, B. (1991) 'What kind of transition and what kind of market in Eastern Europe?' *Most 2,* 9–20.

Commission of the European Communities (1991) *Europe 2000? Outlook for the development of the Community's Territory. A Preliminary Overview.* Brussels: CEC.

Glenny, M. (1990) *The rebirth of History. Eastern Europe in the Age of Democracy.* London: Penguin Books.

Healy and Baker (1990) *European Real Estate Monitor.* Executive Summary.

Hufbauer, G. (1990) 'An overview.' In G. Hufbauer (ed) *Europe 1992. An American Perspective.* Washington DC: The Bookings Institution.

Ifo (1990) 'An empirical assessment of factors shaping regional competitiveness in problem regions.' Cited in European Commission (1991) *Europe 2000,* Brussels.

Illeris, S. (1991) 'Urban and Regional Development in Western Europe in the 1990s; will everything happen in the London–Brussels–Frankfurt–Milan "Banana"?' Paper prepared for the I.G.U. Commission on Urban Systems and Urban Development, Budapest.

Institut für Wirtschaftsforschung (1990) In Commission of the European Communties *Europe 2000? Outlook for the Development of the Community's Territory. A Preliminary Overview.* Brussels: CEC.

Kollontai, V. (1992) 'Some Specifics of Economic Reform in Russia.' Paper presented at the first World-Wide Conference on Planning Science, Palermo, September 8th–12th.

Kuklinski, A. (1992) 'The Future of Strategic Planning in Central and Eastern Europe.' Paper presented at the First World-Wide Conference on Planning Science, Palermo, September 8th–12th.

Kunzmann, K. and Wegener, M. (1991) 'The pattern of Urbanization in Western Europe 1960–1990.' *Berichte aus dem Institut für Raumplanung 28,* Dortmund.

Ludlow, P.W. (1990) 'Managing change: the United States and Europe. East and West.' In W. Brock, T. Hormats, W.W. Norton (eds) *The Global Economy.* New York: W.W. Norton and Co.

MacLaury, B. (1990) 'Foreword.' In G. Hufbauer (ed) *Europe 1992. An American Perspective.* Washington DC: The Booking Institution.

Massey, D. (1984) *Spatial Divisions of Labour.* Basingstoke: Macmillan.

Massey, D. and Meegan, R. (1982) *The Anatomy of Job Loss: The How, Why and Where of Employment Decline.* London: Methuen.

Sassen, S. (1990) 'Economic restructuring and the American city.' *Annual Review of Sociology 16,* 465–490.

Sassen, S. (1991) 'Cities in a World Economy: New-York, London, Tokyo.' Paper presented at Joint ACSP-AESOP congress, Oxford, 8–12 July.

Tickel, A. (1990) Capital cities? Rethinking financial services, University of Manchester: Department of Geography, *Spatial Policy Analysis* W.P. 11.

Thrift, N. and Leyshon, A. (1988) 'The gambling propensity' Bank, developing country debt exposures and the New International Financial System. *Geoforum 19,* 55–69.

van den Berg, L., Klaassen, L.H., van der Meer, J. (1990) *Strategische city-marketing.* Academic Service economie en bedrijfskunde, Schoonhoven.

Wegener, M., Spiekerman, K. (1991) 'The regional impacts of the channel Tunnel.' Paper presented at the Joint ACSP-AESOP Congress, Oxford, 8–12 July.

CHAPTER 4

Economic Reforms in East-Central Europe

Gyula Horváth

Introduction: How Many Europes Can We Speak of?

Unfortunately, it is a common experience that the member countries of the European Communities regard only themselves as parts of Europe. They emphasise their separation from the eastern half of Europe and enter into a self-defensive alliance against the much more dynamic overseas super-economies. Yet there are also a lot of countries whose reference to themselves as being Central European is no accident, because they wish to be distinguished from East Europe and the Balkan. Just as the notion of Europe is not reflected in mere fancies and ideas, we have to regard its internal geographical division, as well as the differences between the various parts of the Continent which derive from their peculiar historical development, as reality. The Continent has been unified by a network of natural, socio-historical and political regions for centuries (Enyedi 1990b).

Nevertheless the marked separation of the western and eastern halves of Europe started as early as the Middle Ages. The regions of Greek orthodoxy and Western Catholicism have run different paths, while the states of Central Europe have been attracted either by the West or the East. The eastern periphery of western-type development was gradually widening in the period of capitalist development, the countries on the Balkan joined organisations of Western-type development at the turn of the nineteenth and twentieth centuries and European development was homogeneous in its main outlines for about 50 years.

It has never been an easy task to respond to the challenges of modernisation in the Eastern European peripheries. The capitalist modernisation effort of the second half of the nineteenth century resulted in half-hearted success. After World War I the small nations manoeuvring between the Russian and German giants were trying to find a way out of the failures by means of nationalist revolutions and the long overdue establishment of independent national identity and statehood, since they found that dependence was the main source of all their troubles. The independent states which were established again or anew, Poland, Czechoslovakia, Rumania, Yugoslavia, and even Hungary having shrunk to one-third of its former territory, formulated euphoristic economic programmes. Frustration caused by World War I led to a rebellion based on the catching-up modernisation programme which ended in failure; instead of following the West, the rejection and annihilation of its values were set as an objective. The countries having joined the German life space deviated from the road of modernisation.

Separation continued after World War II as well. The Stalinist model which held out hopes of economic modernisation caused admiration mixed with shock all over the world. It became an obstacle for keeping up with the other countries, or rather a model of falling behind again even in its improved, reformed post-Stalinist form, in spite of the fact that in the 1950s the modernisation model seemed to be very promising for the underdeveloped countries. In the poor countries which traditionally had low capital accumulation, the new form of state administration increased the centralised incomes many times. It also crushed the hardened social structures which firmly resisted modernisation with ruthless brutality, and dictated a forced pace of economic restructuring with the purpose of the rapid development of the most important element lagging behind, that of industry. By means of equalisation, which for long periods could amount to the equalisation of poverty, some kind of economic democracy was achieved, even if completely lacking the human rights and fundamental freedoms. The redistribution of land and industrialisation created millions of jobs and the regime provided for the elementary social and educational needs of everyone. In spite of this, the countries could not change their positions of 1937–1980 in the ranking of international development. Although their lag was somewhat reduced during the past 40 years relative to the per capita GDP of the USA (13–21% in 1937, 21–32% in 1980), their respective positions on the ranking list of the developed nations did not change (Ehrlich 1990).

With the general appearance of the industrial production systems, however, several processes analogous to those having taken place in Western Europe occurred in East-Central Europe, too. For instance, regular forms of modern urbanisation spread at the time of the state socialist regime (Enyedi 1992a). In the late 1940s this periphery of Europe was predominantly of rural character.

The proportion of the rural population was 80% in the former Yugoslavia and Bulgaria, 70% in Poland and Rumania, 60% in Hungary and 50% in the Czech Republic. In this rural space, urbanisation did not follow the model of the developing countries, but rather that of an earlier period of Western European urbanisation. In general the number of towns with a population of 50–100,000 grew the most rapidly, while the network of the cities formed before World War I did not change. This period of urbanisation, however, also had peculiarities deriving from the character of the state power (Enyedi 1990a).

First, the gap between the town and the village was widening and the pushing of the infrastructure into the background out of ideological considerations, and the reallocating policy of the state, affected the villages adversely. Second, the technical backwardness and the organisational inflexibility also resulting in the collapse of state socialism reproduced the backwardness of the region in terms of the degree of urbanisation. Third, the nationalisation of settlement administration could not subjugate the local societies completely and particularly in the 1980s the urban societies tried to follow the Western European models in collaboration with the urban experts. Consequently, in the formulation of the urbanisation objectives the division of Europe can be observed to a lesser extent today, although there are still significant differences with regard to the instruments and organisational forms.

Under the impact of the 1989–1990 velvet revolutions the totalitarian regimes collapsed. The communist governments of the smaller socialist countries were compelled one after the other to give up power, or at least to share it with the opposition. The political changes brought about the restructuring of the economy. Not only did the small CMEA countries turn their backs on the socialist economic management which had made use of dictatorial methods and set out to build a market economy, but the Soviet Union and its successor states also attempted to get control over the lasting economic crisis by means of reforms and market solutions. With the collapse of state socialism and the disintegration of the imperial frameworks the countries situated in this space had to face a challenge which was unexpected in many respects. While earlier debate was concerned with the option of a more cautious or radical renewal of the socialist economy, after the change of regime these regional societies could start to develop the Western, pluralist economic and political system.

The transfer of the regional and settlement development models of the developed democracies and market economies is made more difficult by the fact that in East-Central Europe the settlement development processes have also come to a critical point. The economic restructuring, the introduction of the market mechanisms, the integration of the ex-socialist countries into the European division of labour and the decentralisation of power all combine to impact upon the future shape of regional policy in this space.

In this chapter a summary of the experience related to the reforms in East-Central Europe is presented, mainly from the perspective of the possible regional political effects of the changes. In addition, attention is paid to how these processes may affect cooperation between the two European regions.

Constraints and Dilemmas of the Economic Change of Regime

The democratic governments of the post-communist countries set themselves the task of the reconstruction and the creation of a market economy in a critical period, because all over Europe:

- the decrease of the growth rate resulted in an economic decline
- the overwhelming majority of the population grew poor, as a consequence of which social polarisation is beyond the extent which is generally characteristic of the market economies
- there was a great increase in unemployment
- inflation rose
- huge external and internal debts were accumulated
- the artificially maintained Eastern European integration, the CMEA, disintegrated and the former member countries were compelled to find new orientations and economic relations in the wider European and international economy
- the regional inequalities increased.

Examination of the constraining factors shows:

1. The model of planned economy which was mainly related to the contemporary Soviet practices and fed mostly on the Marxian ideas was built upon two pillars, those of 'uninterrupted growth' and the new type of man being the subject of the collective power. The system of the planned economy differed fundamentally from the market economy in the respect that the investment decisions were made in central offices, the heavy industry was considered to be the motor of the economic development, the economy-developing role of the infrastructure was undervalued, and, above all, economic management was carried out by a narrow circle, namely the communist party (Kornai 1992).

2. In the central plan management the state socialist governments elaborated numerous detailed programmes, projects and action packages in order to organise production and sales, chiefly in the competitive sector. In the meantime – in contrast with the basic logic of economics – the public infrastructural developments were mere decorations in the state programmes, or the financing of these goods was provided for from private resources. (In a few countries in the 1970s and 1980s, for example, telephone provision, water supply for the population and sewage disposal.) It is not easy for the state to make a withdrawal in Western Europe either, if a sector or region is in crisis, particularly if the government is expected to adjust the deficient functioning of the market according to the social common law. In East-Central Europe the governments having come to power proposed cost-reducing programmes, while at the same time not resisting the customary propensity to overspend the state budget.

   In addition to the already regular budgetary deficit this psychological pressure greatly limits the decentralisation of administration and of the allocation of the market resources. The main objectives of the decentralisation policy of the transitory period is illustrated in Figure 4.1 (Dostál, Illner, Kára and Barlow 1992). Nevertheless, restructuring is progressing at a different pace in the individual countries due to political and economic factors and the insufficient development of the vertical system of public administration.

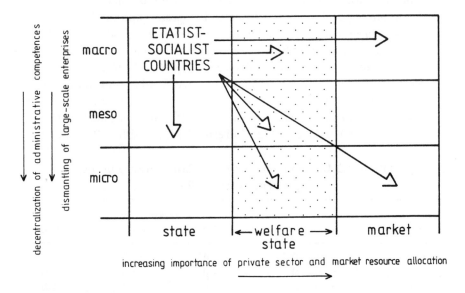

Source: Dostál *et al.* 1992, p.8.

Figure 4.1. Objectives of the decentralisation policy

3. The general crisis emerging in the Central-East European space, and the change of regime, is accompanied unavoidably by the disappearance of the less competitive agents of the economy, and, consequently, by tensions in employment, society and politics. The complex costs of the transformation to the new economic models of restructuring are indicated by the extent of the losses in growth (Table 4.1).

Table 4.1 Growth rates of GDP in East-Central Europe, per cent

Countries	1950–1959	1960–1969	1970–1979	1980–1988	1989	1990	1991	1992
Bulgaria	6.0	5.2	2.3	1.2	-0.4	-9.1	-17	-10
Czechoslovakia	3.8	2.4	2.0	1.2	1.0	-0.4	-16	-7
Hungary	3.8	3.1	2.3	1.1	-0.2	-3.3	-10	-4
Poland	2.7	3.2	2.6	-0.2	0	-11.6	-9	-2
Romania	4.8	4.2	4.4	0.8	-0.4	-7.4	-14	-13

Source: National statistics

4. The most important trouble spot is represented by unemployment. The former CMEA countries were unprepared both with regard to the social safety net and the required institutions and resources (Table 4.2). On the basis of the growth rates it can be predicted that unemployment will continue to rise in future years, and furthermore, the inter-regional differences will also widen. Unemployment has also become the most significant regional issue in East-Central European countries. The unemployment rates of the backward and developed regions show triple, even fourfold differences from place to place. For example, compared with the 6.4% unemployment rate of Prague in the Czech Republic, Eastern Slovakia had a much higher unemployment rate in 1991; in Hungary the rate was 6.6% in Budapest compared with 22% in the northeast counties in May, 1993; in Poland there were differences of similar magnitude at the end of 1992 (Dostál et al. 1992, Gorzelak 1993, Horváth 1993).

Table 4.2 Unemployment rates in East-Central Europe, per cent of labour force

Countries	1989	December 1990	1991	1992
Bulgaria	0	1.4	10.0	14.8
Czechoslovakia	0	1.0	3.3	7.0
Hungary	0.5	1.6	8.3	12.0
Poland	0.3	6.1	11.1	13.6
Romania	n.a.	n.a.	6.0	8.5

Source: National statistics

5. The economic change of regime is made difficult chiefly by high inflation (Table 4.3) and the foreign debt burdens in all the countries. The external financial position of the five East-Central European countries had already deteriorated significantly in 1990, prior to the collapse of the trade with the Soviet Union. Their total gross debts had grown from 80 billion to 90 billion US dollars (85% of this amount made up of the debts of the Czech Republic, Slovakia, Hungary and Poland) and the various indices of indebtedness have also deteriorated (Gibb and Michelak 1993).

6. The majority of the economic troubles of the small East-Central European countries were due to the collapse of the CMEA. The liberalisation of foreign trade and the restructuring of the foreign relations have resulted in the drop of exports (Table 4.4). Until 1992 Hungary managed to increase its exports temporarily – by means of state subsidies – but reductions were expected in subsequent years.

Table 4.3 Inflation rates in East-Central Europe
(percentage change in consumer price indices)

Countries	1989	1990	1991	1992	1993*
Bulgaria	6.4	26.3	334	90	60
Czechoslovakia	1.4	10	58	11	†
Hungary	17.1	28.4	35	21	15
Poland	251	586	70	40	35
Romania	0.9	4.2	161	200	95

*Preliminary estimates
† Czech Republic: 25 per cent; Slovak Republic: 50 per cent.
Source: PlanEcon Business Report, 20 January 1993

Table 4.4 Foreign trade turnover in East-Central Europe, billion USD

Countries	1981	1988	1989	1990	1991	1992*
Export						
Bulgaria	10.7	17.2	16.0	13.3	3.8	3.3
Czechoslovakia	14.9	14.9	14.4	11.9	10.9	11.8
Hungary	8.8	9.7	9.6	9.7	10.3	10.7
Poland	14.5	13.9	13.5	14.3	14.4	14.0
Romania	11.1	11.4	10.5	5.9	4.1	4.0
Import						
Bulgaria	10.8	16.6	14.9	12.9	3.0	3.6
Czechoslovakia	14.6	14.6	14.3	13.3	9.9	12.5
Hungary	8.7	9.1	8.8	8.8	11.5	11.0
Poland	16.8	12.2	10.0	9.5	14.2	13.5
Romania	11.0	7.6	8.4	9.1	5.6	5.4

* Preliminary data
Source: OECD, Economic outlook. December, 1992

7. The ideology of the regional and settlement development policy of state socialism (the classical Marxist theory, the utopian urbanistic conceptions and theory of planning) as well as the related objectives (proportional development, moderation of the civilisational differences between the town and the village, the regionally equal allocation of the free or heavily subsidised social allowances) have lost ground and the shaping powers of the market economy launched a new differentiation.

The dramatic cutback of state subsidies, changes in the geographical and foreign trade guiding principles, the disintegration of the major companies with multiple plants have all affected the central regions and the peripheries.

Although restructuring also adversely affected the traditional growth poles, their formerly diversified economy and relatively more complex socioeconomic functions meant that the regions of the large cities can arrive at the end of the restructuring process in a relatively stronger position than the monocultural industrial regions and rural areas. The spread of the market economy and the establishment of the modern economic structure can be observed in the voivodeships of Warsaw, Krakkow, Poznan and Wroclaw in Poland; in the Budapest metropolitan area and the Northeast-Transdanubian regions of Hungary;

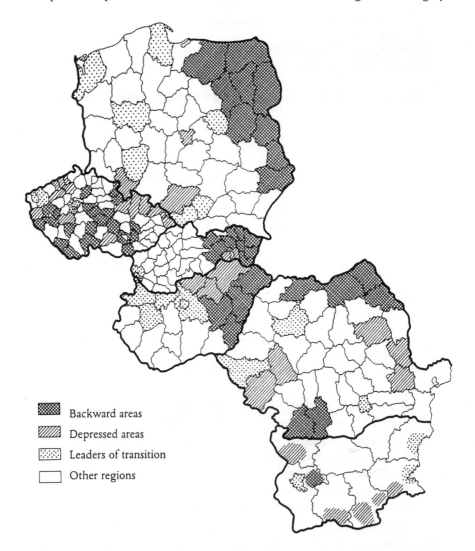

■ Backward areas
▨ Depressed areas
▦ Leaders of transition
□ Other regions

Source: Blåzek and Kára 1992, Gorzelak 1992, Horváth 1992

Figure 4.2. Typology of regions in East-Central Europe

in the neighbourhood of Prague, Karlovy Vary and Bratislava in the former Czechoslovakia (Figure 4.2). In these regions the number of private businesses greatly exceeded the national average; the share of the foreign capital and the service sector (mainly as a result of the growth of business and financial services) slowly became the dominant sector of the economy. These regions can be credited with most innovations, the production of new goods and participation in international economic cooperation.

The 'flagships' of restructuring have formulated ambitious development programmes, particularly in the regions of the capitals – asserting their superiority in the political decision-making more often than not – where they have tried to follow a post-industrial development path and become modern multifunction metropolises of the Western European type and integrated into the network of European cities. If the endeavours of the capitals to become internationalised are not coupled with a decentralised regional policy and the invariable deregulation of the unitary construction of the government, then in the future there will be an intensification of the contrast between the capital and the provinces (provincial cities), or maybe the rise of federalist regional movements.

The obvious losers of the restructuring, however, are the formerly strongly supported citadels of the working classes, namely the centres of the extracting, heavy and light industries. The cities of Lódz, Katowice (Poland), Ostrava (Czech), Koτice (Slovakia) Miskolc, Salgótarján (Hungary) and their agglomerations bear the typical signs of recession which include: the high unemployment rate, the high proportion of companies becoming bankrupt, difficulty in the conversion of the vocational skills of the labour-force, the migration of the progressive labour-force, and the serious impairment of the environment.

The market mechanism has also affected the rural areas with an underdeveloped and weak economic structure. In the regions which were at a disadvantage historically anyway – chiefly in the ones along the eastern border (the voivodeships of Olsztyn, Suwalki, Siedlice, Biala-Podlaska, Chelm and Zamosc in Poland and Eastern Slovakia, Szabolcs-Szatmár-Bereg, Hajdú-Bihar and Békés counties in Hungary) – the earlier slow economic progress has been replaced by a significant decline. In the course of the earlier central industrialisation hundreds of plants with a low technological level and which were moved there from the core regions on the basis of social considerations have been closed. Furthermore, the output of the food industrial plants situated close to the Soviet recipient market has declined to one-fifth to one-tenth of its former output.

In East-Central Europe the days of uninterrupted growth, rapid industrialisation and the perceivable rise of living standards are over. The reserves of growth have come to an end. The beginning of a new era is also justified by a reversal in the regional processes.

The elaboration of the content of regional policy to replace regional planning, the identification of the organisational system and instruments, and the representation of this spatial policy as an independent socioeconomic field of force and its integration within the process of modernisation is feasible but dependent upon the type of strategy adapted in East-Central Europe. One alternative is a regional policy based on the dominant role of the state and a decentralised system of institutions. The other solution is a policy which departs from regional initiatives and the decentralisation of the instruments of state commitments. The second approach is the determining tendency of Western European development, even in those countries where the ruling political forces advocate the greater role of the state in the regulation of the market processes. Because of the regionalisation of European integration, the re-evaluation of the role of regional decision-making centres in the international division of labour and the geopolitical position of East-Central Europe (Horváth 1992), a cooperative, restructuring-oriented and innovative regional policy may become an effective strategy in modernisation. Of course, the possibility that the necessary conditions for this may not be created in each country or region in the long run has to be reckoned with. Therefore, it is probable that for a long time a combination of the traditional Western European regional policy of the 1970s–1980s and elements of the new regional political paradigms will be characteristic of the East-Central European regional development strategies.

Regional Political Reform and Public Administration

If regional policy in East-Central Europe is regarded as an essential element of modernisation, it is necessary to examine its organisational structure as well. The former decisive organisational form of regional development was the powerful central planning office at the peak of the hierarchical planning apparatus in all the countries. The regional developments depending upon the central capital investments and the social welfare policy of the state did not require a system of institutions being active at regional level and cooperating with a number of interrelated agents. The interests of state redistribution and central will were asserted most effectively by the vertically subordinated organisations. Thus, state logistics determined the regional–administrative division as well.

Even though formally, and with regard to operational functioning, the socialist public administration was not much different from that of the developed democracies, the dominant organising principle, the so-called 'democratic centralism' and the omnipotence of the communist party resulted in a peculiar functioning in public administration. The organs of local power were practically – especially in the first three decades of extensive industrialisation and settlement development – ruthless executors of the central will, completely leaving out of consideration the regional endowments of the developments. As dictatorship became softer in a few countries – for example, in Poland and Hungary – local initiatives started to gain more and more ground. As a result, in these countries the civic values (the tertiary sphere, private initiatives) could also appear in the field of urbanisation in the 1980s.

Yet the structure of public administration and the number of its levels were changed several times in the East-Central European countries during the 40 years of the communist regime. The reason for this is to be found in the actual tasks of the construction of society. When the authorities regarded the social reorganisation of agriculture as its main assignment – in the 1950s – the most important units of state administration were the settlements and accordingly the socialist state management elaborated new forms and organisational solutions focusing on them. When, however, industrialisation and the planning of inter-settlement migration became a priority of state organisation, then the reorganisation (political but not functional) of the territorial–regional administrative units was a task of utmost importance.

Although the changes in the administrative influence of central management derived from common economic and political objectives, the precise form of public administration exhibited great variation. The transformation of public administration took place in several stages after the communist take-over. The organisational system of the bourgeois public administrations in the period before the transformation reflected historical traditions. Public administration was made up of 10 provinces, 95 districts and 2000 communes in Bulgaria; 3 regions, 269 districts and 142,000 communes in Czechoslovakia; 27 counties, 113 districts and 3000 communes in Hungary; 16 voivodeships, 264 districts and 14,609 communes in Poland; 58 provinces, 421 districts and 6248 communes in Rumania (Hoffmann 1971). In the early 1950s this three-level hierarchic administrative structure suited the system of councils which had been formulated on the Soviet model and the changes taking place affected first of all the territorial level on the basis of the 'Divide and rule!' principle. In the following three decades more and more administrative reforms were effected – with the exception of Hungary – and the basic logic of organisation, the centralised management, remained unaltered (Table 4.5).

After the change of regime the East-Central European state construction went through significant changes of content with the hierarchic system of councils with its executive character being replaced by the self-governmental structure. The laws of self-government created the constitutional bases for the decentralised execution of power. Today the local governments already have the constitutional safeguards of their independence in both organisation and decision-making. Significant changes have also occurred in the financing of the local governments.

In spite of these advantageous changes, the public administrative units which can be found (at the mesolevel) between the central government and the settlements still await their role to be defined. It is a general phenomenon in East-Central Europe that these levels – mostly to counterbalance the negative role they used to play in the former regime and their extremely strong political and redistributing functions – have only insignificant licences of self-government. The territorial level was either abolished (in the Czech Republic and Slovakia) or formed the unambiguous basis of the role of state influence (in Poland, Bulgaria and Rumania), or

Table 4.5 Summary of changes in administrative units in East-Central Europe

Countries	Pre-communist pattern Number of				First period of communist era 1950–60 Number of				Second period of communist era, 1970–1980 Number of			
	regions	provinces	districts	communes	regions	provinces	districts	communes	regions	provinces	districts	communes
Bulgaria	–	10	95	2000	–	27	867	1833	–	27	–	291
Czechoslovakia	3	–	269	14200	–	10	108	11000	–	19	107	3026
Hungary	–	27	113	3169	–	19	128	3100	–	19	107	3026
Poland	–	16	264	14609	–	17	391	5245	–	49	–	2417
Romania	–	58	421	6248	–	16	146	6150	–	39	–	2942

Source: Hoffman 1971, Gorzelak 1992, Dostál and Kára 1992, Horváth 1989

even though it has self-governing functions (in Hungary), its influence on the regional development process is negligible.

The further development and improvement of public administration at the intermediate level in East-Central Europe can be justified by the following factors:

1. The disintegrational phenomena that can be experienced in the sphere of self-government point to the fact that the legal and interest-related linkage points of the system are lacking. The notion of the model of self-government building exclusively from the bottom and voluntarily proved to be mistaken and unrealistic.

2. Because of the one-level system of self-government the tasks of regional development remained unattended to, and although the decentralised organs of the state are trying to fill this gap, the part of the decentralised state administration entering the vacuum of the intermediate level of self-government faces tasks alien to its organisation. In particular, its sectorally divided structure has resulted in the lack of coordination, information and conciliation of interests.

3. The disintegrated nature of the system of local government and the dysfunctions of the decentralised public administration have intensified the centralising efforts of the central government and in the administrative units the beginnings of a competition between the state and the self-governing models have appeared.

4. The tendency of the nationalisation of the intermediate level is in contrast with the European integrative processes, and this absurdity can be eliminated only by means of the establishment of an intermediate level of self-government.

5. An important task facing the territorial public administration in the future might be the representation and protection of the idea of inter-regional cooperation against the wishes and demands of central governmental institutions. It has to be taken into consideration that the Europe of regions – as one of the guiding principles of European integration – is possible only in the case of the cooperation between territorial units of relatively similar competence and complexity.

If an important role is assigned to the intermediate units in the regional policy of East-Central Europe in the future, then the issue of the present division at the intermediate level comes into the debate. The size and economic potential of the current counties, voivodeships and districts is too small for them to become basic units of the decentralised regional policy (Table 4.6). Thus, it is no accident that conceptions concerning the establishment of new territorial administrative units have been formulated (Figure 4.3). It can be expected that in the future regional-isation will become stronger in several countries which will elicit the reformulation of the division of labour between the centre and the provinces (Bennett 1992, Geshev and Chavdarova 1982, Gorzelak 1992, Horváth 1993).

Table 4.6 Territorial-administrative structure in East-Central Europe, 1993

Countries	Number of mezo units	Average surface area, sq km	Average population, thousands
Bulgaria	9	12,322	997
Czech Republic	76	1,671	137
Hungary	19	4,896	542
Poland	49	6,381	774
Romania	39	6,090	588
Slovak Republic	38	1,290	138

Source: National statistics

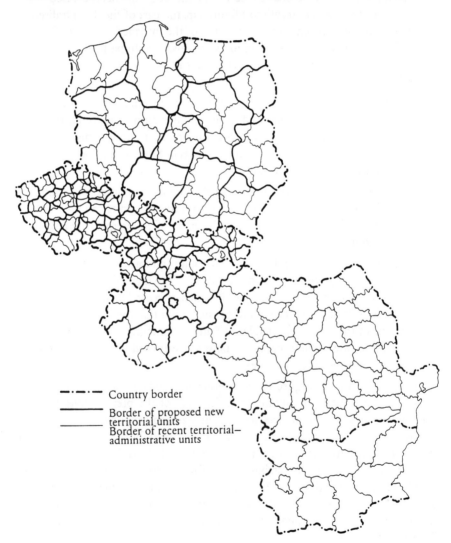

Country border

Border of proposed new
territorial units
Border of recent territorial–
administrative units

Figure 4.3 Proposals for new regional administrative units

Key to Modernisation: The New East–West Cooperation

The East-Central European countries are incapable of achieving modernisation either by themselves, or by means of spatial cooperation and collaboration. For this some external power is needed which can be ensured only by the essential renewal of the whole system of East–West cooperation. Failure to modernise this space may threaten the whole of Europe as a consequence of the level of dependency developed so far. The fact that this point has not been fully realised demonstrates considerable historical short-sightedness.

The Western attitude to the East-Central European countries can be grasped in two perceivable conceptions and one non-existing, but desirable, idea:

1. One kind of behaviour is non-interference which manifests itself in an aversion to the confused relations of the space and the conflicts taking place, as well as the fear of and desire for protection from their spread. All this is ably illustrated by the western attitude in connection with the civil war going on in the former Yugoslavia.

2. Although the other conception appreciates the transformation that has taken place in the East-Central European countries, beyond the moral recognition, the West does not wish to give assistance in the modernisation by making the required resources available. The situation of the German eastern provinces shows that these countries are thereby forced into a peculiar vassalry status. The financial assistance is aimed at the moderation of the conflicts and the short-term management of crises and are devoid of any specific perspective or long-term goal.

3. Third, an unheard of, yet extremely desirable, course of action on the part of the West would be an understanding of the need for the modernisation of this space – or at least of the Visegrád Three, Slovenia and Croatia – by means of efficient assistance and initiative involving collaboration in its realisation. This is not enough for a breakthrough by itself, since the economic policies of modernisation at the national and regional levels is also required, but it represents an important prerequisite.

The historical task of the modernisation of East-Central Europe makes the institutional cooperation of the East and the West unavoidable. The only tangible product of the possibility of cooperation which has a strategic significance is the widely debated treaty of association of the Visegrád Three with the European Communities.

The treaty of association and the circle of the eligible countries shows deliberation on the side of the West. The countries which are to enter the integration have obtained the promise of the possibility of actual joining – that is of the recovery of the economy – but for this they have to become economically and politically suitable. The most important question, namely, how they can become suitable, is left without a reply in the treaty. It is like being caught in a trap, since the outcome expected on the eastern side is at once the requirement set up on the western side: modernisation.

The cooperation between the eastern and western spaces of Europe has both a past and a future. From the aspect of the West the expediency of the establishment of connections and participation in the modernisation of the Central and Eastern European space can be justified not only by a system of negative arguments. There is no doubt that the political crisis, the threat of civil war, the processes generated by internal disintegration, the strengthening migration, and the start of a new migration of nations puts the safety of the West at stake and requires a response. Detachment is untenable because of all the phenomena which carry the danger of an ecological disaster (nuclear warheads, nuclear power stations, chemical plants, etc.). But beyond the imminent dangers East-Central Europe is at the same time a vast potential market the value of which is enhanced by geographical proximity, historical and cultural values shared with the West, as well as the results of the cooperation achieved so far. However, this market should first have the ability to purchase! This space may well contribute to Western Europe becoming more able to cope with world economic competition and also respond to the challenges raised by its own modernisation.

The consolidation of the political and economic relations of East-Central Europe requires both prompt assistance and long-term help. A short-term task of primary importance is to stop the destruction of the society which exists there, because the results that have been achieved in the field of political transformation and the change of regime can be endangered by a deepening economic and social crisis. In the interest of relieving the social tensions and moderating the rise of unemployment immediate external help is needed in the temporary financing of the huge budgetary deficit that can be experienced in all the countries of the Central-Eastern space.

What are the chances for East-Central Europe of the end of separation and of becoming an equal partner of the unified Europe? At a time of such fundamental changes pondering on the future involves obvious risks, yet it is possible to make some assumptions concerning the last decade of our century.

There may be several alternative scenarios (Enyedi 1990a). These may be presented as follows:

- Complete or partial integration with East-Central Europe, with the modernised realisation of the confederative dreams not affecting the state sovereignties (through Eastern-Central European or Balkan and/or Central European integration).
- Integration of the Central European small states with Germany.
- The Alps-Adria integration as a partial counterbalance of Germany.
- The gradual integration of both halves of Europe, etc.

Complete integration may come into being only in contiguous spaces. Integration is not merely close economic (corporal) intertwining, but also linkage of the infrastructural networks, systems of settlements and – through work, education, culture, medical treatment and friendly visits – the civilian societies.

The term 'geopolitical reality' was merely a euphemism in the political usage of the past years: it substituted the statement that the Soviet Union was to be feared. Although today there is no need to be afraid of the Soviet Union any more, this does not alter the geographical situation of East-Central Europe. The 'Ferry Region' has approached the West once again, its pieces – the small countries – being united more out of necessity than by solidarity. It is quite probable that external dependence might continue and Germany could obtain the role of an external power again. It can be hoped that this intermediary region of Europe will break with not only the past forty years but the past seventy years as well. For this reason it is hard to approve of the separation from the Balkan countries. The whole of East-Central Europe is an internal market of 120 million consumers, and the integration between these small countries might reduce external dependence. Certainly the East-Central Europe pictured by quite a few observers as one being based on the strong solidarity of the democratic states of this space is rather hazy and uncertain at the moment. But at least it will be constructed from the desirable elements of the future and not the fragments of the repainted past.

References

Bachtler, J. (ed) (1992) 'Socio-economic situation and development of the regions in the neighbouring countries of the Community in Central and Eastern Europe.' Final report to the European Commission. Brussels, Commission of the European Communities. Directorate-General for Regional Policies.

Bennett, R J. (1992) 'European administrative reforms: dimensions for analysis of diversity'. In P. Dostàl et al. (1992) pp.139–148.

Blàzek, J. and Kára, J. (1992) 'Regional policy in the Czech Publik in the period of transition'. In F. Gorzelak and A. Kuklisski (eds) pp.78–94.

Dostál, P., Illner, M., Kára, J. and Barlow, M. (eds) (1992) *Changing Territorial Administration in Czechoslovakia. International Viewpoints.* Amsterdam, University of Amsterdam, Charles University of Prague, Geographical Institute of the Czechoslovak Academy of Sciences.

Dostál, P. and Kára, J. (1992) 'Territorial administration in Czechoslovakia'. In P. Dostal et al. (1992) (eds) pp.17–32.

Ehrlich, É. (1990) 'Országok versenye, 1937–1986' ('Competition among countries, 1937–1986'). *Közgazdasági Szemle 1*, 19–43.

Enyedi, Gy. (1990a) 'Specific features of urbanisation in East-Central Europe.' *Geoforum 2*, 163–172.

Enyedi, Gy. (1990b) 'A kelet-közép-európai régió.' ('The eastern and central European region'). *Magyar Tudomány 4*, 393–401.

Enyedi, Gy. (1992) 'Urbanizáció Kelet-Közép-Európában' ('Urbanisation in East-Central Europe'). *Magyar Tudomány 6*, 685–693.

Geshev, G. and Chavdarova, G. (1992) Research project on local self-government and administrative-territorial division of Bulgaria. Paper prepared for International Workshop on Local Democracy. Krakow, 24–27. March, 1992.

Gibb, R.A. and Michalak, W.Z. (1993) 'Foreign debt in the new East-Central Europe: a threat to European integration?' *Environment and Planning C: Government and Policy 1*, 69–85.

Gorzelak, G. (1992) 'Polish regionalism and regionalisation.' In G. Gorzelak and A. Kuklinski (eds) (1992) pp.465–488.

Gorzelak, G. and Kuklinski, A. (eds) (1992) *Dilemmas of Regional Policies in Eastern and Central Europe*. Warsaw: University of Warsaw. Regional and Local Studies 8.

Gorzelak, G. (1993) 'The regional patterns of Polish transformation.' Report prepared for the European Policies Research Centre, University of Strathclyde. Warszawa, University of Warsaw.

Hoffman, G.W. (ed) (1971) *Eastern Europe: Essays in Geographical Problems*. London: Methuen.

Horváth, Gy. (1987) *Development of the regional management of the economy in East-Central Europe*. Discussion Papers 5. Pécs: Centre for Regional Studies.

Horváth, Gy. (1989) 'A regionális gazdaságszervezés fejlïdése és intézményei' ('Development of organisation of regional economies and its institutions'). Budapest: Akadémiai Kiadó.

Horváth, Gy. (1992) 'A regionális közigazgatás és az európai folyamatok' ('Regional administration and European processes'). *Európa Fórum 4*, 71–86.

Horváth, Gy. (1993) 'Regional socio-economic development in Hungary'. Prepared for the Project 'Regional Development in Poland, Hungary and Czechoslovak Republics'. Pécs: Centre for Regional Studies.

Horváth, Gy. (ed) (forthcoming) *Development Strategies in the Alpine–Adriatic Region*. Pécs: Centre for Regional Studies.

Kornai, J. (1992) *The Socialist System: The Political Economy of Communism*. Princeton: Princeton University Press.

Part Two

European Community Post 1992
Regions in Competition

CHAPTER 5

The Regional Impact of the Internal Market
A Comparative Analysis of Traditional Industrial Regions and Lagging Regions[1]

Michel Quévit

Introduction: Beyond the Classical Approach to the Regional Impact of the Completion of the European Internal Market

The studies carried out, particularly those on behalf of the European Community, concerning the regional impact of completion of the Internal Market generally conclude with a pessimistic vision from a spatial perspective. In a simplified version, they are summed up in the following statement: 'the main effect of completion of the European Market will be to concentrate economic activity in a smaller number of places where cost reductions and scale savings are used to the best advantage' (PA Cambridge Economic Consultants 1988). The authors reach the conclusion that increased aid to the less-favoured regions will be necessary, whilst advising that they be better adjusted to local realities than in the past. It is from this perspective of 1992 that the decision was taken by the European Community to double the Structural Funds. Such an attitude is relatively common. Consequently, it is not a matter of questioning the decision, which derives from the rule of equity, but knowing whether the appreciable quantitative effect of that measure will have a qualitative effect through more favourable economic position-ing of the regions concerned, bearing in mind the economic and technological changes engendered not only by the dynamics of completion of the Internal

---

1   An earlier version of this paper appeared in *Regional Studies 26*, 4.

Market, but also by techno-industrial changes in the highly industrialised countries.

The approach taken in this chapter, therefore, is to focus on the current relations between spatial development and industrial changes. It objects to the neo-classical analysis, because it does not really take into account the predominant integration of science and technology in productive systems in future decades of development of the industrial economy. For proper perception of regional developments, it is necessary to link the impact of the Internal Market to techno-industrial development. In this context, the Single Market can present new development opportunities for the regions of the Community.

Within this conceptual framework, the purpose of this chapter is to examine some theoretical, empirical and policy issues raised by the completion of the Internal Market in relation to the regions of the Community. The first section examines the results of costs of non-Europe studies, the emphasis being on the theoretical approach to the Internal Market and on some lessons raised by the studies from a regional perspective. The second section presents an analysis of the sectoral impact of the Single Market focusing on issues of policy adjustment. The third and fourth sections examine the sectoral impact of the completion of the Single Market for two specific categories of regions, the traditional industrial regions and the lagging regions of the community. The last section considers possible innovative policy adjustment scenarios for the orientations of regional policy.

Regional Impact of the Completion of the Internal Market: Some Lessons from the cost of Non-Europe Studies

The direct effects of the lifting of NTBs: a positive and immediate impact on the global economy

In general, the theoretical approach of studies relating to the assessment of the impact of the lifting of non-tariff barriers (NTBs) is based on the existence of economic advantages linked to the removal of trade barriers and market distortions which can occur in two particular situations: one where existing comparative advantage may be exploited; the other where there is an absence of comparative advantage for products and the advantages result from an intensification of competition. The approach is based principally on the more fundamental studies on the theory of international trade (e.g. Dixit and Norman 1980, Corden 1984, Baldwin 1984).

From a regional point of view, it can be assumed that the direct effects of the lifting of NTBs will be positive, either for the traditional industrial regions (RECTI) or the lagging regions (Objective 1 regions) of the Community, in that firms will benefit from the lowering of production costs. However, differences could occur relating to the structural components of the productive fabric of these regions.

A series of studies under the supervision of the Commission to assess the economic costs of these diverse barriers seems to confirm this hypothesis. The following findings are particularly noteworthy. The costs of customs procedures are of major importance for SMEs (between 30% and 45% higher than for the large businesses) and in countries where the administrative procedures are relatively more extensive (Ernst and Whinney 1987). Also, the direct effect of opening government markets on capital equipment apply, above all, in the following areas: industrial boilers (reduction of 20%); turbine generators (12%); electric engines (20%); and the telephone industry (30–40%) (Atkins 1987).

More specifically, studies of several industrial sectors (food products, pharmaceutical products, car manufacturing, textiles and clothing, construction material and telecommunications equipment) highlight the importance of the sensitivity of the national economies to the probable effects of the SEM according to their sectoral specialisation. These studies indicate that the direct effects of the SEM are beneficial for most regions. Of course, a more detailed analysis is needed to confirm this hypothesis, inasmuch as these sectoral findings are too global, and they do not integrate the very great differences which may exist at the sub-sectoral level along the entire industrial production chain (see Quévit, Houard, Bodson and Dangoisse 1991, Buiges, Ilkovit and Lebrun 1990).

The indirect effects of the completion of the Internal Market

According to completed studies, the creation of the SEM will have integration effects of three kinds. First, a reduction of costs will be achieved by better exploitation of production units through technical economies of scale or range and comparative advantages through increases in volume and inter/intra-industry restructuring processes. Second, price competition pressure (above all in protected sectors) by way of diverse mechanisms will lead to: encouragement to increase efficiency (reduction of the X-inefficiency, i.e. of internal inefficiency); rationalisation of industrial structures; construction of a more adequate price system in relation to real production costs (price/cost margin); and adjustment between industries effected by the interplay of comparative advantages. Third, the non-price effects of increased competition will encourage businesses to improve their organisation, to increase the quality and variety of their products, to innovate production processes and, on the macroeconomic level, to intensify innovative flow relating to product and processes.

From a regional perspective, the results of these studies suggest differential regional effects of the SEM. In general, there are only limited opportunities for regions to generate technical economies of scale in industry because of the incidence of sectors where demand is stagnating or sectors of low technology products. Many SMEs will find it difficult to pass the minimum efficiency size threshold. There are also few possibilities for many regions to generate technical economies of scale in services, except for those which have good urban infrastructure, and the peripheral geographical position of many regions is an obstacle to non-technical economies of scale aiming at the reduction of transport costs.

Porter (1985) rightly notes that the impact of the completion of the Internal Market will be of a different nature according to the structural characteristics of a firm's sector of activity. The completion of the Single Market represents an opportunity for firms situated in a specialist or volume environment, but the impact in an environment of a fragmented type would be limited, except to change the rules of the competition and to move to industrial production for standardised products (Emerson 1990).

It is a primary requirement that efforts be made to increase knowledge of the structural environment of the regions. A first such attempt appears in this chapter in the sections devoted to the sectoral impact of the Internal Market on industry in the Community countries and their adaptation to the traditional industrial regions (RETI) and the lagging regions of the Community.

The Sectoral Impact of the Completion of the Internal Market

Buiges et al. (1990) identify forty industrial sectors as likely to be the subject of NTBs affecting intra-Community trade. This concerns industries which are currently protected by NTBs and where these barriers prevent the exploitation of economies of scale or permit the retention of wide price discrepancies between the Member States. These sectors represent 50% of the value added of the Community and are more or less equally spread among Member States (see Table 5.1).

Table 5.1 Weight of the forty identified sectors at Community level

Country	Share in industrial value added	Share in industrial employment
Ireland	59.6	43.3
Germany	54.6	54.5
France	53.4	50.8
United Kingdom	52.5	50.0
Belgium	48.8	50.1
Italy	47.7	48.6
Netherlands	47.0	44.9
Portugal	45.3	48.1
Greece	44.8	45.4
Spain	40.9	39.1
Denmark	39.6	39.4

Source: Commission of the European Communities

With respect to structural achievements and comparative advantages of productive systems, a new differentiation is appearing between the economies of the southern and northern countries in the EC, based on an examination of their comparative advantages in relation to three structural characteristics – capital intensity, labour intensity and R&D. On the basis of forty sectors sensitive to removing NTBs and a redistribution of groups of countries with comparable achievements in all sectors (i.e. those which are mainly strong or weak), five groups of sectors may be identified: capital and R&D intensive sectors; capital but not R&D intensive sectors; labour-intensive sectors; skilled labour-intensive sectors; and less labour and capital intensive sectors (Table 5.2). According to this typology, a differentiated redistribution between the countries of North and South is again apparent with comparative advantage for the northern countries in R&D and/or capital-intensive sectors and comparative advantages for the southern countries in labour-intensive sectors.

Table 5.2 Comparative advantages of each Member State in the forty sectors: relative export/import ratio in the five groups

Country-group	B+L	DK	D	GR	E	F	IRL	I	NL	P	UK
Capital and R&D-intensive sectors	110	61	118	25	85	105	112	65	103	49	109
Capital-intensive sectors	147	216	83	83	118	105	143	120	310	41	85
Skilled labour-intensive sectors	83	101	197	27	68	152	41	120	88	31	130
Labour-intensive sectors	75	88	37	196	379	71	52	345	52	416	87
Less capital and labour-intensive sectors	141	108	186	29	53	103	48	189	89	36	137
Comparative advantages											
Capital intensity	X	X			X		X		X		
Labour intensity				X	X			X		X	
R&D intensity			X			X	X				X

Source: Commission of the European Communities

Inter-industrial and intra-industrial scenarios are distinguished in the relationship between the diversity of productive systems and the dynamic effects of the SEM suggested by Buiges *et al.* (1990),in that they separate out two intra-Community trade scenarios in the linkage between the idea of comparative advantage – that of economies of scale and product differentiation. An inter-industrial scenario is where integration in the Internal Market would favour specialisation in the relatively efficient sectors or those which intensively use abundant resources. If similar products are involved, the lifting of NTBs will favour the geographic concentration of production according to the comparative advantages of the country or region. An intra-industrial scenario is where integration could, where products are differentiated, favour specialisation in different kinds of products on an intra-Community scale. According to the authors, the lifting of NTBs will affect countries and sectors in different ways depending upon whether inter-industrial or intra-industrial type trade dominates. This distinction is important for a regional perspective to the extent that, before Greece, Spain and Portugal joined the EC, intra-Community trade was principally of an intra-industrial type, with the exception of southern Italy (Padoa-Schioppa 1987).

However, with the arrival of southern countries in the Community, trade by these countries with the rest of the Community has been mainly of an inter-industrial type. More precisely, four sectors have been identified which are almost exclusively of the inter-industrial type: wine (Portugal, Spain, Italy and France); the footwear industry (Portugal, Spain, Italy and Greece); clothing (Portugal, Italy and Greece); and machine-tools (Italy, Germany and Spain). It is important to note that more extensive analysis of the situation of the southern countries shows a coexistence within the same country of two scenarios, for example in Spain.

The comparative analysis of the sectoral impact of the SEM on Community countries suggests the existence of at least three types of region:

1. Regions of high achievement exclusively in inter-industrial type trade. This is a category characterised by a significant degree of non-skilled and skilled labour-intensive sectors.

2. Mixed regions with high achievements in inter-industrial type trade but which have intra-industrial type trade sectors. These are regions which consist of labour-intensive sectors and capital-intensive sectors.

3. Regions of weak structural achievement in inter-industrial type trade which excludes them from the benefits of the completion of the Internal Market.

The Impact of the SEM on the Traditional Industrial Regions (RETI)[2]

The principal challenge of the Single Market for the RETI

Two salient characteristics of the productive fabrics of the RETI make these regions vulnerable to the SEM: over-representation of the metal-working industry within their industrial fabrics; and their specialisation in stages upstream of production in which they concentrate two and three times more than the EC as a whole. As

---

2   This part is based on the study entitled *The Social and Economic Consequences of Completion of the Internal Market on the Traditional Industrial Regions (RETI) of the European Community* dealing with the industrial and regional impacts of the Europe-wide market and the formulation of recommendations to help the regional productive fabrics concerned adjust to the implications of the Single Market. The study covered the following RETI regions: Nord-Pas-de-Calais; North Rhine-Westphalia, the Basque Region; South Yorkshire; Strathclyde; Wallonia; and West Yorkshire. This summary has been written by Stefan Bodson, Jean Houard and Michel Quévit. The analysis is more fully developed in Quévit *et al.* (1991).

they are largely mature industries with low previous and potential demand growth and are exposed to fierce competition from within and outside Europe, a reasonable assumption might be that future strategies should involve investment in rationalisation.

This assumption is confirmed overall by panels of regional experts in the RETI study, which tend to indicate that the main thrust of capital spending and R&D in the RETIs' principal industrial sectors over the past five years has been process rather than product-centred. In this regard, the most that can be said to have occurred is a marketing adaptation of the product line rather than any real radical innovation.

Therefore, whilst the effort made to transform the RETIs' principal (and traditional) productive activities cannot accelerate the growth rates of those industries, they should facilitate their future optimisation in terms of added value and cost-effectiveness. It is also of interest that the decision-making centres in these activities tend mainly to be locally-based (except for the steel industry in the two British regions concerned), unlike the better-positioned activities in the RETI portfolio (medium to high growth potential and technological transformation), the main representatives of which most often tend to be operating units of national or international groups. The greater volatility conferred on these latter activities by this status means that the traditional industries remain the 'beam and buttress' of regional development.

The second structural component of relevance to the assessment of the regional impact of the SEM on traditional industrial regions is the RTD potential of the RETI. The impact on RTD to be expected from completion of the Internal Market can be summarised as three major changes. First, the growing importance of non-physical factors in the manufacturing process will confront most sectors of industry with major technological changes. The impact of these technical upheavals is likely to be far greater for the RETI than for other regions of the Community due to their extreme dependence on industries whose production remains too tightly focused upstream of their respective industrial sectors. It is thus essential that the RETIs' RTD thrust should focus more on better-positioned product innovations downstream of the industrial sector.

Second, the scientific and technological competitiveness of the industrialised countries will lead to RTD capacities consolidating around European partnerships through inter-company cooperation schemes with research laboratories on a transnational basis. Such forms of cooperation will be increased, in particular, by the development of outsourcing between major companies and smaller firms on high-technology projects. The relative weakness of the RETIs' RTD capacity compared with the standards required to compete in the technology market with the USA and Japan is a major hindrance on their integration as a positive component of the new scientific and technological dimension ushered in by the Single Market.

Third, the expansion of the major Community programmes, coupled with harmonisation of higher education systems, will contribute decisively to the creation of a European research space, characterised by mobility and interlocking cooperation between university institutions on precise scientific targets, in the fields of both basic and pre-competitive research. The densely concentrated supply of science and technology training is an asset for the RETI, but only if accompanied by measures to retain them in the region in the long term.

The RETIs' economic potential and the impact of the SEM

The sensitivity of the economic potential of RETI can be assessed in relation to direct and indirect inputs. Determining those activities most sensitive to the direct effects of the SEM (dismantling of non-tariff barriers, including customs, standards and public contracts) by their contributed weight to regional employment provides no clear grounds for differentiating the RETI from the EC as a whole. Whilst harmonisation of standards will have by far the most significant impact on the RETI, it will have a similar impact on the Community average. The same applies, though with a markedly less significant impact, to the abolition of custom controls and the simplification of trade-related procedures. By contrast, the RETI will be most affected by the liberalisation of public procurement (due to the comparatively larger presence of firms in this sector), by harmonisation and by the planned long-term dismantling of traditional public intervention programmes, with the manifest exception of R&D programmes, with which the RETI are comparatively less involved than other regions.

Indirect impacts may be more significant. There is a relatively high proportion of industrial operations in the RETI which are sensitive to standardisation and the opening-up of protected markets and public purchases essentially the traditional type which have often received massive public assistance in recent years and which are less outward-looking to external markets than are Community industries on average. This makes the RETI vulnerable to two types of interlocking strategy which may be implemented by actors exogenous and endogenous to the region. The first strategy is the quest for technical economies of scale at production unit level, spurred by mutual recognitions of standards and the opening-up of the most protected markets, particularly public purchases. SMEs and independent larger firms are thus in competition here both with one another and with larger integrated firms whose established international presence gives them an immediate competitive edge.

The second strategy is the search for non-technical economies of scale (R&D, marketing, financial administration) and economies of learning. Spurred by increased competition fuelled in turn by quality considerations, the R&D effort and rapid product replacement (to top-of-range standards), this strategy will bring the specialised subsidiaries of financially-integrated international groups into fiercer competition with SMEs in search of specific market niches, placing a twofold burden on small firms to renew their product lines and diversify their markets.

In consequence, the productive fabrics of RETI will be very specifically affected by the indirect impact of the SEM induced by these strategies which, it can reasonably be assumed, will be operationalised. Other things being equal, the assumption from the foregoing is that the impact will take the form of a strengthening and acceleration of the centrifugal trends of recent years, resulting in further compartmentalisation between large and small firms, between firms in traditional industries and those whose core business is in new activities and/or service provision, and between firms with regionally-based decision-making centres and subsidiaries of foreign groups with no real management independence. For this reason, adjustment policies should chiefly be geared towards re-aggregating and optimising existing assets and resources.

In conclusion, the RETI's regions can be mainly characterised by intra-sectoral exchanges, but dominant sectors intensive in capital will be very vulnerable to the indirect effects of the SEM because of their relatively low R&D capacities. Nevertheless, these regions will be likely to position themselves more positively than the less-favoured regions towards the SEM in so far as they comprise industrial sectors where scale economies can still be achieved.

The Main Impacts of the Completion of the Internal Market on the Objective 1 Regions

With regard to the direct effects of the lifting of NTBs on trade, the regions will benefit from the general movement towards lower costs but they will be more directly concerned by lifting of specific NTBs. The Objective 1 regions will be more sensitive to the lifting of barriers increasing costs than to the lifting of restrictions to market access (Emerson 1990) for several reasons: the importance of SMEs in their productive fabric; less immediate opportunities for economies of scale; and a low degree of sectoral specialisation dependent on government markets (with the exception of certain export subsidies or quota systems and tariff barriers in some countries). This tendency is confirmed by the evolution of the effects of specific NTBs.

As indicated in the study of Buiges et al. (1990), concerning the southern countries, the Objective 1 regions are mainly concerned by the impact of 1992 on sectors with medium NTBs (Group 4). For most of these regions, 1992 will have only a small impact on sectors with high technology linked to public markets. However, familiar differences appear when the national positions are examined.

The Italian regions are clearly more sensitive to the 1992 impact on the sectors with high NTBs, especially those with high technology linked to public markets, both traditional and regulated, than on sectors with medium NTBs. In Spain, the sectors with medium NTBs dominate, but the relative importance of sectors linked to the regulated public markets in Andalucia and the Canaries is notable. In the

Portuguese regions, the 1992 impact will also be stronger for those sectors with medium NTBs. However, there will be a sensitive impact of high-technology sectors linked to public and regulated markets in the Algarve. Lastly, Ireland shows a dual configuration between regions essentially characterised by sectors with NTBs and regions highly influenced by the joint presence of these sectors with high technology sectors and sectors linked to traditional public markets or regulated ones like the Midwest, the West and, to a lesser degree, Donegal and the North West. The North East is a special case, where the presence of sectors linked to traditional public markets or regulated markets is significant.

The main indirect effect of the Internal Market on the Objective 1 regions is related to the effects of phenomena of size. In particular, there is generally little scope for many Objective 1 regions to generate technical economies of scale in industry sectors where demand is stagnating or sectors of low-technology products. Modest economies of scale are possible in the food, drink and tobacco sectors, in textiles and clothing, leather and wood articles, but there may be greater opportunities for economies of scale in the distribution and marketing of certain sub-sectors of farm produce. Many SMEs operating in the Objective 1 regions may find it difficult to pass the minimum efficiency size threshold. In the service sector, there are no opportunities for most Objective 1 regions to generate technical economies of scale except for those which have good urban infrastructure because of the predominance of non-market services over market services, and structural weakness in the supply of services to businesses. Lastly, there is the problem of the peripheral geographical location of many Objective 1 regions with regard to non-technical economies of scale aiming at the reduction of transport costs.

Structural performance of sensitive sectors and vulnerability of Objective 1 regions to the effects of the SEM

The productive fabric of the Objective 1 regions in general is vulnerable with respect to the completion of the Internal Market. Amongst the strong regions, only one, the Midwest, has a configuration of intra-industrial type and is thus well-positioned to face the impact of 1992. The other strong regions are inter-industrial in nature: Norte, Puglia or, with a dual configuration, Murcia, Castilla-La Manche, South West and Campania. Most of the other regions (21 out of 38) are in a vulnerable or threatened position (Table 5.3).

However, some of the mixed regions (10) have vulnerable and strong sectors coexisting: Communidad Valenciana, Abruzzi, Centro, West, Sicilia and Calabria, regions with a dual configuration of intra and inter-industrial type; and Extramadura, of essentially inter-industrial type.

The result of these different statements is that most of the Objective 1 regions must, as a matter of urgency, develop adjustment policies that go beyond the classical inter-industrial exchange scenarios. To stay in an inter-industrial scheme by making profits from the comparative transition cost advantages would make them even more vulnerable to intra-community competition, developing countries

Table 5.3 Level of vulnerability of the productive fabric of Objective 1 regions facing the SEM

	Vulnerable or strong but threatened	Strong	Mixed	Insignificant
Inter-industrial outline	Algarve Central Macedonia East Macedonia Thessalie West Greece Islands and others Greek regions	Norte Puglia	Extramadura	
Intra-industrial outline	Asturias Castilla-Leon Molise Lisbon	Midwest	Alentejo Sardenia South-East	
Dual	Andalucia Galicia Basilicata Peloponnese Nord-Est Donegal NW Midlands East Attica Central Greece	South West Campania	C. Valenciana Castilla La Mancha Abruzzi Centro Murcia West Sicillia Calabria	Canaries

or competition from Eastern Europe. The development in these regions of the intra-industrial scenario, centred essentially on the exogenous contribution of foreign firms with high technological potential, will maintain and/or reinforce the dualism of regional economies by isolating the endogenous potential of these regions from the growth process.

Accordingly, two more innovative adjustment scenarios are proposed. One is of the inter-industrial type, the other of the intra-sectoral type; both scenarios avoid the dangers described above. In this context, the Objective 1 regions have room for improvement in the enforcement of their policy in so far as (for most) they could combine innovative adjustment scenarios of inter-industrial and intra-industrial types and try to establish complementarities and synergies between these two approaches. For the regions dominated by inter-industrial exchanges, it is important to note that an inter-industrial adjustment that upgrades regional specialisation is perfectly accessible in the perspective of Internal Market completion.

Plurality of Adjustment Scenarios Adapted to the Regions

Probable adjustment strategy for the regions to the inter-industrial and intra-industrial scenarios

The adjustment strategy of most regions will follow the classical inter-industrial or intra-industrial scenarios if dynamic regional policies are implemented. The classic inter-industrial scenario is that of a region whose structural achievements are characterised by low-skilled, labour-intensive sectors. In this scenario, the removal of NTBs will encourage industries to increase their production in areas where they have a comparative advantage and they will, therefore, aim to increase their inter-industrial specialisation. This policy is reinforced by the existence of low wage costs. From this point of view, following the removal of NTBs, the behaviour of economic agents will favour the improvement of the internal capacity of the business but principally the adaption of production processes and not intra-Community cooperation. They will remain oriented mainly towards the domestic market and/or towards intra-Community exports of simplified and traditionally well-made products.

Such a scenario has a certain number of short-term advantages to the extent that companies draw maximum immediate profit from the lifting of the NTBs and north–south relocation movements are favoured. Nevertheless, this type of scenario is not without risk in the medium term. As is already the case with industries in certain Objective 1 regions, these regions must eventually contend with competition from developing countries and changes in Eastern Europe.

The classic intra-industrial scenario is where regions choose to support development of capital and R&D-intensive sectors. The lifting of NTBs allows more concentrated exploitation of economies of scale and an increase in competition which will increase pressure for product differentiation. The behaviour of economic agents aims jointly at an intensive investment policy in R&D (technological creation type), highly-qualified human resources and the development of intra-Community technological partnerships at the level of pre-competition research. This long-term scenario has its dangers, especially for the Objective 1 regions which must rely on the contribution of foreign investment in advance industries and the attraction of multinational companies. There is a risk, therefore, of the scenario leading to a dualisation of the regional productive fabric between high-performance technology sectors and less-competitive local industries whose adjustment costs can be very heavy for regional economies such as Ireland.

Adjustment policy aimed at innovative inter-industrial and intra-industrial scenarios

The vulnerability of the productive fabric of regions facing the SEM suggests that it is imperative for most of the regions to develop adjustment policies which allow them to avoid the negative effects of industrial strategies associated with the two classical scenarios described above. To face the necessity of by-passing the classical adjustment schemes, two alternative scenarios are proposed and labelled as innovators because they belong to approaches that produce a double dynamic: the

Table 5.4. Proposal of dynamic adjustment scenarios adapted to the problem of Objective 1 regions

	Classic inter-industrial scenario	Inter-industrial innovative scenario	Intra-industrial innovative scenario	Classic intra-industrial scenario
Regional structural achievements	Dominance of non-qualified labour intensive sectors	Dominance of qualified labour intensive sectors	Dominance of sectors intensive in capital and in average technological content	Dominance of capital intensive and high technology sectors
Method of industrial development linked to the comparative advantages and IM impact	Increased industrial specialisation	Upgrading of the range of products, specialist products in great demand	Technological niches Tailored products	Product differentiation
Strategy of businesses in view of NTB	Improvement of internal capacity with emphasis on the innovation of production processes	Improvement of internal capacity with emphasis on product innovation, technological transfers	Modern management: technological expertise, technological product adaptation, technological partnerships and inter-company cooperation	Increase of R&D investments, technological production, international technological partnership
Marketing strategy	Priority orientation towards the domestic market	Initiation of intra-Community exchanges and growth of market sectors	Initiation of intra-Community trade for target products and tailored products	Technical and non-technical economies of scale, intra-industrial strengthening, oligopolistic control
Risks and advantages	Short-term advantages: cost/margin. Medium and long-term risks: competition of less developed countries and Eastern countries	Medium-term advantages: Control of intra and extra-Community market sectors. Long-term danger: competition of new less-developed countries	Medium-term and long-term advantages of growing population	Dependence on foreign investments and increase in the division of the regional productive fabric high adjustment costs

Anticipated evolution: change from an inter-industrial type of economy to an intra-industrial type of economy

valorisation of the existing regional economic potential; and the taking into account of structural logic determined by the creation of an internal market. One belongs to the inter-industrial logic, the other to the intra-industrial logic (Table 5.4).

The inter-industrial innovative scenario is based on classic inter-industrial trade, in which the regions profit from the opportunity of lifting NTBs to integrate with products of a higher value added in the context of homogeneous and traditional production (upgrading of the range). The behaviour of economic agents will remain centred principally upon the improvement of internal company capacity but favour policies of investment in production innovation and technology transfer. In view of this, the business manager will simultaneously develop partnership cooperation with other businesses and technology transfer institutions on the local and intra-community plane, notably in the area of technological trade and distribution. The objective will be to increase the share of the intra and extra-community market. In view of this, the regions will be able progressively to improve their specialisation in more capital-intensive sectors. Such a scenario is more particularly suited to Objective 1 regions which are, from the outset, more dependent on qualified and non-qualified labour-intensive sectors.

The intra-industrial innovative scenario is one in which the regions will try to profit from the lifting of the NTBs to increase the competitiveness of capital and qualified labour-intensive sectors progressively to integrate them in intra-industrial economic trade, based on existing human and technological resources. The final objective sought is product differentiation. To achieve this, the economic agents will favour agreements of intra-Community cooperation with the aim of increasing the technological content of their products. They aim to establish themselves in technological niches and/or in tailored products. They will try progressively to enter into pre-competitive European research partnerships with advanced technology businesses and research institutions. Particular attention is given to the training of highly-qualified employees and local labour to meet the new technological requirements of the business by developing cooperation with institutes of higher education. In view of this, the regions will be able to improve the achievements of their productive fabric in the capital and technology-intensive sectors. This scenario is more particularly suited to the RETI or the Objective 1 regions which possess capital-intensive sectors with a minimum of technological capacity (such as research centres and universities).

References

Atkins, W S. (1987) *The Cost of Non-Europe in Public Sector Procurement.* Reading: Atkins Management Consultants.

Baldwin, R.A. (1984) 'Trade policies in developed countries.' In R.W. Jones and P.B. Kenen (eds) *Handbook of International Economies 1.* Amsterdam: North-Holland:.

Buiges, P., Ilkovitz, F. and Levrun, J-F. (1990) 'The sectoral impact of the Internal Market.' *European Economy* (Social Europe, special issue). Brussels: CEC.

Corden, M. (1984) 'The normative theory of international trade.' In R.W. Jones and P.B. Kenen (eds) *Handbook of International Economies* I. Amsterdam: North-Holland.

Dixit, A. and Norman, V. (1980) *Theory of International Trade.* Cambridge: Cambridge University Press.

Emerson, M. (1990) *1992, La Nouvelle Économie Européenne; une Évaluation par la Commission de la CE des Effets Économiques de l'Achèvement du Marché Interieur.* Bruxelles: De Boeck Université.

Ernst and Whinney (1987) *The Cost of Non-Europe; Border-Related Controls and Administrative Formalities.* Brussels: CEC.

PA Cambridge Economic Consultants (1988) 'The regional impact of policies implemented in the context of completing the Community's Internal Market by 1992.' *Final Report, DG XVI,* Commission of the European Communities, Brussels.

Padoa-Schioppa, T. (1987) 'Efficiency, stability and equity: a strategy for the evolution of the economic system of the European Community.' Report of a study group appointed by the European Communities, Brussels.

Porter, M. (1985) *Competitive Advantage.* New York: Free Press.

Quévit, M., Houard, J., Bodson, S. and Dangoisse, A. (1991) *Impact regional 1992: les Regions de tradition industrielle.* Bruxelles: De Boeck Université.

CHAPTER 6

The Economic Role of Regional Governments in the European Community

David Newlands

Introduction

Within the European Community (EC), there is a new enthusiasm for active regional governments. The Commission has a vision of a 'Europe of the Regions' in which there would be a reasonably homogeneous regional structure across Europe. This view has been strengthened by the increasing acceptance of the principle of subsidiarity which now informs much of the debate about the allocation of functions between the different levels of government within the EC. While this concept is open to various interpretations, there appears to be a common assumption that certain functions will be guaranteed to subsidiary levels of government, including regional authorities (Adonis and Tyrie 1991, Spicker 1991). What is not clear from the concept of subsidiarity is what those functions should be.

The economic functions of regional governments is also a neglected topic in the academic literature. While there has been much discussion of the role of smaller local authorities (Helm and Smith 1989), and the literature on 'fiscal federalism' has analysed at some length the financial relationships between national and regional level governments in federal states (Oates 1991), there has been less consideration of the wider economic role of regional governments, especially in non-federal states. To some extent, this gap is now being filled (Bennett 1990a) but much remains to be done in detailing the appropriate functions of a regional tier.

This chapter explores the range of theoretical arguments concerning the possible economic functions of regional governments and then brings these arguments to bear on the experience of the five largest EC states – Germany, France, Italy, Spain and the UK – and the regional policy of the EC itself.

The Economic Theory of Regional Government

The stabilisation, distribution and allocation functions

Much economic theory of the respective roles of the market and the government derives from a neoclassical perspective. Within this, government is assumed to operate at two levels, central and local. The neoclassical model is incomplete and unconvincing but provides a convenient starting point.

Neoclassical theory recognises three government economic roles. Musgrave (1959) called these the stabilisation, allocation and distribution functions. The stabilisation function is concerned with macroeconomic policy and the distribution function with the redistribution of income and other resources. It is generally argued that these two functions should be confined to national government, or rather the highest level of the structure of government (King 1984). The openness of regional or local economies means that macroeconomic management is infeasible. Indeed, this is becoming true of national economies. At present, a whole range of macroeconomic functions are being transferred from member states to the EC.

The argument that redistributive policies are most appropriately carried out at national or supranational level partly reflects the view that it should be a single level of government which is assigned the role of determining the extent of income redistribution. Otherwise, it is quite likely that redistributive policies pursued independently by a number of levels of government would conflict. In addition, the case for the assignment of redistributive functions to the national or supranational level reflects the costs which might arise if local redistributive policies provoked substantial population movements. However, while the distributional priorities of government are most appropriately set centrally, implementation may be carried out more efficiently at a lower level of government. Thus, in practice, the administration of much redistributive spending, for example on health care or education, may be decentralised.

According to neoclassical theory, the main economic role of sub-central government relates to the allocation function. This arises because the conditions under which a market economy would yield an optimally efficient allocation of resources are so stringent (Helm and Smith 1989). Individuals have to be fully informed about the choices open to them. There should be no monopoly power, no externalities and no public goods. Property rights have to be perfectly defined and costlessly enforced. Both capital and labour have to be perfectly mobile. Since the market fails to meet these strict conditions, government intervention may increase allocative efficiency. The performance of government depends on its capacity to respond sensitively to the needs and preferences of individuals and communities and on its ability to obtain and process the necessary information.

An important element in the ability of governments to process information and make the appropriate decisions is their organisational structure. Specifically, decentralised government is likely to be better informed about the preferences of particular individuals or communities and better able to reflect those preferences. Thus, it can be argued that sub-central governments use resources more efficiently than either the market or central government in undertaking expenditure at the local level.

Both regional and local authorities have a role to play in the provision of public services but there are certain services which are more appropriately provided by a regional tier of government. Regions may be able to capture administrative economies of scale and avoid complex externalities while still reaping the gains from better information about local preferences. Due to their greater size, regions will face fewer constraints from migration than local authorities. Moreover, the balance of advantage between regions and smaller local authorities may not be stable but rather may be shifting in favour of regional government (Firn and MacLennan 1979). As people move towards a greater uniformity of tastes, so distinctive patterns of individual preferences are more likely to be identifiable at the regional rather than the local level.

These arguments have important implications for the financing of sub-central government. Specifically, central government grants may play several distinct roles. First, there may be administrative economies to be reaped from central government collecting taxes and then allocating grants as necessary to finance the activities of local authorities. Second, grants are a recognition of the interest that central government or people in other areas might have in specific aspects of an authority's spending. For example, spending on education may need to reflect national priorities as well as local preferences. Third, grants can be used to combat fiscally induced migration, of firms or individuals, if a suitable non-mobile tax base cannot be identified. Finally, and most importantly, grants are a mechanism for the equalisation of differential needs and resources.

In each case, regions will probably be less reliant on grants than local authorities. Regions are better able to exploit economies of scale in tax collection. They are more likely to be able to internalise externalities. They will generally confront less fiscally induced migration. While grants may still be required to equalise inter-regional differences, these are less marked than the disparities between local government areas.

The growth function

According to neoclassical theory, the principal role of local government lies with the allocation function. This argument is generally applied within a central–local government structure but with a little stretching it can be extended to cover a regional tier of government.

The principal flaw of the neoclassical model, however, is that it exaggerates the effectiveness of market mechanisms and diminishes the economic importance of government. This is true of the stabilisation, distribution and allocation functions which neoclassical theory concedes as legitimate roles of government. Moreover, the neoclassical model fails to recognise the potential for government to raise the dynamic efficiency and technological capability of the economy. Economic development policy constitutes a further dimension of government economic activity and is termed here the growth function.

The growth function does not fit easily into Musgrave's tripartite division. It occupies distinct ground between macroeconomic policy and service provision. On the one hand, macroeconomic policy is a means of achieving a more stable level of utilisation of the economy's productive capacity. It is concerned with stabilisation around the trend rather than the trend itself. On the other hand, while economic development policy could be viewed as a public good and thus included under service provision intended to achieve a more efficient allocation of given resources, this is not a satisfactory perspective since it confines the argument to a largely static framework. The importance of economic development policy is precisely as a means of increasing dynamic efficiency.

The growth function of government can be justified as a response to three instances of market failure to ensure optimal dynamic efficiency. First, risk aversion by lenders or industrialists may inhibit the pursuit of risky projects and so constrain technological innovation. Second, imperfect information may prevent the identification of profitable market opportunities and thus restrict the rate of growth. Third, the existence of externalities means that certain business services will be under-provided by the private market.

A role for national or supranational government in pursuit of the growth function does not necessarily imply any such role for regional government. Indeed, it has traditionally been considered that decentralised 'economic development expenditures are purely diversionary "zero sum" effects in a game which disproportionately burdens those localities which have the least resources to play the game' (Bennett 1990b, p.221). However, new arguments for giving regions more autonomy in economic development policy have arisen from a recognition of the changing nature of production in capitalist economies.

The relative advantage of large-scale, mass production methods seems to be declining. Small-scale, flexible methods of production can now compete more effectively. There is increased innovation and more market diversification. There is more reliance on subcontracting and the use of internal markets within the firm. These changes have variously been identified as a shift from organised to disorganised capitalism, from mass production to flexible specialisation, or from Fordism to post Fordism (Piore and Sabel 1984, Lash and Urry 1987, Harvey 1989). The universality of these trends should not be exaggerated. Mass production, mass markets and economies of scale are still very important in many sectors.

Nevertheless, there has been a shift in the balance of production and this has significant implications for the determinants of growth.

Those local and environmental factors which regional governments can influence have increased in importance. Regions are thus in a position to evolve distinctive development policies which reflect local knowledge and opportunities. Strategies for prominent sectors of production are important because, in each sector of the economy, alternative development paths exist with different implications for employment, the nature of technology and working conditions, and the environment (Commission of the European Communities, 1991a). Technology initiatives may be a further significant element of regions' economic development policies. Regional development agencies or similar bodies appear to be useful vehicles in the implementation of appropriate economic development policies. They have been employed in an attempt to tackle all three market failures referred to above, providing capital, advice and services.

Decentralised economic development policy may be greatly constrained by the active pursuit of distributional objectives. Drawing upon German experience, Zimmerman (1990) has argued that:

> distributional issues are easy to perceive and lend themselves to direct and visible remedy by public action. In contrast, growth (or at least sustained high level income) needs allocational instruments which work over a long time, are less visible, and imply present saving for future returns, which means no 'public benefits' for a national government with a more short term political perspective. If this is true, the existence and safeguarding of strong sub-national regional governments can be interpreted as an institutional provision to secure a share of resources for the national growth objective. Regional growth can shift to those regions which are able and willing to accommodate to the necessities of a growth orientation. (p.251)

Regional Government in European Community Countries

The centrality of economic development policy to the rationale for regional government helps explain the experiences of different countries. The cases of Germany, France, Italy, Spain and the UK are reviewed briefly here.

West Germany had eleven powerful, constitutionally entrenched regional governments or Länder. Following reunification, five Länder have been recreated in the former East Germany. The responsibilities of the Länder include education, cultural affairs, and local government. Moreover, the promotion of economic development has long been a decentralised area of policy in Germany. Most Länder have their own regional programmes and industrial development agencies (Littlechild 1982). On the other hand, there has been some centralisation of functions and finance, largely as a result of attempts by the federal government to increase the extent of regional redistribution. The federal government operates a regional policy, mainly concerned with infrastructural improvements, in conjunction with the Länder (Bartels 1981). In addition, an equalisation fund was established in 1969 although this and other mechanisms of redistribution between the Länder is under enormous strain from the reunification process.

In contrast to the German experience of greater centralisation over the last forty years, the powers of decentralised government have been significantly strengthened in France, Italy and Spain.

The twenty-two French regions were originally designated in 1955. At first, their only function was to provide the framework for the regional dimension of the National Plan. However, they gradually gained in authority and the Socialist government's decentralisation reforms in the 1980s greatly extended the role of the regions. The regional councils, which have been elected bodies since 1986, play an essential role in the elaboration of regional development plans which are then married to the functional and sectoral plans of the National Plan. In addition, the French regions have other functions in the encouragement of economic growth (Tuppen 1988). They have responsibility for vocational training and adult education. They administer two French regional policy grants and are also empowered to finance or guarantee loans, provide industrial sites and arrange business advice.

While there has been some genuine decentralisation of government functions in France, central government maintains tight control of regional finances. Regional governments receive the revenues from a car registration tax and can levy certain minor taxes but are otherwise largely dependent on central government grants. The system has the potential to be redistributive, from rich to poor regions, but the extent of any redistribution appears to be small (Prud'homme 1990).

In Italy, the Republican Constitution of 1948 provided for five 'special' regions and fourteen (subsequently increased to fifteen) 'ordinary' regions although the creation of the latter took until 1970. A crucial factor in the implementation of this regional structure was that 'regionalism tended to dovetail with another important reform movement – economic planning. The obvious inadequacy of local provincial and communal economic planning and the growing awareness of the need for a firmer and wider spatial base for regional planning favoured the establishment of the regional councils in 1970' (King 1987, p.177). Apart from social and cultural provision, the regions' powers largely concern physical planning and economic development policy. The twenty Italian regions vary considerably in size and it has been the largest regions which have gone furthest in implementing strategic economic plans. The five special regions have wider responsibilities and financial resources than the ordinary regions but, with the exception of Sicily, they are among the smaller regions.

Regional governments in Italy do not have independent taxation powers. Almost all regional finances are state grants. While the allocation of funds has generally favoured the poorer regions in the South, the relative economic advantage of the Northern regions has persisted. Thus, as in France, regional decentralisation has not succeeded in significantly reducing regional inequality (Rey and Pola 1990).

In recent years, Spain has moved rapidly towards a system of regional government. Decentralisation was viewed as an essential element in the return to democracy after the death of Franco. In 1979, Catalonia and the Basque Country became the first two 'autonomous communities' created under the new Spanish Constitution. Fifteen other autonomous communities were created between 1981 and 1983. The exclusive powers of the Spanish regions include cultural affairs, housing, town planning and environmental protection. Economic development policy is among the powers shared between the central and regional governments. Many of the autonomous communities have started offering incentive packages and undertaking promotion in order to attract foreign investment.

The Spanish regions are financed from a variety of sources. They retain the revenues from certain taxes levied by central government, and derive income from their own local taxes, rates and surcharges, but otherwise are heavily dependent on tax-sharing grants from central government. It has been argued that this fiscal system detracts from the regions' efficiency both in providing services and in encouraging economic development (Sole-Vilanova, 1990). On the other hand, there is evidence that it is a powerful means of redistributing income in Spain (Castells 1990).

The UK is exceptional among the larger EC states in not having a network of elected regional authorities and provides an instructive contrast with France, Italy and Spain, other unitary, previously centralised, states of broadly comparable size.

In the 1960s, the British experience fitted the general European trend rather well. A regional planning system based on Regional Economic Planning Councils was introduced. These Councils operated within eleven regions – Scotland, Wales, Northern Ireland and eight regions of England. Although the Councils lacked formal powers and finance, they were precisely the type of regional advisory body which, in other countries, gradually generated their own territorial demands and allegiances. However, the regional planning framework in the UK failed to develop into a system of regional government. While the Regional Economic Planning Councils were regional bodies, their principal function was to carry out a central policy, the National Plan. When the National Plan foundered, much of the rationale for the Councils disappeared. They were finally abolished in 1979, apart from the one in Scotland (Keating 1989).

Some of the larger local authorities might still have formed the basis of a regional tier. However, the abolition of the Greater London Council and the English metropolitan councils in 1986 has meant that few local authorities in the UK are now of the size to attempt the strategic policies and economic development efforts pursued by regional governments in other European countries. Nevertheless, while there are no elected regional governments, there is some decentralisation of state functions in the UK (Brunskill 1990). The Scottish, Welsh and Northern Irish Offices are, in effect, regional administrations. Within England, the Departments of Employment, Trade and Industry and Environment maintain a network of regional offices.

The Role of Regional Government in EC Regional Policy

There are very considerable regional disparities within the European Community. The ten least developed regions have an average per capita income of less than one third that of the ten most developed regions. Moreover, while inequalities narrowed a little in the 1960s and 1970s, they widened again in the first half of the 1980s (Commission of the European Communities, 1991b).

EC regional policy was reformed in 1989 in recognition of the fact that the likely effects of the completion of a single market will be to widen regional disparities throughout the EC still further. It was agreed that the Structural Funds of the EC, which comprise the European Regional Development Fund, the European Social Fund and the Guidance Section of the Agricultural Fund, be doubled in real terms by 1993. There is to be greater coordination of the three different Structural Funds and they now target specific Community priorities rather than national priorities. The other principal change is that there is to be a move away from financing individual projects to programme finance. Programmes are to be based on regional development plans submitted by national governments but, in most EC countries, drawn up by regional governments. The regional level tier of government is thus to become central to the formulation and implementation of EC regional policy.

Several different reasons have been given for increasing the direct involvement of regional authorities (Council of Europe 1990). The most commonly cited argument is that this will lead to a better understanding of local needs in the formulation of development plans. It is in this respect that the principle of subsidiarity has most influenced the reform process. However, there are also more pragmatic considerations. In particular, by channelling funds directly to regional and local authorities, the Commission hopes to ensure that EC funds are wholly additional to national funds.

Despite these developments, there are still a number of serious obstacles to the building of an institutional framework within which regional governments can be involved in EC regional policy. For a start, not all member states have regional government structures. Furthermore, at present, Germany and Belgium, both federal states, are the only two EC countries which have a formal machinery for involving regional authorities in the EC decision-making process. While the intention is that, in future, regional development plans will be drawn up by the regions themselves, in the past there has often been comparatively little consultation with regional and local authorities (Council of Europe 1990). The only new developments to emerge from the Maastricht summit were agreements to conduct a further review of EC regional policy and to create a Committee of the Regions.

It is unlikely that the strengthening of EC regional policy and the increased role of regional governments will be sufficient to tackle regional disparities within the EC. While the Structural Funds are to double in size to 14 billion ecu by 1993, the Padoa-Schioppa Report estimated the increases in capital formation necessary to achieve an additional percentage point in the growth of GDP in the lagging regions of the EC to be between 55 and 76 billion ecu (Padoa-Schioppa 1987). Moreover, the positive effects of regional policy may be outweighed by the impact of the completion of a single market. While changing methods of production mean that the ability to service mass markets may not be of overriding importance, it is still true that the already more developed regions are better placed to exploit economies of scale, external economies, and conditions of rapid technological change. There is a definite possibility, therefore, that the formation of an integrated EC market will lead to a further widening of regional disparities between the richer and poorer regions of the EC (Williams, Williams and Haslam 1991).

Conclusion

The appropriate economic functions of regional governments include the provision of various goods and services which the market can be expected to under-provide. However, while this allocation function is important, the distinctive role of regional governments relates to the enhancement of the dynamic efficiency of the economy,what has been termed here the growth function.

The experience of the five largest European Community states suggests two important conclusions. The first is to confirm the expectations of economic theory that the central economic role of regional governments lies in the sphere of planning and economic development policies. The economic powers of regional governments in Germany, France, Italy and Spain all reflect the growth function. It is the limited support which planning and economic development policies command in the UK which is the most important single economic factor in explaining the failure of a regional structure of government to develop there. The other important conclusion concerns the conflict between efficiency and equity concerns. Economic theory suggests that a regional structure of government may bring several efficiency gains both in the provision of public services and in the operation of planning and economic development policies. However, it does not necessarily ensure an equitable distribution. If anything, decentralisation may exacerbate regional inequality. As the cases of Germany and Spain demonstrate, it is possible to operate effective redistributive mechanisms but these constrain the autonomy of regions and may threaten the efficiency gains of a regional structure.

These same themes are relevant to the regional policy of the EC as a whole. The reform of EC regional policy, together with its growth in importance relative to the regional policies of individual member states, will reinforce the economic role of regional governments. However, the risks are that the completion of the internal market of the EC will make it increasingly difficult for regional governments to effectively apply planning and economic development policies, and that efficiency considerations will prevail over equity concerns.

The vision of a 'Europe of the Regions' is attractive: 'geographically decentralised, economically competitive, politically pluralist, with a refreshed democratic life that draws upon diverse provincial and national identities' (Garside and

Hebbert 1989, p.13). However, at least in economic terms, there are considerable obstacles to the realisation of this vision. Despite the expanded role and increased powers of regional governments throughout the EC, the increased competition between regions which will result from further political and economic integration is likely to reinforce the economic advantages of stronger regions over weaker ones.

References

Adonis, A. and Tyrie, A. (1991) 'What kind of European Union? Some Community reforms for the 1990s.' *National Westminster Bank Quarterly Review,* May, 47–54.

Bartels, D. (1981) 'Conceptions and strategies on regional development in the Federal Republic of Germany.' In G. Hoffman (ed) *Federalism and Regional Development.* Austin: University of Texas Press.

Bennett, R. (ed) (1990a) *Decentralisation, Governments, and Markets.* Oxford: Clarendon Press.

Bennett, R. (1990b) 'Decentralisation and local economic development.' In R. Bennett (ed) *Decentralisation, Governments, and Markets.* Oxford: Clarendon Press.

Brunskill, I. (1990) 'The regeneration game – a regional approach to regional policy.' *Institute for Public Policy Research.* London.

Castells, A. (1990) 'Financing regional government and regional income distribution in Spain.' In R. Bennett (ed) *Decentralisation, Governments, and Markets.* Oxford: Clarendon Press.

Commission of the European Communities (1991a) *Europe 2000: Outlook for the Development of the Community's Territory.* Brussels: CEC.

Commission of the European Communities (1991b) *The Regions in the 1990s: Fourth Periodic Report on the Social and Economic Situation and Development of the Regions of the Community.* Brussels: CEC.

Council of Europe (1990) *The Impact of the Completion of the Internal Market on Local and Regional Autonomy.* Brussels: Council of Europe.

Firn, J. and MacLennan, D. (1979) 'Devolution: the changing political economy of regional policy.' In D. MacLennan and J. Parr (eds) *Regional Policy: Past Experience and New Directions.* Oxford: Martin Robertson.

Garside, P. and Hebbert, M. (1989) 'Introduction.' In P. Garside and M. Hebbert (eds) *British Regionalism 1900–2000.* London: Cassell.

Harvey, D. (1989) *The Condition of Postmodernity.* Oxford: Basil Blackwell.

Helm, D. and Smith, S. (1989) 'The decentralised state: the economic borders of local government.' In D. Helm (ed) *The Economic Borders of the State.* Oxford: Oxford University Press.

Keating, M. (1989) 'Regionalism, devolution and the state, 1969–1989.' In P. Garside and M. Hebbert (eds) *British Regionalism 1900–2000.* London: Cassell.

King, D. (1984) *Fiscal Tiers: The Economics of Multi Level Government.* London: George Allen and Unwin.

King, R. (1987) *Italy.* London: Harper and Row.

Lash, S. and Urry, J. (1987) *The End of Organised Capitalism.* Cambridge: Polity Press.

Littlechild, M. (1982) 'Germany.' In D. Yuill (ed) *Regional Development Agencies in Europe.* Aldershot: Gower.

Musgrave, R. (1959) *The Theory of Public Finance.* New York: McGraw Hill.

Oates, W. (1991) *Studies in Fiscal Federalism.* Aldershot: Edward Elgar.

Padoa-Schioppa, T. (1987) *Efficiency, Stability and Equity: A Strategy for the Evolution of the Economic System of the European Community.* Brussels: CEC.

Piore, M. and Sabel, C. (1984) *The Second Industrial Divide.* New York: Basic Books.

Prud'homme, R. (1990) 'Decentralisation of expenditure or taxes: the case of France.' In R. Bennett (ed) *Decentralisation, Governments, and Markets.* Oxford: Clarendon Press.

Rey, M. and Pola, G. (1990) 'Intergovernmental relations in Italy: recent institutional and financial developments.' In R. Bennett (ed) *Decentralisation, Governments, and Markets.* Oxford: Clarendon Press.

Sole-Vilanova, J. (1990) 'Regional and local government finance in Spain.' In R. Bennett (ed) *Decentralisation, Governments, and Markets.* Oxford: Clarendon Press.

Spicker, P. (1991) 'The principle of subsidiarity and the social policy of the European Community.' *Journal of European Social Policy 1*, 1, 3–14.

Tuppen, J. (1988) *France Under Recession 1981–86.* London: MacMillan.

Williams, K., Williams, J. and Haslam, C. (1991) 'What kind of EC regional policy?' *Local Economy 5*, 4, 330–346.

Zimmerman, H. (1990) 'Fiscal federalism and regional growth.' In R. Bennett (ed) *Decentralisation, Governments, and Markets.* Oxford: Clarendon Press.

CHAPTER 7

The Spatial Impact of the Social Chapter

Mike Danson

Introduction

As the economies of the regions of the European Community react to the restructuring processes generated by the advent of the Single European Market and other global influences, so underlying divisions in the labour market are coming more to the fore with consequences for local communities and groups in the societies around Europe. Anticipating this tendency, and with an expectation that 1992 will benefit the Community overall (Cecchini 1988), there is an appreciation in the European Commission that there will be dimensions of spatial and social disadvantages to these developments.

However, despite a long history of identifying, prescribing and analysing the impact of regional and local economic problems on individuals and social groups in much of the developed world, there appears to have been relatively little attention paid to the spatial impact of the social dimension of the Single Market. This paper attempts to at least open up this area for consideration and, whilst not claiming to present a definitive thesis, does provide a framework for debating the issues. The paper focuses on the traditional, industrialised areas of peripheral western Europe (and is based on work in one of the most deprived of all these areas: the East End of Glasgow), to demonstrate how the policies and programmes of the Social Chapter may impact on such areas and therefore shows how such analysis could be undertaken. The diversity of the regional problem around the Community and the critical role of national governments in implementing the Chapter mean that a unique, ubiquitous model cannot be applied for all 'objective' regions affected. To extend this speculative research to other nation states and to other types of region would therefore require specific data, system-defining characteristics and evaluations, which must be beyond the scope of this contribution.

Nevertheless, the main conclusions of this chapter are that there will be a *spatial* dimension to the Social Dimension of 1992 and that this secondary set of effects should not be ignored. The lessons of the last decade in the UK are that underlying social, cultural and political factors are often identified, in retrospect, as crucial in the failure of national policies to succeed throughout all regions and social groups. The reverse is as likely to happen in the case of the Social Chapter – with the absence of a regional dimension to the analysis a critical omission.

It should be noted that this paper has been updated since the Maastricht Treaty was concluded, though not ratified. Crucially, although proposals were adopted for a Social Chapter of the Treaty, one country, inevitably the UK, excluded itself from coverage by this chapter and others, most notably the Danes and the French, have failed to support Maastricht at all convincingly. This suggests that the operation of the market and the interaction of economic and social factors and policies, in the manner set out below, will be as important in determining the ongoing development of the social dimension of 1992 as any set of agreements.

Further, there must surely be lessons for the analysis of the spatial impact of the social dimension from the deteriorating situation in the former state of Yugoslavia, the rising tide of long established but long forgotten 'isms': racism, anti-semitism, sexism, tribalism, intolerance based on creed and religion, in the former USSR and Eastern Europe – in what were considered developed and progressive central and western parts of the continent. Might it be argued that promoting social cohesion without consent, against a background of increasing unemployment and failed expectations, threatens 1992 as much as a market-driven solution alone to the realisation of the European ideal?

It is presumed that the reader is well aware of the institutions of the European Community and of the broad progress that was made towards 1992. Also the Social Chapter itself is dealt with only briefly here, and interested readers are referred to the comprehensive studies of the history of the social dimension of the European Community by Teague (1989), Grahl and Teague (1990) and Silvia (1991). Rather the paper is structured as follows. The first section offers an economic framework in which to analyse the potential effects of the Social Chapter and 1992, highlighting the different views of commentators on the importance of segmentation and flexibility in factor markets. The second section addresses the economic background of traditional industrial areas and the likely effects of the Single European Market on their futures. This is followed by a consideration of the social dimension of 1992 and an introduction to the potential spatial impacts of the Social Chapter. The final two sections deliver an agenda for action for disadvantaged communities to ensure they do not fall further behind in the coming decades, and a proposal for increasing general support for the ideals of the Social Chapter, as originally developed.

Economic and Industrial Structure

Most, if not all, developed economies have been steadily moving towards a new industrial structure based not on large assembly plants (car factories, steel mills, heavy engineering shops), but rather on more diversified forms of production – with more small and medium enterprises, service sector jobs, and flexible forms of production (see, for example, Atkinson 1984, Holland 1976, Massey 1985, Danson 1982, 1991). These various forms of flexibility are matched in the job structure: with *core* positions providing high and stable wages, good career prospects, trade union organisation, good training and skill acquisition opportunities, good holidays, hours, and conditions; and a *periphery* of low wages, unstable employment and unemployment, poor prospects, non-unionised labour, low and poor training, and poor conditions, hours, holidays and discipline (Figure 7.1).

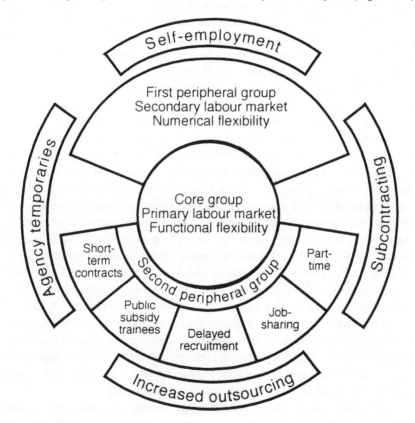

Figure 7.1. The flexible firm (Atkinson 1984)

The distribution of these core and periphery jobs is not even across the country nor, of relevance to this paper, across the European Community. In particular, since 1945 the history of old industrial areas (the 'Objective 2' regions of the EC) has been marked by a tendency for the core jobs to decline locally, with a loss of relatively well paid, skilled and unionised employment, in parallel with the loss of indigenous control over the companies established in these communities. In many cases this has been followed by their subsequent redundancy and closure – of coal, steel and engineering firms, food, drink and tobacco companies, and so forth. In the particular instance of Glasgow, over the last 15 years under the public sector initiatives of the Glasgow Eastern Area Renewal (GEAR) project, this period of decline has been partially compensated by a growth in periphery jobs located in small, service companies employing people in low-paid, non-unionised, low-skill occupations. Many of these small firms are owned and managed by non-local residents, whilst the majority of jobs in older plants have also become relatively low paid and are now located in the branch plants of state-owned and multinational companies. This long period of decline and degradation of the disadvantaged communities in such economies does not just affect the workforce or population during its employment: because of the structure of the welfare state and the class system in most of developed Europe, poverty and deprivation continue into unemployment, sickness, disability and old age.

Whilst most commentators would recognise and accept such a description of the industrial structure of the constituencies of the European Community, in many ways it obscures the nature of the true debate over the Social Charter. The social dimension of the EC has for long been an ideological battleground (see, *inter alia*, Addison and Siebert 1991, Teague 1989, Silvia 1991). This has led to relatively little advancement in adopting social programmes or standards across the Community. With the proposal for a Social Charter came an intensification of this struggle between the 'free-marketeers' and the 'regulators'. Based on neoclassical economic foundations, the former stress the role of the free market in maximising welfare and securing market adjustments with the greatest speed and fluency. In particular, they highlight the need to remove labour market rigidities and in-flexibilities and to promote deregulation (Addison and Siebert 1991, Lindbeck 1985, Giersch 1985). This school has also been important in influencing sections of the media, *The Economist* for instance, governments, especially the UK Conservative Party of the last decade, and employers. Adopting their *laissez-faire* and flexible strategies should lead, it is argued, to the creation of competitiveness, wealth and jobs. Confounded with such ideology are references to the importance of national differences in industrial relations traditions, labour market institutions, training systems, and to national sovereignty and subsidiarity.

On the other side of this great but muted debate are those who support regulation and controls on markets: a disparate group who stress need for intervention in factor and product markets. They include the European Commission itself, Trades Unions in the core regions and industries (but see Silvia, 1991, for a discussion on the limitations on their powers and influences), organisations such as the UK Low Pay Unit, most member states at least superficially, and some employer associations. For some of these actors the reasons for intervention come from a desire to restrict the size of the labour supply, so ameliorating the unemployment problem; for others this will secure the place of their members in a high-wage–high-productivity–high-investment environment protected from threatening competition. The protagonists on this side seek to promote social cohesion, see the objectives of the Social Charter as legitimate and worthwhile in their own right, consider them necessary if the common market is to work effectively (Cripps 1987), and as valuable in preventing social dumping: '…potentially adverse and retrogressive effects of a deregulated and decentralised European labour market' (Teague 1989).

Much of the debate has concerned and been absorbed with considerations of the different time scales and different theoretical bases for these two paradigms. The neoclassical or libertarian approach assumes that either all markets are perfect or if not, that it does not matter, and that all economic and welfare relationships are made transparent through the market. By also implicitly accepting that negative feedback predominates, they are able to use static equilibrium techniques to analyse the probable effects of the Social Charter on factor markets (see Addison and Siebert 1991, UK Department of Employment 1991, for instance). Indeed, given our lack of knowledge of what may happen in the changed situations of the single European market anyway, it is perhaps the only way to conceive of being able quantitatively to investigate such effects. Nevertheless, as with much of the work on the likely effects of 1992, there is a pretence of positive economics. The Department of Employment publications on the implications of the Social Charter provide an interesting and forthright example of such an approach, with their briefing papers for UK Ministers. Undoubtedly, however, the problem of the counterfactual is paramount but ignored here: a rigorous econometric-based study of the impact of the Social Charter is not possible because the characteristics which define the present economic system are meant to change under the integration of the market.

How companies respond to 1992 will determine its success, and how employers, unions, workers and governments react to the social action programme will influence its effectiveness. In this paradigm labour frequently disappears as a unique commodity, entering into the analysis merely as another factor of production. In these terms of dehumanisation, labour, and indeed entrepreneurs, are incapable of reacting to the environment so that Vibert (1989) and Addison and Siebert (1991) can ask what possible relevance information and consultation by enterprises with their employees can have on a market, and how management structures can affect the freedom of companies to make decisions.

In brief, the neoclassical approach stresses the need to deregulate markets in isolation as well as in totality, with fundamental differences between individuals' life chances and rewards due to their freely taken choices and innate abilities.

In complete contrast the interventionists stress, though usually implicitly, the central roles of monopoly and monopsony power, segmentation, institutions and the new models of flexibility in describing and prescribing the European market.

They identify positive feedback mechanisms as critical in creating artificial barriers to progression and adjustment (see Vietorisz and Harrison 1973 for analogous arguments in the USA). In labour market cases this would lead to, for instance, secondary and periphery workers being faced with low or negligible returns to human capital investments, hence low attachment to the firm or occupation, and so to destructive turnover. Therefore this suggests, by extension, the possibility of radically different responses to market signals in different circumstances, such as higher wages and improved conditions under the provisions of the Social Chapter. In contrast to the neoclassical concern with short-term cost minimisation, dynamic readjustments to changing business environments are being introduced. Similarly, the linkages between labour supply and labour demand are not recognised or are dismissed by those opposed to a social action programme (Addison and Siebert 1991), while they should form a cornerstone of the efficiency arguments of the Commission. (Addison and Siebert nevertheless correctly point out that the European Commission is remarkably reticent at suggesting such grounds for the Social Charter.)

Flexibility in companies may have been overplayed as an expansionary concept in any event according to some commentators (Grahl and Teague 1990). In terms of the neoclassical definitions of the perfect market, risk, uncertainty, monopoly power, poor information and externalities will all have a role to play in undermining the potential benefits of deregulation and liberalisation of the labour market. Experience in Britain in the 1980s suggested that flexibility often led to defensive strategies by companies with risks and instabilities passed onto employees in successive rounds of cost reductions. Elsewhere in Europe, but especially in Germany, the opposite course can be discerned with enterprises adopting a virtuous spiral of high skill, high productivity, high value added and high investment in products, designs, technology and skills.

Rather than rigidities, the idea of the social dimension would have the potential to create increased flexibility through quality enhancement and innovation throughout the Community in the long term, if this reasoning held true. Reversing the UK's argument (Department of Employment 1991), there would be economic progress *only* through social progress.

Single European Market and 1992

The creation of the Single European Market in 1992 by the European Community compounded and added to these processes of change as they impact on the traditional industrial areas across the EC.

In aggregate, the European Commission has forecast that the creation of a competitive, integrated market could increase GDP across the Community by about 5%. However, the European Commission also believes that this could only be accomplished in the context of a Community-wide expansionary economic policy programme promising the full employment of labour and other resources.

Thus 'it is necessary...that the credibility of these favourable expectations of (5% growth) be supported by a well coordinated, growth orientated macroeconomic policy. If this is not done, the market liberalization process risks generating defensive and negative reactions, in which case the viability of the programme could be threatened' (Commission of the European Communities 1989).

In the absence of such a reflationary programme and a package of countervailing powers to counteract economic concentration and centralisation, there must be concern that the economies of the old industrial areas of the EC may suffer net losses from the completion of the single integrated market. With their higher inherent transport and communications costs and peculiar industrial historical legacies, such areas on the geographical periphery have the most to lose from an unplanned approach. It is therefore vital that all sections and enterprises of these regional communities are fully prepared to respond to these developments.

The single market and the policies leading to the completion of the internal market will not so much set in motion new developments as, in the words of the Scottish Development Agency (1989), 'for individual companies bring both threats and opportunities' and for peripheral industrial regions in general accelerate existing trends. The most important of these include:

- the growth of multinational companies, built on an ability to exploit large markets through economies of scale

- industrial restructuring, with an associated loss of indigenous control over production, investment, employment and linkages

- increased specialisation in production, with more subcontracting, and continuous change in processes, markets, etc.

- a tendency for regions with concentrations of 'traditional industries' to be at a competitive disadvantage.

The comprehensive report for the Commission on the impact of 1992 on the traditional industrial regions by Quévit, Houard, Bodson and Dangoissa (1991) analyses in detail how many of these developments will affect such areas. It is sufficient here, however, to note that this background to their economies will become more apparent as we move further into the 1990s. In particular, for areas where decline has been endemic for over two decades (such as the East End of Glasgow), the internationalisation of business, the growing dominance of the multinational corporations (the real powers and movers behind the single European market), the drift to the capital region (the south-east in the UK) of the better paid and higher function jobs in management, finances and services (albeit interrupted in the last few years), and the promotion of the regional capital (Glasgow) as a post-industrial city based on tourism and culture will all exacerbate the geographical divisions and decline of the national/regional (Scottish) and local (East End) economies. At the same time the ability of the local authorities, Scottish and UK governments to influence and direct the economy in the future will become more difficult because of the EC's regulation of industrial and trading policies. So the

EC now controls many of the instruments of economic policy, demand management, subsidies, regional policy, public contracts, etc. Many regional, infrastructural and training schemes now also are funded by the European Regional Development Fund and the European Social Fund, so that the EC sets the agenda for training, industry and business development, etc.

The impact and relevance of the Social Chapter for these sorts of communities should therefore be considered in these contexts, whilst remembering that this area (the East End of Glasgow) continues to suffer from massive unemployment (over one-third of men are without work), and deep-rooted and extensive poverty and deprivation. At the same time the communities of this part of Glasgow have less control over their own economies and lives than at any time in the last two centuries. Finally we should note that the regulations introducing the Single European Market, and therefore limiting and restricting the ability of this community and its political bodies to direct the economy, are binding on the local and national governments of the European Community, but, because of UK government actions under multinational companies' pressure, the Social Chapter is being implemented through advisory and not binding directives.

The Social Charter

Against the background of industrial and local economic restructuring across the European Communities and the imminent acceleration of these processes with the advent of the single integrated market, the EC has proposed a set of measures – the Social Charter – to benefit all workers in the EC, but especially those in the periphery, in both geographical and economic terms. By definition the people of the East End and other disadvantaged communities would seem set to benefit from its provisions. That said, the Social Charter is not intended to turn-around the economy of this or other communities, rather it is intended to safeguard, to provide a safety net (see for example the DHSS (Department of Health and Social Security) schemes of the 1970s) and to promote 'social cohesion'. Under the present political climate these programmes are not to be introduced for their own worth, but for their role in ensuring public acceptance of the expansion of profit through the completion of the single, integrated market across Europe.[1]

The Social Charter is thus to be seen as an amelioration to the effects of 1992, yet because it is in many ways to be a voluntary set of directives and because of the relative strengths of the economic and social forces, the charter will not be able to counter the major effects of the industrial, trade and financial impacts of the former.

---

[1]   Brief guides to the Social Charter are given in, for example, *News Brief* (Low Pay Unit 1990), but more comprehensive accounts are available from the Commission, national governments, and more academic articles (for example Grahl and Teague 1990).

As the Social Charter develops and as some of its components become subject to directive or regulation status, so the advice, research and campaigns of the Commission, unions and special interest groups will improve. However, with a few notable exceptions, for example the Low Pay Unit and the Child Poverty Action Group, much of the literature at present available is too optimistic on the status or potential impact of the proposed changes. For instance, although at least two British trade unions have produced worthy, well written documents on the Charter (GMBATU 1990, USDAW 1991), in many ways they appear to have confused suggestions of developments with actual legislation. The Charter is just that: a publication or set of documents which chart out possible and desirable changes to national and EC rules and regulations; as yet, few if any of these are actually in force, and if and when they are introduced, it will be in the form of non-binding directives. As these will not be automatically adopted into UK legislation, further problems arise in seeing the potential benefits of the Social Charter. For instance, examples of areas covered by the Charter are low pay and sex discrimination: yet already we have laws and regulations in Britain to protect the low paid and women at work, but the long-term impact of the equal opportunities legislation of the 1970s has been underwhelming and the proportion of the workforce on low pay has risen inexorably throughout the last decade. Laws alone will not eradicate many of the evils of the labour market under capitalism, not least because of who monitors and polices the law in reality. As these present restrictions on the rights of employers and the market have not changed nor sought to undermine fundamental power relations in work and society, we must be aware that a system of European programmes and policies on the same basis – and monitored and policed by national governments, as proposed – will be equally successful.

Social Dumping or Social Plinthing

Around Europe there is a broad consensus that problems will arise in attempting to impose minimum standards across the EC in social security provision, labour laws, industrial relations practice, etc. This can be explained in two ways. Firstly, 'social dumping' – richer regions with higher standards are concerned that these will be downgraded to the lowest common denominator and/or jobs will be lost to southern Europe, Ireland and, in the future, to Eastern Europe. One option to overcome this, at least to an extent, would involve shifting the burden of financing social welfare onto general taxation and away from employers, having obvious effects on the standards of living of most people in such regions. Secondly, even the imposition of low minimum standards of social provision would represent an unacceptable burden on the poorly developed businesses of the poorer regions of Europe, at least in the short to medium term.

A brief review of the EC league table on legislation and provision for the unemployed, low paid, retired, disabled and other disadvantaged, already shows the UK as one of the poor nations of the EC, appearing just above Greece, Spain,

Portugal and Ireland, with especial gaps over control of employers. An avoidance of the 'social dumping' implicit above would suggest that our position in this table will not improve over the coming decade. Rather the position of the East End in Glasgow may in fact deteriorate further. Thus the single market will increase competition for jobs between regions of the EC, and, given relative wages and social protection in the UK compared with the rest of peripheral Europe, we may reasonably expect:

- a loss of jobs to the south and the Mediterranean regions

- because of this threat of relocation, an intensified downward pressure on wages in internationally traded sectors

- a tendency to adopt implicitly a low-wage, anti-trade union regional economic strategy to capture and secure jobs and plants.

It is interesting to compare this series of threats with the historical conditions Ulman identified as being necessary to promote unions in the USA to amalgamate and cooperate across the continent and so reduce their traditional weakness in the face of mobile and informed capital (Ulman 1966, 1975).

The history of the social dimension of the European Community has been tortuous, as comprehensively described by Teague (1989), Grahl and Teague (1990), Addison and Siebert (1991) and Silvia (1991). Given the opposition of the UK government in particular, but also other Member States, employers and professionals outwith the European Commission, there must be a real concern that successful efforts to adopt minimum standards fully backed by binding EC-wide legislation will be restricted to Health and Safety matters. Apart from these positive moves the threat must be of deregulation and deterioration rather the opposite, as originally proposed under the Social Charter.

For the disadvantaged communities of the traditional industrial regions of the EC, already peripheralised by the restructuring of the last two decades and suffering the 'new poverty' of low pay, secondary employment and self-perpetuating deprivation (Bruce 1991), the Social Action Programme seems to offer tentative hopes but concerted threats. Against the background set out above, and with a substantial experience of initiatives, programmes and the benefits of other economic development interventions (see Danson 1988 and GEAR Appraisal Group 1987 for some discussion of this), the reality of 1992 and the Social Chapter may well be very different from those anticipated by its authors or opponents. Without a fully developed social accounting framework (Madden 1989) and a complete analysis of how regional economies will respond to the challenges of 1992, any presentation of the possible ultimate effects of the implementation of the Social Action Programme must be speculative at best. The reactions of individual industries, enterprises and agencies themselves are not objective processes, following automatically from the stimulus of the integration of the European market. Whether specific companies, cities or occupations will benefit from these developments will depend on the interaction of the operation of markets and social actors in particular circumstances, and in a way that cannot be determined by blanket macroeconomic modelling of national labour markets (see, for example, Department of Employment 1991).

That there will be an impact on different sectors in communities such as the East End of Glasgow seems apparent, but the form and nature of this effect are less discernible. We would argue, however, that without a 'social plinth' or floor of living standards, for many the imposition of unfettered market forces would be literally catastrophic. Along with the problems of the market outlined above, the original distribution of abilities, education and training facilities, capital endowments, and other characteristics of locations will all continue to have profound effects on the likely futures of the peripheral communities. Without a macroeconomic policy of expansion under 1992 (Commission of the European Communities 1989), and with a partial implementation of the Social Charter, the balance of prospects could be a deepening of poverty as predicted by the UK government. The possibility of promoting a citizens' Europe would be more achievable under planned expansion and a social action programme.

Opportunities for Hope?

The above depressing picture appears, almost without exception, as holding out little prospect for the East End and other disadvantaged communities of EC-sponsored improvements in the lives of ordinary, working class people. There are very few binding pieces of legislation being proposed to assist in the implementation of the Social Charter: no minimum wages nor guaranteed pensions across the Community, with even (UK) Wages Councils' rates not protected, raising the threat of downward pressure on even these poverty levels. However, exactly because the UK is such a poor protector of its low-paid, temporary, part-time, home-based, unemployed, disabled, retired, etc. workers we can expect some benefits from the provisions and philosophy of the Social Charter. Improved freedom of movement for workers should allow the residents of Europe's industrial periphery to migrate to more prosperous parts of the EC, although, as in the past, this may make the position of those left behind even worse. But to enable workers to seek career opportunities elsewhere in Europe, there must be a large expansion and improvement in language teaching and facilities for all locally. Secondly, the European Commission and certain social actors are determined to implement as much of the Charter as possible, and innovative ways are being explored to achieve this.

So, although the UK government, amongst others, may be able and willing to block the passage of binding legislation directly, the Commission is beginning to use the competition aspects of the Treaty of Rome to ensure the implementation of some parts of the Social Chapter. Thus, the Commission has been investigating the use of part-time workers by (West) German companies at different rates and conditions to full-time employees as being anti-competitive compared with the position in the Netherlands, where all workers have similar protection and rights regardless of how many hours they work. As such practices are against the provisions of the Treaty they can be outlawed by the Commission, and so, through the back door, protection for peripheral workers improved across the Community. Thirdly, in a similar vein of promoting competition, trades unions across the EC are attempting to have labour clauses included in public contracts, so that pay protection, hours of work, pension rights, etc. can be guaranteed for health workers, local authority staff and others subject to contracting out of services and competitive tendering. Other proposals that may be introduced through binding legislation would protect young people over the hours of work, and fair wages for women and ethnic minorities as contract compliance regulations used to (and still do in the USA and other competitor countries).

But in general, as argued above, the Charter will not be implemented through regulations or even directives. Other areas of the Charter may be introduced piecemeal country by country, with EC laws being tested in the European courts or simply overriding national laws; instances of this of late in the UK have included pension rights for women, and DSS regulations, which were found to be illegally opposed to the higher level Community legislation.

More important, the Social Chapter provides a set of potential improvements to the quality of life for millions of citizens in Europe. As with previous charters: the Declaration of Arbroath, the American Declaration of Independence, the nineteenth century Chartists, the Reform Act, and so forth, change comes sometimes through negotiation, but more often than not through struggle, and in particular through struggle at the workplace. In the special circumstances of the single European market and the contexts referred to in the early part of this chapter, it seems all the more essential that trades unions cooperate across the continent, within companies, industries and federations to press for the implementation of the Social Charter. At the same time the workers of the new Europe should take regard to the threat of the establishment of 'Fortress Europe', with the downgrading and degrading of jobs, incomes and lives in the rest of the world (both Silvia 1991 and Teague 1989 demonstrate the limitations of the unions in such negotiations, however).

Other struggles in the history of the working class in Glasgow have been built around not the workplace but the home, with the role of women crucial in establishing better housing, fair rents and improvements in the provision of housing, education and other areas of social life. Although the main objectives of the Social Charter are based around the workplace, there are again important measures to be implemented in these wider spheres – education, nursery provision, pensions, access for the disabled, etc. It is therefore important that debates over the Charter are not perceived as the exclusive territory of civil servants, parliamentarians, trade union officials and employer representatives nor hijacked by such exclusive groups.

Concluding Lessons for the East End Communities

In the short term, the representative bodies of the East End, by joining and assisting in the campaigns and lobbies of organisations such as the Low Pay Unit, the Child Poverty Action Group, and Community-wide groups, should work towards the implementation of the Charter. Direct lobbying of MEPs, MPs, local authorities, employers and trades unions are complementary to this. Insisting that local authorities, for instance, support the spirit of the charter by instituting improved language facilities, working conditions and pension rights could be a first step in this process. Seeking to establish links with similar community groups across the EC is likewise a positive initiative that can be taken. In the medium term the East End and similar devastated communities should attempt to attract more core employment, with the associated improvement in incomes and security. Without stronger action and community involvement, this would not be achieved through the normal channels and this was meant to be the objective of the GEAR (Glasgow Eastern Area Renewal) project. So the history of official attempts at promoting business development suggests something more will be necessary on this occasion if the area is not to fall even further behind prosperous Europe. In the long term the East End and similar communities around the EC and beyond can only benefit from the single European market with the abolition of the apartheid of core and periphery jobs.

It appears to us that to achieve the above, to ensure the implementation of the Social Charter, the communities of the East End should look to their history. The Chapter and its development show remarkable similarities to the Beveridge proposals of the 1940s. Originally published in 1942 as the blueprint of the Welfare State, these were progressively watered down by the Civil Service, politicians and other members of the establishment so that ultimately the social provisions implemented formed an incoherent strategy to combat poverty and deprivation. The attacks on the welfare state in the 1980s were made much easier by this early dismantling of the structures of the programmes and policies envisaged by Beveridge. However, although the philosophy of the welfare state was under systematic and sustained attack throughout its early years, and its formative stages in particular, many of the provisions of the original plans were implemented in a fairly strong form. This was achieved through strong, committed and vociferous campaigning by the labour movement during the later years of World War II to ensure the introduction of the Beveridge proposals. Nothing less than a similar level of unremitting and wholehearted campaigning seems necessary if the aspirations and hopes of the East End of this city and of other working class communities are to be realised. The people of this area can benefit, but the implementation of the Social Charter will be an ongoing process requiring ongoing struggle through lobbying, campaigning and other initiatives. At a time when these communities are already under severe economic attack the prospect of further activity must be naturally unwelcome; however, just as the European Community likes to promote the single European market in terms of the costs of non-Europe, so the costs of non-campaigning are too high and the potential benefits too great to ignore.

References

Addison, J. and Siebert, S. (1991) 'The Social Charter of the European Community: evolution and controversies.' *Industrial and Labour Relations Review 44*, 4, 597–625.

Atkinson, J. (1984) 'Manpower strategies for the flexible firm.' *Personnel Management,* August, 28–31.

Bruce, A. (1991) 'The impact on poverty.' Mimeo CEI Consultants, Edinburgh.

Cecchini, P. (1988) *The European Challenge. 1992: The Benefits of A Single Market.* Aldershot: Wildwood House.

Commission of the European Communities (1989) *Action Programme in the Field of Employment, Industrial Relations, Social Affairs and Training.* Brussels.

Cripps, L. (1987) 'The social policy of the European Community.' *Social Europe 1,* 51–57.

Danson, M. (1982) 'The industrial structure and labour market segmentation: urban and regional implications.' *Regional Studies 16,* 4, 255–266.

Danson, M. (1988) 'GEAR: not failed but flawed.' *Local Work No 7.* Manchester: The Centre for Local Economic Strategies.

Danson, M. (1991) *The Scottish Economy: Revisiting the Development of Underdevelopment, Economics and Management.* Working Papers No 17. Paisley: Paisley College.

Department of Employment (1991) *The United Kingdom in Europe: People, Jobs and Progress.* London.

GEAR Appraisal Group (1987) *A Job Half Done.* Glasgow: GAG.

Giersch, H. (1985) 'Eurosclerosis.' *Kiel Discussion Papers 112.* Kiel: Kiel University.

GMBATU (1990) *Getting Ready for the European Social Charter.* Surrey: GMBATU.

Grahl, J. and Teague, P. (1990) *1992 – The Big Market. The Future of the European Community.* London: Lawrence and Wishart.

Holland, S. (1976) *Capital Versus the Regions.* London: Macmillan.

Lindbeck, A. (1985) 'What is wrong with the West European Economies?' *World Economy 8,* 153–170.

Low Pay Unit (1990) *News Brief.* London: Low Pay Unit.

Madden, M. (1989) 'A social accounting framework.' Mimeo. Paper to the ESRC Urban and Regional Economics Seminar Group, Glasgow.

Massey, D. (1985) *Spatial Divisions of Labour.* London: Macmillan.

Mosley, H. (1990) 'The social dimension of European integration.' *International Labour Review 129,* 2.

Quévit, M., Houard J., Bodson S. and Dangoissa A., (1991) 'The regional consequences of completion of the 1992 internal market: the case of The Traditional Industrial Regions (RETI).' Mimeo, RIDER, Louvain-la-Neuve.

Scottish Development Agency (1989) *1992 – Opportunities and Threats for Scottish Businesses.* Mimeo. Paper to Regional Studies Association Scottish Branch AGM.

Silvia, S. (1991) 'The Social Charter of the European Community: a defeat for European Labour.' *Industrial and Labour Relations Review 44,* 4, 626–643.

Teague, P. (1989) 'Constitution or regime? The Social Dimension to the 1992 project.' *British Journal of Industrial Relations 27,* 310–329.

Ulman, L (1966) 'The rise of the National Trade Union: The development and significance of its structure, governing institutions, and economic policies.' Cambridge, MA: Harvard University Press.

Ulman, L (1975) 'Multinational unionism: incentives, barriers and alternatives.' *Industrial Relations 14*, 1, 1–31.

USDAW (1991) *Europe 1992: The USDAW Workbook.* Manchester: USDAW.

Vibert, F. (1989) 'Europe's Constitutional Deficit.' *IEA Inquiry 13.* London: IEA.

Vietorisz, T. and Harrison, B. (1973) 'Labour market segmentation: positive feedback and divergent development.' *American Economic Review 63,* 366–376.

CHAPTER 8

The Single European Market
Implications for Local and Regional Authorities

Trevor Hart and Peter Roberts

Introduction

This chapter aims to review the implications of the Single Market for local and regional authorities and to identify the essential elements of a successful response. The approach followed is one which looks beyond the 282 measures making up the Single Market programme, to also include the five companion policy areas in the Single European Act. This is not only because the Commission has stressed that the Single Market Programme should not be viewed in isolation from the other five objectives of the Single European Act (Commission of European Communities 1986, 1987), but also because these other objectives are, in many cases, of equal importance to the workings of local and regional authorities.

It is possible to identify a wide range of impacts on local and regional authorities, some more direct than others, arising from the realisation of these six policy objectives. At one end of the range there are the local and regional economic impacts of the '1992' process, which will provide a changed economic context for the authorities to operate in and will have consequent impacts on the delivery of some services – in particular, economic development. At the other extreme, there are a number of direct impacts on the way authorities carry out their functions. Some of these impacts are very directly related to legislation making up the Single Market programme and will affect, for example, the standards the authorities have to apply or the procedures they have to adopt.

In practice, most departments and functions of local and regional authorities are subject to a mixture of these more and less direct impacts. To illustrate the implications of 1992 for local and regional authorities, two examples have been chosen: the purchasing function, which illustrates many of the sorts of impacts resulting from legislation and programmes directly affecting the ways authorities operate; and economic development, which allows some of the less direct impacts to be explored, and enables some specific consideration to be given to the accompanying policy areas in the Single Act.

The Single Market and Regional Economies

The Cost of Non-Europe

In order to provide some scientific analysis of the size and nature of the costs of European fragmentation and the benefits on offer following the removal of barriers, the Commission launched a programme of research ('The Cost of Non-Europe'). The significance of these studies – which are essentially concerned with estimating the overall benefits which will be generated by improving the international competitiveness of the EC – lies in how the benefits which have been postulated will be spatially (and, to a certain extent, socially) distributed, and where any adjustment costs accompanying their generation will fall. The White Paper (CEC 1985) recognised that a consequence of completing the Internal Market may be that existing discrepancies between regions could be exacerbated. This somewhat disturbing possibility was subsequently underlined by a survey of 9000 businesses in the EC (CEC 1990a), which found that the most positive views of the impact of the Single Market were held by firms in the more prosperous regions, while companies in 'problem' regions were least likely to have a clear view of the potential impact.

It is worth bearing in mind that the estimates of benefits should be interpreted 'as potential and conditional, not inevitable' (Emerson 1988, p.95), in that the realisation of benefits to a significant extent depends on the successful redeployment of resources (particularly labour) made redundant in the process of adjustment to new trading conditions. The short run costs of this rationalisation and restructuring process were recognised by Cecchini (1988), who forecast job losses of up to 500,000 in the first year following the implementation of the Single European Market.

The Cost of Non-Europe team did not attempt any estimate of the geographical distribution of these costs or benefits, and this attracted criticism from a number of quarters. However, Emerson (1988) pointed out that 'difficult as it is to estimate the aggregate gains...this task is relatively manageable compared to that of forecasting its distribution by country or region' (p.21). Studies which have considered the question of the regional impact of the Single European Market have tended to place emphasis on the consequences which flow from the uneven structure and distribution of industry between regions, and the varying vulnerability of different sectors to the changes accompanying the Single Market.

Sectoral impacts

The variable potential vulnerability of individual sectors has been considered by the Commission in a study of 100 manufacturing industries, and a categorisation (CEC 1988) of potential vulnerability identified a number of sectors most at risk:

1. Those rapidly growing, high technology industries, such as computers and telecommunications equipment, which operate under high non-tariff barriers (such as arise through restrictive public procurement practices and standards setting), which will need to operate at a larger scale (through mergers and other forms of restructuring) to be fully competitive with their US and Japanese counterparts.

2. Industries such as pharmaceutical and boilermaking, characterised by high non-tariff barriers, low import penetration and wide price dispersion, where restructuring and rationalisation is to be expected.

3. Industries such as shipbuilding, industrial chemicals, clothing, and motor vehicles, which operate behind less substantial non-tariff barriers and are subject to greater import penetration, but where significant economies of scale remain possible.

The geographical distribution of such vulnerable sectors is of concern to local and regional authorities, but they will also be concerned to learn which businesses in their area are well placed to take advantage of the opportunities offered by the Single Market. By and large these will be businesses which are not dependent on any form of protection for their success, are international in outlook and activity, are well informed about the impacts of the Single Market and have accounted for these impacts in their business strategy, and above all are internationally competitive: such businesses are more likely to be large than small.

Although the Commission's analysis concentrated on manufacturing industries, it is clearly the case that a number of important service industries are directly affected by the 1992 proposals: prime examples are road transport and financial services. Likely outcomes for such industries include an acceleration of trends already in evidence, leading towards a growing internationalisation of operations and structures. The quest for international competitiveness is likely to lead to similar structural adjustments as have been postulated for manufacturing sectors, and in particular mergers and acquisitions and labour force reductions. In addition to their concern about possible negative impacts of '1992' on their service sectors, local and regional authorities are likely to be particularly interested because of the perceived importance of the service sector in local economies – as the major source of expected job growth, and because of the potential synergies between well-developed producer services and production industries.

The Single European Act and the regions

While the Commission's analytical work focused on the consequences of the Single Market Programme, it is the case that implementation of the other policy areas of the Single European Act may have differential impacts on the economies of regions. Two examples may be cited. Firstly, the benefits and costs of the progress towards economic and monetary union has recently been the subject of a study by the Commission (CEC 1990b). While the study does not come to any clear conclusion about the spatial impact of policy, it does suggest that the transitional adjustment costs for higher inflation countries may be significant: experience would suggest that already disadvantaged regions are less able to 'adjust' and may well bear a disproportionate share of the costs of implementing the policy. Secondly, although the 'social dimension' is designed to ensure that workers share in the benefits of the Single Market, some commentators feel that certain proposals within the Social Action Programme may have a negative impact on employment. Proposals on atypical work (essentially concerning part-time and temporary workers) will, it is felt, have a particular negative impact on employment in industries such as tourism and clothing which tend to employ a large proportion of such workers: employment in such industries tends to be regionally concentrated and often offers employment to otherwise vulnerable groups in the labour market.

Regional competitiveness

The preceding paragraphs have largely focused on the way particular sectors are affected by 1992 and the effects on regions consequent on variations in industrial structure. Of equal importance is a region's capacity to take advantage of the opportunities offered by the creation of the Single Market, and in particular its attractiveness as a location for investment. In a consideration of the regional aspects of 1992, Tyler (1990) defines the factors determining an area's attractiveness as including '...relative accessibility...to the axis of economic development of the Community, the quality of infrastructure of the area concerned, the characteristics of the labour force and their relative cost, the environmental attractiveness of the area and a range of other factors including government urban and regional policy incentives' (p.64). In relation to the first of these factors, while a precise definition of the 'axis' of the Community remains somewhat elusive, it is clear that peripherality will become a more significant disadvantage in relation to the stimulation of those industries which value the importance of close proximity to collaborators, customers and suppliers, and in particular to manufacturers who place an increasing importance on 'just-in-time'.

A study for the European Commission (CEC 1990a) of the factors shaping regional competitiveness highlighted two factors in particular: businesses questioned across the Community identified the availability of qualified labour as the factor to which they accorded the highest priority for improvement; while the availability of modern communications systems was the most frequently cited strength of a region. Similarly, a study under the FAST programme (Illeris 1989) of the regional development of services – the major source of new employment in the Community – pointed to the presence of 'proper human resources' (p.102) as being decisive for the successful development of service industries: attributes noted included 'entrepreneurial spirit and innovative capacity...and labour forces with high professional qualifications' (p.133).

Viewed in the context of the acceleration by the '1992' process of the internationalisation of business and the enhanced geographical mobility of investment, regions will need to ensure that they are those which offer the most competitive local conditions if they are to gain the potential benefits of the Single European Market. A careful appraisal of the position of the region with respect to the sorts of factors noted above is an important first step in the process.

Thus there are a number of regional dimensions to the completion of the '1992' process, many of which can have fundamental impacts on the fortunes of a region's economy and consequently affect the context in which local and regional authorities operate. Because of the broad range of the impacts under consideration, a local representative body is particularly well placed to assess the nature and direction of the changes which may ensue, to evaluate the preparedness of the region to take advantage of the opportunities offered by the Single Market, and, in the context of its economic development responsibilities, to initiate appropriate policy responses.

The Single Market and Local and Regional Government

A number of commentators (see, for example, Roberts, Thomas, Hart and Campbell 1990, Bongers 1990) as well as local government associations (e.g. CCRE/IULA 1988) have assessed the likely impact of 1992 on local and regional authorities' functions. These impacts range from administrative issues affecting day-to-day operations, to those which are more closely aligned with the broader role of the authority. Impacts of the first type principally concern Community legislation (particularly the Directives which make up most of the Single Market Programme) which, when transposed into national law, impose *obligations* on local government, and procedures for the delivery of services have to be adapted accordingly. Impacts of the second type are, as far as local and regional authorities are concerned, less direct and consequently the authorities usually have considerable *discretion* in framing their response. It will be apparent that many activities have to face a mixture of these 'obligatory' and 'discretionary' impacts.

New legislative obligations

Perhaps the clearest example, from a list of significant length, of Single Market changes to which authorities are *obliged* to respond is the revised public procurement legislation. In brief, the most widely relevant legislation comprises:

- The *Supplies Directive*, applying to all contacts for the purchase of supplies which have a value of over 200,000 ecu.

- The *Works Directive*, covering all public works contracts with a value of over 5 million ecu.

- The *Services Directive*, covering the procurement of most services by public bodies; generally, there are similarities with the supplies legislation.

- The *Utilities Directive*, covering public services such as water, energy, transport and telecommunications.
  Where they exist, European standards must be specified, and, depending on the type of contract, up to 77 days may be needed to satisfy EC requirements for the advertisement of contracts.

- Finally, a *Compliance Directive*, aimed at ensuring that Community procedures are being followed and at introducing a means of redress for tenderers.

The general philosophy behind the legislation is that there are substantial efficiency gains to be made by removing restrictive practices in public sector purchasing and that lower costs will follow from the opening up of the market. However, the greatest economic benefits are to be gained by liberating the purchasing approach of major public sector monopolies, and the shape of the legislation to a certain extent reflects this. Thus, in the UK local authority context, there is, as yet, no discernible evidence of any cost savings or a broadening of the supplier base by the inclusion of non-national based firms. From this UK experience, the major impacts on purchasers seem to have been:

- the need to be aware of the extended timescale associated with contracts above the thresholds

- the need to take care with specification where new EC standards are involved

- the need to take a systematic approach to identifying and recording criteria for the award of contracts, in the light of the increased stress on compliance.

Overall, there are not insignificant cost implications associated with following the new procedures, because of the extra administrative burdens involved. The current purchasing philosophy in local government (in the UK, reinforced by recent national legislation) is one of the keen pursuit of value for money, and this does not sit very comfortably with the rather bureaucratic approach dictated by the legislation.

This example serves to illustrate the nature of the impact of EC-originated legislation on the operations of local and regional government. Firstly, there is a need to keep informed about the development of EC legislation. Although, once it is part of national law, official or professional channels tell authorities about changed obligations, any attempt to influence the shape of legislation requires a more determined effort to gain information. Indeed, it is possible to argue that the current legislation could be more in tune with the workings of local government if it or its representative organisations had been more closely involved in the original drafting. Forward planning within the authority will also benefit from the early availability of information: for example, the 'contracting out' of a service (say to some form of direct service organisation) may seem less attractive if it would bring its supply within the scope of the proposed Services Directive. Secondly, the EC legislation can give rise to a need to change procedures or more fundamentally adapt ways of working. Some EC-originated changes in technical standards will prove little more burdensome than earlier nationally-originated changes, while others can lead to more fundamental changes. In the UK, perhaps the most striking example of having to change methods of working is in the field of Trading Standards, where, broadly speaking, the adoption of EC regulations and methods has resulted in a switch away from exercising control over products at the point of sale towards control, inspection and advice at the place of production. This shift towards assisting producers with their 'quality assurance' has placed new and increased demands on Trading Standards Departments, and serves to underline the third impact – that of the potential demand on resources associated with the obligation to respond to EC-originated legislation, which will affect a wide range of functions in all member states.

Economic development and other local considerations

There are many areas where local authorities have considerable *discretion* in framing their response to the impact of EC policies, regulations or programmes, with the most readily apparent being their involvement in local economic development. The possible economic impacts of 1992 and their regional expressions have been reviewed above. Clearly, local and regional authorities have a variety of responses they can consider in attempting to cope with the structural adjustment which may occur and attempting to realise the benefits which may be available to the region. These can range from analytical work identifying potential sectoral and structural effects, to interventions to either help improve the competitive position of existing industry or to help generate alternative sources of employment to replace that lost in restructuring.

Interventions of the first type involve encouraging the development of a European dimension to all services to business – information, advice, training services – including making particular efforts to help small and medium sized enterprises who have generally been found to be the least well prepared to face the impact of 1992. More broadly, the authority will want to assess how European integration is affecting the competitiveness of their area as a location for business. It is the case that some areas of the EC will be growing faster than others, and it is thus of some importance where an authority is located adjacent to the more dynamic regions of the Community.

As well as providing a favourable working environment and location for businesses already established in the region, authorities will also wish to consider questions of regional competitiveness in the context of inward investment from other EC and third countries, which will not only be seeking the best located sites within Europe (including Eastern Europe) but will also be seeking locations which offer the best quality hard and soft infrastructure, greatest innovative capacity, and the most attractive social and physical environment. It is a well established role of local and regional authorities in their economic development activity to evaluate and to seek to improve some or all of these factors, but in the future development of strategy and the setting of priorities it is clear that the changes brought about by the Single Market will be an important consideration.

In the context of actually or potentially mobile investments which will accompany the completion of the Single Market, Boisot (1990) suggests that regional authorities should develop their policy responses and interventions on the basis of being competitive *with* other regions, implying that new interventions should be assessed not only in terms of the absolute benefits they will confer on the region, but also in terms of the competitive advantage it will confer over potential rival regions. However such interventions are evaluated, there is clearly a relationship between these activities and the remaining policy areas and related programmes of the Single European Act.

Research and technological development

The Commission's Research and Development Framework Programme (1990–1994) has a value of 5700 million ecu, about 39% of which is devoted to information technology. While the reason for the existence of EC R&D programmes is the need for the Community to become and stay competitive with the USA and Japan, the local authorities' interest is perhaps more closely related to the uneven distribution of R&D between regions of the Community. The five weakest economies in the twelve account for only 10% of R&D activity and similar disparities can be observed between regions within states. Clearly, the narrowing of such differences will be a major interest of local and regional authorities. Many of the EC R&D programmes are complementary to local authorities' economic development aspirations, and there is an increasing interest among authorities in this field. This can take the form of direct participation in programmes such as SPRINT, STRIDE and Energy Demonstration, or indirect involvement through alerting other local actors to the potential of the broad range of programmes and perhaps assisting with the forging of transnational links. However, up to now there is little evidence of a high level of local government involvement, with most activity being at the alerting/brokerage level.

Coordinated action on the environment

The protection and enhancement of environmental quality and the conservation of natural resources are major and growing concerns of the EC. This is a trend which is paralleled in local government. The impact of EC environmental policies will be felt by authorities in three ways. Firstly, there are a number of direct impacts on authorities' activities, including the control of development through the operation of a planning system (particularly given movements towards a wider use of EC-inspired environmental impact assessment); responsibility for environmental standards (particularly in the broad fields of environmental quality-related matters such as drinking water, effluent disposal and safety in the workplace, rather than matters such as plant and animal health); and the standards to be observed in the authorities' own operations, such as waste incineration. Secondly, a quest for higher environmental standards – in many cases EC measures have tended to set standards which operate at or above previously defined national standards – can have significant impacts on businesses in the local authority's area, not all of whom will be able to adapt to controls and processes and remain viable. Thirdly, EC policies and programmes of positive action can support and complement an authority's aims of advancing environmental standards for their area. Maintaining an awareness and involvement with Commission environmental concerns can therefore be expected to become increasingly important for local authorities; indeed, the proposed Fifth Environmental Action Programme – 'Towards sustainability' (CEC 1992a) – explicitly identifies the role local and regional government might play in the achievement of the Community's environmental objectives.

The social dimension

The 'social dimension' of the internal market is of interest to local and regional authorities from three perspectives – that of affecting their own employment practices; as a means of support in areas where they have assumed a role of advocacy or practical assistance on social issues, particularly for disadvantaged groups; and for any impacts it may have on levels of employment. The dozen areas noted in the Social Charter do not clearly fall into these three groups, but the first is particularly relevant for proposals on health and safety, freedom of movement and vocational training, while the second has a particular focus in the area of equal treatment (of men and women). (See Chapter 7 for further discussion of this issue.)

Strengthening economic and social cohesion

This final area of policy in the Single Act brings the focus back to the local authorities' involvement with the Community's Structural Funds. These have always been a means of support for local economic development with the initial emphasis being on assisting the provision of basic infrastructure and training the unemployed. The reform in the operation of the funds enshrined in legislation enacted in 1988 (CEC 1989) brought some changes in emphasis and some changes in procedures for local authorities. The emphasis of the ERDF is now more sharply focused on the provision of 'productive infrastructure', while the growing recognition of the importance of continuing training (throughout working life) as a key to success in the quest for enhanced competitiveness is reflected in the development of programmes like FORCE under the ESF. The Commission's proposals (CEC 1992b) following Maastricht continue to pursue the same basic objectives, but greater emphasis is given to tackling the problems of the poorer regions of the Community.

Local and regional authorities and community decision-making

Only two member states – Belgium and Germany – have developed formal machinery to involve regional authorities in the formulation of national positions on Community policies. In many ways, it seems only natural that local and regional bodies should develop an enhanced role vis-à-vis the Community, as it is often these authorities which are most directly concerned with and most directly feel the effects of Community activities: many examples to support this thesis have been set out above.

Of particular interest to local authorities is the influence they can hope to exercise over the decision-making process for the structural funds. The 1988 regulations governing the operation of the funds make mention of consultation and partnership between the Commission and national, regional and local authorities in 'the preparation, financing, monitoring and assessment of operations', but any optimism this has given rise to has not been born out by experience. It has been pointed out in a report prepared by Caldiroli for the Council of Europe (1990) that 'there was insufficient consultation with local and regional authorities – or none at all – in the preparation of regional plans...and the Community Support Frameworks [indicative financing plans] were prepared without any direct intervention of local and regional authorities' (p.36): indeed, it is only under ERDF Article 10 actions that there is a clear role for local authorities. The development of greater influence in these matters is, as Caldiroli puts it, 'an ambitious objective but well worth fighting for' (p.37). The development of an increasing number of active partnerships between cities and regions across the Community (both with and without Commission assistance) and the creation of the 'Committee of the Regions' proposed in the Maastricht Treaty represent significant moves towards this objective.

However, it is the case that many national governments remain unsupportive, or in some instances overtly hostile, to local and regional authorities' efforts to establish effective cross-frontier cooperation. Putting support behind representative bodies for regional and local authorities, and making greater efforts to forge interregional links, may be a means by which sub-national government bodies can help overcome the 'democratic deficit' in the Community – not this time that between elected members and the legislative process, but that between the legislative process and the localities affected by its consequences, and that between Community programmes and those responsible for their effective implementation. (See Chapter 6 for further discussion of this issue.)

Conclusion

This chapter has sought to indicate the wide ranging implications of '1992' for local and regional authorities, both in terms of how the economic fortunes of their geographical base may be affected (which in turn will be reflected in their economic development policies and activities), and in terms of how they will need to change their ways of working in carrying out their functions. At this operational level, local and regional authorities will, among other things, have to:

- interpret and apply new standards – for example, for safety equipment
- adopt new procedures, as is the case with the new public purchasing legislation
- develop new ways of working, with (in the UK) the Trading Standards service an example of where this has already taken place
- inform staff about the changes and provide necessary training
- monitor and assess the developing influence of the EC, to ensure preparedness.

Turning to the wider regional economic impact of the Single Market, the authorities' interest and concern is, as Begg (1989) puts it, 'to end up amongst the winners rather than the also-rans' (p.374). An essential precursor to the positive action that this implies is clearly analysis, not only of the impact on sectors of business represented in the region, but also the quality and availability of business support infrastructure, and in particular those support services which have a European emphasis. In terms of maintaining or enhancing the competitive position of the region, authorities will need to develop an awareness of the attributes and strategies of 'rival' regions, as well as developing strategies and programmes to improve those factors which are likely to act as attractants to business investment. In all Member States there are actors who will need to be mobilised by the authorities in developing a high standard of supporting infrastructure, but there are also wide variations between the Member States in the competencies of local and regional authorities – ranging from the highly centralised administration in the UK, to the more autonomous regional bodies in Spain and France.

While the Community resources which are available through the structural funds may seem small in the context of potential demand, they can be important in mobilising action and in levering resources from other sources. There is therefore a need for local and regional authorities, as a very minimum, to maintain an awareness of EC strategies and programmes, but there is also a need to adopt a more active role and to engage with the Commission in the hope of influencing the shape of programmes to reflect the problems and requirements of their region.

At first sight there thus seems to be a substantial potential task for local and regional authorities. What is certain is that most functions of authorities will feel the impact of the Single Market in some way, and the wide-ranging nature of these impacts argues for a response being developed on a corporate and coordinated basis.

An important first step must be to improve the awareness and understanding of the nature and content of the Single Market programme and the Single European Act. In many instances, these efforts will need to cover such matters as how the Community's legislative process works and how it becomes effective at a domestic level, as well as grasping the importance of individual programmes and items of legislation. Having raised awareness and improved understanding, it is important that decisions on how to react to 1992 are taken in the correct context – that of the existing strategic management process of the authority. Thus, consideration of Single Market impacts must take place alongside a consideration of other issues affecting services and functions and within existing strategies for service delivery. Given that 1992 is a process which, in some senses, has been in train since 1957 and that its impacts will certainly not have been completely realised by 1 January 1993, some analysis of how the authority has been affected up to now by EC legislation and programmes may be helpful in informing the development of an appropriate strategic response. Of course, the objective of the White Paper was to accelerate the process, so there is an added urgency for local and regional authorities to address the task of strategy development.

In addition to developing a wide-ranging view of the likely 'internal' impacts – on their day-to-day operations – and 'external' impacts – on business, and other local interests in the geographical area in which they are based and whose interests they serve – authorities could usefully develop a clear understanding of the available resources – internally and externally – which will be of particular assistance in tackling Single Market issues. This will include experience and skills gained in dealing with EC programmes and in adapting to EC legislation, and other forms of technical expertise in a range of matters relevant in an integrated Europe. This will be particularly important in an environment of scarcity of resources and accelerating demands for services.

The method of working which is implied by the analysis is in many ways the antithesis of the bureaucratic approach which is frequently ascribed to local and regional government. While it is true that some authorities can point to the establishment of European offices, to 1992 studies which have been undertaken, and the inclusion of a European focus in their economic development strategy, stress needs to be placed on carefully integrated internal corporate working, focused on systematically defined internal and external strategic objectives, developed with a clear knowledge of the regional competition, implemented in concert with other important local actors, and based firmly in a European (rather than a national or more parochial) context. How far the existing organisational culture of local and regional government is able to meet these challenges will to a significant extent determine the success or failure of a region in the Single European Market.

References

Begg, I. (1989) 'The regional dimension of the "1992" proposals.' *Regional Studies 23*, 4, 368–376.

Boisot, M. (1990) 'Territorial strategies in a competitive world: the emerging challenge to regional authorities.' *European Management Journal 8*, 3, 394–401.

Bongers, P.N. (1990) *Local government and 1992*. Harlow: Longman.

CCRE/IULA (1988) *1992 et les enjeux pour les collectivites territoriales.*

Cecchini, P. (1988) *The European Challenge: 1992 – the benefits of the single market*. Aldershot, Hants: Wildwood House.

Commission of European Communities (1985) 'White Paper from the Commission to the European Council.' *COM(85) 310 final,* June 1985. Brussels: CEC.

Commission of European Communities (1986) *Bulletin of the European Communities, Supplement No. 2*. Single European Act. Brussels: CEC.

Commission of European Communities (1987) 'Making a success of the Single Act: a new frontier for Europe.' *COM(87)* 100 final. Brussels: CEC.

Commission of European Communities (1988) 'The social dimension of the internal market.' Special Edition of *Social Europe*. Luxembourg: Office for Official Publications of the European Community.

Commission of European Communities (1989) *Guide to the reform of the Community's Structural Funds.*

Commission of European Communities (1990a) *An empirical assessment of factors shaping regional competitiveness in problem regions*. Luxembourg: Office for Official Publications of the European Community.

Commission of European Communities (1990b) 'One market, one money.' *European Economy 44*. Luxembourg: Office for Official Publications of the European Community.

Commission of European Communities (1992a) 'Towards sustainability: a European Community programme of policy and action in relation to the environment and sustainable development.' *COM(92) 23 final 2*, March 1992. Brussels: CEC.

Commission of European Communities (1992b) 'From the Single Act to Maastricht and beyond: the means to match our ambitions.' *COM(92) 2000 final,* February 1992. Brussels: CEC.

Council of Europe (1990) 'The impact of the completion of the internal market on local and regional autonomy.' *Studies and Texts Series 12*. Strasbourg: Council of Europe.

Emerson, M. (1988) 'The economics of 1992: an assessment of the potential economic effects of completing the internal market of the European Community.' *European Economy 35*.

Illeris, S. (1989) *Services and regions in Europe* (A report from the FAST programme of the EC). Aldershot, Hants: Gower.

Roberts, P., Thomas, K., Hart, T. and Campbell, A. (1990) *Local authorities and 1992*. Manchester: Centre for Local Economic Strategies.

Tyler, P. (1990) '1992 and the local authority response.' *Local Economy 5*, 1, 55–68.

Acknowledgment

This paper is to a large extent based on work carried out for the Centre for Local Economic Strategies inproducing 'Local Authorities and 1992', and in preparing a contribution to the 'European Municipal Directory' (21st Century Publishing, 1991, London)

CHAPTER 9

European Financial Integration
The Search for an 'Island of Monetary Stability' in the Seas of Global Financial Turbulence[1]

Andrew Leyshon and Nigel Thrift

Introduction

The process of economic and political integration within Europe is a highly complex and multi-faceted phenomenon. Nevertheless, most interpretative accounts of the integration process line up into one of two opposing schools of thought. On the one hand, there are those accounts which view the process as one of *liberalisation*. As captured by the slogan, 'Europe is now open for business', a previously inward-looking and regressive constellation of national economies has apparently been opened up to competitive forces to create a single economic market running the length and breadth of Western Europe. Considerable economic efficiency gains have been, and will continue to be, realised as formerly protected markets are 'purged' and forced to adjust to a pan-European level of competitiveness, as weaker firms and institutions fade and die, bequeathing their markets and revenues to stronger and fitter economic agents (Thompson 1992). This interpretation of events gained ascendency throughout the 1980s, due in large measure to the primacy of neo-liberal ideology within the states of the EC and their

---

1 Our sub-title refers to the comment made in 1965 by Otmar Emminge, Deutsche Bundesbank directorate member: 'I would like to put the question of how the intended "internal market relationships" across the Common Market can be reached if, within the individual regions of this large internal market, currencies keep fluctuating?... Our next goal must be to make the European Economic Community an island of monetary stability' (quoted in Marsh 1992, p.228).

advocacy and installation of the Single European Market programme, which culminated in the 'bonfire of controls' ignited on 1 January 1993 (Grahl and Teague 1989, 1990).

However, the story of European integration can also be told in quite a different way. According to an alternative interpretation, European integration is not really a process of liberalisation at all, but one of consolidation. Although the interventionist capacity of the state is being eroded, this is seen to be part of a wider process of regulatory syncretism, a process of 'creative destruction' by which regulatory frames are being broken at a national level only to be reconstructed and consolidated at the level of the EC. Such a process might well allow EC states to reclaim at a collective level at least some of the economic and political sovereignty lost due to the globalisation of capital and economic exchange. In this sense, European integration may be seen as a process of enclosure in the face of globalising social and economic relations.

These two accounts may be described as competing discourses; descriptions which reflect in their vocabularies and language differing ideological and political positions, each of which attempts to make sense of and justify the extensive restructuring imposed upon the economic and political institutions of EC states in recent years. What is interesting about these two accounts of the European integration process is not so much the relative veracity or validity of their claims. On their own terms and in substantive terms they can both be seen to be accurate to varying degrees. Rather, it is the way in which the process of economic and political change can be seen at various times to reflect *both* positions, leading to a process that is at once liberalising *and* consolidating which demands our attention. Changes have been made to European regulatory structures and institutions which have served to increase regulatory control over economic activity at one turn, to be followed by moves which have then loosened control at another. This dialectical process is possible because the processes of economic and political liberalisation and consolidation are both means to a common end. The broader project which ultimately drives the integration process is geopolitical, or more accurately, geoeconomic. The process of European integration – by whatever means – is seen to be desirable because it will increase the influence of European political and economic institutions in relation to those of the United States and Japan (Cutler, Haslam, Williams and Williams 1990, Streeck and Schmitter 1991). However, it remains to be seen whether an integration process informed both by motives of liberalisation and consolidation can succeed, or whether the tensions between these contradictory tendencies will merely serve to destroy the ambitious geoeconomic project of European integration before it has a chance to reach fruition.

We have undertaken an initial investigation of the tensions between the project of consolidation and of liberalisation within the process of European integration elsewhere (Leyshon and Thrift 1992). There we focused primarily upon the process of financial liberalisation, by means of an analysis of the Single European Market project. In this chapter we turn our attention to the much longer-run process of financial consolidation within the integration process, by means of an investigation of the process of European monetary integration. The chapter is divided into two main parts. In Part I we focus upon the global financial system as the context within which the processes of European monetary integration have unfolded. In Part II we go on to consider the dynamics of European monetary integration in more detail, analysing them against the background of important structural transformation within the global financial system.

Part I – The Global Context

Financial order and disorder – European monetary integration and the breakdown of International Monetary Regulation

The process of financial consolidation has a relatively long history in Europe. Since the 1960s, in often disparate, infrequent and at times counter-productive initiatives, the majority of EC states have been engaged in a collective search for new mechanisms of monetary coordination to replace those lost following the collapse of the Bretton Woods system (Grahl and Teague 1989, 1990). This search was mainly driven by defensive and exclusionary motives. The aim was to protect the productive bases of the leading EC economies from the damaging effects of financial perturbation and speculation, by means of coordination between the internal and external monetary policies of EC states.

Thus, the process of European financial consolidation has taken the form of increased monetary integration, which can be seen as a means by which EC states sought to reassert their structural power within the world economy, both in relation to international capital and to non-European economies (Gill and Law 1989, Strange 1991). From the late 1960s onwards the structural power of European states was significantly eroded in the face of the growing power of international capital and the intensification of geoeconomic competition within the world economy as the United States abandoned its role as governor of the post-war system of regulation by moving ever more to a 'competition state' footing (Cerny 1991, Leyshon 1992). Through ever more effective monetary integration EC states have sought to transform Europe into an 'island of stability' within the world economy by building a new monetary order of sufficient size and power to defend European accumulation within the global context of an intensified level of geoeconomic competition and an ever more predatory and powerful international financial system.

The collapse of the Bretton Woods order is crucial to this story, for the process of European financial consolidation may be seen as a regional solution to the collapse of global monetary order. We will now consider the role and importance of the Bretton Woods system and the reasons for, and implications of, its downfall.

The Bretton Woods inheritance

That the Bretton Woods system provided the foundation for the unprecedented period of economic expansion enjoyed by core capitalist countries after 1945 is acknowledged by writers from a diverse range of theoretical perspectives (for example, Aglietta 1979, Lipietz 1987, Cox 1987, Piore and Sabel 1984). The actual mechanisms and precise *modus operandi* of the Bretton Woods system need not concern us here, and are in any case well documented elsewhere (see Black 1977, Brett 1985, Cohen 1977, De Grauwe 1989, Scammell 1987, Walter 1991). It is sufficient at this point to note that through its fixed exchange rate system and associated international institutions of economic adjustment, the Bretton Woods system served as an international regulatory anchor within the post-war world economy, providing a framework for the flow of trade and capital.

Three reasons in particular help explain why the post-war regulatory order was so effective, albeit for a relatively short period of historical time. The first was the way in which the system reconciled the construction of coherent national economies with a more or less open trading system. The second was the way in which the regulatory order effectively discriminated in favour of one fraction of capital over another, by prioritising national industrial capital over financial capital (Gill 1992, Leyshon 1992), thereby helping to promote social cohesion and political compromise around what one commentator has described as 'the politics of productivity' (Maier, quoted in Gill and Law 1989, p.478). Third and finally, the operational success of the post-war regulatory order was due in large measure to the way in which it was underwritten, governed and ultimately guaranteed by the United States. According to Gill (1992), these characteristics enable us to interpret the post-war order 'in terms of a hegemonic congruence…between the dominant social forces, social structures and forms of state across space and time: that is, operating at both the domestic and international levels, and lasting in the metropolitan capitalist states for roughly the period 1945–1970' (p.271). This congruence included 'ideas (including theories, ideologies and social myths, as well as intersubjective meanings), institutions (such as state, market and international organisation) and material capacities (productive power and military might) [which] came together to create the relatively integral historical conjuncture of *pax americana*' (p.271). This internationally regulated space, in which nation-states were tied one to another through reciprocal exchanges of money, goods and services, and overseen by a set of institutions such as the IMF, World Bank and the General Agreements of Tariff and Trade (which existed both to supervise and manage processes of adjustment within the international economy), nevertheless contained a number of destabilising contradictions and flaws which ensured that the 'regulatory fix' of Bretton Woods was to be of only limited duration (Leyshon 1992, pp.257–259).

There were three particularly important problems. First, there was a contradiction between the pursuit at a national level of welfarism-orientated accumulation strategies, which tended to run in tandem with fairly expansionary monetary policies, and the existence at an international level of an adherence to an anti-inflationary logic of economic adjustment, expressed at first through the IMF and then, following the rise in the structural power of financial capital from the late 1950s onwards, through the foreign exchange markets. The ability of financial capital to 'discipline' states pursuing investment-eroding expansionary economic policies, by cancelling future investment and withdrawing existing funds, forced states to question the wisdom of inflationary strategies of economic adjustment (Gill and Law 1989).

This was linked to the second problem. The perceptions of space which informed the post-war order were highly flawed, given that they tended to reify the state form and assume that the borders of the state were coterminous with the boundary of 'the economy'. The post-war order contained an assumption that the international economic system was precisely that, *inter-national*; that is, a system based on the exchange of capital, goods and services between a constellation of national economic agents within different countries. This geographical interpretation of the international economy ignored the tendencies towards cross-border capital accumulation *within* the boundaries of multinational and transnational corporations, tendencies which were already manifest within the first half of the twentieth century. This interpretation tended to overestimate the structural power of individual nation-states, particularly as regards their ability to manage the process of accumulation at a national level. At the same time, this interpretation led to an underestimation of the ability of private sector corporations to increase their structural power *vis-à-vis* the state through use of international space, by moving or by merely threatening to move activities from one country to another, in a process of 'regulatory arbitrage' (Dicken 1992a). This capacity has severely circumscribed the regulatory autonomy of all but the largest and most powerful nation states.

Third, and finally, there was a contradiction between the role of the United States as both the guarantor of this regulatory order on the one hand, and its existence as a competitive geoeconomic entity in its own right on the other. The central role of the dollar within the international financial system and the overwhelming dominance of the productive base of the USA within the post-war world-economy meant that it took much longer before international financial capital generated sufficient structural power to be able to challenge and discipline the USA in the way it could other states. However, US monetary expansion was such that this ensured a rapid growth in the stock of world monetary reserves, which significantly empowered international financial capital in relation to nation-states and other fractions of capital. It was this more than anything which served to undermine the post-war system of monetary regulation.

To date the discussion has been conducted at a fairly abstract and theoretical level. We now want to substantiate some of these arguments through a more concrete examination of the spatial and organisational dynamics of financial capital in the post-war period. We seek to illustrate how the 'design faults' in the Bretton

Woods system created 'spaces' into which financial capital could expand and develop beyond the surveillance of nation-state regulation. Thus, the growing structural power of financial capital can be linked to a process of 'deterritorialisation', as financial capital increasingly began to operate in ways and places that in a functional sense existed outside the extant structure of international economic regulation.

Financial capital and the deterritorialisation of regulatory space: money and credit in the post-war international financial system[2]

The nature of credit provision within the post-war international financial system has undergone a continual process of evolution, in response to the pursuit of capital accumulation on an international and increasingly on a global scale (Clarke 1988), as well as to changes in the framework of financial regulation constructed by nation-states and supranational regulatory authorities. The deterritorialisation of credit provision during this era should be viewed as a historical process, representative of the unravelling of the structure of international financial regulation described earlier. It is possible to partition this historical process into successive periods, in which the principal mode of credit provision was characterised by distinctive organisational and spatial characteristics. Each of these periods revolves around particularly important disjunctures in national and international financial structures.

THE FIRST PERIOD: LATE 1940s TO LATE 1950s

In this period, credit was for the most part advanced in the form of credit money, denominated in domestic currency, and was created by the expansion of the balance sheets of banks. In spatial terms, credit provision was largely nationally bounded, which served to consolidate the functional dominance of credit money as the primary mode of credit provision. The free circulation of financial capital was discouraged, for fear that this would disrupt the reconstruction of Western European economies, which was being undertaken via the generalised application of nationally-centric Keynesian policies of demand management, and fuelled by the Marshall Plan (see Part II). The full reopening of the foreign exchange markets in 1958 facilitated the growth of international portfolio investment, the absence of which in the earlier post-war period had seen capital markets remain relatively underdeveloped. The limited supply of funds entering capital markets made this form of credit provision relatively expensive, ensuring that securitised forms of credit provision played only a minor role during this period.

---

2   This section is drawn in large part from Leyshon and Thrift (1992).

THE SECOND PERIOD: LATE 1950s TO LATE 1970s

In this period, credit was still predominantly advanced in the form of credit money, although the volume of securitised credit increased strongly over this period, a product of the growing volume of international portfolio investment which found its way into capital markets, and the growing importance of institutional investment organisations such as pension funds and insurance companies in systematically organising this investment.[3]

However, from the late 1950s onwards there was a marked transformation in the spatial dimensions of the process of credit creation. Anomalies between the structures of financial regulation in the United States and in Europe encouraged the export of financial capital from the USA to European financial centres (Strange 1988, Thrift and Leyshon 1988, Urry 1990). The growth of the 'euromarkets', which developed for the most part in the City of London, saw the emergence of off-shore credit-money markets denominated largely in expatriate US dollars, which were then pooled into loans by the international banks which flocked to the City to participate in these new debt markets. The volume of funds in the euromarkets increased rapidly from the late 1960s and early 1970s onwards as money continued to flow overseas from the USA. The export of money from the USA was further accelerated by domestic policy measures introduced to speed up the rate of capital accumulation within the US economy and through the cheapening of credit, and pumping demand into the economy.[4]

The mid to late 1970s marked the zenith of this phase of credit creation within the international financial system, and revealed the growing divide between processes of credit creation and structures of regulatory control; the former were largely conducted at an international scale, whereas the latter operated at the level of nation-state. The ability of financial institutions to advance credit largely unconstrained by the dictates of good banking practice led first to a series of financial crises as banks began to extend credit beyond the capacity of borrowers

---

3   The state often played an important role in facilitating the rise of international investment institutions to positions of importance within the circuit of financial capital. For example, in Europe, where state intervention in the accumulation process was highly developed, the level of employment supported by the nationalised industries meant that the pension funds organised by these industries were responsible for handling very large volumes of capital (Davis 1991). Moreover, the international Keynesian–Fordist settlement, where rising levels of industrial productivity were balanced by a greater distribution of surpluses to the personal sector to support consumption, was responsible for producing higher levels of disposable income, which often found its way into the circuit of financial capital via the purchase of insurance policies.

4   The cheapening of credit led to a marked increase in the volume of money circulating within the US economy, and as a consequence of capital export, also within the rest of the international financial system, leading to a marked increase in the volume of extant global monetary reserves (Parboni 1981). The euromarkets, into which these funds predominantly flowed, expanded still further after 1974 as OPEC nations deposited the super-profits they derived following the steep rise in oil prices.

to pay it back, and then, in response to these crises, to the tentative organisation of forms of supranational financial regulation, designed to overcome the spatial mismatch between the processes of credit creation and the framework of regulatory control over the credit system.[5] But, efforts to reassert regulatory control over the international financial institutions participating in the off-shore credit markets at this time were both too little and too late. An over-extension of credit and an important disjuncture in the trajectory of global macroeconomic development was to usher in a new era of credit provision within the international financial system.

Until 1971 the USA was ultimately constrained in the extent to which it could push domestic accumulation by cheapening credit because of the link between the dollar and gold established at Bretton Woods. Cheap credit had the effect of increasing the volume of dollars in circulation, making the promise made by the USA to convert dollars into gold ever harder to keep. To prevent the growing number of dollar holders from cleaning out the US gold reserve, the gold window was unilaterally revoked by the USA in 1971. This decision had the additional short-term benefit to the USA of easing of the cost of credit within the domestic economy, thereby encouraging accumulation. At the same time, the severing of the link between the dollar and gold destroyed the fixed currency exchange rate system, one of the cornerstones of the Bretton Woods system, and enabled the USA to push down the value of the dollar in relation to other currencies simply by increasing the supply of dollars, which helped improve the competitiveness of US productive capital in world markets.

THE THIRD PERIOD: LATE 1970s TO LATE 1980s

A third phase of credit creation within the post-war international financial system began to emerge in the late 1970s, but was only really fully installed in the early 1980s. As the world economy entered the 1980s, the international credit system was still based on the creation of 'intermediated credit', with the large international banks booking loans on their balance sheets. However, during the 1980s, both the principal process of credit creation, and the spatial dimensions of this process, were transformed. The functional transfiguration of the credit-creation process was propelled by a sea change in US monetary policy from the late 1970s onwards. Problems of rising inflation combined with growing selling pressure on the dollar in the foreign exchange markets to encourage the USA to check its policy of monetary laxity which it had long used to drive domestic accumulation. Interest rates began to rise, making credit more expensive, and so cooling demand within the domestic economy. The 'high interest rate, strong dollar' policy was extended still further as the Reagan administration pursued a defence-led expansion of the economy through the use of imported money; high interest rates attracted in the

---

5   The collapse of the German Herstatt Bank in 1974 is generally recognised as the catalyst
    which spurred national financial regulators to move towards the creation of more unified,
    multinational standards of financial regulation (Dale 1989).

globally mobile international financial capital were needed to fund the project (Lipietz 1989, Thrift and Leyshon 1988).

However, the rise in US interest rates was transmitted through the rest of the international financial system, and pushed debt repayments on intermediated credit to crippling levels. Developing countries, which had borrowed heavily in the euromarkets during the 1970s, found they were unable to pay the interest, let alone the principal, on the debt they had accumulated. The breaking of the developing country debt crisis set off a series of reactive developments within the international financial system which helped install a new regime of credit creation. On the one hand, investors chose not to invest their money with banks, for fear that the banks were too heavily implicated in the developing debt crisis for their money to be absolutely safe. Instead, investors increasingly began to lend their money directly to borrowers, through the purchase of securities and various forms of commercial paper. On the other hand, the shift to off-balance-sheet financing was consolidated by renewed post-crisis attempts by financial authorities to impose multinational regulatory safeguards upon bank lending, by insisting upon higher capital-to-asset ratios, which further curtailed the capacity of banks to engage in asset-based expansion. In the search for profits, banks began to engage in fee-earning activities, which did not expand their balance sheets. These activities, which included the issue of securities for borrowers, created new problems for regulatory authorities, for not only was the creation of credit via securitisation more difficult to constrain by conventional means of financial regulation, but the process of disintermediation also set in train a wave of financial innovation, which greatly multiplied the ways in which borrowers could gain access to credit. Many of the new financial instruments were highly esoteric, often beyond the control of the regulatory authorities, and sometimes also beyond their comprehension.

The transformation of the process of credit creation was paralleled by a reorientation of the spatial movement of credit flows. During the 1970s credit flows moved primarily between the industrialised, OPEC, and developing nations, in a process of 'financial recycling' which was organised in the euromarkets and mediated by international banks. Following the debt crises, the developing countries were subjected to a process of exclusion from international credit markets, cut off from the supply of new funds by their financial position. This saw the international financial system experience a process of spatial concentration, as the circulation of credit was increasingly restricted to a cohort of core industrial nations. In particular, financial flows began to move in response to a new process of recycling, which was necessitated by the widening budget imbalances emerging between industrialised nations. The largest imbalance opened up between the USA and Japan, which resulted in large volumes of funds being diverted from Japan to the USA, with the bulk of this money being placed in securitised investments. In consequence, financial, economic, and geopolitical relations between the two most dominant national economies began to exercise an increasingly pervasive influence upon the trajectory of world economic development. In the new international financial system of the 1980s, New York performed a role akin to global financial sink, as money was sucked in to fund the growing deficit, while Tokyo acted as a financial fountainhead, providing the liquidity which helped lubricate processes of accumulation (Leyshon 1993). The flows of financial capital moving between Japan and the USA became the dominant feature of the international financial system of the 1980s, and saw both New York and Tokyo assume the position of the world's premier financial centre at different times during the decade.

Despite the growth in the structural power of financial capital following the development of this new international financial system, in the mid-1980s much of Europe displayed a marked degree of financial stability. This stability did not occur by chance; it was the product of a long process of financial consolidation by which European states have sought to act in a co-operative and coordinated way to counteract the power of international financial capital. It is to the process of European financial consolidation during the post-war period that we turn in Part II of this chapter.

Part II – The European Dimension

Creating a 'Zone of Stability' – the fall and rise of European Monetary Integration

Although the process of monetary integration within Europe has waxed and waned at various times during the post-war period, according to David Marsh (1992) 'the dream of European economic and monetary union (EMU) is almost as old as the European Community itself' (p.228). The 1980s and early 1990s saw monetary integration come to assume a new prominence in European affairs as it was returned to the forefront of the European policy agenda. In many ways, monetary integration became a totem around which advocates of consolidation within Europe coalesced during this period. The line of argument advanced by those in favour of monetary integration went broadly like this. In return for the surrendering of a large degree of 'nominal' economic and political sovereignty, monetary integration would deliver to European states a real measure of collective and therefore 'effective' sovereignty within the context of the global economy. Monetary integration would in turn pave the way for a more integrated and more autonomous European economy and polity.

In this sense, the movement towards monetary integration within Europe can be interpreted as a geoeconomic process which contains both defensive and offensive elements. It is a defensive process, in as much as one of the purposes of integration is to defend intra-European processes of capital accumulation from destabilising exogenous forces. But at the same time, monetary integration is also an offensive geoeconomic process. The coordination of macroeconomic conditions across the region required for full integration will serve to further bind the national economies of the EC together so that they rise and fall in lockstep with one another, thereby creating a pan-regional economy. This fusion would then require the EC to speak with a single voice in geoeconomic debates and disputes with the United

States and Japan. In the past, EC states were forced to take a subservient role in discussions with the United States of by virtue the latter's far greater economic muscle. But a fully integrated Europe would be at least the economic equal of the United States, and in some respects, its economic superior (Table 9.1). In this sense, the creation of a single European currency, through the process of monetary integration, can be seen as a means by which the EC can put to an end the long-held, but already decaying, financial and economic hegemony of the United States.

Table 9.1 The European Community in the World Economy

	GDP		Trade*	
	Billion ecu	% of OECD total	Billion ecu	% of World total
EC12	4700	34.4	430.7	16.1
United States	4300	31.5	386.9	14.5
Japan	2550	18.7	218.5	8.2

* Trade is measured by (imports + exports)/2, excluding intra-EC exports and imports for the Community
Source: D. Gros and N. Thygsen, (1992) European Integration: From the European Monetary System to European Monetary Union, London; Longman, Table 9.1.1, p.293

In many ways, the new prominence given to monetary integration seemed to run at odds with the discourse of liberalisation that had informed most debates on the issue of European integration during the 1980s. While the process of *market integration* seemed to offer the prospect of a deregulatory spiral across a set of competing national economies leading to the erosion of the power of the state, the movement towards *monetary integration* seemed to offer the possibility of re-regulation and the reassertion of state power at the level of the EC as a whole. The centralisation of monetary policy which would inevitably flow from monetary integration would permit a regulatory syncretism by which EC states could begin to effectively counter the structural power of international financial capital. Thus, on the one hand, the creation of a single European currency would do much to limit the capacity for financial capital to engage in spatial arbitrage within the Community, and act as an effective deterrent to the rapid switching of 'hot money' between European states. On the other hand, meanwhile, full monetary union would do much to speed the construction of more effective prudential financial regulatory structures within the EC, a process that was actually pioneered by the European Community in 1972 when the 'Groupe de Contact' was created to act as a forum within which EEC bank regulators could seek to counter the tendency for financial institutions to engage in international regulatory arbitrage (Llewelyn 1989).

The greater prominence given to this consolidationist theme within the European integration process helps explain the growing opposition to the European project by a vocal but not altogether surprising alliance of neo-liberals and nationalists. Nationalists at least have been fairly consistent in their opposition to European integration at any level, being motivated in large part by xenophobic fears and delusions of the real level of economic and political sovereignty possessed by individual nation-states (Lipietz 1992, p.127). The sense of outrage expressed by neo-liberals is more recent, and betrays a belated recognition that liberalisation has never been the sole item on the agenda for the European Commission. Indeed, the 1992 programme succeeded in revitalising the process of European integration, which had stalled badly during the mid-1970s. It was only by drawing up a neo-liberal agenda to which the more powerful northern European states could give their support, that the European Commission, which has a long history of social democratic leadership, successfully got the integration bandwagon rolling again (Grahl and Teague 1989).

It must be emphasised that there is considerable doubt over how effective any newly created political institutions would actually be in delivering greater powers of intervention to a newly formed EC state within the deregulated environment of post-1992 Europe (Streeck and Schmitter 1991). Even so, to believe that the process of market integration in Europe could have proceeded unencumbered by calls for the closer monetary and political integration that would pave the way for the delivery of interventionary powers was surely to deny the durability and tenacity of the consolidationist theme running through the politics of the European integration programme.

The creation of a more stable monetary platform within the European arena as a base upon which processes of capital accumulation could be played out is a central part of the consolidation process. Indeed, we would argue that the process of European economic integration has proceeded fastest when there has existed a regulatory framework to govern and control the monetary environment within Europe. To expand upon this proposition, we now propose to outline the history of the process of European monetary integration. For reasons of consistency and comparison, we will use the same historical periodisation used in our earlier analysis of the post-war international financial system. We do so because we agree strongly with Grahl and Teague (1990, 101) who have argued that an analysis of the process of European monetary integration must proceed against the contextual background of the 'rise and decadence' of a post-war international system 'centred on the US dollar, and regulated under US hegemony'.

THE FIRST PERIOD – LATE 1940s TO LATE 1950s

During the 1950s, Europe achieved a fairly high level of monetary integration. However, integration was largely a product of external pressure exerted by the United States as part of the process of economic reconstruction and redevelopment. The scale of the economic imbalance between the United States and the war-damaged European economies effectively prevented the immediate installation of the multilateral trading system envisaged under the Bretton Woods agreement. The problem lay in the use of gold as the signifier of absolute value within the international system. The US dollar served as the link between the international monetary system and this ultimate source of value, and was exchangeable into gold on demand at $33 per ounce. All other currencies were to be aligned against the dollar at fixed, but in necessary adjustable, exchange rates. In theory, this would make the 'true value' of non-dollar currency holdings transparent, which could be realised by conversion into dollars and then into gold.[6]

In the context of the immediate post-war period, however, the re-establishment of convertible national currencies proved highly problematic. The main problem was that the link to gold meant that the dollar became 'good as gold' and operated as an absolute standard itself (Lipietz 1987, 144). The strength of the dollar and the relative weakness of the European currencies saw the development of the 'dollar gap', which deterred European states from participating in the multi-lateral trade required by the Bretton Woods system. The dollar gap manifested itself in the following ways:

> Most countries would have been in serious difficulties with their overall balance of payments if they had allowed unrestricted multi-lateral trade because in most countries the demand for imports, especially for goods from the dollar area exceeded by far the limited supply of exports. All European countries tried therefore to earn surpluses in gold, US dollars or any currency convertible into dollars. If any individual European country had tried to make its currency convertible unilaterally it would have rendered its currency equivalent to the US dollar with the result that all the other countries would have attempted to earn a surplus in their bilateral trade with it. (Gros and Thygsen 1992, p.5)

Indeed, this precisely was what happened in 1947 when the UK re-established sterling's convertibility with the dollar, which lasted all of seven weeks before a balance of payments and foreign exchange crisis forced a hasty retreat.

The failure of this unilateral move towards reintegration with the international financial system led to a more collective European response, albeit one that operated in parallel to the US programme of economic aid to Europe extended via

---

6   The central role afforded to the dollar was in the end to prove critical in undoing the Bretton Woods system, in that a national currency was inserted in place of a truly deterritorial numeraire (Leyshon 1992).

the Marshall Plan (1948–1952). In 1950 the European Payments Union (EPU) was established, based in large part upon a blueprint provided by Belgian economist Robert Triffin, a prominent critic of the gold standard system (Thompson 1990). The EPU allowed states to re-enter multilateral trade but protected national currencies from direct competition with the dollar. The solution to the problem of the dollar gap was simple but effective. The EPU introduced a multilateral convertibility system, whereby the surpluses and deficits accruing from multilateral trade were not settled immediately through the transfer of currencies or gold, but were netted within the EPU zone. In this way, European countries could enter into trade with the knowledge that running up a deficit would not lead to an immediate and catastrophic haemorrhage of currency and specie. Thus, the EPU can be seen to have operated as a form of a regional credit system, whereby deficit countries were given time to trade their way out of a deficit, the cost of which was collectively carried by the more successful participants in the system.

The success of this system depended upon restrictions placed upon the convertibility of European currencies into dollars. The willingness of the USA to subscribe to this policy, which ran counter to its short-term economic interests, was of course part of a longer-term project: to give European economies time to recover sufficiently so that in time they would be strong enough to be able to compete within a multilateral capitalist trading system along the lines drawn up at Bretton Woods (Grahl and Teague 1990, Thompson 1990). As recovery proceeded the proportion of deficits repayable in specie and dollars steadily increased (De Grauwe 1989). By 1958, European states were trading sufficiently strongly to allow full convertibility and to permit the break-up of the EPU, despite counter arguments in favour of the retention of the EPU (Gros and Thygsen 1992). As the operation of the EPU ended the Bretton Woods system began in earnest, and the foreign exchange markets, which during the 1950s had been largely preoccupied with intra-European currency movements and speculations (Ferris 1960), switched their attention to dollar trading, and so a new phase in the international financial system began to unfold (see above).

The EPU provided an important demonstration of both the possibilities and the problems of monetary integration within Europe. The EPU had a successful record of managing monetary relations within Europe over a relatively long period of time, during which productivist modes of regulation were installed and operated with considerable success.

The netting procedure effectively insulated accumulation processes in Europe from the discipline of the wider international financial system. Moreover, one of the arguments for the extension of the EPU was clearly geoeconomic and geopolitical in nature, in that the EPU could have continued to provide a Western European forum for policy coordination at a time when Europe fragmented into members of the EEC, signatories of the European Free Trade Area (EFTA) Agreement of 1958 and those few who did not participate in either trading agreement (Gros and Thygsen 1992, p.8).

However, the operation of the EPU also saw the emergence of difficulties in the form of centrifugal tendencies which would come to dog later attempts to forge monetary integration in Europe. For example, even in the 1950s it was clear that the different economies of Europe were moving at different speeds and along markedly different trajectories. For example, the German economy recovered from immediate post-war crises to quickly settle into a pattern of anti-inflationary economic growth and export success, the early 1950s seeing the first in a long sequence of current account surpluses. The demonic status of the 1923 inflation and its economic, social and political consequences saw monetary stability in post-war Germany become an objective of the first order, which was successfully realised under the stewardship first of the Bank deutsche Länder (BdL) and then the Deutsche Bundesbank from 1957 (Kennedy 1991, Marsh 1992). The monetary stability achieved through this central commitment to anti-inflationism, while at times being costly in terms of unemployment, has proved critical in laying the foundations of an innovative, production-orientated economy (Eltis, Fraser and Ricketts 1992). Over a long period of time German interest rates have been low enough and stable enough to encourage firms to borrow long-term, and critically, to encourage banks to lend long-term. Elsewhere in Europe, such monetary stability proved much harder to achieve since recourse to a centralising and inflationary logic as a means of adjustment out of economic crisis was not proscribed the way it was in Germany.

The 1950s also bore witness to the destabilising influence of the UK upon the process of financial integration in Europe. The eagerness of the City of London to reclaim its former glory as the world's premier international financial centre combined with the 'globalist' rather than 'regionalist' outlook of the UK authorities (Gros and Thygsen 1992, p.27) to ensure that inclusion within such a cooperative monetary venture such as the EPU was undertaken somewhat grudgingly. The aspirations of the UK government and the City were always much wider than Europe, which meant that the UK has always found it difficult to come to terms with the process of financial integration in Europe. The UK made a second unsuccessful attempt to establish full convertibility with the dollar in 1955, while in the late 1970s, despite encouragement from the other parties in the endeavour, the UK rejected the option of joining the EMS at its inception (see below).[7]

THE SECOND PERIOD: LATE 1950s TO LATE 1970s

As we have argued above, the EPU can be seen as an institutionalised credit system, which was particularly advantageous to deficit countries. The demise of the EPU in 1958 meant that European states were suddenly faced with the much harsher adjustment processes of the Bretton Woods system as prosecuted by the IMF (Brett

---

7   Indeed, the eagerness to find an international currency to take the place of sterling led the City to propagate the market in eurodollars in London, which in turn played an important part in destabilising the Bretton Woods system of international monetary management.

1985, Galbraith 1975). However, the transition from the EPU to the Bretton Woods system was actually achieved in a fairly painless manner. Indeed, the platform of monetary stability that the system provided served to facilitate the deepening and widening of economic integration in Europe called for in the Treaty of Rome, signed by six European states in 1957. But as the 1960s wore on, and as international monetary instability increased, European states began to cast around in search of alternative models of monetary regulation to hold together the economic integration which had been achieved in earlier, less turbulent times.

FROM MONETARY STABILITY TO INSTABILITY: THE LATE 1950s TO EARLY 1970s

During the early years of its operation Bretton Woods seemed to be a more than adequate substitute for the EPU. Indeed, European exchange rates were sufficiently stable to underpin the creation both of a European customs union and the Common Agricultural Policy (CAP). However, this stability proved to be short-lived, as almost from its full installation in the late 1950s the Bretton Woods system began to be undermined. During the 1950s the international monetary instability had been caused by the 'dollar gap'. In the 1960s monetary stability was destroyed by a 'dollar overhang' (Gros and Thygsen 1992). The return to full convertibility saw the empowerment of the foreign exchange markets and a marked increase in international portfolio investment. As described above, large volumes of money began to flow out of the USA into the euromarkets, as financial capitalists sought higher returns on their dollar investments in Europe. At the same time, the supply of dollars in the world economy continued to increase as the USA pursued expansionary policies at home to fuel economic growth and pay for its geopolitical adventures in Indo-China.

The new potency of international financial capital during this period saw the rise of a deflationary or fractioning logic operating at an international level, which promoted forms of economic adjustment which was strictly at odds with the centralising logic being pursued by most Western European governments at a national level (Leyshon 1992). In this way, the mid-1960s can be seen as the zenith of autocentric capitalism within Europe (Lipietz 1987, p.46), for thereafter modes of regulation would increasingly come to reflect the logics of adjustment emanating from the international financial system.

The first signs of the growing structural power of international financial capital and of the dangers that this development posed for the international monetary order emerged in the late 1960s. From 1967 onwards the foreign exchange markets became ever more volatile. Investors and dealers began to expose the contradictions of a fixed-exchange rate system comprised of a large number of disparate national economies each moving at different rates of economic growth and along divergent economic trajectories. The first currency to be subjected to a speculative assault was sterling in 1967, to which the UK government responded with a 15% devaluation. Then, in the space of one month in 1969, the French franc was devalued by over 11% whilst the Deutschmark was revalued by almost 10% (Marsh 1992).

This sharp realignment of the two main currencies of the European Community came as something of a shock to the European integration project, revealing as it did the extent to which the institutions of economic and political integration were critically dependent upon a monetary stability over which the European states had little control or influence. In the wake of the realignment, all the old certainties seemed to melt away. Not even the cornerstone of the integration process, the Common Agricultural Policy (CAP), seemed safe. Agricultural prices within the Community were denominated in European Units of Account (EUA), a universal 'green' currency. However, the method by which the value of the EUA was calculated revealed the way in which the monetary stability and institutions of the Bretton Woods system had been taken as given, for one EUA was defined as being equivalent to the gold value of one US dollar. Therefore, any devaluation or revaluation of European Community currencies led to a depreciation or appreciation against the EUA, which had obvious implications for agricultural prices.

The devaluation of the franc and the revaluation of the deutschmark threatened to so destabilise the underlying patterns of agricultural production and trade between France and Germany that the CAP was effectively remade, so that it reflected changed circumstances.

> In order to maintain process at different levels a complicated system of 'Monetary Compensatory Amount' (MCAs) had to be introduced...which helped keep French food prices below the Community average...(and kept) the prices for German producers above the Community average. Since these MCAs were really tariffs and import subsidies they effectively compartmentalised national agricultural markets. The Community recognised this and the MCAs were therefore supposed to be temporary, but since exchange rates continued to move throughout the following two decades new MCAs were created as the old ones were slowly dismantled. (Gros and Thygsen 1992, p.11–12).

The 1969 realignment was merely the forerunner of a systemic crisis within the international monetary order, the break-up of which was to usher in a new era of volatility and turbulence within the international financial system (Thrift and Leyshon 1988, Hubner 1991).

THE 'SNAKE'

As the old system of international monetary management closed, so, in Europe at least, there began a search for an alternative. This search was motivated by a desire to defend the projects of integration, such as the CAP and the customs union, from the turbulence induced by the monetary instability that followed in the wake of the United States' shift to a more overtly geoeconomic footing and by the relentless rise in the structural power of international financial capital. When in 1971 the

United States closed the 'gold window'[8] it was clear that the condition of the Bretton Woods system had become critical, although it took two more years before the system finally became inoperative. In March 1973, when the foreign exchange markets reopened under a 'floating regime' after a two-week period of closure, it was clear that a major turning point in international financial systems had passed.

The ending of the dollar's official role as the anchor and the benchmark of the international monetary system enabled the United States to drive down its value in the foreign exchange markets in order to stem imports and deliver a competitive advantage to US exporters. The uncoupling of the dollar in this way also encouraged the United States to accelerate monetary expansion at home, for no longer did the printing of dollars carry any threat to the United States gold reserve (Leyshon 1992).

This geoeconomic initiative had serious consequences for Europe. As we have seen, even under the fixed exchange rate system it was becoming increasingly difficult to maintain the parities of European currencies. Now that the value of the dollar was 'managed', parities became even more volatile. This problem was made even worse by the tendency for international investors to use the deutschmark as a refuge of value in the face of the long-term decline of the dollar. The two currencies became inversely related so that 'the weakness and volatility of the dollar tended to be massively disruptive of internal economic relations (in Europe)' (Grahl and Teague 1990, p.106). It was in response to such externally-generated uncertainty that European states began to cast around for an alternative mechanism of macroeconomic stabilisation during the 1970s.

The disruptive potential of monetary turbulence was such that even by 1970 the European Community had already drawn up an ambitious plan for full economic and monetary union (EMU) – the Werner Report – which was to be implemented by 1980. However, as Gros and Thygsen (1992) pointedly observe, this initiative did not really represent an attempt to construct an independent system of monetary management. Rather, it was more an attempt to stabilise European currencies within the existing Bretton Woods system, since the Werner Report did not prescribe the need for separate European monetary institutions. When the switch from fixed to floating exchange rates came, European states were faced with a dual dilemma. Not only had the system of international monetary stabilisation been swept away, but the regional solution contained within the Werner Plan became impossible because of its implicit dependence upon the institutions of Bretton Woods.

Attention now became focused upon a mechanism to which European states had first turned in 1972. In the Smithsonian Agreement of December 1971, by which the United States ended the link between the dollar and gold, the permitted range of currency fluctuation within the fixed exchange rate system increased. In

---

8   The right to convert dollars into gold.

order to counter the monetary volatility which this would induce within Europe, the Spring of 1972 saw EC countries introduce the system of cooperative exchange rate management which became known as the 'snake', through which they sought to limit intra-European currency fluctuation.[9]

While the 'snake' did provide some benefit in protecting underlying intra-European trade by limiting the range of permitted intra-European currency movements, the costs and benefits of this system of monetary stabilisation were distributed unequally across the Community, which meant that the system itself proved to be fairly unstable. The instability and inequality of the system stemmed from the fact that the 'snake' was, in essence, 'a lopsided system, with the German economy accounting for more than two-thirds of the collective GDP of the group, and the DM as the only significant international currency' (Gros and Thygsen 1992, p.35). The costs tended to be borne by Germany's partners in the system, particularly as the inverse relationship between the dollar and the deutschmark meant that a decline in the former translated into a rise in the latter. Therefore, bouts of US devaluation during the 1970s imposed considerable economic and social costs on EC countries. Membership of the 'snake' required that they defend the parities of their currencies against the deutschmark, which meant extensive intervention within the foreign exchange markets and/or the imposition of higher rates of interest at home. The former option meant the loss of reserves, while interest rate increases had implications for domestic economic growth. A further cost was an erosion of price competitiveness in relation to US producers, as European currencies drifted upwards against the dollar along with the deutschmark.

The benefits of the 'snake', meanwhile, tended to accrue to the German economy and to German firms. With the deutschmark the dominant currency within Europe, Germany was able to avoid the costs of intervention and interest rate management which were imposed upon its partners. Clearly, the steady revaluation of the deutschmark against the dollar posed problems for German producers, but in the end these problems proved surmountable in a way that proved more difficult for the other countries participating in the 'snake'. The strength of the deutschmark and of the German economy directly enabled the holding down of interest rates which, in combination with the close links between financial and industrial capital in Germany, helped German firms fund what Grahl and Teague (1990) describe as 'a vast process of industrial restructuring':

---

9   The name of the system stems from the metaphor of a snake moving through a narrow
    tunnel, the tail of which could only move up and down between the floor and the ceiling of
    the tunnel. It was hoped to replicate this movement by limiting the fluctuation of European
    currencies against the dollar. The number of countries participating in the 'snake' increased
    from 6 to 10 shortly after its inception following the accession to the EC of the United
    Kingdom, Ireland and Denmark, and Norway's entry into the 'snake' (but not the EC) (Gros
    and Thygsen 1992).

> rapid technical innovation held down costs and maintained competitiveness
> for complex products, particularly factory equipment and other investment
> goods; meanwhile German companies used the strong deutschmark to carry
> out enormous foreign investments, moving labour-intensive production
> processes to countries with lower wage costs. (p.107)

It was far more difficult for Germany's partners to respond in this way. With weaker
currencies and more inflationary domestic economies, interest rates tended to be
higher, which in turn militated against the comprehensive technological overhaul
to which German firms subjected themselves. Moreover, as recent research makes
clear, the German economy possesses a network of institutions of economic
adjustment which are lacking or only partially developed in other EC countries
(see, in particular, Cooke and Morgan 1990, Cooke 1992). In Germany these
institutions have arisen over a long period of time alongside a series of 'embedded'
conventions and social norms (Granovetter 1985, Zukin and DiMaggio 1990,
Grabher 1993, Herrigel 1993), such as the commitment to low inflation and to
social order and consensus, which helps facilitate the competitiveness of the
German economy within an international context. As Thompson (1992) has
argued, this 'institutional variability counts. And in as much as it is "structurally"
embedded it is very difficult to shift' (p.139). It also means that it is difficult to
replicate, particularly in periods of economic retrenchment. The paucity and
poverty of institutions of economic adjustment and restructuring among Germany's partners ensured that the 'snake' was not only an unbalanced system of
monetary stabilisation but also a highly volatile one, both in terms of exchange
rates and membership. Between 1972 and 1979 there were nine separate episodes
of revaluation and devaluation while several countries were forced to leave the
'snake' because of the severe domestic costs of maintaining international currency
stability.[10]

The weakness of the 'snake' as a mechanism of international monetary stability
has largely been attributed to its timidity. The system sought to maintain monetary
stability without the requirement that all participants equally share the costs of
this task. The responsibility tended to fall upon those states with the weaker
currencies who were required to maintain parities with the much stronger
deutschmark. There was no reciprocal requirement that the German government
of the Deutsche Bundesbank ensure that increases in the deutschmark were
sufficiently managed so that they did not disturb the system (Gros and Thygsen
1992). In other words, the system was a sort of half-way house; not a truly

---

10 The UK was the first to leave never to return, less than two months after joining the system in
    the wake of yet another foreign exchange crisis. Italy left the system in 1973 while Sweden
    joined in 1973 only to leave again in 1977. Both Denmark and France left the system to
    rejoin later. Indeed, the franc left and rejoined the system three times (Gros and Thygsen
    1992, Table 1.1).

international system of coordination, yet more than merely a set of national responses.

The operation of the 'snake' in the mid-1970s was concomitant with the nadir of the post-war project of European integration, a synchronism that was not altogether coincidental, and which helps explain why the 'snake' was never anything more than a partial response to international monetary stability. According to Streeck and Schmitter (1991), the mid-1970s represent the 'dark age' of the European integration process, being 'a time when European national elites seemed to believe as a matter of course that the supranational European institutions they had set up in the 1950s and 1960s, embedded in a relatively stable world order, could not serve as a useful tool (sic) for the restoration of that order and that therefore everybody had to find their own solutions' (p.144). However, these national 'solutions' were destined to fail, mainly because they simply involved a more intensive implementation of those institutions, conventions and social norms that had been utilised during the earlier period of international regulatory order. In the absence of suitable institutions and mechanisms of international stability much greater emphasis was placed upon controlling and disciplining domestic economies:

> ...governments almost everywhere experimented with 'social contracts' of all sorts. These agreements served as a homemade replacement or functional equivalent for the now defunct set of international institutions that had in the past provided at least some form of stability for and among competing capitalist nations by, for example, imposing and enforcing external 'balance of payments constraints' that helped governments keep domestic 'discipline'. To an important degree, concentration in the 1970s must be understood as a sometimes desperate turn to domestic political and institutional resources in a search for solutions to what really were international problems. (Streeck and Schmitter 1991, p.143)

The difficulties of this task have been well documented, not least by the burgeoning literature on regulation theory and flexible accumulation (for example, Lipietz 1987, 1992, Harvey 1989, Gertler 1988, 1992, Tickell and Peck 1992, Peck and Tickell 1992, Dunford 1990). Even in the heyday of Keynesianism, the validity of a construct such as 'the national economy' was highly questionable (Boss 1990, Leyshon 1992); by the 1970s the tendency towards the 'globalisation' of economic relations (Levitt 1983, Gordon 1988, Dicken 1992b) meant that modes of social regulation which depended upon more autocentric forms of economic development were faced with severe difficulties (Swyngedouw 1989).[11]

---

11 An important exception to this rule was Japan, which exercised a fierce regulatory defence of its economy from outside forces until US geoeconomic pressure forced it to capitulate during the 1980s (see Leyshon 1993).

The growing awareness of the extent to which the 'effective sovereignty' of European states had been undermined by the progressive internationalisation of the regime of accumulation prompted two main political responses. The first, introduced initially at a national level, was to lead to the introduction of the discourse of liberalisation into the European integration process. Governments across Europe began to question the relevance and appropriateness of those national institutions, conventions and social norms that had developed in parallel to the now all but defunct international institutions of regulatory order. Although the extent to which these national modes of social regulation were overhauled and overthrown varied markedly from state to state (Thompson 1992), neo-liberalism gained sufficient momentum across Europe for the EC to use the neo-liberal advocacy of reregulation as the spark by which the process of European integration could be rekindled during the 1980s (Grahl and Teague 1989, 1990). The second response was more in keeping with the long tradition of the integration process, and fell more clearly under the rubric of consolidation. From the late 1970s onwards, a number of European states embarked upon a more concerted and sophisticated attempt to establish monetary stability within Europe. The creation of the European Monetary System (EMS) in 1979 signalled the beginning of a new phase in the history of monetary relations in Europe. Indeed, we would argue that the EMS was critical to the furtherance of economic and political integration within Europe during the 1980s, in that it not only provided the necessary monetary stabilisation to encourage economic integration, but also, through its example of international monetary cooperation, provided a blueprint for even closer monetary and political integration.

THE THIRD PERIOD: LATE 1970s TO LATE 1980s

The next period of post-war European monetary history is dominated by the EMS. The EMS evolved out of the 'snake' but represented a significant advance on the earlier model of monetary stabilisation, being a much more coordinated and cooperative system. The bilateral parities of the 'snake' were to be replaced with a system of multilateral parities, with all currencies being measured against the European Currency Unit (ECU), the value of which was an expression of a 'basket' of EMS currencies. Currencies were allowed to move against the ECU, but only within set ranges of variability. Should a currency move above or below its permitted range this triggered intervention in the foreign exchange markets to bring the currency back in line. The use of the ECU as the numeraire of the EMS was intended to ensure that a movement in just one currency in the system necessarily meant a counter-movement in all the other currencies (Grahl and Teague 1990). In this way, currency fluctuation had systemic implications requiring an unprecedented level of collective responsibility and action. The rationale for this mode of operation was to avoid currency fluctuations being the sole responsibility of states with weaker currencies, as was the case during the operation of the 'snake'. The introduction of the principle of collective responsibility in the arena of exchange rate management contributed to the later success of the EMS, which delivered to Europe a level of monetary stability unknown since the mid-1960s.

The EMS owes its creation to a Franco-German geoeconomic response to the prospect of ever increasing turbulence and volatility within the international macroeconomic environment. The election of US President Jimmy Carter in 1976 seemed to signal a continuation of the combined policies of domestic expansion and forced devaluation of the dollar in the foreign exchange markets. The omens for the 'snake' were not propitious, given the inverse relationship between the dollar and deutschmark. In Germany it was feared that without a stronger link between the deutschmark and the other currencies in the 'snake' then the system would collapse, resulting in a sudden and violent revaluation of the deutschmark against European currencies, damaging the export-orientated German economy. Therefore, it was very much in the interests of the German economy and polity to seek to establish a more effective system of monetary integration to replace the 'snake' (Gros and Thygsen 1992). Given that the call for a system such as the EMS was quickly interpreted as an opportunity to forge within Europe a path of economic development more resistant to US geoeconomic pressure, it was hardly surprising that the German government found a natural ally in France, which had long advocated such a path.[12]

Emboldened by the European Community's attempt to revive the European integration process by advocating closer economic and monetary ties under the presidency of Roy Jenkins, the German and French governments submitted a proposal for the construction of a European Monetary System for consideration by the European Council in 1978. By 1979 the system was in operation.

The principal aim of the EMS was to create a 'zone of monetary stability' within Europe, thereby realising a long-held aim of the consolidationist project for Europe. The EMS was to act as a kind of monetary 'flotation platform' in the turbulent seas of the foreign exchange markets; while the platform would rise and fall in relation to the value of non-EMS currencies, on the platform itself a relative calm would prevail. The implicit hope was that this defence against disruptive exogenous forces would promote a more autocentric form of development across the EMS area which could proceed relatively unhindered by dollar-induced financial perturbations.

The original plans for the EMS called for the creation of a parallel institution, the European Monetary Fund (EMF), the purpose of which would have been to provide institutional support to the exchange rate mechanism (ERM) of the EMS:

> A European Monetary Fund (EMF) was to take over a substantial part of the gold and dollar reserves of member central banks, issuing ECUs in return. A

---

12 For example, in the 1960s France exchanged its dollar reserves for gold as 'a public gesture of distrust in American leadership' (Grahl and Teague 1990, p.104).

hierarchy of responsibilities would then emerge: the supranational EMF would conduct the external policy of the system, deciding for example when to buy or sell dollars against the EC. National central banks would manage the relation between their own currencies and the ECU, by constraining domestic monetary policies in order to preserve the given parities. The EMF would finance national balance of payments equilibria in ECUs when the central bank concerned was unable to do so, or would signal the need for a collective adjustment of parities if devaluation seemed necessary. In external negotiations the EMF would represent Western Europe in the reconstruction of the world payments system...(the) general aim would be a reassertion of social control over international relations. (Grahl and Teague 1990, p.124).

However, despite the grand ambition and the laudable intentions, the EMF was never established, nor did the ecu take the prominent position planned for it, a turn of events which was to have long-term implications for the trajectory of development within the EMS.

The EMF was effectively blocked by opposition within Germany, and in particular within the Bundesbank. The original EMS model promised to reduce the effective level of control that the Bundesbank wielded over the German economy. The fear was that the EMF would respond to the structural problems faced by the less competitive countries in the EMS by introducing a more expansionary and inflationary model of adjustment. This was incompatible with the anti-inflationary model which had served the German economy well during the post-war period. The opposition to the institutional stage of the EMS within Germany in general, and by the Bundesbank in particular, was such that the EMF was 'quietly shelved' in 1980 (Gros and Thygsen 1992, p.34). The failure to establish the EMF ensured that processes of economic adjustment within the EMS would be governed by a deflationary logic in line with German demands, while the failure to back the ecu with an appropriate monetary institution meant that while the ecu was the *de jure* lead currency in the EMS, the *de facto* lead currency was the deutschmark. In this way the rearguard action mounted by the Bundesbank succeeded in turning 'the original concept (for the EMS) on its head by making the strongest currency the yardstick for the system' (Karl Otto Pohl, former President of the Bundesbank, quoted in Marsh 1992, p.233), making the EMS a far more asymmetrical system than was ever intended.

Through the EMS, the Bundesbank's commitment to price stability was transmitted to the other economies in the system. This effectively locked EMS states into a process of 'competitive disinflation' in order to maintain stability. EMS participants were forced to bring their macroeconomic indicators more into line with those of Germany to prevent the expensive and destabilising bouts of devaluation and revaluation that would otherwise be necessary. The difficulties of achieving convergence ensured that in its early years the EMS was anything but a zone of stability. Between 1979 and 1983 there were no less than seven episodes of realignment as member states struggled to move their economies onto a more deflationary path, balancing the quest for international stability with the management of their domestic economies. However, between 1983 and 1987, the EMS entered a more stable period, when only four realignments were required, and inflation within the EMS began to approach German rates (Table 9.2).

Table 9.2 Disinflation in Europe, 1974–1989: average rates of inflation

	1974–78	*1979–82*	*1983–86*	*1986–89*
EMS	9.9	10.4	4.6	2.3
EC non-EMS	16.3	16.1	12.6	6.6
Europe non-EC	8.4	8.8	5.2	3.7

Note: Europe non-EC includes Switzerland, Norway, Sweden, Finland, but not Austria, since that currency is linked to the deutschmark.

Source: D. Gros and N. Thygsen, (1992) European Monetary Integration: From the European Monetary System to European Monetary Union, London; Longman, Table 4.1.4, p 112.

It was no coincidence that during this later period of monetary stability the project of European integration gathered pace, both in the form of the Single European Market programme and in the call for full Economic and Monetary Union. The EMS appeared to provide the necessary framework of stability within which the neo-liberal re-regulatory project could unfold. At the same time, the EMS also seemed to provide the platform for those consolidationists seeking to forge monetary integration within Europe. However, the liberalisation of capital flows, which formed part of the creation of the Single European Market, was to usher in a 'new EMS' in the late 1980s which was much less stable (Haldane 1991, Gros and Thygsen 1992). By the late 1980s, it became clear that the EMS was in crisis. There were growing fears that the demands of the 1992 programme would place unbearable pressures upon the EMS, as the drive for liberalisation undermined the ability of the member states to hold the exchange rate system together. These concerns helped usher in a new phase in the history of monetary relations in Europe.

Between a Rock and a Hard Place: European Monetary Union and the Crisis of the EMS

The essence of the emerging crisis of the EMS in the late 1980s revolved around the so-called 'impossibility theorem'; that is, the impossibility of reconciling a system of fixed exchange rates with both independent monetary policies and free capital mobility:

> The logic of the theorem is straightforward: with full mobility capital will always flow from a country with lower interest rates to one with higher rates – unless there is a risk of exchange rate movements. Thus, with completely

fixed exchange rates, a differential in interest rates will be unsustainable as the country with lower rates will undergo an unlimited outflow of funds. Eventually one of the three things will have to give way – the exchange rate, the difference in policy, or the freedom of capital movements. (Grahl and Teague 1990, p.129).

As preparation for the 1992 programme saw the easing of restrictions on capital between EMS countries, so the system begin to take on a new and destabilising dynamic. As anticipated by the 'impossibility theorem', money began to flow into higher inflation countries in anticipation of higher rates of interest. This inward movement of money moved the currencies of countries such as Italy and Spain to the top of their bands in the exchange rate mechanism, which in turn forced some relaxation in monetary policy, which had the unwanted effect of giving a further push to inflation (Haldane 1991). This development destabilised the EMS in two ways. Firstly, it ran counter to the deflationary logic upon which the German-dominated EMS had been grounded since its inception. Secondly, the option of revaluing the currencies bumping up against the top of their bands was now more dangerous given the ease by which money could now move through the EMS; the fear was that if realignments occurred too frequently then the benefits of the exchange rate system would be lost, for it would only serve to encourage speculative attacks within the EMS.

The danger that the EMS might collapse under the weight of its internal contradictions proved a powerful spur to the European Commission, which under the stewardship of Jacques Delors revived its long-held consolidationist plans to move towards full monetary union in Europe. The EMS came to be seen not as an end in itself, but more as a stage along a process of economic harmonisation, involving a more explicit linking of monetary policies at a supranational scale, culminating in a process of full Economic and Monetary Union. If the EC could achieve monetary union, then the struggle towards the stabilisation of monetary relations in Europe would be seen to have been in vain and would mark a significant advance in the EC's geoeconomic ambitions. However, Marsh argues that the move towards EMU was also motivated by geoeconomic struggles within the EC itself, and in particular between Germany and France. EMU, by creating an institutional framework for monetary management missing in the EMS, would limit the autonomy of the Bundesbank, and in so doing, would also reduce German economic and financial hegemony in Europe:

> The Bundesbank realised more quickly than the politicians that the plan for European monetary union was above all a means of undermining German power. Accurately summing up the political power-play with the Paris government Pohl (the Bundesbank president) complained consistently that France was trying to 'get a grip on the D-Mark'. As Wilhelm Nolling president of the Landeszenttralbank in Hamburg put it in early 1991: 'We should be under no illusions – the present controversy over the European

monetary order is about power influence and the pursuit of national interests. (Marsh 1992, p.236).

Spurred on by German desires to keep the EMS together and by her partners' wishes to create a more equitable monetary order in Europe, the Delors committee produced its plan for EMU in April 1989. The report presented a three-stage plan towards monetary union and was a clear statement by the EC that it was determined to pursue a path towards full economic and monetary union, to be completed before the end of the 1990s. The Maastricht Agreement, signed in December 1991, was a further step on the road towards this goal.

However, the consolidationist ambitions behind the process of EMU have begun to run into trouble in the early 1990s. It proved more difficult than expected to persuade national governments to give up what limited sovereignty they still have in favour of a more effective sovereignty at a trans-European level.[13] This, combined with the neo-liberal leaning of several EC states, meant that the trans-European mode of social regulation envisaged at Maastricht was a pale shadow of those national modes of social regulation which operated for much of the post-war period (Lipietz 1992). Indeed, the Delors plan itself leaned more towards the right than the left, being 'above all concerned with the control of the money supply and, in the monetarist style, via this with the control of inflation' (Grahl 1991, p.141). To a large extent, the deflationist stance reflected the need to ensure that the German government and Bundesbank were on board the EMU train, by insisting that before any EC country could participate in EMU they had to meet fairly strict convergence criteria relating to price stability, the 'sustainability' of budgetary positions, exchange rate stability within the EMS and long-term interest rates around the EMS average (*Bank of England Quarterly Bulletin* 1992). The setting of these criteria effectively paved the way for a 'two-speed' or 'two-tier' Europe (Leborgne and Lipietz 1990). As far as the Bundesbank and the German Government were concerned:

> European monetary union had to be 'two-speed'; otherwise it would not happen at all. Low inflation countries could proceed along a fast track and join as soon as monetary union was established. Higher inflation countries...would have to wait. In the EMS, full membership had been restricted to those countries wishing to stick to German-style *Stabilitatspolitik* and it worked well. If EMU had any chance of functioning, it would have to follow the same principle of refusing membership to the laggards in the inflation stakes until their economic performances had improved (Marsh 1992, p.238).

---

13 At the time of writing, it is not sure whether the treaty will be ratified by the governments of all the EC members. Nevertheless, this does not mean that EMU will not go ahead. The treaty allows for the creation of a two-speed Europe in matters of monetary integration. Integration can proceed with as few as two states.

By 1992 the prospects of even this pale version of financial consolidation being implemented in Europe looked distinctly unpromising. The summer and early autumn of that year witnessed the near breakdown of the EMS, the foundation upon which EMU was to be built. The catalyst for this crisis was the process of German unification in 1989. This caused an inflationary surge which destabilised the German economy, and in turn the entire EMS. The link between unification and the EMS crisis has been clearly outlined by King (1992):

> The impact of unification was to raise demand – for both consumption and investment – in the eastern Länder without any corresponding immediate increase in output. Much of this increased demand was for goods produced in the western part of the country. Unification led, therefore, to a change in the balance between aggregate demand and aggregate output, or, to put it another way, to an increase in the difference between domestic investment and national saving. In turn this implied a temporary reduction in the net trade surplus... The classical recipe in this situation is a nominal appreciation of the currency. Under a system of floating exchange rates the economic shock of German unification would have led to an appreciation of the deutschmark – thus providing the incentive to switch demand from Germany to its trading partners... But in the ERM changes in parities have costs in the form of reduced credibility in the new parities and the member countries of the ERM decided that even the German-specific shock of unification did not justify a change in exchange rates. (p.327)

Therefore, as German interest rates rose to counter the inflationary pressures emanating from the east, holding the EMS together proved more and more difficult. By mid-1992 the centrifugal pressures pulling the EMS apart seemed irresistible. In order to counter capital mobility to Germany and to maintain exchange rate parities, interest rates across the EMS rose to new heights. The deflationary shocks caused by these interest rate hikes began to have serious social and economic effects across the community. To maintain monetary stability within the EMS, member states had to pay heavy costs in their domestic economies. The growing tension between the external commitment to the EMS and the political costs of internal economic decline created a fertile ground for international financial capital, as money manager capitalists began making speculative attacks on the weaker currencies in the system in the hope of a devaluation against the deutschmark. Based on the findings of subsequent journalistic investigations, Hutton (1992a,b,c) has argued that in order to save the EMS, and to avoid the ultimately inflationary expense of propping up the system through intervention in the foreign exchange markets, the Bundesbank offered to lower German interest rates, but only if this were linked to a general realignment of the system with a revaluation of strong and devaluation of weak currencies in the system. In effect, this would have meant a revaluation of the deutschmark, the guilder and the Belgian and French francs against all the other currencies in the system. According to Hutton (1992a), the possibility of such a realignment was blocked by the UK at a summit of European finance ministers held in Bath in early September 1992:

> The economic logic (for realignment) was obvious but there were constraints. Britain could not let France join Germany, and almost certainly Belgium and Holland, in moving upwards, leaving the pound to move down with the less strong currencies...(but the)...UK was willing to consider a general realignment with the mark appreciating against all other ERM currencies. (p.11)

In the wake of this stalemate, speculative pressure on the Italian lira increased which encouraged the German authorities to open bilateral talks with their Italian counterparts to discuss a bilateral realignment. This bilateral move, which was accomplished with a marginal reduction in German interest rates, was clearly in the short-term interests of both Italy and Germany; the Italian government could ill afford the cost of intervention in the foreign exchange markets, while the German government was concerned that 'the marks they were now printing to lend to the Italians to sell to currency speculators would end up in the Frankfurt money markets, undoing 18 months of effort to hold down the growth of German money supply and raising, as the Bundesbank saw it, an acceleration in the inflation', (Hutton 1992a, p.11). But this bilateral move was interpreted by the foreign exchange markets as a precedent. This belief was reinforced by a somewhat injudicious comment by the president of the Bundesbank, to the effect that he doubted very much whether the existing parities in the EMS could survive for very long (Hutton 1992b). The foreign exchange markets began to pick off the weaker currencies in the EMS one by one. Between 15 and 16 September 1992 the UK government spent over half its monetary reserves (over £11 billion according to one estimate) buying sterling to defend its EMS parity, only to admit defeat by ignominiously withdrawing the currency from the EMS altogether.[14] This was then followed by speculative attacks on the lira, peseta, escudo, punt and French franc. Only the latter managed to hold out, thanks to massive intervention in the foreign exchange markets by the Bundesbank, motivated by the sure knowledge that if the markets were able to dislocate the central parity in the EMS, between the deutschmark and the franc, then the credibility of the system as a source of monetary stability in Europe, already seriously weakened, would perhaps be completely destroyed. At the time of writing this link is still intact, but is one which has been massively disruptive of internal social and economic conditions in France as the country has been subjected to a large deflationary shock caused by the determined defence of the 'franc fort'.

---

14 This reckless attempt to defend a clearly overvalued currency was in effect a massive, if unintentional, state subsidy to the financial sector. The profits made in these two days were sufficient for several banks to wipe out substantial losses incurred on non-performing corporate and property loans.

As Hutton, Keegan, Elliot and Brummer (1993, p.8) argue, the asymmetry of the EMS meant that it was quickly transformed from a vehicle of monetary stability into 'a monster', whereby the dominance of the deutschmark forced member states to share the costs of unification.[15] In the wake of the EMS crisis, German's partners found themselves caught between a rock and a hard place. Should they attempt to hold out against devaluation in the hope that German interest rates would begin to fall both to preserve the credibility of the EMS and the timetable towards EMU? Or cut and run to ease the strain on domestic financial and industrial capital? The dilemma was exacerbated by a growing feeling that time was running out for EMU, particularly in the wake of German unification:

> In the equation of German emotions, the dominant fear is that of German might. Ex-Chancellor Helmut Schmidt recognises the worries – at home and abroad. A man who has campaigned for years for a single currency, Schmidt says that the quest for Europe's money is a race against time. If EMU is not accomplished before 2000 Schmidt says, then it will not happen at all. By the end of the 1990s, he predicts, one of two things will have happened. Either the D-Mark will have been replaced by the Ecu. Or else it will be the 'dominating, overwhelming currency because of the overwhelming formation of capital in a state of 80 million Germans'. By then, he says, Germany will have recovered from the turbulence of unification, and the country will be in 'a position of great leverage over the whole of Europe' – and neither the German government, nor the German financial community, will wish to give it up. (Marsh 1992, p.255)

Conclusions

The difficulties of balancing the interests of 'actual existing' nation-states with the gains that might be realised from ceding power to a supranational monetary authority has loomed large in the European project of financial integration. This problem has dogged the integration project almost from the very outset. The success of the EPU during the 1950s was due in large part to the imposition of such a supranational monetary authority by the USA in the interests of wider 'regional' stabilisation. Pan-European interests took priority over more narrow national interests, as the more successful states in the system effectively subsidised the less successful states through the institutionalised credit that the system provided. The projects of monetary integration which developed in the 1970s and 1980s were relatively weakly developed in comparison, due to the failure of EC states to fully endorse the creation of a monetary institution which would assume the regulatory authority vested in national institutions. For Grahl and Teague (1990, pp.118–126), the failure to implement the institutional phase of the EMS

---

15 For a dissenting view see Brittan (1993).

(the EMF) was a lost opportunity, both for Europe, in that the EMF would have helped Europe develop a more sympathetic form of adjustment than the deflationary logic imposed in its absence, and for the wider international community. The failure to develop the ecu as a leading international currency also prevented the EC becoming a powerful 'ecu bloc' which could have acted as an effective counterweight to US-induced monetary and financial instability within the global financial system.

Admittedly, the EC's programme for full economic and monetary union by the end of the 1990s does seek to create a set of supranational monetary institutions, although the likelihood of EMU conforming to the original blueprint and timetable has been cast into doubt in the wake of German unification. But even if it were to do so, EMU as currently envisaged may well introduce a new destabilising dynamic into development processes within the EC. As German unification has plainly illustrated, monetary integration in itself is no panacea for uneven development. As Lipietz (1992) argues in the German case, 'monetary integration changed nothing':

> The sudden linking of such divergent price systems and levels of productivity raised tensions even more, ruined thousands of individual concerns in the East and sent the unemployed fleeing westwards. (pp.154–5)

While the economic polarities of northern and southern Europe are not as extreme as those of western and eastern Germany, the parallels are clear. Indeed, the logic of deflationary adjustment to which the planned independent European Central Bank (ECB) will be wedded, along the lines of the Bundesbank, will do nothing to unfreeze the geography of uneven development in Europe following EMU.[16] The creation of an independent central bank, the remit of which will be to achieve price stability across Europe, begs the question as to how the EC will tackle problems of uneven development. Given the difficulties that the German government has faced in mobilising support for reconstruction among its western population, the difficulties facing the EC in this task should not be underestimated.[17] Indeed, this, combined with the chill winds of competition blowing through the European financial services industry in the wake of the Single European Market programme, is likely to have quite serious implications for local economic development in several European regions. For example, as in the case of successful regions such as Tuscany in Italy (Amin and Thrift 1992, p.579), regional

---

16 The association between level of economic development and relative adherence to a deflationary logic has been recognised for a considerable period of time. For example, Galbraith (1975) points to the geographical schism that opened up in the United States during the nineteenth century between those capitalist elites in the more developed east, who were wedded to a deflationary conservatism, and those in the less developed mid-west and west, who wished to see a more permissive monetary regime.

17 The poverty of the social dimension in the Maastricht Agreement illustrates the difficulties the EC faces in this area.

economies of international importance have emerged at least in part due to the role played by localised banking and savings systems, which have served to pool local savings for relatively low cost investment-related loans. However, the reregulation of financial services markets in Europe has forced regional financial institutions to compete for funds on a national and increasingly an international level. This development has engendered processes of capital and centralisation among the European financial system, as smaller and 'less efficient' regional financial institutions have subsumed into national and international organisations (see Begg, Chapter 10 of this volume). This has already resulted in an inevitable 'distancing' of regional financial institutions from the economies with which they were formerly integrated. Moreover, the credit on offer to firms in the regions of Europe will increasingly reflect prevailing rates of interest in Europe, which will in turn reflect the anti-inflationary stance of the European central bank of the future.

It is of course possible that peripheral states and regions in a Europe characterised by monetary union will seek recourse to economic autonomy that they will still possess in fiscal policy, the responsibility for which will remain located at a sub-EC level (Healey and Levine 1992). In the absence of EC-wide fiscal rules, it is not hard to imagine governments resorting to heavy borrowing and spending in order to stimulate economic growth, if only for reasons of short-term political expediency. The consequences of such behaviour, particularly if it is adopted by more than one state, is that it could set in train a competition for funds in Europe's capital markets, forcing interest rates to rise. Therefore, even if the EC realises its long-cherished dream of European economic and monetary integration by the end of the 1990s, one is forced to question just how long an 'integrated Europe', based upon institutionalised uneven development, upon a hegemonic logic of deflationary economic adjustment, and accompanied by spiralling interest rates, would remain integrated.

Coda

Shortly after this paper was delivered for publication the crisis of the ERM took a new turn. The Franco-German alliance finally gave up on the defence of the Franc Fort in the face of further speculative activity within the foreign exchange markets. After two days of turmoil and a weekend of crisis meetings between EC finance ministers and central bankers, on 2 August 1993 the margins of currency fluctuation within the ERM were widened from 2% to 15%. While this decision enabled the franc to fall against the deutschmark, thereby calming the markets, and allowed EC ministers to argue that despite everything the ERM remained in place, the system had become but a pale shadow of its former self (for an anatomy of the crisis, see Leyshon 1993).

While the crisis of the ERM may not have killed the long-cherished dream of creating a stable monetary platform in Europe, twenty years after the first European experiments with monetary coordination the path towards currency union looked as rocky and treacherous as it ever had been.

Acknowledgements

The authors would like to thank Jonathan Pratt and the editors of this volume for their comments on an earlier draft of this paper. The usual disclaimers apply.

References

Aglietta, M. (1979) *A Theory of Capitalist Regulation: the US Experience.* London: Verso.

Amin, M. and Thrift, N. (1992) 'Neo-Marshallian Nodes in Global Networks.' *International Journal of Urban and Regional Research 16*, 571–587.

Bank of England Quarterly Bulletin (1992) 'The Maastricht agreement on economic and monetary union.' Bank of England Quarterly Bulletin *32*, 64–68.

Black, S.W. (1977) *Floating Exchange Rates and National Economic Policy.* New Haven: Yale University Press.

Boss, H. (1990) *Theories of Transfer and Surplus: Parasites and Producers in Economic Thought.* London: Unwin Hyman.

Brett, E.A. (1985) *The World Economy Since the War: The Politics of Uneven Development.* London: Macmillan.

Brittan, S. (1993) 'The battle for the "Franc Fort".' *Financial Times*, March 11, 22.

Cerny, P.G. (1991) 'The limits of deregulation: transnational interpretation and policy change.' *European Journal of Political Research 19*, 173–196.

Clarke, S. (1988) *Keynesianism, Monetarism and the Crisis of the State.* Aldershot: Edward Elgar.

Cohen, B.J. (1977) *Organising the World's Money: The Political Economy of International Monetary Relations.* London: Macmillan.

Cooke, P. (1992) 'Regional innovation systems: competitive regulation in the New Europe.' *Geoforum 23*, 365–382.

Cooke, P. and Morgan, K. (1990) *Learning Through Networking: Regional Innovation and the Lessons and Baden-Wurttenburg.* Regional Industrial Research Report No 5. Cardiff: Department of City and Regional Planning, University of Wales College of Cardiff.

Cox, R. (1987) *Production, Power and World Order: Social Forces in the Making of History.* New York, NY: Colombia University Press.

Cutler, T., Haslam, C., Williams, J. and Williams, K. (1990) *1992 – The Struggle for Europe* Leamington Spa: Berg.

Dale, R. (1989) 'International financial regulation.' In K. Button and D. Swann (eds) *The Age of Regulatory Reform.* Oxford: Clarendon Press.

Davis, E.P. (1991) 'The development of pension funds – an international comparison.' *Bank of England Quarterly Bulletin 31*, 380–390.

De Grauwe, P. (1989) *International Money: Post-War Trends and Theories.* Oxford: Clarendon Press.

Dicken, P. (1992a) 'International production in a volatile regulatory environment: the influence of national regulatory policies on a spatial strategies of transnational corporations.' *Geoforum 23*, 303–316.

Dicken, P. (1992b) *Global Shift: The Internationalisation of Economic Activity*. Second Edition. London: Paul Chapman.

Dunford, M. (1990) 'Theories of regulation.' *Environment and Planning D: Society and Space 8*, 297–321.

Eltis, W., Fraser, D. and Ricketts, M. (1992) 'The lessons for Britain from the superior economic performance of Germany and Japan.' *National Westminster Bank Quarterly Review*, February, 2–23.

Ferris, P. (1960) *The City*. London: Victor Gollancz.

Galbraith, J.K. (1975) *Money: Where it Came, Where it Went*. London: Penguin.

Gertler, M.S. (1988) 'The limits to flexibility: comments on the post-Fordist vision of production and its geography.' *Transactions, Institute of British Geographers, NS 13*, 419–32.

Gertler, M.S. (1992) 'Flexibility revisited: districts, national states, and the forces of production.' *Transactions, Institute of British Geographers, NS 17*, 259–278.

Gill, S. (1992) 'Economic globalisation and the internationalisation of authority: limits and contradictions.' *Geoforum 23*, 269–283.

Gill, S. and Law, D. (1989) 'Global hegemony and the structural power of capital.' *International Studies Quarterly 33*, 475–499.

Gordon, D. (1988) 'The global economy: new edifice or crumbling foundation.' *New Left Review 168*, 24–64.

Grabher, G. (1993) 'Rediscovering the social in the economics of interfirm relations.' In G. Grabher (ed) *The Embedded Firm: On the Socioeconomic of Industrial Networks*. London: Routledge.

Grahl, J. (1991) 'Economies out of control.' *New Left Review 185*, 170–183.

Grahl, J. and Teague, P. (1989) 'The cost of neo-liberal Europe.' *New Left Review 174*, 33–64.

Grahl, J. and Teague, P. (1990) *1992 – the Big Market: The Future of the European Community*. London: Lawrence and Wishart.

Granovetter, M. (1985) 'Economic action and social structure: the problem of embeddedness.' *American Journal of Sociology 91*, 481–510.

Gros, D. and Thygsen, N. (1992) *European Monetary Integration: From the European Monetary System to European Monetary Union*. London: Longman.

Haldane, A.G. (1991) 'The exchange rate mechanism of the European monetary system: a review of the literature.' *Bank of England Quarterly Bulletin 31*, 73–82.

Harvey, D. (1989) *The Condition of Postmodernity*. Oxford: Basil Blackwell.

Healey, N.M. and Levine, P. (1992) 'Unpleasant monetary arithmetic revisited: central bank independence, fiscal policy and European Monetary union.' *National Westminster Bank Quarterly Review*, August, 23–37.

Herrigel, G.B. (1993) 'Power and the redefinition of industrial districts: the case of Baden-Wurttemburg.' In G. Grabher (ed) *The Embedded Firm: On the Socioeconomic of Industrial Networks*. London: Routledge.

Hubner, K. (1991) 'Flexibilisation and autonomisation of worked money markets: obstacles for a new long expansion.' In B. Jessop, H. Kastendiek, K. Nielson and O.K. Pedersen (eds) *The Politics and Flexibility: Restructuring States and Industry in Britain, Germany and Scandinavia*. Aldershot: Edward Elgar.

Hutton, W. (1992a) 'Inside the ERM crisis: The Chancellor, the banker, and deaf ears in Bath.' *The Guardian*, November 30, 11.

Hutton, W. (1992b) 'Inside the ERM crisis: Black Wednesday Massacre.' *The Guardian*, December 1, 15.

Hutton, W. (1992c) 'Inside the ERM crisis: Nothing but the actualite?' *The Guardian*, December 2, 19.

Hutton, W., Keegan, V., Elliot, L. and Brummer, A. (1993) 'Rebuilding Britain: The Agenda for Economic Recovery.' *The Guardian Supplement.*

Kennedy, E. (1991) *The Bundesbank: Germany's Central Bank in the International Monetary System.* London: RIIA/Pinter.

King, M. (1992) 'Europe in the 1990s: the economic perspective', *Bank of England Quarterly Bulletin 32*, pp.324–331.

Leborgne, D. and Lipietz, A. (1990) 'Avoiding a two-tier Europe.' *Labour and Society 15*, 177–199.

Levitt, T. (1983) 'The globalisation of markets.' *Harvard Business Review,* May–June, 92–102.

Leyshon, A. (1992) 'The transformation of regulatory order: regulating the global economy and environment.' *Geoforum 23*, 249–267.

Leyshon, A. (1993) 'Crawling from the wreckage: speculating on the future of the European Exchange Rate Mechanism.' *Environment and Planning A*, 25.

Leyshon, A. (1994) 'Under pressure: finance, geoeconomic competition and the rise and fall of Japan's post-war growth economy.' In S. Corbridge, R. Martin and N. Thrift (eds) *Money, Power and Space.* Oxford: Blackwell.

Leyshon, A. and Thrift, N. (1992) 'Liberalisation and consolidation: the Single European Market and the remaking of European financial capital.' *Environment and Planning A 24*, 49–81.

Lipietz, A. (1987) *Mirages and Miracles: The Crises of Global Fordism.* London: Verso.

Lipietz, A. (1989) 'The debt problem, European integration and the new phase of world crisis.' *New Left Review 178*, 37–50.

Lipietz, A. (1992) *Towards a New Economic Order: Postfordism, Ecology and Democracy.* Cambridge: Polity.

Llewelyn, D.T. (1989) 'The changing structure of regulation in the British financial system.' In K. Button and D. Swann (eds) *The Age of Regulatory Reform.* Oxford: Clarendon Press.

Marsh, D. (1992) *The Bundesbank: The Bank that Rules Europe.* London: Heinneman.

Parboni, R. (1981) *The Dollar and its Rivals.* London: Verso.

Peck, J.A. and Tickell, A. (1992) Local modes of social regulation? Regulation Theory, Thatcherism and Uneven Development.' *Geoforum 23*, 347–363.

Piore, M. and Sabel, C. (1984) *The Second Industrial Divide.* New York: Basic Books.

Scammell, W.M. (1987) *The Stability of the International Monetary System.* London: Macmillan.

Strange, S. (1988) *States and Market.* London: Pindar.

Strange, S. (1991) 'An eclectic approach.' In C.N. Murphy and R. Tooze (eds) *The New International Political Economy.* Boulder, CO: Lynne Reiner.

Streeck, W. and Schmitter, P.C. (1991) 'From national corporatism to transnational pluralism: organised interests in the Single European Market.' *Politics and Society 19*, 133–164.

Swyngedouw, E. (1989) 'The heart of the place: the resurrection of locality in an age of hyperspace.' *Geografiska Annaler 71B*, 31–42.

Thompson, G. (1990) 'Monetary policy and international finance.' In B. Hindess (ed) *Reactions to the Right.* London: Routledge.

Thompson, G. (1992) 'The evolution of the managed economy in Europe.' *Economy and Society 21*, 129–151.

Thrift, N. and Leyshon, A. (1988) 'The gambling propensity': banks, developing country debt exposures and the new international financial system.' *Geoforum 19*, 55–69.

Tickell, A. and Peck, J.A. (1992) 'Accumulation, regulation and the geographies of post-Fordism: Missing links in regulationist research.' *Progress in Human Geography 16*, 190–218.

Urry, J. (1990) 'Globalisation, localisation and the nation-state.' *Lancaster Regionalism Group Working Paper 40*, University of Lancaster.

Walter, A. (1991) *World Power and World Money: The Role of Hegemony and International Monetary Order*. Hemel Hempstead: Harvester Wheatsheaf.

Zukin, S. and DiMaggio, P. (eds) (1990) *Structures of Capital: The Social Organisation of the Economy*. Cambridge: Cambridge University Press.

CHAPTER 10

The Impact on Regions of Completion of the European Community Internal Market for Financial Services

Iain Begg

Introduction

Although it is manufacturing industries which have been most extensively analysed in relation to the likely impact of the single market (for example, Buigues, Ilzkowitz and LeBrun 1990, Mayes 1991; or, at a regional level, Quévit 1992), some of the most profound changes will occur in the services sectors, and especially in financial services. Despite the difficulties which emerged in the process of ratification of the Maastricht agreement, the integration of the financial services sector will be given an additional impetus by the move towards monetary union (Giovannini and Mayer 1991). The advent of the single market can be expected to affect not only the spatial allocation of activity and employment in the sector, but also the quality, price and availability of services in different localities. This will have a number of consequences for the different regions and cities of the EC and will lead to competition between regions for shares of this key sector of activity.

During the 1980s, the financial services sector was amongst the most dynamic in the EC economy, and consequently had a major influence on relative regional prosperity (as Marshall 1988 shows for the UK). On the whole, regions where leading financial centres are located not only have high levels of GDP per capita and relatively low unemployment, but also experienced above average rates of growth. As Figure 10.1 shows, the sector increased its share of employment in all Member States of the EC except Spain during the 1980s, providing some compensation for the decline of manufacturing. The growth of the sector was

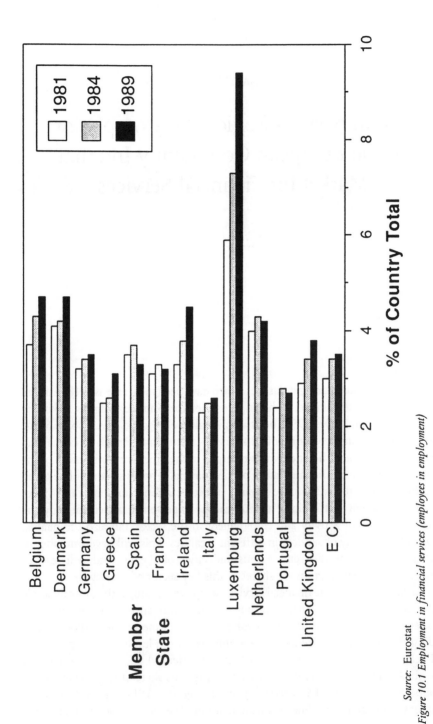

Source: Eurostat
Figure 10.1 Employment in financial services (employees in employment)

particularly noticeable in Luxembourg, where it has become a major source of foreign earnings. Among the less-favoured Member States of the Community, Ireland stands out for the weight of its financial sector which is more akin to that in the more prosperous countries in character.

This chapter considers how closer economic integration will affect the financial services sector in the regions of the EC. It draws on interviews carried out in each country of the Community (more fully reported in Begg 1990, 1992) with managers of financial entities, trade associations, regulators and public officials. These sought to explore how the advent of the Single Market would affect the regional distribution of activity and employment in financial services.

The next section reviews the Single Market proposals in the light of other changes in the financial sector (defined here to cover banking and other credit institutions, merchant banking and corporate finance, life and non-life insurance, and securities trading and markets[1]) and their regional implications. This is followed by a discussion of factors affecting the location of activity in financial services and a description of the regional pattern of employment in the sector. The remaining sections appraise the outlook for different sorts of regions and financial centres in the 1990s.

Economic Integration and the Changing Face of Financial Services

Measures to open up the EC market for financial services feature prominently in the '1992' programme. They include directives which explicitly affect the sector, as well as complementary measures which alter the wider economic environment in which the sector operates (for a good summary of these, see House of Commons 1989). In banking, insurance and investment services, there will be a switch from host to home country regulation of financial entities. This will mean that once a bank, for example, is licensed to take deposits in one country, it can operate in other Member States – the so-called banking 'passport'. These changes are expected to lead to greater competition in the more heavily protected markets and to bring about reductions in the cost of financial services. According to the research done for the Cecchini (1988) report, up to one-sixth of the aggregate gains from completion of the internal market may be achieved in financial services.

More generally, the financial sector faces a major transformation brought about not just by the Single Market measures, but also by the effects of forces for change which will alter methods of doing business, the internal organisation of financial entities and the character of the market for financial services. A key influence has been the internationalisation of many segments of the sector. This has increased the presence of foreign-owned financial entities in domestic markets, intensifying

---

1   This definition excludes business services such as accountancy or corporate legal services which often go hand-in-hand with financial services, although many of the findings and conclusions can be applied to these complementary services.

competition. This trend can also be expected to affect regional markets (see Leyshon and Thrift, Chapter 9 of this volume). Disintermediation – the replacement of financial intermediaries by direct dealing between lenders and borrowers – has been another important trend, as both depositors and lenders seek more advantageous arrangements.

Deregulation and other changes in the supervisory framework for financial services have both led *and* accommodated the other trends, and have led to market liberalisation, although many of the regulatory changes do in fact amount to reregulation, rather than a bonfire of rules (Dale 1992). In parallel, technological developments, as the OECD (1992) has noted, 'have stimulated the fading of technological barriers between countries and sectors' and must be expected to continue to affect location decisions, forms of service delivery and demand for labour (Rajan 1990).

Technology and the increasingly segmented and specialised nature of key professions have combined to alter the character of 'production' in the sector, as well as stimulating innovation. The exploitation of advanced technologies not only places new demands on staff, but also shifts the basis of competition as financial entities are obliged to 'industrialise' their processes. This has contributed to a reappraisal of the location needs of different functions within the sector, with the result that there is both greater scope and greater willingness to separate functions geographically. London, for example, has lost a proportion of processing activity to other locations in the UK. Further restructuring is taking place because of mergers and acquisitions activity, much of it prompted by '1992' and other institutional developments. Cosy domestic cartels have been swept away in most leading countries, to be replaced by much more cut-throat competition. In a number of market segments, the sophistication of customers has reinforced this trend, but has also encouraged the drive for innovation. As other sectors have become internationalised, the need for the financial sector to develop in parallel has been evident.

One specific objective of the '1992' programme, generally, is the perceived need for Europe to be able to compete on equal terms with the USA and Japan. In the financial services sector, this can be expected to reinforce the quest for financial centres of world stature able to compete effectively in global markets. However, because there are various agglomeration economies in the sector, the EC can only sustain a limited number of global centres. Following the rapid growth of the sector during the 1980s in most OECD countries, there were many new entrants, with the result that there is now excess capacity and low profitability in many market segments. This 'financial fragility', as OECD (1992) has described it, is expected to lead to greater competitive pressures on financial entities. This points to a probable rationalisation in the financial services sector as the single market is completed, which is bound to affect the regional allocation of activity in the sector, so that the location attributes of the different financial centres will come under scrutiny.

The Location Attributes of Financial Centres

A range of different characteristics of financial centres will influence their attractions for the financial sector (Begg 1992). On the whole, it is major cities (though to a vastly greater degree in some than others) which have the greatest concentration of activity in financial services – especially wholesale and corporate services – although because of the need for a retail presence, there is a tendency for employment in the sector to be widely distributed across the urban system. Even at the retail end of the sector, however, certain cities are relatively specialised in providing regional or national central administration functions. Such a pattern has been observed in the USA by Noyelle and Stanback (1984), and may, to some extent, serve as a model for what to expect in the single European market.

In most EC countries, there is a clear hierarchy in the provision of financial services. There is generally a recognised 'financial capital' which usually contains the Central Bank and the principal regulatory organisations,[2] the country's main stock exchange, and a wide range of financial entities. Typically, such centres also have disproportionate shares of complementary business services and it is common, as Goldberg, Helsley and Levi (1989) found for the USA, for the headquarters of leading companies to be correlated with a high intensity of financial sector activity. The evidence suggests that the pattern is much the same in Europe, and it is to be expected that mergers triggered by the move towards a single market would add to this concentration, in the financial sector and in other sectors. A comparison of European cities by Brunet (1989) shows that London and Paris stand out for the number of head offices of multinational corporations, and he notes how they are dominant in their respective countries.

There are also secondary financial centres which either specialise in certain types of financial services, or perform 'regional capital' functions across a range of financial services, with branch offices of leading financial entities. Further down the regional/urban hierarchy, the functions performed within the financial sector consist largely of retail delivery of the services. A few smaller cities have unusually high concentrations of employment in the sector where they are home to particular financial entities (the eponymous building societies in the UK, such as the Halifax, being good examples). More recently, the increasing need for processing of financial transactions has stimulated the creation of what are in effect financial factories. Time-sensitive operations such as cheque clearing need to be close to the bank branches they service and are consequently usually located near or in major financial centres. Processing of credit card transactions or insurance claims is less urgent and can often be farmed out to lower cost locations. These and other 'back-office' functions can be seen as yet another element in the hierarchy of financial services. Transport and communications infrastructures play an important

---

2   Italy is the obvious exception.

part in attracting activity of this sort, as well as the availability of middle-grade clerical labour.

As the European financial services market becomes more integrated, it is probable that the *nationally* determined spatial hierarchy will alter gradually to become a pan-European one, paralleling that in the USA where three cities – New York (pre-eminently), Chicago and Los Angeles – are at the top of the financial hierarchy, while other cities specialise in 'lower-order' services within regions of the USA (Noyelle and Stanback 1984). London, along with Tokyo and New York, has acquired a global role in the wholesale and large corporate banking markets, which complements its global role in insurance markets. This accords with an emerging trend towards global cities carefully documented in Sassen (1991). France, the Netherlands and Germany are also keen to see their respective financial capitals assuming a greater role in external markets. Such roles need not embrace the full range of financial services. Luxembourg, for example, capitalising on its fiscal and regulatory regime, has developed a niche in savings 'products' and specialist banking. Eastern Europe may, provided telecommunications infrastructure is upgraded, compete effectively for processing activity.

The Regional Distribution of Employment in Financial Services

A broad picture of the regional distribution of financial services can be obtained by looking at data on the sector's share of total employment in each region relative to the EC average. Table 10.1 presents data on the relative regional concentrations of paid employment in financial services (defined as NACE classes 81 and 82 – the services of credit and insurance institutions). This shows that there are a number of regions which stand out as being very specialised in employment in the sector. These are, predictably, the regions containing the EC's principal financial centres, such as Amsterdam (West-Nederland), Brussels, Frankfurt (Hessen), London (South East) and Paris (Ile de France).[3] The dominant role of financial services in employment in Luxembourg is also apparent. In all countries, there is a substantial gap between the leading one or two regions and the rest. In many instances, the leading regions owe their prominence to the fact that they have 'cornered' much of their respective countries' financial sector activity, the extreme case being Brussels.

---

3   It should be noted, however, that regional boundaries can have a marked effect on the location quotient. Thus, Hamburg and Brussels, both of which are compactly defined city regions with no hinterland of rural areas or smaller towns, have unusually high location quotients. By contrast, London accounts for less than half of the paid employment in the South East of England, and consequently has a relatively lower location quotient.

Table 10.1 Relative regional concentrations of employment in financial services (Wage and salary earners, location quotients, EUR-12 = 1.0, 1986)

Belgique	1.35	Ireland	1.13
Vlaams Gewest	0.85	Italia	0.74
Region Wallonne	0.73	Nord Ovest	0.80
Bruxelles	3.57	Lombardia	0.95
Danmark	1.28	Nord Est	0.64
BR Deutschland	1.04	Emilia-Romagna	0.88
Baden-Württemberg	0.99	Centro (I)	0.72
Bayern	1.10	Lazio	1.15
Berlin	0.77	Campania	0.49
Bremen	1.01	Abruzzi-Molise	0.45
Hamburg	1.77	Sud	0.38
Hessen	1.45	Sicilia	0.56
Niedersachsen	0.91	Sardegna	0.48
Nordrhein-Westfalen	0.95	Luxembourg (Grand-Duché)	2.41
Rheinland-Pfalz	0.86	Nederland	1.25
Saarland	0.83	Noord-Nederland	0.93
Schleswig-Holstein	0.85	Oost-Nederland	0.96
Ellada	0.89	West-Nederland	1.53
Espana	1.05	Zuid-Nederland	0.97
Noroeste	0.87	Portugal	0.82
Noreste	0.93	United Kingdom	1.02
Madrid	1.67	North	0.63
Centro (E)	0.92	Yorkshire and Humberside	0.82
Este	1.11	East Midlands	0.67
Sur	0.77	East Anglia	0.88
Canarias	0.70	South East	1.37
France	1.00	South West	1.06
Ile de France	1.68	West Midlands	0.70
Bassin Parisien	0.70	North West	1.00
Nord-Pas-de-Calais	0.72	Wales	0.80
Est	0.74	Scotland	0.91
Ouest	0.95	Northern Ireland	0.62
Sud-Ouest	0.82		
Centre-Est	0.72	EUR-12	1.00
Méditerranée	0.85		

Note: Regional data derived from Eurostat, except for Germany where the regional breakdown is based on social security records. Germany only includes the 11 Western Länder. The figures shown are for NACE classes 81 and 82 – the services of credit and insurance institutions

The location quotient measures the ratio of the share of employment in the region to the same share for the country as a whole. An LQ greater than 1 signifies that the region is relatively specialised in financial services

Source: Eurostat, Bundesanstalt für Arbeit, Nuremberg

On the whole, the financial services sector in the EC is most concentrated in regions which are comparatively favoured both within countries and between countries, and is less prominent in most problem regions. Many financial institutions are, nevertheless, geared to serving regional markets, especially in market segments like housing finance and provision of capital to farmers and to small firms. From the perspective of regional development, completion of the internal market therefore raises important questions about how the evolution of the sector in the 1990s will affect regional economies.

At the other end of the spectrum, the regions with the fewest jobs in financial services are in peripheral areas, such as the South of Italy, Northern Ireland, and Southern Spain. These regions are either mainly rural in character, or contain urban centres which appear to have been unattractive to the financial sector (for example, Campania). However, the sector is by no means insignificant in any region. This is, in part, because a fair proportion of employment in financial services is in retail service delivery and this requires proximity to customers. Other banking and insurance functions (such as credit card or insurance claims processing, wholesale banking or fund management) tend to locate according to different criteria. It is largely these functions which account for regional disparities in the concentration of financial services employment. In some regions, the presence of a number of medium-sized establishments can boost the regional location quotient. For example, employment in insurance is relatively high in the Ouest region of France (in Pays de la Loire and Poitou Charentes, rather than Bretagne) because major companies are located in these regions. Some regions benefit from having second-tier financial centres, examples being the Este region of Spain (Barcelona) or Scotland (Edinburgh). Ireland's relatively high number of jobs in financial services is accounted for partly by the presence of 'back-office' jobs in processing.

The differences between Member States in the scale of financial sector employment stem from two offsetting influences. The first is the efficiency of service provision. As Smith (1992) demonstrates, establishing how efficient and competitive the financial services sector is in a particular country is far from easy. However, some of the data in OECD (1989) suggest that Spain may be 'overbanked' in the sense of having either too many banks or too many bank branches for the business they conduct, whereas in Italy, a comparative lack of branches may be an explanation for the low level of employment. In Northern Europe, Germany and Denmark stand out for the density of their branch networks, indicating that rationalisation brought on by competitive pressures associated with completion of the internal market could have a greater impact than in other countries.

The second influence is the diversification and competitive position of the sector in the country. Smith's (1992) findings suggest that the UK has a lead over its EC partners in a number of key market segments, which not only helps to explain why there are relatively more jobs in financial services than in some other countries, but also suggests that they have a higher productivity.

In terms of the classifications used by the European Commission to designate regions for policy assistance, it is clear that Objective 1 regions (regions which lag behind the Community in their stage of economic development) are relatively low in financial services employment. Many regions which have had problems of industrial decline (the Objective 2 regions), such as Wallonie, are similarly lacking. Only Ireland appears somewhat out of place, having a relative specialisation in financial services despite being one of the four least prosperous member states. It is worth noting that all the major air transport hubs (Amsterdam, London, Brussels, Frankfurt and Madrid) are also areas in which financial services are prominent.

The Single Market and European Financial Centres

The financial services sector varies significantly in structure from country to country, and the survey work suggested that these differences will have a bearing on the regional impact of the single market. In Germany, for instance, the large number of regional banks may be unsustainable in the face of growing external competition. Smaller, specialised credit institutions, such as the Cajas in Spain or the Building Societies in the UK can expect intensified competition, despite the general view that the low cost bases of these financial entities should work in their favour. In the Mezzogiorno, external influences are expected to cause rapid change, possibly entailing local job losses. At the same time, as the Banca D'Italia (1990) notes, the need to adapt to change may accelerate improvements in the sector and thus the service provided to local enterprises. Given that interest rates charged in the single market Mezzogiorno have been shown (SVIMEZ 1991) to be consistently higher than in the Centre-North of the country (partly reflecting greater credit risk), this would be good for bank customers.

Many barriers to a true single market will remain in place beyond 1992, some of which will be the result of restrictions that continue to be applied by member states of the EC (Bank of England 1989). Survey respondents stressed the importance of having indigenous staff involved in selling and administration of financial services, and the virtual impossibility of entering retail markets without access to an existing distribution network. Some of these residual barriers may diminish, but it was generally considered unlikely that a market entrant could establish a meaningful retail presence from scratch.

A possible typology for categorising the roles of different cities and their surrounding regions has been derived from the research as a description of the way the European financial system will evolve, and is shown in Table 10.2. Its purpose is to suggest what a European urban hierarchy in financial services might look like once the transition to a single European financial area is complete. It is, inevitably, somewhat speculative, given the uncertainty about the timing of economic and monetary union and the possibility that the EC will extend to incorporate EFTA or Eastern European countries. Six categories of financial centres are distinguished, although there is bound to be disagreement about the precise

allocations of cities and it is accepted that some cities are on the margin between
two categories.

Table 10.2 Typology of European financial centres in a unified European market

Type of centre	Characteristics	Cities in the category
Node of global financial system	Diversified services; good communications; HQs of major financial entities; to lesser extent, high volume securities and forex markets; branches of foreign banks etc.	London; Paris and Frankfurt
Diversified European centres	Significant cross-border business; HQs of major financial and non-financial companies; critical mass in markets; air and telecoms links; location of regulatory organisations; wide range of complementary business services.	London, Paris, Frankfurt; scope for Amsterdam, Milan Madrid and possibly Brussels
Specialist European centres	Strong in niche markets; critical mass of specific labour skills.	Edinburgh, Luxembourg; Dublin gaining ground
National centres with limited international business	Presence of several leading financial entities; complementary services; mix of general and specialist financial services, some financial markets and regulatory functions.	Amsterdam, Brussels, Rome, Milan Madrid, Athens, Hamburg, Lisbon, Munich, Barcelona, Dublin, Lyons
Regional centre	Wide range of regional offices; mix of business services; some financial HQs back-offices.	Dusseldorf, Hannover, Berlin, Bordeaux, Lille, Marseilles, Rotterdam Eindhoven, Turin, Bologna, Palermo, Naples, Liege, Antwerp, Salonika, Oporto, Bilbao, Valencia, Malaga, Bristol, Leeds, Glasgow, Liverpool, Belfast, Birmingham
Specialist national centres	Centre for processing activity or presence of a major financial entity.	Halifax, Utrecht, Norwich, Mons for example
Retail outlet	Predominantly retail distribution of financial services.	Other cities and towns

The first category is perhaps the most straightforward. With the global financial system centred on three nodes, of which Tokyo and New York are two, there is probably only room at present for one representative from Europe.[4] At present, that role is fulfilled by London, which qualifies on the strength of its non-European international business in banking, insurance, securities, related financial services, and interbank services. Although other cities, notably Paris, are positioning themselves to challenge London, the survey work indicated that the critical mass that London has achieved should enable it to maintain its pre-eminence, a point emphasised by the Deutsche Bank in evidence to the House of Commons (1989):

> We believe that there will only be room for one predominant global financial centre in Europe and that London already has a clear advantage in this respect. The City offers a pool of capital, human talent and technological resources which is unmatched in Europe at present. This is unlikely to be equalled by any other centre unless the obvious advantages are put to waste or self-imposed hurdles erected. (p.28)

It is also probable that Paris and Frankfurt, as well as London, will consolidate their positions as leading European centres as competitive pressures from completion of the internal market push some financial entities to shift higher level functions to these areas. For all three top centres, there is some threat from congestion, though this would be expected to result more in the relocation of lower-level functions within companies than of major entities in their entirety. Nevertheless, as the recent experience of London has shown, net job losses may well occur in the leading centres because of cost pressures (although much of this benefits the regional hinterland). Amsterdam, Madrid and Milan currently lag behind the leading three in scale and scope of financial services, and could either retreat to more specialist roles or make the quantum leap to the 'first division'.

Changes and jockeying for position are likely to be most evident amongst cities which are currently mainly geared to domestic markets. In Spain, for example, a concentration of specialised financial services is already occurring, with the rationalisation of the country's four stock exchanges and market entry favouring Madrid (Ahijado, Clapes, Begg and Planelles 1991). Germany, similarly, is seeing some move to consolidate in Frankfurt, although the aftermath of unification and change in Eastern Europe may provide a boost to Berlin's claims as a financial centre. These trends are, however, kept in check by strong regional identities which will ensure that substantial amounts of financial services activity remain in cities such as Barcelona or Munich. Belgium has seen a gradual drift towards the leading financial centre (Brussels), but may also face a loss of some higher level financial services to nearby 'European' centres, notably Paris. The likely choice of Frankfurt to be the location for the European Monetary Institute and, probably, the European

---

4   The criteria suggested by Sassen (1991) to designate global cities may, in time, come to apply to certain other EC cities.

Central Bank, can be expected to provide a fillip to financial services employment, possibly at the expense of rival centres such as London.

Regional financial centres may be those in which the most pronounced changes of fortune occur. Those, such as Leeds or Lyons, which are doing fairly well and which have the advantage of being the location of a number of head offices, could stimulate their respective regions, while cities which lose ground (as Bilbao or Liverpool appear to be doing) could make the transition to the single market more difficult for their regions. Some cities are attempting to respond proactively. Dublin, for example, has an ambitious programme to heighten its appeal to the international fund management community. This includes a major city centre property initiative and the offer of tax incentives to inward investors aimed at making Ireland an alternative to Luxembourg or Edinburgh. Dusseldorf has benefited from being a favoured location for Japanese financial entities which may, however, bring it into competition with other German cities. Amsterdam, buoyed by the presence of Schipol international airport, is attempting to establish itself as an alternative to the three leading cities.

Where financial services activity is mainly retail, the weight of opinion was that the impact of '1992' will be muted. Older industrial cities in towns, or those which lack a tradition of financial services activity, may be constrained in this way. Some smaller cities may, however, gain from the establishment of back-office 'factories' – the Bank of Scotland facility in Dunfermline processing credit card transactions, and now employing over a thousand staff, being a good example. In others where the presence of a single large financial entity has been the mainstay of financial sector employment, the employment outlook will depend on what happens to that major employer. This would have knock-on effects on the supportive business services in the region if the result was a loss of managerial functions.

Conclusions on the Prospects for Different Types of Regions

As the European market is progressively opened-up, cross-border links between financial entities are bound to increase. Most of the largest financial entities are based in the more favoured regions of the Northern EC countries, and this may presage a concentration of the top levels of management and control in these regions, possibly to the detriment of Objective 2 regions. Market entry may assist the Objective 1 regions to achieve more rapid development of their financial sectors than if they were restricted to internal development by providing a form of 'technology transfer'. To the extent that this improves the cost and quality of services to enterprises in these regions it should encourage economic development.

From a policy perspective, the impact of the single market on the less-favoured regions of the EC is a central issue (PA Cambridge Economic Consultants 1990). The research reported here suggests it is likely to have three main effects:

1. There will be market growth, especially in the less-developed regions which have relatively low incomes, although this effect will be muted in regions such as Calabria which are judged to be vulnerable to the general competitive effects of '1992'. This income elasticity of demand effect is not expected to be so pronounced in the Objective 2 and Objective 5b regions, since many of them are already well-served for financial services.

2. To the extent that the intensity of competition increases in the single market, there will be pressure on financial entities to rationalise. This will be necessary to improve productivity so as to meet the more intense competition that will come to characterise the retail end of the sector as obstacles to external entry are reduced.

3. There may be market niches that less-favoured regions can hope to fill, notably back-office functions. Ireland, with relatively attractive communications infrastructure and a good supply of clerical labour, is well-placed, but few Southern regions of the Community share these attributes and are less likely to benefit from such functional relocations.

Overall, however, the research suggests that the benefits of completion of the internal market for financial services will accrue disproportionately to existing financial centres which tend to be in the more prosperous and rapidly growing regions of the European Community. It is also likely that a more explicit European hierarchy in the provision of financial services will develop, and that, as a result, some of the existing financial centres will lose ground to more competitive rivals.

References

Ahijado, M., Clapes P., Begg, I.G. and Planelles, J. (1991) *El impacto del mercado interior europeo sobre la economia de Madrid.* Madrid: Communidad de Madrid.

Banca D'Italia (1990) *Il Sistema Finanziario nel Mezzogiorno.* Rome: Banca D' Italia.

Bank of England (1989) *The Single European Market: Survey of the UK Financial Services Industry.* London: Bank of England.

Begg, I.G. (1990) *Completion of the EC Internal Market for Financial Services: Consequences for the Scottish Economy.* Research Report No. 1, The Scottish Foundation for Economic Research: Glasgow.

Begg, I.G. (1992) 'The spatial impact of completion of the EC internal market for financial services.' *Regional Studies 26,* 333–47.

Brunet, R. (1989) *Les Villes Européenes.* Paris: La Documentation Française.

Buigues, Ilzkowitz and LeBrun (1990) 'The impact of the internal market by industrial sector: the challenge for the member states' *European Economy,* Special Issue. Luxembourg: CEC.

Cecchini, P. (1988) *The European Challenge: 1992, The Benefits of the Single European Market.* Aldershot: Wildwood House.

Dale, R. (1992) *International Banking Deregulation: The Great Banking Experiment.* Oxford: Blackwell.

Giovannini, A. and Mayer, C. (eds) (1991) *European Financial Integration.* Cambridge: Cambridge University Press.

Goldberg, Helsley and Levi (1989) 'The location of international financial activity: an interregional analysis.' *Regional Studies 23*, 1.

House of Commons (1989) *Financial Services and the Single European Market*. Fifth Report of the Trade and Industry Select Committee, HC 256. London: HMSO.

Marshall, J.N. (1988) *Services and Uneven Development*. Oxford: Oxford University Press.

Mayes, D.G. (ed) (1991) *The European Challenge*. Hemel Hempstead: Harvester-Wheatsheaf.

Noyelle, T.J. and Stanback, T.M. (1984) *The Economic Transformation of American Cities*. Totowa NJ: Rowman and Allanheld.

Organisation for Economic Co-operation and Development (1989) *Competition in Banking*. Paris: OECD.

Organisation for Economic Co-operation and Development (1992) *Banks Under Stress*. Paris: OECD.

PA Cambridge Economic Consultants (1990) 'The Regional Consequences of completion of the internal market for financial services.' Unpublished report to the European Commission.

Quévit, M. (1992) 'The regional impact of the single market: a comparative analysis of traditional industrial regions and lagging regions.' *Regional Studies 26*, 349–60.

Rajan, A. (1990) *1992 A Zero-Sum Game*. London: Industrial Society Press.

Sassen, S. (1991) *The Global City: New York, London, Tokyo*. Princeton: Princeton University Press.

Smith, A.D. (1992) *International Financial Markets: The Performance of Britain and its Rivals*. Cambridge: Cambridge University Press.

SVIMEZ (1991) *Rapporto 1991 Sull' Economia del Mezzogiorno*. Rome: Il Mulino.

CHAPTER 11

European Integration and Public Finance
The Political Economy of Regional Support

R. Ross MacKay

Introduction

'Is there any point to which you would draw my attention?'
'To the curious incident of the dog in the night-time.'
'The dog did nothing in the night-time.'
'That was the curious incident,' remarked Sherlock Holmes. (Doyle 1951)

What does not happen can add to understanding. For Sherlock Holmes the clue was the dog that failed to react, the hound that did not bark in the night. In the context of European integration it is, therefore, the lack of response to the MacDougall Report which may be the key to understanding the difficulties in trying to reconcile closer economic and monetary union with regional balance. Regional fiscal transfer (support of weaker regions) played a trivial role in the European Community prior to the report's publication in 1977. Its role remains negligible in the early 1990s, in spite of clear recommendations to the contrary and major steps towards closer union.

Regions lack many of the instruments that can be applied at national level to create employment, to add to demand, to manage the economy and move it closer to the production possibility frontier. As national groupings progress along the spectrum that ranges from independent nations to common markets to economic union and common currency, national markets become increasingly open and vulnerable to competitive pressure. Ability to act independently, to protect home industry, is reduced: nations become more like regions. At regional level deliberate economic policy comes into play to counter regional imbalance. Measures and instruments have evolved, over time, to cushion and guide weaker regions within nation states. The key response is fiscal transfer from richer to poorer regions. This appears to be common to all developed economies (though in notably varying degree and form). Regional fiscal transfer (budget equalisation) would, the MacDougall Report anticipated, play a central role in Europe, as the Community moved towards closer economic and monetary union.

The MacDougall Report points to the need for changes in the scale and direction of the Community Budget. In the late 1970s that budget came to less than 1% of Community GDP, was dominated by agriculture and had limited redistributive power (as between richer and poorer regions). The Report recommends (1) that the Community Budget rises to between 2 and 2.5% of Community GDP at a stage called 'pre-federal integration' and to between 5 and 7% of GDP when real political federation emerges (MacDougall Report, Vol 1, p.14) and (2) that the pattern of expenditure is altered to adopt a clear redistributive role as between richer and poorer parts of Europe. Almost seventeen years later, the Community Budget remains at less than 1% of Community GDP, is still dominated by agriculture, and still lacks clear regional focus. The Commission accepts (1) that market forces will not bring regional balance, (2) that economic benefits are the cement of the community: to hold the union together those benefits must reach all parts and (3) the need to devise and finance measures that contain regional inequality. There remains a gap between image and reality. The most important aid to regional balance at national level (fiscal transfer from richer to poorer regions) remains of trivial importance at Community level. What has not happened is at least as important as what has.

Other parts of this chapter outline the implications of 1992 for regional balance (Section 2), summarise the evidence of the MacDougall report on fiscal transfer within federal countries and nation states (Section 3) and briefly explore the trend of regional inequality, the role of regional policy and touch on the vexing question of additionality, or its absence (Section 4). Finally (Section 5) we account for the absence of regional fiscal transfer within the Community.

1992 and Regional Divergence

> The extent of the American domestic market, unimpeded by tariff barriers, may have something to do with the matter... Taking a country's economic endowment as given...the most important single factor in determining the effectiveness of its industry appears to be the size of the market... Not area or population alone, but buying power, the capacity to absorb a large annual output of goods. (Young 1928, pp.532–3)

The above explanation of American prosperity, strongly influenced by Adam Smith's *Wealth of Nations* (1776), is a reasonable introduction to the argument for a single European market. 1992 involved the reduction of non-tariff barriers which limit competition and distort trade within the Community. The European Community of 12 nations could become the largest single market in the world industrial world.[1] The vision which lies behind the move to a single European market claims:

1. The potential for prosperity remains frustrated as long as Europe 'remains a fragmented market' (*European Economy* 1988, p.25).

2. Non-tariff barriers protect inefficient producers and distort competition within the Community.

3. The extended market which follows from removal (more realistically reduction) of physical, fiscal and technical barriers would, in certain key sectors, allow units of efficient scale to emerge.

4. Delay in proceeding to a single market has contributed to slow growth in the Community economy in the 1970s and 1980s.

The poor record of the Community is highlighted by notably faster growth (and lower unemployment) in the United States and Japan.

Reducing non-tariff barriers involves trade creation. In doing so it eliminates the least efficient producers. Consumers in all parts of the Community benefit. The key question is what will happen on the supply side? How will producers, particularly those in the more peripheral and poorer regions, fare, given that restructuring is part of trade creation?

Reducing barriers to trade adds to the process of creative destruction where old values and old capital (human as well as physical) are destroyed and new values and new capital (human and physical) emerge to take their place. But the new values and new capital are not necessarily in the same community, the same region, or even in the same country. The single European market finds new sources of value. The process of structural change involves adjustment costs which may be considerable.

The process of competition – which was encouraged by 1992 – has two effects. First, it selects between superior and inferior locations and trade routes according to existing potential. This reallocation of market areas and redistribution of production in favour of the most efficient and best located firms (static impact) implies geographic specialisation and concentration of production. Selection is more likely to benefit the core than the periphery of the Community.

The second effect (dynamic impact) follows from concentration and expansion of production in selected locations. Internal and external economies of scale and scope develop in particular locations, providing advantages that are more than temporary. Internal and external economies of scale protect those locations that gain an initial advantage. Positive and negative feedbacks emerge in response to

---

1   The population (including East Germany) is 1.4 times the population in the United States and 2.6 times the population of Japan. The GDP of the 12 is approximately equal to the US GDP and 1.9 times the Japanese GDP.

expansion and decline. To a certain degree, success and failure are self-perpetuating.

The contrast between regions involves a 'process of circular and cumulative causation' (Myrdal 1957) which is closely connected to increasing returns: these benefits to scale are broadly defined to emphasise external economies, or a support structure. This includes transport and communications, the encouragement of skill and know-how, the availability of complementary services, differentiation in product and process.

The reinforcement of success and failure points to real problems for those who see the market as the all-important source of harmony: the forces which frustrate regional equilibrium are natural, pervasive, ingrained. They are more powerful than is commonly realised. Our myopia is partly explained by the focus of economics. The problem that conventional economics normally addresses is (to paraphrase Schumpeter) how capitalism (the market) administers existing resources. The real problem is how resources are created and destroyed. The conventional question is essentially static, it takes resources as given and explains how resources are effectively allocated at a given level of adaptability. The adjustment problem is dynamic and more complex than allocating reward according to existing potential. Economic policy cannot ignore the broader forces which determine change in potential over time and these include the signals sent to different parts of the economy.

There are three key themes which connect 1992 to regional matters. First, the benefits from trade, the gains from competition, are unevenly distributed by the market. The expectation is that income and employment will concentrate at the centre of the Community rather than the periphery. Closer union adds to regional divergence, as well as Community prosperity.

Second, the Community cannot be indifferent to distribution of reward. The Commission accepts that economic benefits are the cement of an economic community. That union is unstable if economic benefits are confined to the centre. The Commission advertises its consistent concern for the regions and underlines the need to '[strengthen] the Community's economic and social cohesion and, in particular, to reduce the gap between the different regions and the backwardness of the least favoured regions' (EC Commission 1987a, p.6). If 1992 yields sufficient gains to raise income and product in the Community as a whole, it ought to be possible to use part of these gains to ensure improvement even in the periphery. The objective is, to use a Commission phrase, to 'help the disadvantaged regions to catch up'. The political contract between weaker and stronger parts of the Community involves the weak regions accepting the full force of competition and the stronger regions providing assistance to raise the level of resource endowment in the weaker regions towards usual Community standards. The contract is more complex than leaving all to market forces.

Third, to give effect to the implicit contract, implies the emergence of mechanisms that have evolved to protect weaker regions within nation states. The most important of these is regional fiscal transfer – that is, support for weaker regions.

Regional Fiscal Transfer – The MacDougall Report

> A region which forms part of a political community, with a common scale of public services and a common base of taxation, automatically gets 'aid' whenever its trading relations with the rest of the country deteriorate. There is an important built-in fiscal stabilizer. (Kaldor 1970, p.345).

Fiscal transfer may be regarded as compensation to weaker regions for being notably vulnerable to competition.[2] The region cannot devalue, reduce interest rates, impose quotas, or act independently to raise the level of demand to a level which ensures that regional resources are fully utilised. The level of demand in a

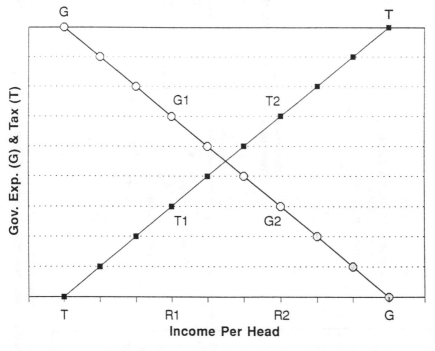

Figure 11.1 Public finance as a regional stabiliser

---

2   Fiscal transfer can also be regarded as an attempt to ensure that payment of taxes at the same rates in different regions will ensure similar levels of service. Unless transfers were made, taxpayers in richer regions would get away with lower tax burdens (or receive higher levels of service) than taxpayers in poorer areas. See Oates (1972) and Buchanan (1950).

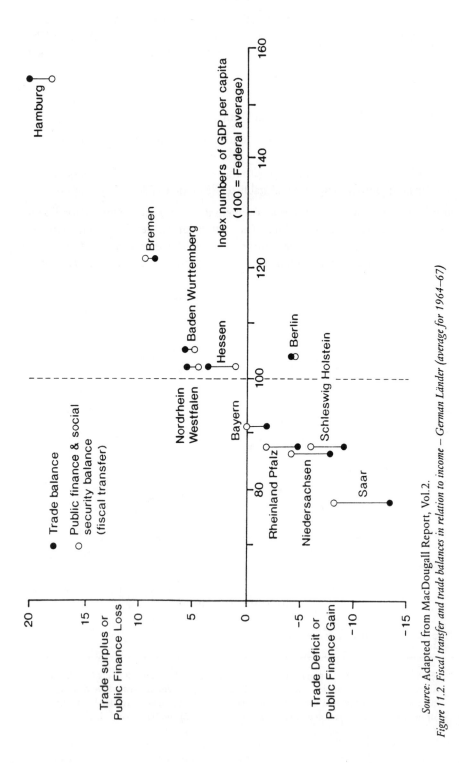

Source: Adapted from MacDougall Report, Vol.2.

Figure 11.2. Fiscal transfer and trade balances in relation to income – German Länder (average for 1964–67)

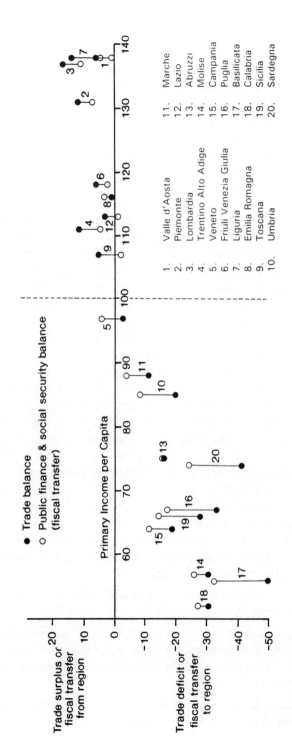

Source: Adapted from MacDougall Report, Vol.2.

Figure 11.3. Fiscal transfer and trade balances in relation to income – Italian Regions (average for 1971–73)

nation state will always be a compromise, leaving margins of unused resources which differ as between regions.

The theory of regional fiscal transfer (Kaldor's automatic 'aid' to weaker regions) is illustrated in Figure 11.1. Two functions of regional fiscal transfer are implicit in the figure. First, low income regions gain more from government expenditure (GG in the figure) than they pay in tax (TT in the figure) – the net transfer is shown by G1 T1 in Figure 11.1. Second, a loss of regional income will add to government expenditure in the region and reduce taxation. Protection of low income regions emerges naturally as a product of tax and welfare in all advanced economies. Moreover, given a shock to the regional economy, the budget balance reacts sympathetically without the need for conscious decision. Tax payments fall in the region that has lost income and social security expenditure rises, thus providing an automatic cushion which works to limit the overall reduction in demand in the declining regional economy. Transfer has two functions: it redistributes income and it acts to absorb shocks to the local economy.

Figures 11.2 and 11.3 are taken from the MacDougall Report. They indicate that the reality of regional fiscal transfer is close to the model of Figure 11.1. Figure 11.2 shows the relationship between fiscal transfer and (a) income per head, (b) trade balance for German Länder. Figure 11.3 shows the same relationships for Italian regions. In both Germany and Italy regions with high income per head have fiscal losses (they pay more in taxes than they receive in services and benefits); low income regions have fiscal gains (they pay less in taxes than they receive in services and benefits). There is a remarkably close relationship between income per head and scale of fiscal transfer in both countries (Berlin is an exception). Figures 11.2 and 11.3 also illustrate that low income tends to go with trade deficits. In effect, in both Germany and Italy, the region that loses its export base automatically receives a degree of protection from the tax and welfare system. Standards of consumption in declining areas are protected by the tax and welfare system. The fiscal stabilisers are built-in – they respond naturally to industrial decline. The reality of fiscal transfer (in Germany and Italy) is remarkably close to the model provided by Figure 11.1.

Tables 11.1 and 11.2 outline the MacDougall Report evidence for four federal (Table 11.1) and three unitary (Table 11.2) states. The general picture that emerges from the MacDougall Report is as follows:

1. Regional economies are notably open and highly vulnerable. Significant loss of 'export base' is more likely for the region than the nation.

2. The region is in no position to counterbalance trade problems with trade-barriers, or devaluation, or interest rate reduction. In compensation for loss of independence, trade and income decline lead to fiscal compensation.

3. There is continuous redistribution of income from richer to poorer regions. Net flows of public finance in the range of 3–10% of regional product

Table 11.1 Fiscal transfer – federations

	Numerical measures				Qualitative comment			
	Average reduction in per capita income differentials	Per capita tax revenue of poorest region (as % of nation) — Before fiscal transfer / After fiscal transfer	Fiscal transfer range of outflow(-) and inflow (+) in relation to regional product	Effect on regional inequalities in per capita income	Nature of transfer	Means	Strength and intention of regional tax equalisation	Objectives
Australia	53			Redistribution more powerful than in other federations	Vertical (from central government)	Financial grants and special grants biased to poorer States	Explicit and clear fiscal equalisation	Redistribute revenue according to tax capacity and needs
Canada	32	62 / 88		Significant	Vertical	Central government pays equalisation grants	Explicit and clear fiscal equalisation	Reduce differences in revenue as between poor and rich states
West Germany	29	88 / 98	-17 to +8 (1964–67)	Clear	Horizontal (above revenue) revenue Länder) pay transfers to low revenue Länder	Tax sharing (modest role for) federal grants	Explicit and clear system ensures that poorest Länder has tax capacity which reaches 97.5% of West German average	Public sector revenue and expenditure flows contribute considerably in equalising regional per capita income and in preventing regions becoming 'bankrupt' when trade balance in deficit
USA	28			Below average and and not as consistent as for other countries	Vertical	Revenue sharing law weighted according to 1. Population 2. General tax effort 3. Relative income	Limited relatively small first step in redistribution	Complex criteria lead to compromise results which lack clarity
Summary	35 (average of the above)							

Equalisation systems 'proper' identified in Australia, Canada and West Germany. Open-ended funding to ensure that fiscal capacity of states equalised (to varying degrees). Intergovernmental grants and/or tax sharing achieve relatively large redistributive effects with relatively small amounts of expenditure. As much as one-half to two-thirds of civic expenditure left in control of lower levels of government. Equalisation systems in federations are relatively open or transparent. They are explicitly voted or negotiated on a geographical basis. The federal system ensures considerable independence and autonomy at state level.

Source: Drawn from Vols 1 and 2 of MacDougall Report

Table 11.2 Fiscal Transfer – unitary states

	Numerical measure			Qualitative comment			
	Average reduction in per capita Income differential (%)	*Fiscal transfer range of outflow (-) and inflow (+) in product (%)*	*Net inter-regional transfer in relation to GDP*	*Tax*	*Public expenditure*	*Total transfer*	*General*
France	54	? to + 11	?	Slightly progressive as between regions. A rise of 10% in per capita income involves an increase of 12.6% in per capital public revenue	Substantial redistribution. Public expenditure programmes and social security	Very substantial redistribution effect	Regional redistribution is *not* deliberate and takes place through the tax and expenditure systems, with *little or nothing known* about the relevant mechanisms
Italy	47	-11 to +28	4.2	Redistributive power slight	Redistributive power considerable. 12x as strong as for tax. Public expenditure programmes and social security	Substantial redistribution against a background of pronounced regional inequality. A relatively low inter-regional transfer (col 3) serves to offset almost half of regional differences in income	Pattern of resource transfer from rich (North) to poor regions (South). Flows from the North offset trade surpluses and flows into the South offset trade deficits. Most striking aspect of regional trade balances and fiscal flows is their high level
United Kingdom (Great Britain)	36	-5 to +16 (-5 to +8)	3.7	Mildly progressive as between regions. A rise of 10% in per capita income involves an increase of 11% in per capita public revenue	A more powerful force for equalisation. Public expenditure programmes and social security	Strong redistribution. Highly correlated to per capita regional output	Two functions of inter-regional movement of public funds. First, *reducing regional inequality.* Second, *stabilising regional income and employment*
Summary	46 (average of above)			In unitary states a large part of the total redistribution between regions is invisible or opaque. It is rarely measured and evolves automatically from the nature of tax and social security in advanced countries. High incomes go with high tax payments and low incomes with generous receipts of centrally provided services and transfer payments. Public finance flows prevent poorer regions from going 'bankrupt' and maintain a region's effective demand.			

Source: Drawn from Vols 1 and 2 of the MacDougall report.

(income) are common for low income and high income regions. Net flows of up to 30% of regional product occur in exceptional circumstances.

4. The flows reduce regional income inequalities by an average of 40% in the countries studied.

5. Public finance plays a major role in limiting cyclical fluctuations. 'One-half to two-thirds...of loss in primary income...may be automatically offset'. through lower taxes and higher benefits (MacDougall Report Vol 1, p.12).

6. Regional policy (narrowly defined) is relatively unimportant, at least in expenditure terms.

7. The nature of redistribution varies from country to country. There is no clear role model. There is more variation (as between countries) in the instruments of redistribution than in the changes it brings in inter-regional income differences.

8. Redistribution at European Community level is negligible.

The pattern outlined by the MacDougall Report gives substance to Hirschman's claim (1958) that 'non-market forces are not necessarily less automatic than market forces' (p.63). In unitary states (like the UK) these non-market forces are all the more impressive for emerging 'as a consequence of the normal activities of government, possibly without any explicit expression of intent, and probably without any statistical calculation' (Wilson 1975, p.19). In France 'inter-regional distribution is not deliberate and takes place...with...little or nothing known about the relevant mechanisms' (MacDougall Report, Vol 1, p.31).

The transfers, both hidden and open, are of particular interest to economists in the Keynesian tradition. They imply that balance between spread effects (forces that reduce regional inequality) and backwash effects (forces that add to regional inequality) depends, in large part, on the nature of the fiscal adjustments that emerge to counter recession and redistribute income and opportunity. They also imply that fiscal transfer has a role to play within the Community.

The 'need for redistribution' (MacDougall Report Vol 1, p.60) emerges because economic integration is expected to add to Community wealth and to regional diversity with 'some areas being net losers' (MacDougall Report Vol 1, p.25). A clear and explicit system of redistribution is required, 'to divide the gains from integration in a politically acceptable way' (MacDougall Report Vol 1, p.60). If it does not emerge, the process of integration falters, the continuity of European union is threatened.

To achieve the minimum response appropriate to 'pre-federal integration' the Report recommends a menu which includes (i) budget equalisation (fiscal transfer) for weak member states to bring fiscal capacity up to 65% of Community average, (ii) cyclical grants to local or regional government, (iii) counter-cyclical aids for weak member states and (iv) a community unemployment fund. In order to sustain a programme designed to counter extremes of income distribution within the community, the Community budget would have to rise to between 2 and 2½% of Community GDP (from 0.7%) (MacDougall Report Vol 1, pp.16–17). Transfer (budget equalisation) 'would have to be not only strongly redistributive, but also capable of a sensitive and large-scale response to short-term changes in the economic fortunes of regions and states' (MacDougall Report Vol 1, p.20).

The actual process of integration takes a notably different form. The entry of Spain, Portugal and Greece adds to regional inequality (and implies larger transfers between different parts of the Community). The Community Budget remains below 1% of Community GDP and is not strongly redistributive between regions. The remarkable fact is that next to no progress has been made. If explicit transfers are required to sustain integration and avoid 'secession and dissolution' (MacDougall Report Vol 1, p.60), the Community is more vulnerable now than in 1977, when the MacDougall Report delivered its reasoned plea for public debate and political consensus on the mechanisms of transfer within the Community.

Unemployment, Social Security and Regional Policy – UK Experience

> Regional policy…(excluding budget equalisation systems and general public investment in roads and schools etc.) provides only a relatively minor component of the overall financial redistribution process.' (MacDougall Report Vol 1, p.37)

Regional policy is only a small component of regional fiscal transfer. The implication is that regional economists may have underplayed the importance of other supports to regional income – including benefit systems.

Table 11.3 shows UK male unemployment in the 1970s and 1980s. As unemployment rises, it climbs more quickly in the Outer (peripheral) than in the Inner Regions. Unemployment rises in all parts, but concentrates in the regions where unemployment is already high (MacKay and Jones 1989). The unemployment gap between Outer and Inner Regions climbs from around 2 percentage points in the 1970s to 6 percentage points in the 1980s (close to 7 percentage points 1985– 89).[3]

---

3   Higher unemployment, a weaker regional policy and greater reliance on market forces have
    seen regional imbalances grow in the 1980s. Another influence is growing trade with Europe.
    Prior to entry into the European Community, barely one-third of what the United Kingdom
    sold and bought overseas went to, or came from, the rest of the Community; today it is more
    than half, and by the year 2000 it is expected to climb to the EC average of more than
    three-fifths. Closer union provides a locational advantage for the Inner Regions, the South
    East in particular. Development concentrates on the parts of Britain already under pressure
    and there is no policy to disperse demand from the South East. 1992 and the Channel Tunnel
    are not linked to better road and rail systems which could spread wealth and opportunity
    (MacKay 1991).

Table 11.3 Male unemployment[1] rate[2] – inner and outer regions

	Average for	
	1970–79 (%)	1980–89 (%)
United Kingdom	4.9	12.9
Outer Regions[3]	6.3	16.3
Inner Regions[4]	3.8	10.4
Outer less Inner Regions	2.5	5.9

[1] Unemployment consistent with current 'claimant count' from 1975
[2] Narrow definition – unemployment as percentage of employees in employment and unemployment
[3] Outer Regions – Northern Ireland, Scotland, Wales, North, North West, Yorkshire and Humberside
[4] Inner Regions – South East, East Anglia, South West, East Midlands, West Midlands
Source: Employment Gazette (including Historical Supplements)

Table 11.4 Social security – inner and outer regions
(Social security as share of household income)

	Average for years	
	1970–79 (%)	1980–89 (%)
United Kingdom	9.4	12.8
Outer Regions	11.0	16.1
Inner Regions	8.7	11.0
Outer less Inner Regions	2.3	5.1

Source: Family Expenditure Surveys

Table 11.4 denotes two trends implicit in automatic stabilisation and regional fiscal transfer within advanced economies. As unemployment climbs, the importance of social security benefits increases in all parts: the increase is more significant in the regions which experience severe losses in employment opportunity.

Social security income climbs from less than £1 in every £10 of UK household income in the 1970s, to £1 in every £8 in the 1980s. In both periods the Outer Regions are more heavily dependent than the Inner. The gap is relatively small in the 1970s, but it grows with unemployment.

The growing importance of social security does not follow from government policy. This has sought to reduce dependence on the state and to cut back social expenditure. The trends indicated in Table 11.4 occur in spite of policies which are not notably generous to those separated from opportunity. They indicate the power of automatic stabilisers against a political background which has not been particularly sympathetic to those dependent on the welfare state.

In 1975, social security expenditure per household was roughly £46 per annum higher in the Outer Regions than in the Inner Regions. The extra burden of social security expenditure in the Outer Regions translates into a total cost of approximately £380 million to the National Exchequer. By 1985, social security expenditure per household was roughly £328 per annum higher in the Outer Regions. The extra burden on the budget climbs to roughly £3000 million per annum. After allowing for inflation, the social security gap between Outer and Inner Regions increases by a multiple of over 3.

Stated differently, the extra burden of social security in the Outer Regions adds to government expenditure a sum equal to only three-fifths of regional aid in 1975; but a sum over five times regional aid in 1985. By the late 1980s, the extra burden of social security in the Outer Regions is probably over eight times regional aid.

There are two opposing trends. Declining significance of regional aid[4] in spite of growing regional inequality) and growing importance of welfare benefits (in spite of a desire to reduce state dependency). Fiscal transfer between regions takes the form of a growing gap in welfare payments (monetary and real) as between Outer and Inner Regions.

There is evidence, for the United Kingdom, that regional policy can deliver results. In two lengthy periods of active regional policy (1945–51 and early 1960s to mid-1970s) the Assisted Areas of the UK added to their share of national employment and captured a surprisingly large share of industrial expansion. In two lengthy periods of weak or inactive regional policy (1952–59 and from 1976) the Assisted Areas share of national employment fell in nearly every year. (Moore, Rhodes and Tyler 1986, MacKay and Thomson 1979, MacKay 1982).

Effective regional policy relied on controls over industrial location, as well as incentives. Controls have been abandoned and aid levels have dwindled to insignificance in the late 1970s and 1980s. The traditional (and for a time successful) forms of regional policy evolved in conditions which no longer hold. The strategy depended on guiding manufacturing expansion away from regions of full employment to regions with unused resources. In little over a decade the United Kingdom lost 2 million manufacturing jobs and unemployment is high in all regions. With high unemployment and decline in manufacturing, there are fewer, potentially mobile plants. On average these provide fewer jobs. Those jobs fall over time rather than increase. Regional policy increasingly resembles an attempt to fill a doubtful tank from a tap of diminishing cross-section.

Reduced faith in regional policy is not confined to the United Kingdom. It appears to be shared throughout Europe. In Läpple's (1985) words, '…almost every country silently gives up its regional policy'. This is endorsed by a new

---

4   In real terms regional aid lost two-thirds of value between 1975 and 1985. In 1975 regional aid accounted for 0.7% of GDP and 1.6% of public expenditure: in 1985, for 0.2% and 0.4%.

realism which denounces balanced regional development 'as a luxury belonging to an earlier period of economic growth' (p.52).

In the wider European Community, as in the United Kingdom, there is a more difficult setting for regional policy and growing regional inequality. In the Community (as in the UK) the years of slow growth (from 1973) and rising unemployment add to regional divergence. Between 1976 and 1985 (EC Community 1987b, p.62) unemployment rose by 4 percentage points in the 25 Community regions with the lowest unemployment rates. The increase in the 25 regions with highest unemployment was 13 percentage points. The unemployment gap, at the extremes of the Community, tripled in only 10 years. There is a core-periphery pattern to disparity. In relation to the Community average, unemployment rates in the more peripheral regions are almost 50% higher and productivity levels are more than 25% lower (EC Community 1987b, p.47).

The Commission's desire to contain regional inequality is not backed by growing commitment at national level. The Commission has added to adjustment assistance. It intends to double the real resources provided by the three Structural Funds. There is, however, real doubt as to the ability of the Structural Funds to play a role remotely comparable to the role played by fiscal transfer within countries.

There are three cautions. First, doubling the fund can be regarded as a minimum response to entry into the Community of Portugal and Spain. Second, growth emerges from a low level. The Structural Funds accounted for only 0.16% of Community GDP in 1986. Third, there are real problems in devising and implementing a Community response which is effective at regional level. One problem is additionality, or rather its absence. This issue will be explored in greater detail in the following chapter by Barnett and Borooah (Chapter 12).

EC regional spending is channelled through the central governments of Member States. In principle, structural funds from the EC are meant to be on top of each State's own expenditure. They should have an effect at local level, provide extra projects and influence the type of project receiving aid. They are not intended simply to substitute Community funds for national aids.

Two Reports from the House of Lords (1988, 1989) indicate the problems of enforcing additionality. The 'vast majority' of projects allocated assistance by the European Regional Fund, 'would go ahead' without assistance (House of Lords 1988, 9, p.73). Moreover, 'money...is not always passed on directly to the applicant' (House of Lords 1988, p.9). It does not reach private firms. If it is handed over to local authorities and government departments, the amounts awarded are deducted from the relevant budgets. There is little clear return for the effort involved in application.

The UK government is quite open about the absence of benefit to particular firms, regions or departments. Reductions in Treasury expenditure following receipt of Structural Funds are apparently justified 'because Community money comes from the same source as national funds, that is the taxpayer' (House of Lords

1989, p.30). The government claims national, not local, additionality. The Community contributes to expenditure levels, but has next to no impact on who receives assistance. National additionality is impossible to disprove but appears improbable given the trend in regional policy expenditure.

The UK approach converts additionality into a tortuous game. The selection of projects in Britain and their careful scrutiny by EC officials serve no useful purpose. The game militates against local initiative. It provides no recognition of the problems for Outer Regions which flow from closer integration within Europe. It ensures that lower levels of government remain the '"creatures" of central government' (Peacock 1984, p.109). A more direct response is required.

The familiar arguments for 1992, and the broader process of closer economic and monetary union, stress 'gains from trade' which add to overall welfare. Our most appropriate examples of open economic systems – national economies – suggest that reducing barriers to exchange is part of a more complex process. That process involves compensation for enhanced risk. The title of this book is *An Enlarged Europe: Regions in Competition?* The question-mark is appropriate; mechanisms apart from competition must come into play.

Economic systems have different functions – allocative and creative. Economics is not confined to finding the most appropriate use for resources of given potential. It is also about exploring and developing potential by, for example, providing positive signals for labour and capital. The only important function for capital, Schumpeter (1934, p.116) suggests, is to dictate a new direction to production, or to divert the factors of production to new uses. We can at least agree that this is an important quality and one reasonable test to apply to economic systems. Markets, unless guided, respond only to costs and benefits that connect to profit: they have a tendency to emphasise immediate returns. Non-market forces come into play because they identify a broader, perhaps more appropriate, perspective.

Regional transfers are not simply defensive. The market has weak self-establishing and self-correcting properties. Reversals can come with devastating speed, creative destruction implies injury to the wealth-creating capacity of communities. A sustainable market system requires an Aristotelian sense of balance – with neither market nor non-market forces pushed to excess. Automatic stabilisers are natural to advanced, mixed economies. They are a response to a weakness of capitalism. Experience has shown how long it takes to prepare for useful investment. With loss of market and reduced valuation of human and physical capital, built-in stabilisers provide an important 'shock-absorber' role: they provide time and opportunity to adapt to new information. Moreover, it will be much easier to check decline if we intervene at its earliest stage. Without transfer, without guaranteed support early rather than late, cumulative forces of decline may be set in motion which prove almost impossible to check until they have run their course. If we are to be successful, regional transfers must be available before the full impact of decline is visible to the general public.

The approach of this chapter points to three problems with Maastricht. First, the 'convergence' requirements have little relevance to regional convergence and sometimes point in the opposite direction. They stress price stability to the exclusion of any reference to unemployment, or level of economic activity. Second, Maastricht avoids any commitment to the increased funding required to compensate for the risks inherent in restructuring. Third, and connected, if the European Community is to be more than a means to reducing trade barriers, the lack of democratic accountability within the Community cannot be ignored. The great attraction of built-in stabilisers is that, once introduced, they work without conscious political decision, or direction. Their great problem is that they depend on consensus, on shared values, on political institutions to provide the representation that goes with taxation and redistribution. Within nations agreements, understandings and responses have evolved to provide a breathing space for poorer regions and for regions with trade problems. A similar process at Community level has problems. It is impossible if we retain the myth that membership of the European Community is simply about revealing opportunities for exchange which are, at present, disguised.

Regional transfers are important to open economies. Why do they fail to emerge within the Community as national economies become increasingly open to trade and exchange?

Conclusion

> In Europe the worry that economic advance may widen the differentials between advanced and backward regions has inspired new institutions and policies specifically designed to pour resources into the poorer regions and to accelerate their development. The European wide institutions and policies came of course on top of national policies to deal with the problem. (Hirschman 1981, p.279).

The reality is different. The resources provided by the European Community are slight. They are not necessarily additional to national efforts. These are in decline. That decline is set against a background of growing regional inequality.

Fiscal transfer (budget equalisation) appears to be central to economic and monetary union. Transfer is central to the spread effect provided by non-market forces. It gives substance to Hirschman's claim that economic policies emerge naturally, almost inevitably, to counter regional inequality (Hirschman 1958, pp.63–65, p.190).

Substantial development of fiscal transfer was anticipated to hold the European Community together in the process of integration. The mystery is that it remains neglected, unexplored, still-born.

In contrast to a Sherlock Holmes story, no logical explanation can be provided on the basis of what has not happened. Political economy remains untidy. The list of suspects include: (1) 1992 may have been less important than was often implied,

(2) the risks to the periphery have been overstated in this chapter, (3) there is no clear model for budgetary reform, (4) fiscal transfer (budget equalisation) depends on a degree of political unity that is (as yet) beyond the reach of the Community.

Reducing non-tariff barriers does not guarantee a unified market for all goods and services. A space economy remains an economy of imperfect competition. The spirit of 1992 may be more important than the substance. As explanation this is true, but not entirely relevant. 1992 was part of a broader process. That broader process leads to progressive loss by nations of their ability to control trade, exchange rates and monetary and fiscal policy. Loss of control reaches out to embrace nations as well as regions.

This chapter may be guilty of placing excessive emphasis on geography and the core–periphery contrast. Infrastructure and human capital are more important than location in determining relative growth. As Sapir (1990) reminds us, extreme locational disadvantage in Korea (and Japan) has been no bar to accumulating human and physical capital.[5] What is peripheral is not given. It depends on decisions, including those made by the public sector. In a paper, which is clearly informed by the MacDougall Report, Jacques Delors (1989, p.83) develops a similar theme: 'The United States economy has…seen pronounced economic growth at its geographic edges.' The core regions may be more prosperous in Europe, but there is no universal pattern.

The qualification is important, but is a plea in mitigation rather than a convincing alibi. Range of location choice has increased: the part played by nature declines over time (Kaldor 1970). In the early stages of economic development, ideal location was determined by the natural characteristics of places. In the later stages the part played by interaction between producers increases, as does the role of physical and human capital. Greater freedom of location choice does not imply stability, or control. Production has become more mobile in space, but less stable in location. The essence of specialisation implies risk. Exchange value of the individual and of the local community (wages, profits, etc.) are at the mercy of a division of labour which adjusts to competitive forces beyond the control of the

---

5   International comparison is useful in emphasising that human capital is a key resource. The skills, qualifications and resources of the labour force may be even more important than physical capital, even though human capital is not recognised in regional and national accounts. Traditionally regional development policies rely on so-called 'hardware' investment tools such as financial incentives and infrastructure investment to create jobs. A more ambitious approach embraces 'software' development tools, that is job skills to sustain a momentum that may also require capital investment. The weaker regions may prove to be those with labour surplus (unemployment) and labour shortage. The scarcity relates to quality – to education, to qualifications, to job skills and training which are essential to economic development. The essential arguments for regional policy link to the above. They stress that human capital, like physical capital, is both a consequence and a source of economic development. Also, development of human resources, realisation of potential, is unlikely if the centres of growth concentrate on the same privileged growth space.

individual and the local community. An extended market produces uncertainty as well as wealth.

The great attraction of fiscal compensation is that it produces automatic support given industrial decline. Fluctuations in personal incomes are evened out, without the need for conscious policy response. Moreover, compensation is as Jacques Delors claims (1989), 'both a product of, and source of the sense of national solidarity which all relevant economic and monetary unions share' (p.84).

Delors (1989) also points to our third clue: 'There is no apparent model on which all integration efforts seem destined to converge' (p.82). Budget reform can follow a number of different evolutions. The national models provide considerable contrasts in the way fiscal transfers emerge. In some countries transfer is explicit, open, acknowledged. In others they remain hidden, rarely measured, a source of surprise. Once again true, but a plea of limitation rather than a full explanation. While there are many plausible models (see MacDougall Report) there is one common result. All advanced economies rely on fiscal transfer. In the countries studied, fiscal transfer reduces regional income inequalities by an average of 40%. In the Community the redistributive power of the budget remains insignificant. It appears difficult to envisage economic and monetary union without a degree of fiscal compensation. The real mystery relates not to the absence of a complete system, but to zero progress.

There is merit in Hirschman's claim that a determined effort will be made to pull weaker regions out of stagnation. Non-market forces emerge to support weaker regions within countries – surely we can rely on their evolution within the European Community. The fear that closer union adds to regional inequality invites response.

There are, however, obvious differences between individual countries and the European Community. The latter lacks independent sources of finance and the political integration that provides the background for taxation and distribution. Financial and democratic deficits flow from a common source. The sense of solidarity that binds different parts of a nation together is not as strong between nations. We reach the paradox that perhaps explains the logical action which fails to surface. Closer union may require fiscal support for weaker regions: fiscal transfer depends on closer union.

The absence of effective regional transfer within the Community has many partial explanations, but political themes are more important than economic. Closer union between countries provides a difficult test for Hirschman's claims. Fiscal transfers (equalisation mechanisms) compensate for loss of independence, but their counterpart, 'is a mature political structure with a federal government and parliament and other federal agencies' (MacDougall Report, p.61).

References

Buchanan, J. (1950) 'Federalism and fiscal equity.' *American Economic Review 40*, 583–599.

Commission of the European Communities (1977) *MacDougall Report*, Report of the Study Group on the Role of Public Finance in European Integration, Vol.1, General Report, Vol. 2, Individual Contributions and Working Papers. Luxembourg: Office for Official Publications of the European Community.

Commission of the European Communities (1987a) 'Reform of the Structural Funds.' *Communication 87*, (376).

Commission of the European Communities (1987b) Third Periodic Report from the Commission on the Social and Economic Situation and Development of the Community (The Regional Report), Com (187k) 230 Final, Brussels: CEC.

Delors, J. (1989) 'Regional implications of economic and monetary integration' pp. 81–89. In Committee for the Study of Economic and Monetary Union, *Report on Economic and Monetary Union in the European Community*. Luxembourg: Office for Official Publications of the European Community.

Doyle, Sir Arthur Conan (1951) *Sherlock Holmes – selected stories*. London: Oxford University Press.

European Economy (1988) 'The Economics of 1992.' March, 35.

Hirschman, A.O. (1958) *The Strategy of Economic Development*. New Haven: Yale University Press.

Hirschman, A.O. (1981) 'Three uses of political economy in analysing European integration.' In A.O. Hirschman *Essays in Trespassing: Economics to Politics and Beyond*. Cambridge: Cambridge University Press.

House of Lords (1988) Select Committee on the European Communities, Reform of the Structural Funds, Session 1987–88, HL Paper 82.

House of Lords (1989), Select Committee on the European Communities, Transport Infrastructure, Session 1988–89, HL Paper 84.

Kaldor, N. (1970) 'The case for regional policy.' *Scottish Journal of Political Economy 17*, 337–48.

Läpple, D. (1985) 'Internationalisation of capital and the regional problem.' In J. Walton (ed) *Capital and Labour in the Urbanised World*. London: Sage.

MacKay, R.R. (1982) 'Planning for balance: regional policy and regional employment – the United Kingdom experience'. In W. Buhr and P. Friedrich (eds) *Planning Under Regional Stagnation*. Baden-Baden: Nomos Verlagsgesellschaft.

MacKay, R.R. (1991) 'The Channel Tunnel and the regions.' In R.R. MacKay *The Future of Railways and Roads*. London: Institute for Public Policy Research.

MacKay, R.R. and Jones, D.R. (1989) *Labour Markets in Distress: the Denial of Choice*. Aldershot: Gower Press.

MacKay, R.R. and Thomson, L. (1979) 'Important trends in regional policy and regional employment – a modified interpretation.' *Scottish Journal of Political Economy 26*, 3, 233–260.

Moore, B., Rhodes, J. and Tyler, P. (1986) *The Effects of Government Regional Economic Policy*. Department of Trade and Industry. London: HMSO.

Myrdal, G. (1957) *Economic Theory and Under-Developed Regions*. London: Duckworth.

Oates, W.E. (1972) *Fiscal Federalism*. London: Harcart Brace Jovanovich.

Peacock, A. (1984) 'Tax sharing: the West German example.' In T. Wilson (ed) *Fiscal Decentralisation*. Printed by David Green, Kettering, for the Anglo-German Foundation.

Sapir, A. (1990) Discussion on Krugman, P.J. and Venables A.J. 'Integration and the competitiveness of peripheral industry'. In C. Bliss and J.B. De Macedo (eds) *Unity with Diversity in the European Economy; the Community's Southern frontier.* Cambridge: Cambridge University Press.

Schumpeter, J.A. (1934) *The Theory of Economic Development.* Cambridge, MA: Harvard University Press.

Schumpeter, J.A. (1943) *Capitalism, Socialism and Democracy.* London: Unwin University Books.

Smith, A. (1776) *An Inquiry into the Nature and Causes of the Wealth of Nations.* I. Cannon (ed) London: Methuen, 1904.

Wilson, T. (1975), 'Economic sovereignty.' In J. Vaizey (ed) *Economic Sovereignty and Regional Policy.* London: Gill and Macmillan.

Young, A. (1928) 'Increasing returns and economic progress.' *Economic Journal 38,* December *38,* 527–42.

CHAPTER 12

The Additionality (or otherwise) of European Community Structural Funds

Richard R. Barnett and Vidya Borooah

Introduction

The Single European Act is best known for its commitment to the completion of the internal market. But the prospect of such an internal market led to fears among the poorer regions, located mainly on the western and southern fringes of the Community, that it would lead to a greater concentration of wealth in the Community's core economies, the so-called 'golden triangle'. In response to these fears the Single European Act included an article on social and economic cohesion:

> In order to promote its overall harmonious development the Community shall develop and pursue its actions leading to the strengthening of its economic and social cohesion. In particular, the Community shall aim at reducing disparities between the various regions and backwardness of least-favoured regions'.[1] (EC Commission 1986, p.13)

The Act lays down that the Community is to achieve these objectives via the use of the structural funds, that is, the European Regional Development Fund (ERDF), the European Social Fund (ESF) and the guidance section of the European Agricultural Guidance and Guarantee Fund (EAGGF(Guidance)). Towards this end the structural programmes have been reformed and the funds available have been doubled.

---

1 Throughout this chapter we use the term 'Community' when referring collectively to the institutions of the European Community.

In the process of reforming the structural funds, the Community has assumed greater control over the distribution of the funds. This greater control has taken two principal forms. First, the funds are to be concentrated on a limited number of priority objectives and on regions of greatest need. And it is the Community, rather than Member States, who decides on the criteria for establishing priority objectives and regions of greatest need. Second, 'additionality' has become a legal requirement. Additionality is the idea that community funds should not substitute for monies that would otherwise have been spent by Member States in the relevant policy area. Instead, it is intended that these funds should lead to an increase in expenditure in the Member States of an amount at least equal to that received from the Community.

Additionality had, in fact, been a concern of the Community for some time. For example, the preamble to the regulation establishing the ERDF in 1975 states that:

> the Fund's assistance should not lead Member States to reduce their own regional development efforts but should complement these efforts. (EC Council of Ministers 1975, p.2)

Similarly, the concept of additionality had been emphasised by one of the Commissioners:

> we are anxious to ensure that money from Community sources should be genuinely additional. In other words that things should happen which would not otherwise happen. (Northern Ireland Assembly 1983, p.6)

Although it was expected that Member States would use ERDF funds to complement their own expenditure, there was no legal requirement for them to do so. This changed following the reform of the structural funds. Article 9 of the regulation for the coordination of the structural funds states:

> ...the Member States shall ensure that the increase in appropriations for the Funds...has a genuine economic impact in the regions concerned and results in at least an equivalent increase in the total volume of official or similar (Community or national) structural aid in the Member State concerned... (EC Council of Ministers 1988b, p.5)

In this chapter we discuss various issues that are pertinent to an assessment of additionality. We do this at three levels of increasing generality. Having made additionality a legal requirement, the Community has recently established a procedure for checking that the receipt of structural funds does result in additional expenditure. Our first objective is to provide an assessment of this procedure. Our conclusion is that the procedure that the Community intends to adopt is unlikely to provide a test of the additionality requirement.

The second objective of the chapter is to examine whether the form in which the funds are given – essentially as matching grants – is conducive to the achievement of additionality. In order to address this issue we require a model of budgetary policy. Employing the widely used model of rational budget setting we conclude that we should not expect additionality to necessarily follow as a consequence of the optimising behaviour of Member States. Thus, quite irrespective of the procedure that has been set up to test for additionality, it is possible that there has been a failure in policy design. Given these two negative findings – that additionality is not being tested for and that the nature of the funds is not necessarily conducive to the achievement of additionality – in the final part of the chapter we broaden our discussion to consider the development of the structural funds in a wider political and economic context. A central question that we address concerns the role that is being played by the structural funds within what might be termed the budgetary politics of the Community. In short our discussion broadens from the economics of the structural funds to the political economy of the structural funds.

Assessing Additionality

Following the passage of the Single European Act, a number of reforms have been made to the structural funds, the main aspects of which can be summarised as follows (EC Council of Ministers 1988a, b):

1. The resources available for the funds are to be doubled in real terms between 1987 and 1993.

2. The funds are to be concentrated both geographically and in policy terms in order to meet a limited number of priority objectives.

3. There has been a further move towards programme support and away from the support of individual projects.

4. Additionality has been made a legal requirement.

These reforms can be seen as a continuation in the development of the Community's regional policy. The Treaty of Rome did not include a Title dealing specifically with regional issues and made no argument for a Community regional policy. Instead, regional policy was to be the prerogative of the Member States and the Community's role was a regulatory one with the Community being empowered to control both the level of regional aid and the form in which it was given by Member States (Swann 1990). With its development, especially the moves towards economic and monetary union and enlargement, the Community has progressively taken steps towards a more proactive and positive role in regional policy. Community funded schemes have been established and control over the distribution of the funds has been moved away from Member States towards the Community. Thus, the general thrust has been towards a positive Community regional policy with greater Community control and the additionality requirement can be viewed as part of this development.

Additionality refers to the idea that Community structural funds should complement, rather than substitute for, monies that would otherwise have been spent by the Member States in the relevant policy area. Although the concept has come to prominence in connection with the Community's structural funds, it has a much wider and more general application in policy analysis. Thus, in its manual on policy evaluation for public sector managers the UK government describes additionality as follows:

> The amount of output from a policy as compared with what would have occurred without the government intervention. The concept of additionality is particularly important in evaluating financial incentives, e.g. grants to industry, tax allowances, employment measures. If you are paying someone to do something which he would have done anyway, there is zero additionality and the incentive is ineffective'. (HM Government 1988, p.26)

This definition brings out the fundamental importance of ascertaining what would have happened in the absence of the policy that is the subject of the evaluation. We might refer to this as the problem of ascertaining the counterfactual. The counterfactual situation is often referred to as the base case and is defined in the UK manual in the following terms:

> Any evaluation of a policy's effects needs to be relative to a base case, i.e. to a statement of what would have happened without government intervention or if the government intervention had taken a different form. Otherwise there is no way of disentangling the effects of a policy from other changes which have occurred as a result of other causes. In many cases the base case may be the continuation of previous policy. It is not usually enough just to describe the starting position or baseline since this would have changed with time anyway. (HM Government 1988, pp.26–27)

Whilst the establishment of the counterfactual is often one of the trickiest parts of any policy evaluation, it is of the utmost importance. The success or otherwise of a policy is to be judged relative to the base case situation.

The simplest approach to policy evaluation is to undertake what Hogwood and Gunn (1984) refer to as a 'before and after study'. In such a study the situation immediately prior to the introduction of the policy is described and is compared with the situation at the point in time at which the policy is being evaluated. But this is the type of study which the UK manual says is 'not usually enough' and about which Hogwood and Gunn (1984) write:

> Despite their superficial attractiveness, simple before and after studies are likely to have a number of unsatisfactory features. (p.229).

Prominent among these unsatisfactory features is the failure to consider other influences on the variables under consideration; for example, other policy changes and changes in the wider social and economic environment. It is now commonplace, and indeed considered best practice, to move beyond before and after studies. Thus, there is now widespread use of experimental and modelling approaches to policy evaluation (Rossi and Freeman 1989). The modelling approach has been central to evaluations of regional policy in the UK with the development and gradual refinement of what are frequently referred to as 'policy on – policy off studies' (Armstrong and Taylor 1985). A model of the relevant policy area is developed and simulations of varying degrees of sophistication are undertaken to ascertain what the level of key variables would have been in the absence of the policy (the policy off situation); these are then compared with actual values of the variables (the policy on period).

Despite widespread recognition of the likely limitations of 'before and after' studies and the development of more appropriate methodologies, the Community's approach to testing for additionality is in terms of a simple 'before and after' study.

In attempting to test for additionality the Community proposes to divide expenditure in each of the recipient Member States into three categories (EC Commission 1991):

1. Community structural funds.

2. Expenditure by the Member State on Community aided programmes.

3. Expenditure by the Member State on programmes similar to those supported by structural funds but not in receipt of Community aid.

Together (1) and (2) represent what is referred to as 'co-financed public expenditure' and (3) is referred to as 'non-co-financed public eligible expenditure'. The sum of (2) and (3) is termed 'national public structural aid' and this includes expenditure by all levels of government in a Member State and also by public bodies and enterprises. The Community's test for additionality is then described as follows:

> The verification of additionality will result from a comparison in real terms (constant prices) of 'national public structural aid' in the base year and in the (Community Support Framework) period. (EC Commission 1991, p.3)

If the national public structural aid in the Community Support Framework period is more than it is in the base year then additionality is said to be verified. It is recommended that base year expenditure is taken as the average of expenditure in 1987 and 1988. The Community Support Framework period can be presented either on a year-by-year basis or as a yearly average.

There are several points to be made here. First, even recognising the limitations of the approach being taken, additionality of structural funds is not being tested for. Instead, it is only the *increase* in funds since 1987–88 that is the subject of scrutiny. This is recognised by the Community in Article 9 of the regulation for the coordination of the structural funds:

> ...the Commission and the Member States shall ensure that the increase in the appropriations for the funds...shall have a genuine additional impact...'
> (EC Council of Ministers 1988b, p.5)

Since the structural funds are to be doubled, the additionality requirement will apply to only half of the total funds allocated. To the extent that a Member State did not treat the funds that it received in 1987–88 as additional, it will not need to do so into the future on funds equivalent to the amount that it received in those years. Clearly, other things being equal, the additionality requirement is a more stringent requirement for a Member State in the following circumstances:

- the greater is the increase in structural funds that it receives
- the more it treated funds as additional in the baseline period 1987–88.

Thus, a Member State that paid scant regard to additionality in the earlier period and receives little increase in funds need not be unduly worried by the new additionality requirement. It can be argued that the UK is in this position (Trimble 1989, Commission of European Communities, Draft CSF for Northern Ireland). Conversely, a Member State that treated Community funds as additional in the earlier period and receives a large increase in funds will have less freedom to use Community funds as it wishes. Even accepting that the Community will be testing only for the additionality of the extra funds, the procedure that they intend to use is open to all the criticisms of such simple before and after studies. In particular there is no attempt to estimate the counterfactual. In this policy area perhaps the most important change that could affect the counterfactual is the Member State's own regional policy (on, say, non-Community aided programmes). A planned reduction in this aid could lead to a Member State being criticised for not complying with additionality when in fact this is not the case. The opposite could be the case for a Member State which plans to increase non-Community aided programmes (for example, by switching money out of programmes aided by the Community).

It has to be recognised, of course, that estimation of the counterfactual is unlikely to be a straightforward matter but this does not excuse the Community's failure to consider the issue. It might be argued that estimation of the counterfactual in this case is either not possible or too costly. To argue the former is to really argue that it is not possible to evaluate the policy. This is no more than to argue that there has been poor policy design: ideally the extent to which policy is capable of evaluation should be one of the criteria for policy selection. With respect to the issue of cost, again ideally the cost of the evaluation process should be considered at the time of policy selection. But also, at a minimum, a simple interview exercise could be carried out at the time the policy is introduced (Rossi and Freeman 1989). The objective of the interview would be to ask Member States how they viewed their own policy as changing over the policy period. This is a poor substitute, however, for a proper attempt to estimate the counterfactual.

Thus, the Community's proposed evaluation procedure is unlikely to test for additionality even in terms of the limited notion of the additionality of the increase in funds that it has set itself. A possible consequence is that blame will be attributed where it is not due and praise will be awarded where it is not justified. This is perhaps the worst of all possible outcomes from an evaluation exercise. It is not clear, though, what sanctions the Community has at its disposal for offending parties.

If the Community is serious in its efforts to test for additionality it is important that it takes its job more seriously. As Shackleton (1991) notes, with the likely development of economic and monetary union there will be further pressures to increase the funds available for Community regional policy. Shackleton writes:

> ...there is a danger that regional and sectoral imbalances will emerge which could threaten the viability of EMU. (p.108)

He then quotes the Delors report to the effect that:

> ...a particular role would have to be assigned to common policies aimed at developing a more balanced economic structure throughout the Community. (p.108)

This echoes the Werner report written some twenty years earlier. It would be pointless to develop a substantial Community regional policy which could effectively be undone by the actions of Member States. Hence the importance of additionality and the need to be able to test for it.

Additionality and Budgetary Policy

The central issue addressed in this section is whether the form in which the structural funds are given is conducive to the achievement of additionality. The funds are currently given as a form of matching grant with the Community paying a proportion of the cost of aided programmes. The effect of such grants is to reduce the tax price of the aided programmes in the Member States. In order to ascertain whether such grants will lead to an increase in spending by an amount at least as great as the structural aid received (and hence whether additionality occurs) requires knowledge of the budget-setting behaviour of Member States.

There is a series of well-developed models of the budgeting process (see, for example, King 1984), the most widely used one of which assumes rationality in budget setting. Since matching grants are essentially price reductions for Member States to carry out regional programmes, of key importance is knowledge of the relevant price elasticities. For additionality to occur the price elasticity of demand for regional expenditure in the Member States must be greater than or equal to one. With a value of one or more for the price elasticity of demand there will be no reduction in 'national public structural aid'. Thus, if the rational budget-setting model is the appropriate one to use, and only empirical work can determine this, additionality will not necessarily follow as a result of optimal budget setting in the Member States. The authors of the influential Padoa-Schioppa report seem to imply that the use of matching grants necessarily assures the achievement of additionality (Padoa-Schioppa 1987); they write:

the Funds would then offer the incentive of matching grants, variable as a function of relative income levels of countries, for suitable programmes of expenditure... The Community subsidy would thus cheapen for the public authority of the recipient region the tax price of the development pro-grammes in question, and therefore help assure additional total expenditure on this function... 'Additionality' would be achieved in a decentralized manner through the working of incentive mechanisms, not by a centralized attempt by the Community to negotiate 'additionality' in relation to budg-etary projections. (p.97)

As our discussion above indicates, this conclusion is not warranted. Matching grants related to relative income levels, or indeed anything else, will not necessarily guarantee the achievement of additionality and thus a decentralised incentive mechanism may not be enough.

If the relevant price elasticity in a Member State is less than one, then to comply with the additionality requirement the State would have to diverge from its optimal budgetary allocation and thereby reduce national well-being. This brings into the open the possible conflict between the welfare-maximising objectives of Member States and those of the Community. Such tensions are at the heart of all discussions of policy setting in multilevel systems of government. But given that the form in which the funds are allocated is not necessarily conducive to optimal budget setting in Member States, perhaps we should not be too surprised if these tensions come to the fore in this policy area.

Before leaving this section we should note that the rational budget-setting model is likely to be applicable only in the long run. In the short run Member States will face both institutional constraints and other policy commitments which may make the achievement of additionality more or less likely. For example, in the case of the UK the way in which public expenditure is allocated to the territories (Northern Ireland, Scotland and Wales) makes the achievement of additionality problematic.[2] Also the fact that structural funds are allocated to national govern-ments, rather than to the regions which qualify for support, means that funds may get 'stuck' in the national treasury and not passed through to the regions.

Additionality and Budgetary Politics

In this section we provide some discussion of the concept of additionality in the wider political and economic context. Any reform of the structural funds inevitably involves a political compromise. Various parties will have entered the discussions with differing agendas and as a consequence are likely to view the role that the

---

2   For a discussion of the allocation of public expenditure to the territories – which is essentially on a per capita basis – see, for example, Likierman (1988). To see the links between such an allocation process and additionality see Northern Ireland Economic Council (1992).

structural funds are playing somewhat differently. The importance that a particular party attaches to the achievement of additionality is likely to depend in part, at least, on the role that it believes the structural funds to be playing.

The structural funds can be seen as performing three types of role. The first of these is a resource allocation role. Over the coming years Community regional policy faces what the authors of the Padoa-Schioppa report refer to as the 'triple challenge' of the Single Market, enlargement of the Community and new trends in industrial technologies. All of these will lead to structural adjustments in the location of economic activity and without an active regional policy there is clearly the possibility that the poorer regions will lose out at least in relative terms. And it seems likely that the 'triple challenge' will lead to structural adjustments which result from inter-industry trade, rather than intra-industry trade as has tended to be the case in the past. To the extent that this is the case the magnitude of the change will be greater (Krugman 1987), thus calling for well-formulated regional policies. Without such policies there is clearly a danger that individuals living in the poorer regions will become marginalised in terms of their participation in economic activity. The poorer regions would become marginal in an economic sense as well as a geographic one.

Economic marginalisation is a source of injustice in modern societies.[3] For Young (1990), justice is an enabling concept and injustices are seen to result when individuals are unable to take a full and active part in society. Thus injustices result from disabling constraints and Young identifies two forms of these, namely oppression and domination. She views marginalisation as a form of oppression and writes:

> Marginalization is perhaps the most dangerous form of oppression. A whole category of people is expelled from useful participation in social life and thus potentially subjected to severe material deprivation and even extermination. The material deprivation marginalization often causes is certainly unjust, especially in a society where others have plenty... Material deprivation, which can be addressed by redistributive social policies, is not, however, the extent of the harm caused by marginalization. (pp.53–54)

Young then refers to further injustices caused by marginalization: dependency on welfare payments (lack of privacy, respect and choice), and the injustice of uselessness and boredom. In terms of the possible marginalization caused by the single market (and other aspects of the 'triple challenge'), there is then a case for redistributive policies. But, as she points out, this is not a complete solution. A further problem, not directly alluded to by Young, is that reliance on welfare payments can lead to the development of a dependency culture.

---

3   Other causes of marginalisation include long-term unemployment, old age and racial discrimination.

Thus, and this is recognised by the authors of the Padoa-Schioppa report, the structural funds have a second role to play in addition to resource reallocation, namely redistribution. Clearly, the objective must be to develop policies which not only redistribute but also serve to stimulate economic activity. In this way the material injustice can be alleviated in the short-run and economic marginalisation avoided in the longer run. It is beyond the scope of this chapter to assess the structural funds against this broader objective. Our point is simply that in any discussion of the structural funds the broader political context in which they are set must be considered.

In considering these broader budgetary politics the structural funds can be seen as playing a third role by at least some parties. This additional role is another form of redistributive policy but this time involves Member States getting their fair share of Community funds. In this context the structural funds are to be seen, in part at least, as a policy instrument designed to help bring about an acceptable allocation of monies from the Community budget to Member States. It is arguable that regional aid has been used as the politically acceptable way of achieving 'juste retour' in the past. Thus, on the eve of joining the Community the UK argued for the establishment of a regional policy at the Paris summit of 1972. In part the motivation for this can be seen as the UK's desire to get its *juste retour* since it received relatively little from the budget-dominating agricultural fund.[4] Regional policy may be a clumsy way of achieving such redistribution (Mawson, Martins and Gibney 1985), but to say this misses the point. Regional policy is a politically acceptable way of achieving such redistribution. The fact that the structural funds are paid into national treasuries, rather than directly to the regions, perhaps represents a further facet of this compromise.

Thus, the structural funds are likely to be viewed differently by different parties. The Community (in the form of the Commission) may well see regional policy as the true objective and for them additionality will be important. In support of this view we might cite the gradual development of a meaningful Community-level regional policy as documented, for example, by Swann (1990). As we noted above and as Swann points out, there has been a steady development of policy away from a largely regulatory role towards a positive Community policy. Against this pressure from the Community, certain Member States will be less interested in the development of such a policy and for them additionality is something to be resisted. We saw in the section on assessing additionality that the current arrangements for testing for additionality are unlikely to be successful. The way in which the procedures for testing for additionality are modified in the future, if at all, will be one indicator of the changing balance of views on the role that regional policy should play within the European Community.

---

4   Of course, in the eyes of a later UK government a 'juste retour' was not achieved and a special rebate scheme was negotiated under the Fontainebleau agreement.

Conclusion

With the movement towards a single market and the concern of the poorer Member States that they might lose from this process, there has been a substantial increase in the Community structural funds. Alongside this increase in the structural funds the Community has made additionality a legal requirement. In this chapter we have examined the concept of additionality at three levels of increasing generality. First, we examined the procedure that the Community has set up to test for additionality. We saw that the planned procedure is in essence a simple 'before and after' study and concluded that as such it is unlikely to provide an adequate test of additionality. We then considered additionality in the context of budgetary policy. Contrary to the views expressed by the authors of the Padoa-Schioppa report we concluded that the form in which the structural funds are given is not necessarily conducive to the achievement of additionality by decentralised (incentive driven) means.

In the final part of the chapter we discussed briefly some of the budgetary politics surrounding the structural funds. We pointed to the differing roles that various parties might see the structural funds as playing. These include arguments concerning redistributive policy, resource reallocation policy and ones related to 'juste retour'. Inevitably, the current form of the structural funds represents a political compromise and the importance attached to additionality depends on the view taken of the main role being played by the funds. One test of the direction in which Community regional policy will develop in the future is the seriousness with which the issue of additionality is taken over the coming years.

References

Armstrong, H. and Taylor, J. (1985) *Regional Economics and Policy*. Oxford: Philip Allan.

EC Commission (1986) 'Single European Act.' *Bulletin of the European Communities*, Supplement 2/86. Luxembourg: Office for Official Publications of the European Communities.

EC Commission (1991) *Information Note on the Verification of the Additionality Principle*, DG XVI. Luxembourg: Office for Official Publications of the European Communities.

EC Council of Ministers (1975) Regulation 724/75.

EC Council of Ministers (1988a) Regulation 2052/88.

EC Council of Ministers (1988b) Regulation 4253/88.

HM Government (1988) *Policy Evaluation: A Guide for Managers*. London: HMSO.

Hogwood, B.W. and Gunn, L.A. (1984) *Policy Analysis for the Real World*. Oxford: Oxford University Press.

King, D.N. (1984) *Fiscal Tiers*. London: George Allen and Unwin.

Krugman, P. (1987) 'European economic integration: some conceptual issues.' In T. Padoa-Schioppa *Efficiency, Stability and Equity*. Oxford: Oxford University Press.

Likierman, A. (1988) *Public Expenditure*. London: Penguin.

Mawson, J., Martins, M.R. and Gibney, J.T. (1985) 'The development of the European Community regional policy.' In M. Keaton and B. Jones (eds) *Regions in the European Community*. Oxford: Clarendon Press.

Northern Ireland Assembly (1983) *Report on the Additionality of the Receipts of European Funds*, Report 46. Belfast: HMSO.

Northern Ireland Economic Council (1992) *European Community Structural Funds in Northern Ireland*, Report 94. Belfast: HMSO.

Padoa-Schioppa, T, (1987) *Efficiency, Stability and Equity*. Oxford: Oxford University Press.

Rossi, P.H. and Freeman, H.E. (1989) *Evaluation: A Systematic Approach*. California: Sage.

Shackleton, M. (1991) 'The EC's Budget in the Move to a Single Market.' *Governance 4*, 94–114.

Swann, D. (1990) *The Economics of the Common Market*. London: Penguin.

Trimble, M.J. (1989) 'Regional policy of the European Community.' In A. Aughey, P. Hainsworth and M.J. Trimble (eds) *Northern Ireland in the European Community*. Belfast: Policy Research Unit.

Young, I.M. (1990) *Justice and the Politics of Difference*. Princeton: Princeton University Press.

CHAPTER 13

The European Community's RECHAR Programme

An Adequate Response to the Problems of Coal Areas?

Stephen Fothergill

Introduction

RECHAR is a programme of European Community aid targeted at coalmining areas. Its aim is to assist economic renewal in EC coalfields that have lost large numbers of jobs in recent years and which suffer from important handicaps to regeneration.

RECHAR (a name derived from the word *charbon*, the French for coal) was the first of a series of 'Community Initiatives' to be announced following the 1988 reform of the EC's Structural Funds. It is also the largest of these initiatives, in financial terms, to impact on 'Objective 2' regions – Europe's older industrial regions. It is therefore valuable to assess its effectiveness not only in terms of its impact on the coalfields but also as a guide to the value of EC regional aid in general.

This chapter examines RECHAR in four stages. The first looks at the origins of the programme. Clearly, major initiatives do not emerge without having first undergone a period of consideration and debate, and it is interesting to consider why the Commission chose to make coal areas its first priority. The second part of the chapter describes the programme, including the involvement of the various EC funds, the range of eligible measures, and RECHAR's context amongst other EC activities. The third part of the chapter evaluates RECHAR against the background of the development needs of coal areas and the organisational obstacles to its effective implementation. Finally, the chapter draws a number of conclusions.

Origins of the RECHAR Programme

Why, when faced with a whole range of possible actions following the reform of the Structural Funds, did the Commission opt to assist coal areas? The answer lies partly in lobbying efforts, partly in the circumstances of coalfield areas, and partly in good luck.

The lobbying for EC aid for coal areas can be traced back to the UK, where the 1984/5 miners' strike was followed by a major round of pit closures. In 1985, local authorities in coal areas throughout Britain formed the Coalfield Communities Campaign (CCC) to press for funds for the economic, social and environmental renewal of their areas. Membership grew quickly to include just about all present-day and former coalmining local authorities in England, Scotland and Wales, irrespective of political complexion.

At an early stage it became apparent that Brussels was likely to be more receptive than Westminster to the call for assistance. However, as a purely UK-based association the CCC carried little weight with the Commission. But by 1988 contacts between the EC's mining regions were developing quickly. In the European Parliament, MEPs from the Community's principal mining areas established an 'Inter-Group' to discuss coal-related matters. On the local authority front, the CCC initiated relations with coalfield local authorities elsewhere in Europe, culminating in a conference in Strasbourg in September 1988, mounted with the Inter-Group's assistance. This established a framework for cooperation, subsequently formalised as EUR-ACOM – the association of local and regional authorities in the coalmining areas of the European Community.

A basis for joint lobbying of the Commission had therefore been established. However, local authorities in mining areas across Europe would not have come together so readily if they had not recognised that they shared common problems associated with the run-down of the coal industry.

The industry is concentrated in five EC states – Belgium, France, Germany, Spain and the UK. In Belgium the coal industry is in terminal decline, with the last pit in the Limburg coalfield scheduled to close in 1992. In France, coalmining has ended in the Nord-Pas de Calais basin and continues only on a reduced scale in Lorraine. In Germany, mining continues in the Ruhr and Saarland, though with lower employment. The Spanish coal industry has traditionally been smaller and more dispersed, with miners in Asturias, Leon, Teruel and elsewhere. In the UK there has been recent coalmining in no fewer than eight regions, but the 'central coalfield' embracing Yorkshire, Nottinghamshire and Derbyshire has dominated the industry for some years.

Table 13.1 shows the change in employment in the EC's coal industry between 1977 and 1992. In absolute terms, the UK has lost by far the most jobs. In

Germany and Spain, where job loss has been less severe, the coal industry has been sustained by substantial subsidies, and there are fears that a reduction in these (encouraged perhaps by EC efforts to promote an internal energy market) will lead to a UK-style contraction. Mining employment continues to fall throughout the EC. In the UK, for example, there are widespread fears that the industry will be reduced to a residual rump of 10 or 12 pits and perhaps 10,000 men by the mid-1990s.

Table 13.1 Employment in the EC coal industry

	1977	1984	1988	1992
Belgium	22,100	19,000	7,100	0
France	72,700	48,900	27,900	20,000
Germany	191,900	169,100	147,700	120,000
Spain	n.a.	48,700	44,200	41,000
UK	292,300	217,500	108,900	58,000
TOTAL*	n.a.	504,400	336,800	240,000

* includes very small numbers in other EC states
Sources: Eurostat, EUR-ACOM

Coalfield local authorities argued that in responding to job losses their areas are handicapped by the legacy of the coal industry:

- Mining areas tend to be dominated by the coal industry and lack a diverse economic base, especially in the service sector.

- Mining areas tend to be divided into large numbers of relatively small and dispersed communities.

- Mining settlements are often isolated from the wider economy and suffer from inadequate roads, housing and community facilities.

- The areas are liable to mining subsidence and have had their environments severely damaged by mining.

- The skills developed in mining do not easily transfer to other industries.

- Young people tend to leave in search of work, leaving behind an older, less skilled and less healthy population.

- Mining areas, in common with other areas dominated by a single large employer, lack an entrepreneurial tradition and tend to have few indigenous small and medium-sized enterprises.

- Mining areas tend to suffer from a bad image which deters inward private sector investment.

Through EUR-ACOM, local authorities therefore argued for a programme of EC aid to focus on the specific problems of coalmining areas. The programme was to be additional to existing EC aid. Proposals to this effect were drafted by the CCC, on behalf of EUR-ACOM, and submitted to the European Commission towards the end of 1988.

An EC-wide alliance of local authorities now had an agreed set of objectives on which to focus its efforts. Luck now played its part. In January 1989 Bruce Millan, a former UK Labour MP, took over as Commissioner with responsibility for regional policy. Whilst Commissioner Millan had previously represented a shipbuilding constituency, he was well aware of the problems of coal areas. At an early stage his attention was drawn to the EUR-ACOM proposals, and he asked his officials to investigate the possibility of such a programme.

From this point onwards progress was rapid. Draft proposals for a programme, now called RECHAR, were debated within the Commission and in European Parliament, which expressed its support. The UK government, which had described its position as 'positively neutral' when the proposals were first mooted, swung to a position of enthusiastic support when it realised that such a programme was a real possibility and that the UK would be the largest beneficiary. The discussions culminated in the formal approval of the programme by the Commission in December 1989. As a Community Initiative within the terms of the reformed Structural Funds, RECHAR did not require the approval of the Council of Ministers and it was never raised in this forum.

Scope and Objectives

To understand the RECHAR programme it is first necessary to explain where it fits into the activities of the European Community.

The EC completed a major reform of its Structural Funds during 1988. Under the new arrangements, intended to operate for five years in the first instance, at least 85% of the EC's main budget for regional aid (the European Regional Development Fund) is spent through mainstream spending programmes. These are the 'operational programmes' drawn up by member states to cover the EC's designated assisted areas, and the national allocation of these funds is determined by negotiation at inter-governmental level. The remaining 15% can be spent on Community Initiatives. These are programmes which the Commission itself decides to establish. They may be targeted at particular types of area (e.g. coalfields) or at particular activities (e.g. technology transfer).

Overlain on this 85/15 split is a second split. Objective 1 regions – Europe's least developed regions, mainly in the Mediterranean countries – receive 80% of the total aid, and Objective 2 regions – older industrial regions experiencing restructuring, mainly in Northern Europe – the remaining 20%. This 80/20 split applies to mainstream operational programmes and to Community Initiatives in total, though each individual Community Initiative need not adopt an 80/20 split.

Outside Spain, most coalfield areas are in Objective 2 regions. RECHAR therefore draws mainly on Objective 2 regions' 20% share of the 15% share of EC regional aid that is reserved for Community Initiatives – i.e. 3% of the total kitty. RECHAR had to be accommodated alongside competing claims for this modest sum, though this does not detract from the fact that it is the largest single programme of, in effect, discretionary spending in Europe's older industrial regions.

Whilst RECHAR is the first of the new Community Initiatives it does have parallels in earlier programmes. In particular, the RESIDER and RENAVAL programmes provide assistance to steel and shipbuilding areas respectively and both pre-date the reform. There are important differences however. Both RESIDER and RENAVAL were introduced as integral parts of EC-led moves to reduce steel and shipbuilding capacity. RECHAR is different in that it is not linked to a programme of rationalisation; rather, its purpose is to compensate for the damage that has already been done to local economies in coal areas. Indeed, local authority support for RECHAR was only forthcoming on the condition that the programme was not linked to an EC-sponsored round of colliery closures. Commissioner Millan and his regional policy directorate (DG XVI) shared the local authority view, though some officials within the energy directorate (DG XVII) favoured linkage to further closures.

RECHAR draws on several EC funds, as was the intention for initiatives launched after the reform. The largest contributor is the European Regional Development Fund (ERDF), reflecting the primary nature of the programme as an economic development initiative. The European Social Fund (ESF) is also making a contribution, mainly towards training measures. The initial allocation from the ERDF and ESF was set at 300m ecu, with a commitment to revise the figure upwards to allow for inflation and additional colliery closures. The exact division between the two funds is determined by the composition of each Member State's plans. ERDF and ESF assistance takes the form of grants – up to 50% of the cost of a project in Objective 2 areas and 65% in Objective 1. The ERDF and ESF contributions cover a four-year period (1990 to 1993 inclusive).

In addition the European Coal and Steel Community (ECSC) is making extra funds available as 'readaptation aids' on a year-by-year basis. 40m ecu of grants was set aside for this purpose for 1990, and 50m ecu in 1991. Readaptation aids include finance for the retraining of redundant miners and for early retirement schemes.

Finally, the Commission agreed to make extra loans available to businesses and local authorities in coal areas to help finance job creation projects. These loans are available at a preferential rate of interest, subsidised by the ECSC. The volume of the loans depends principally on demand, but is expected to exceed 500m ecu over the period of the programme.

The Commission chose to allocate the ERDF and ESF grants in proportion to the number of coalmining jobs lost between January 1984 and December 1990 in the areas eligible for RECHAR. An additional allocation was made for planned job losses, though given the political sensitivity of future redundancies neither the Spanish or UK government was willing to submit details of manpower reductions other than those already announced. Overall, the allocation worked out at approximately 1000 ecu per job lost.

The resulting national allocations were roughly:

United Kingdom	45%
Germany	24%
France	16%
Belgium	8%
Spain	6%
Portugal	1%

At the local or regional scale, the allocation of funds has similarly been guided by job losses during the relevant period. In the UK, for example, the country is divided into eleven operational programme areas for RECHAR purposes. Each of these submitted proposals to the Commission outlining the priorities for development and explaining the use to be made of RECHAR funds. Reflecting the pattern of job loss, the operational programmes for South Yorkshire, the East Midlands and South Wales received the largest financial allocation.

The measures defined by the Commission as eligible for RECHAR grants are:

- environmental improvement
- renovation and modernisation of social and economic infrastructure
- construction of new advance factory units and workshops
- promotion of alternative economic activities, especially small and medium-sized enterprises
- promotion of tourism
- assisting the creation or increased activity of economic conversion bodies
- vocational training
- assistance for the retraining of ex-mineworkers.

Interest rebates on ECSC loans are available for investments in small and medium-sized enterprises and for the reclamation of sites for industrial use. Other loans are available for 'any other measure which contributes to the economic conversion of the area concerned'.

An Assessment

Irrespective of practical problems in disentangling the impact of RECHAR from other events and from other EC aid, it is too early to arrive at a quantitative evaluation. Although RECHAR was agreed in principle at the end of 1989, the operational programmes for Belgium, France, Germany and Spain only received approval in the spring of 1991, and the UK in February 1992. It is nevertheless possible to arrive at an informed assessment of the programme's value under a number of headings.

Eligible areas

In order to qualify for RECHAR an area must have lost (or be anticipated to lose) at least 1000 coalmining jobs since 1 January 1984. It must also fall within an Objective 1, 2 or 5b region as defined for the purpose of EC regional aid. In the majority of coal areas neither of these hurdles is a problem: there has usually been sufficient job loss, and most coal areas in Northern Europe already had Objective 2 status. But the effect of the hurdles has been to exclude a number of coalfields whose sense of injustice at being left out is highlighted by the knowledge that so many others have been included. Three problems can be identified.

First, the EC defines its map of Objective 1, 2 and 5b regions on the basis of relatively large building blocks such as travel-to-work areas (TTWAs). Each of these must meet a number of statistical criteria, including unemployment rates. This is a problem because in several cases there are relatively self-contained mining villages that for statistical purposes fall within larger and more prosperous units. A good example is the mining area within Leeds district in the UK, which comprises an isolated corner of the much larger Leeds TTWA. Lack of Objective 2 status has prevented such areas from receiving RECHAR aid.

In fairness to Commission officials, they were aware of the problem. The Commission extended the Objective 2 map to cover a small group of extra areas, despite the fact that the map was only a year old. Areas that benefit from this extension include Midlothian and Ashfield in the UK, where it was recognised that labour market conditions in the cities of Edinburgh and Nottingham did not reflect circumstances in the neighbouring mining settlements. But significant areas of coalfield decline continue to be omitted because of lack of Objective 2 status. In the UK these include parts of Leeds, southern Nottinghamshire, South Derbyshire, North West Leicestershire, North Staffordshire and Kent.

The second problem concerns the job loss hurdle. As noted earlier, employment in the Spanish coal industry has been propped up by subsidies yet the economic situation in some Spanish mining areas is exceedingly precarious: the coal is the most expensive in Europe, there is already high unemployment, and there is very little other industry. If a hard line had been adopted, few Spanish mining areas would have leapt the job loss hurdle to qualify for RECHAR. To its credit, the Commission again responded with flexibility. The map of RECHAR eligible areas within Spain is probably the cartographical equivalent of creative accountancy, but the outcome is broadly what all the participants had always intended. Nevertheless there remain some omissions, for example in Andalucia.

The third problem concerns the cut-off date for qualifying job losses – 1 January 1984. This was a compromise between those who favoured a programme to pave the way for new closures (and therefore a recent cut-off date with emphasis on anticipated losses) and those who wanted a longer perspective on coalfield decline. Some local authorities, for example, argued that it takes fifteen years or more to recover from the demise of a dominant employer such as coal. Whilst the compromise date ensured that all the post-strike job losses in the UK were included, it excluded some areas where the last mines closed prior to 1984. Few of these areas have recovered totally, and some continue to experience very high levels of unemployment. In Belgium, for example, most of the southern coalfield around Liege is ineligible because of the cut-off date.

Spending

The spending needs of an area is clearly something of an elastic concept. All areas – even the most prosperous – can usually put forward a case for extra resources. As a rule-of-thumb, nevertheless, it is worth comparing the resources allocated to RECHAR with the expenditure that in an ideal world might be allocated to coalfield regeneration.

Table 13.2 presents tentative figures. The numbers of projects required (or area of land, places on courses, etc.) are based on local authorities' own assessment, and the unit cost of schemes reflects typical levels across the EC. Necessarily, all the figures are estimates, but they do give an indication of the scale of funds required to make serious inroads into the development problems of EC coal areas.

The most important point to emerge is just how little can be achieved with even quite large sums. Economic regeneration is not a cheap process. To reclaim derelict land for 'soft' after-use (i.e. landscaping or agriculture) might cost 450m ecu. To reclaim a modest proportion for 'hard' after-use, such as new industry, might cost an additional 560m ecu. Just 150 km of new roads, such as by-passes and links to motorways, might gobble up 300m ecu. In total, the items listed in Table 13.2 come to a sum of just under 4000m ecu. For comparison, the ERDF and ESF grants allocated under RECHAR total just over 300m ecu.

The EC cannot be expected to foot the whole of the bill for the reconversion of mining areas. Even if it were to co-finance all of the measures listed in Table 13.2, its contribution under present rules could be no more than 50% in most areas. The point is simply that RECHAR by itself falls well short of the scale of funding required. Unless substantial funds are also forthcoming from other participants in the regeneration process – particularly national and local government – a real solution to the problems of coal areas is unlikely.

Table 13.2 Reconversion expenditures required in EC coal areas

		million ecu
1.	Environment	
	30,000 hectares of derelict land for landscaping, recreational use at 15,000 ecu per hectare	450
	4000 hectares of derelict land for reclamation for industry, housing etc. at 140,000 ecu per hectare	560
2.	Transport infrastructure 150 km of new roads (e.g. by-passes, links to motorways) at 2m ecu per km	300
	500 km of reconstructed roads at 700,000 ecu per km	350
	Miscellaneous capital investment in public transport	50
3.	Factories and industrial land 10,000 hectares of serviced industrial land (sufficient for c.100,000 jobs) at 30,000 ecu per hectare	300
	1m sq. metres of publicly-provided factory and workshop space (sufficient for c.20,000 jobs) at 400 ecu per sq metre	400
4.	Business support 10 regional innovation and technology transfer centres at 3m ecu each	30
	50 local enterprise centres at 1m ecu each	50
	Aid to SMEs for marketing, product development, business development 10,000 grants at 10,000 ecu each	100
5.	Training 30,000 adults to undertake pre-training courses at 3000 ecu per head	90
	30,000 ex-miners to be retrained to craft standard at 5000 ecu per head	150
	30,000 unemployed to be trained to craft standard at 5000 ecu per head	150
6.	Tourism	
	5 major projects of national significance at 15m ecu each	75
	30 image-building advertising campaigns at 500,000 ecu each	15
7.	Housing	
	100,000 former coal company houses to be brought up to modern standards at 5000 ecu per dwelling	500
	Miscellaneous improvements to residential environments (e.g. new utilities, planting)	100
8.	Social infrastructure	
	Refurbishment of social facilities (e.g. halls, clubs, schools, sports facilities) formerly belonging to coal companies 100 projects at 500,000 ecu each	50

Source: EUR-ACOM

Eligible measures

The list of measures eligible for aid is in fact remarkably similar to that originally proposed by coalfield local authorities through EUR-ACOM. Furthermore, like other EC regional aid, there is considerable flexibility in the RECHAR package. The mix of measures to be implemented in each coalfield is not dictated by Brussels but determined mainly by the operational programmes put forward by local and regional authorities. This is important. In Spain, for example, the dominant requirement is for basic infrastructure: the mining valleys of Asturias and Leon are remote from the main transport network and have no hope of attracting new industry without investment in new roads. In Germany and Belgium the basic infrastructure is mostly in place and the greater need is for training and business support.

If criticism can be levelled at RECHAR it concerns the overall balance of the package. As a programme initiated from within DG XVI, RECHAR is primarily an economic development programme drawing on the ERDF. The social dimension of renewal in coal areas – pre-training, vocational training and social infrastructure – is a secondary concern.

In particular, there is a continuing failure to target ESF training grants spent under Objectives 3 and 4 (aid to the long-term unemployed and young unemployed) at priority areas such as the coalfields. Unlike the modest ESF funds devoted to Objective 2, the larger amounts spent under Objectives 3 and 4 are disbursed widely across all parts of the European Community. Some schemes in coal areas benefit from aid under this heading, but so do schemes in relatively prosperous regions. There is also concern that because of the untargeted nature of this aid it is easily absorbed into national government budgets and it becomes harder to identify additional schemes on the ground.

Questions must also be raised about the role of the European Coal and Steel Community. Established as far back as 1952, the ECSC was framed in an era when the steel and coal industries employed many more people. The ECSC has functioned primarily as a source of grants and loans to steel and coal companies. In recent years it has also provided some assistance to alternative employers in steel and coal areas. RECHAR has taken this shift in emphasis a step further, but arguably not far enough. Now that the coal and steel industries are so much smaller, the ECSC ought to be redefined as a provider of aid for economic regeneration in the areas abandoned by the industries' contraction. The ECSC has a finite life, since the treaty provisions expire in 2002. Potentially, it could have a major and positive role in mining communities during its closing years.

Implementation

The concept of 'partnership' – between the Commission, member states and local authorities – is central to the way in which the reformed Structural Funds are supposed to operate. RECHAR is no exception. If partnership worked well it ought to provide a framework within which EC contributions could be matched by local contributions, and the details of operational programmes could be worked out to the satisfaction of all concerned. To date, the experience has been less happy.

In France, local authorities (communes) in the mining areas have largely been by-passed in the development of RECHAR programmes. The French national government and the reconversion company SOFIREM, which belongs to the state-owned mining company, have been the dominant influences. Partly the problem is one of size. Most communes are very small, which raises difficulties of coordination and resources, though they are the tier of government which most clearly represents the mining areas themselves.

In Spain there has been a similar problem arising from the small size of municipios, the local town councils. In planning the implementation of RECHAR, the Spanish provincial governments have overshadowed their smaller partners.

The failure to achieve partnership is most acute in the UK. Here the problem is not a failure to consult in the preparation of plans: a dialogue between local authorities and the regional offices of central government is well established on European matters. The problem has been an unwillingness to listen. Central government acts as secretariat to the committees that draw up the RECHAR programme, and has final responsibility for submission of the plans. At times it has ruthlessly exploited this privileged position. The aim of the UK government has been to keep the RECHAR programmes as vague as possible, so as to avoid commitments to specific extra projects and, ultimately, to use RECHAR monies as a reimbursement for their own previously planned spending. In general, the more closely the UK government has controlled the drafting, the woollier the proposals and the less acceptable the result to local authorities and the Commission.

Additionality

At the heart of the difficulties in the UK is a dispute over what is known as 'additionality'. Although the UK is an extreme case, additionality is an issue relevant to all regional aid in all EC Member States.

Put simply, additionality occurs where extra money leads to extra spending in the places that are being assisted. The 'additionality problem' is one of ensuring that aid from Brussels, such as RECHAR, is not used as a refund for existing spending or as a substitute spending by national or local government, resulting in no extra activity on the ground.

In all EC states additionality is a question of goodwill and intent as much as detailed regulation. When the Structural Funds were reformed and increased, all Member States signed an agreement to the effect that the additional funds would lead to additional actions. In the regulations covering RECHAR there is also an explicit requirement to demonstrate additionality. In Belgium and Germany there is no problem in achieving genuine additionality because procedures ensure that RECHAR can only be used to finance extra actions. In France and Spain there is also by and large no problem, though the leading roles of central and regional government mean that the financial arrangements are not so transparent.

The UK was quite different: a system of central government financial controls on local authority spending ensured almost total non-additionality. In effect, the RECHAR grants were worthless to coalfield authorities because they could not be used to finance extra projects. Not only RECHAR fell foul of these restrictions: all ERDF aid targeted at UK local authorities – in excess of £1 billion between 1989 and 1993 – was caught in this trap.

The European Commission and UK coalfield authorities were naturally distressed by the way RECHAR money was to be treated, particularly as the UK was set to be the largest recipient. Not surprisingly, RECHAR became the test case over which the European Commission decided to challenge the UK government's failure to adhere to the additionality principle. In April 1991, the Commission decided to withhold the UK's share of RECHAR, pending satisfactory new arrangements. The same threat was later extended to all ERDF payments due to the UK. Politically isolated, the subject of unfavourable publicity, and with a general election looming, the UK government conceded in February 1992. All RECHAR grants could in future be spent on additional projects, and from 1993 onwards the same arrangements would also apply to all other ERDF grants.

The significance of this policy change should not be understated. It represents a sea-change in the UK government's approach. The impact and effectiveness of EC regional aid had previously been undermined by the UK government's actions; henceforward, EC regional aid takes its proper place alongside the UK's own urban and regional policies. RECHAR was the programme that precipitated the new approach. Since the UK is the largest beneficiary not only from RECHAR but also from the EC's fund for Objective 2 areas, the impact is considerable.

Conclusion

So has the RECHAR programme proved to be a worthwhile initiative?

At a practical level, RECHAR is undoubtedly accelerating the economic, social and environmental renewal of coal areas, especially now that the additionality problem in the UK appears to have been resolved. RECHAR is enabling progress in improving infrastructure and skills for modern development. Many projects are superficially mundane – the construction of access roads to new industrial sites for example – but in that respect they are no different to many essential tasks of economic development.

Still at a practical level, RECHAR demonstrates a sensible pragmatism in the way that the Commission approaches regional policy. The Commission recognised that coal areas face severe and distinctive problems, over and above those found in other older industrial areas. There is a lot in the detailed design of the programme – the eligible measures, and the flexibility to determine local priorities – that makes sense. And where partnership in implementation has broken down, the blame generally lies elsewhere than with the Commission. The UK posed special problems over additionality, and to its credit the Commission did not shy away from tackling these. All this augers well for the EC's growing role as the largest provider of funds for regional development.

At a political level, RECHAR has also been a success. In coal areas across the EC, RECHAR is widely perceived as a response to a call for help in tackling problems that local resources alone could not solve. It has shown that the Commission need not be a remote and unresponsive bureaucracy and, more generally, has kindled enthusiasm for the wider project of cooperation on which the European Community is engaged. This shift of attitude is greatest in the UK, where the long-running dispute over additionality, focusing on RECHAR, cast the Commission as the virtuous challenger to the UK government's sharp practice.

But if the RECHAR programme is to be criticised it is in the scale and duration of funding. A four-year programme with a modest budget is insufficient to arrest and reverse the economic decline that has been occurring in so many of Europe's coalmining areas for so long. Some coalfields – South Wales and North East England for example – have received regional aid in one form or another continuously for nearly fifty years but still have unemployment well above the national and EC average. Moreover, coalfield regeneration is a moving target: as new jobs are created, further mines close creating fresh unemployment. As noted earlier, the EC's coal industry has already shed nearly 100,000 jobs since the RECHAR programme was first conceived, and further losses seem inevitable.

It is not clear that the Commission has yet learned that regional aid must be substantial and sustained if it is to be genuinely effective. The European Community has been going through a period of rapid evolution, which has fostered a preoccupation with new structures, new initiatives and wider powers. By comparison, activities that are already up and running, such as RECHAR, tend to lose their glamour. The real test of Brussels' commitment to the regeneration of coalmining areas, and perhaps the seriousness of its whole approach to regional development, will come as the present RECHAR programme draws to an end during 1993. Will RECHAR be renewed, or will it be shelved? If the Commission wants to have more than a fleeting impact on Europe's coalfields, a second phase of the programme will undoubtedly be necessary.

Part Three

The Transformation Process in Eastern and Central Europe

CHAPTER 14

Spatial Inequality in Gorbachev's Era

Gennady I. Ozornoy

Introduction

The year 1991 enters history as the year when the USSR, the major multi-ethnic communist state, ceased to exist. Its sudden and largely unexpected implosion has created a growing sense of uneasiness, insecurity and perplexity in the international community. Both politicians and analysts in the West seem to be perplexed most by an apparent irrationality in the replacement of established political-administrative units by a score of new states, often of questionable viability. Evidently, the West finds it difficult to come to grips with a wave of nation-states formation because an image of nationalism as a basically irrational and anachronistic movement still prevails in the Western mentality.

But there is a logic to the breakdown of the Soviet Union and, more generally, of all multi-ethnic Soviet-type societies (e.g. Czechoslovakia, Yugoslavia). Its understanding requires not only an analysis of the general factors responsible for the persistence and periodic resurgence of nationalism throughout the twentieth century (Gellner 1983, 1990, Hobsbaum 1990), but also a close examination of the reasons for the rise of nationalism and separatism specific to Soviet-type societies. In the case of Gorbachev's USSR, such an analysis pre-supposes a probing into the role played in these processes by the outcomes of the Soviet policy response to the problems of unequal development and spatial inequality.

This chapter examines the issues of inter-republican disparities in the levels of economic development in the former Soviet Union on the eve of its collapse. It begins with an overview of the major findings by the earlier salient Western studies of the outcome of Soviet regional policies, and proceeds with an analysis of recent evidence of inter-republican disparities in levels of economic development. The following section focuses on the institutional policies and levers available for the reduction of spatial economic inequality within a highly centralised system of management. The final section examines evidence of inter-republican economic relations and trade balances, as well as developments related to the failed attempt by Gorbachev to prevent the disintegration of the USSR's national-economic complex or to reform the entire economic and financial framework of spatial and nationality policies.

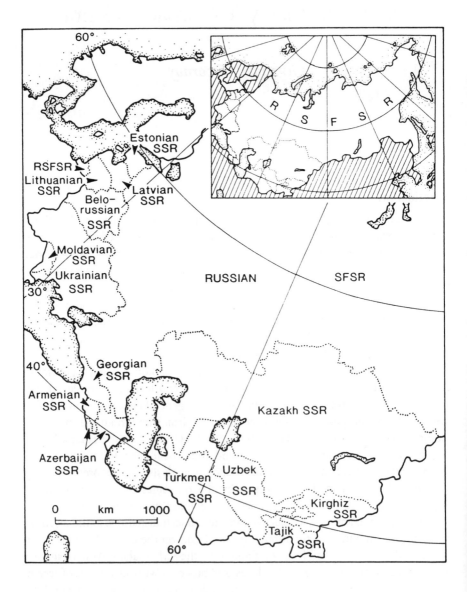

Spatial Inequality in Levels of Economic Development

For most of the Soviet period, official policy statements have declared the objective, *inter alia*, to be to even out levels of economic development and equalise living standards among the USSR's diverse nationalities and regions. Consequently, Soviet economic planning has attempted to reconcile the salient spatial discrepancies between the distribution of resources, population and economic activities across 15 constituent republics (see Figure 14.1 and Table 14.1).[1] Yet, the issues of spatial inequality have always remained of secondary importance, and the primary focus has been on overall economic development, with most planning conducted on a sectoral basis. Decision-making powers have been vested, until very recently, with the central authorities in Moscow; the regional sections in the

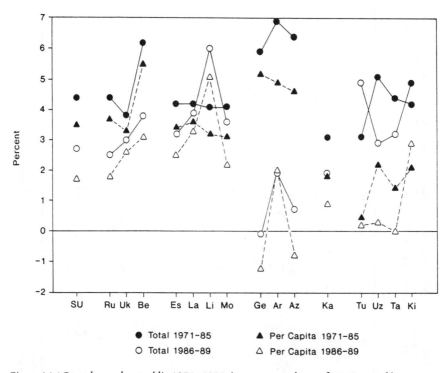

Figure 14.1 Growth rates by republic 1971–1989 (average annual rate of NMP growth)

---

1   In recognition of national differences, the former USSR was divided administratively into 15 union republics, each associated with one of the larger Soviet nationalities. As seen from Table 14.1, these republics differed in area, population and economic activities. For instance, in 1989 over 60% of net material product was generated in the RSFSR alone, with another 20% originating in the Ukraine and Belorussia. In industry and agriculture, these republics together accounted for 85.1% and 73.3% of total value added, respectively.

Table 14.1. USSR: basic characteristics and indicators, by republic, 1989

	Territory[1]	Population	Percentage urban	Fixed assets	Net material product (NMP) (as percentage of total NMP by sector)				
					Total	Industry	Agriculture	Construction	Transport/Communication
USSR	100.0	100.0	66	100.0	100.0	100.0	100.0	100.0	100.0
Slavic									
RSFSR	76.2	51.3	74	61.8	61.1	63.7	50.3	62.5	65.6
Ukraine	2.7	18.0	67	15.2	16.2	17.2	17.9	13.5	13.8
Belorussia	0.9	3.6	66	3.4	4.2	4.2	5.1	3.4	2.9
Baltic/Moldavia									
Estonia	0.2	0.5	72	0.7	0.6	0.7	0.7	0.6	0.7
Latvia	0.3	0.9	71	1.1	1.1	1.1	1.3	0.8	1.4
Lithuania	0.3	1.3	68	1.4	1.4	1.1	2.0	1.5	1.1
Moldavia	0.2	1.5	47	1.1	1.2	1.1	1.9	0.9	0.8
Caucasus									
Georgia	0.3	1.9	56	1.4	1.6	1.5	2.1	1.6	1.0
Armenia	0.1	1.1	68	0.8	0.9	1.2	0.7	0.8	0.6
Azerbaijan	0.4	2.5	54	1.5	1.7	1.7	2.3	1.8	0.9
Kazakhstan									
Kazakhstan	12.1	5.8	57	5.9	4.3	2.5	6.4	6.0	6.7
Central Asia									
Turkmenistan	2.2	1.3	45	1.0	0.8	0.5	1.3	1.2	0.8
Uzbekistan	2.0	7.0	41	3.3	3.3	2.4	5.5	3.8	2.7
Tadzhikistan	0.6	1.8	32	0.7	0.8	0.6	1.3	0.9	0.5
Kirgizia	0.9	1.5	38	0.7	0.8	0.6	1.4	0.8	0.5
Composition by regions									
Slavic	79.8	72.9	73	80.4	81.5	85.1	73.3	79.4	82.3
Baltic/Moldavia	1.0	4.2	62	4.3	4.3	4.0	5.9	3.8	4.0
Caucasus	0.8	5.5	56	3.7	4.2	4.4	5.1	4.2	2.5
Kazakhstan	12.1	5.8	57	5.9	4.3	4.4	6.4	6.0	6.7
Central Asia	5.7	11.6	40	5.7	5.7	4.1	9.5	6.7	4.5

Source: Goskomstat SSSR (1990a, p.17, pp.19–24)
[1] USSR territory includes 127,000 square kilometres for the White Sea and the Sea of Azov, not included in the area of individual republics.

five-year and annual plans were traditionally mere summaries of sectoral developments compiled by republics and economic regions. Moreover, since the early 1970s, the Soviet leadership has not explicitly addressed the theme of reducing regional economic disparities, even though central planners have continued to effect differential economic growth through investment allocations among republics (Ozornoy 1991a).

The outcome of Soviet policies in the reduction of inter-republican differences in levels of economic development has been widely discussed by Western sovietologists. It is generally agreed that considerable progress was made in the pre-war and early post-war years in reducing the immense spatial economic inequality that had existed when the USSR was formed. Most studies dealing with more recent periods conclude, however, that since the late 1950s little more has been accomplished to reduce inter-republican differences in levels of economic development.[2] Indeed, in the decade of the 1960s, per capita investment was no higher in the republics with the lowest per capita income than in the more-developed ones (Whitehouse 1972).[3] Furthermore, although during the 1960–75 period industrial output grew at higher rates in historically less developed republics (Central Asia, Transcaucasus) than the national average, this did not reduce the regional disparities in output per capita, because of the high birth rates in those same republics (Ozornoy 1985). A similar conclusion is indicated by examination of inter-republican disparities in such measures of living standards as income and consumption per capita for the same period (McAuley 1979, pp.303–10). These findings suggest that by the mid-1970s, Soviet regional policies had not equalised levels of economic development between the union republics.[4]

A general loosening of control over information since the mid-1980s resulted both in the updating of the evidence of the development gap among union republics and important statistics on the outcomes of decisions concerning spatial resource allocations made in, and enforced by, Moscow since the early 1970s. This also provided valuable insights into the realities of a republic's role in determining its own economic destiny. Initially, these revelations were followed by increased demand by the republics and regions for greater decentralisation in economic decision-making, but later they became associated with growing nationalism and separatism among various titular ethnic groups, and finally led to the collapse of

---

2   The various Western studies are summarised in Schiffer (1989, pp.233–41).
3   That two southern republics, Kazakhstan and Turkmenistan, did receive higher than average
    investment per capita is attributed primarily to the development of mineral and fuel deposits
    in those republics.
4   The development gap among union republics may be shown to have grown. In general,
    however, conclusions regarding the direction of change in inter-republican disparities have
    depended not only on the methodology and measures applied but also on an understanding
    of the systematic biases of Soviet statistics (Bahry and Nechemias 1981, Ozornoy 1985, Ch.
    II).

the USSR. Recent evidence on these inter-regional disparities in levels of economic development is presented and commented on below.

Table 14.2 USSR: per capita net output (NMP) by sector by republic, 1989 (USSR = 100)

	Total	Industry	Agriculture	Construction	Transport/ Communication	Other
USSR	100	100	100	100	100	100
RSFSR	119	124	98	122	128	130
Ukraine	90	95	99	75	77	80
Belorussia	117	117	144	96	82	107
Estonia	117	121	124	101	125	107
Latvia	119	123	134	85	146	103
Lithuania	110	89	152	118	87	108
Moldavia	81	70	126	56	50	77
Georgia	86	79	113	86	54	76
Armenia	80	102	65	67	54	61
Azerbaijan	70	69	94	74	37	50
Kazakhstan	74	44	111	104	117	61
Turkmenistan	61	37	104	97	62	33
Uzbekistan	47	35	79	55	39	34
Tadzhikistan	43	31	70	50	27	34
Kirgizia	53	42	91	54	32	33

Source: Goskomstat SSSR (1990d, pp.34–9)
Population at beginning of 1989 from: Goskomstat SSSR (1990a, p.17)

The Soviet official measure of economic development – net material product per capita (NMP) – discloses sizeable differences in the relative levels between republics (Table 14.2).[5] According to this measure, in 1989 inter-regional disparities in aggregate NMP per capita ranged from 43% of the Union average in Tadzhikistan to 119% in both the Russian Federation (the RSFSR) and Lithuania. In the southern tier of the USSR, six out of eight union republics had development levels that were measured at two-thirds or less than that of the RSFSR. On a per capita basis, the RSFSR, Belorussia and the Baltic republics are considerably more advanced and the Central Asian republics considerably less advanced than the rest.

---

5   Unlike the national accounts for most countries prepared according to the UN System of National Accounts, Soviet national accounts are prepared in accordance with the System of Balances of the National Economy that exclude depreciation and the output of most so-called non-material services (banking and insurance, medical care, education, scientific research, housing, and government services). This means that levels of output implied by traditional Soviet indicators such as national income produced (also referred to as net material product or NMP) understate the true level of economic activity.

Industrial net output per capita in the RSFSR, Estonia, Latvia and Belorussia is three to four times that in Central Asia. The leading agricultural producers on a per capita basis are Lithuania and Belorussia, followed by Latvia, Moldavia and Estonia. Despite their agricultural focus, Uzbekistan and Tadzhikistan trail all other republics except Armenia in agricultural value added per capita.

From 1970 to 1985, development gaps relative to the RSFSR and Baltic republics narrowed considerably for the Transcaucasian republics and Belorussia, but widened for Central Asia (Figure 14.1).[6] In the period 1986–89, NMP per capita grew more rapidly in the Baltic republics, the Ukraine and Belorussia than in Kazakhstan, Uzbekistan, Tadzhikistan, Azerbaijan, and Georgia. Reflecting their high birth rate, however, the Central Asian republics matched or exceeded the all-union pace in aggregate NMP growth for the same period.

Other crucial evidence on relative levels of development is provided by data on the extent of urbanisation, the proportion of industrial/construction and agricultural sectors in total employment, and the proportion of and growth rates of fixed productive assets by republics. The Central Asian republics and Azerbaijan consistently ranked far below the RSFSR, the Ukraine, Belorussia and the Baltic republics. The highest proportions of urbanised population occurred in the RSFSR, Estonia and Latvia, where they ranged from 71% to 74% (Table 14.1). Urbanisation is one of the areas in which Soviet modernisation failed to meet its objective of homogenising peoples and areas. In four Southern-belt republics, the urbanisation gap, relative to the USSR average, is wider today than in 1926 (Azerbaijan, Georgia, Uzbekistan, Tadzhikistan), while some have come only a little closer to the average (the Ukraine, Belorussia, Kazakhstan, Kirgisia, Turkmenia).[7]

---

6   In the absence of market prices, one should be aware of well-known and serious distortions related to the use of the official Soviet measure of value added – net material product (NMP) – in analysing inter-republican productivity differentials. The republican value added figures are easily distorted by domestic pricing decisions and changes in the allocations of turnover taxes (Nove 1986, Ch. 12, Ozornoy 1985, Ch. II). However, the general productivity differentials seem to be confirmed by commodity breakdowns disaggregated by republics (Goskomstat SSSR 1990a, 17, pp.338–41). Recent (1989) Soviet data on the republican shares in output of the 'most important industrial products' show that the share of a Central Asian republic in Soviet industrial output rarely exceeds its population share and is usually considerably less, while the RSFSR and the Ukraine typically have more than proportionate shares, especially in heavy industries. Belorussia stands out as an important producer (over 10% of the Soviet total, or roughly three times its population share) of electric motors, dairy equipment, fertiliser, synthetic fibres, and an assortment of consumer durables. The Baltic republics, and to a lesser extent Moldavia, are major producers, on a per capita basis, in light industry, food-processing, building materials, paper (except Moldavia), and certain machines and consumer durables. The Transcaucasian republics and Kazakhstan stand in between Central Asian and European republics, with their relative emphasis on light industry, machine building and (in the case of Kazakhstan) bulk heavy industry and building materials.

7   The results of the 1926 census are given in Kozlov (1982, p.100).

The high proportion of the labour force engaged in industry and construction ranged from 39% in Armenia to 42% in the RSFSR and Estonia. In Central Asia, Azerbaijan and Moldavia the corresponding figures were 21–28%, the share of agriculture was more than one-third of the total. In Tadzhikistan and Turkmenia it exceeded 40% (Figure 14.2).

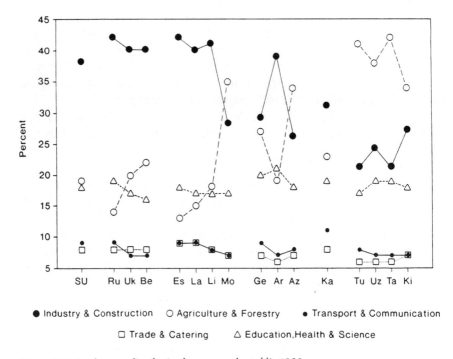

● Industry & Construction   ○ Agriculture & Forestry   • Transport & Communication
□ Trade & Catering   △ Education,Health & Science

Figure 14.2 Employment distribution by sector and republic 1989

Considerable variations can be observed, also, in the employment status of the labour force across republics (Table 14.3). In 1988, state enterprises and collective farms employed 72–80% and 5–12%, respectively, of the total labour resources in the Slavic and Baltic republics, as compared with 52–62% and 9–19% in the Central Asian republics. At the same time, only 1–3% of the labour force in the former republics was engaged primarily in private activity versus 9–14% in the latter ones. Labour force participation rates are lower in the southern tier republics (except Georgia), than in the European part of the USSR. This reflects not only the greater share of students and draftees in the population, but also cultural pressures on women in the southern republics to stay at home and raise large families (Lubin 1984, Pankratova 1990). Recent official Soviet statistics reveal pronounced inter-republican and ethnic differentials in labour force participation between Muslim and non-Muslim women. Thus, in 1989 the proportion of women among workers and employees ranged from 52% to 55% in the republics of the European USSR versus 39–49% in the predominantly Muslim areas. These differences were only partly offset by the higher percentage – from 43% to 55%– of Muslim women among those employed in collective farms (Goskomstat SSSR 1990a, 1991b). The lower official participation rates in the southern republics may also reflect a greater proclivity on the part of their nationals to engage in various aspects of the informal sector and black market (Grossman 1989, Muk-omel' 1990).

Table 14.3 USSR: labour force by employment status
by republic, 1988 (percentage of total for republic)

Republic	Total labour resources	Employed total	Employed in:				
			State enterprises	Collective farms	Private activity	Students	Other[1]
USSR	100	85	75	7	3	7	8
RSFSR	100	86	80	5	2	7	7
Ukraine	100	86	72	12	2	7	7
Belorussia	100	87	74	11	1	7	6
Estonia	100	85	76	8	2	7	8
Latvia	100	87	76	9	2	7	7
Lithuania	100	86	73	10	2	8	7
Moldavia	100	87	67	13	7	7	6
Georgia	100	88	74	8	6	7	5
Armenia	100	81	70	3	8	8	12
Azervaijan	100	81	56	8	6	8	22
Kazakhstan	100	70	75	3	3	8	11
Turkmenistan	100	82	52	19	11	9	9
Uzbekistan	100	76	55	11	11	10	14
Tadzhikistan	100	77	53	11	14	10	13
Kirghizia	100	80	62	9	9	10	11

Source: Goskomstat SSSR (1989b, p.30)
[1] Includes housewives, soldiers, religious functionaries and the unemployed

The employment figures in Table 14.3 miss, however, marked inter-republican differences in the recent explosion of cooperative establishments producing goods and services. Data show that over the 1987–1990 period, an additional 3.2% of the labour force shifted its primary employment status to that of cooperative employee (Goskomstat SSSR 1991a, 97). Latvia, Armenia and Georgia stood out as centres of cooperative activity. In relative terms, cooperative employment was higher in the European USSR than in Central Asia (Goskomstat SSSR 1990a, 269).

In terms of concentrations of specialists and scientists, the Central Asian republics ranked at the bottom while the Slavic and Baltic republics exceeded the national average (Figure 14.3). Generally, the regional distribution of skilled labour in the USSR reflected that of industrial production. However, two republics –

Armenia and Georgia – displayed unexpectedly high concentrations of specialists and scientists relative to their level of industrial development. This discrepancy in labour supply and demand might have been partly resolved by the mobility of this group (Gibson 1991). In recent years, however, the republican authorities, especially in the Baltic and Central Asian republics, have typically tried not so much to attract skilled labour from outside as to cultivate it from within. In the Baltic republics, such a policy shift – aimed at slowing a troublesome decline in titular nationality majorities – has been justified by the low birth rates and a rapid ageing of the titular population (Belkindas 1989, Krumin'sh 1990). In the Central Asian republics, by contrast, it is high birth rates, especially in rural areas offering both an inferior education and limited employment opportunities, that have produced the above shift in skilled labour policy (Rumer 1989, Mukomel' 1990).[8] Inadequate education and employment opportunities, coupled with cultural pressures on Muslim women to have many children and to care for large families, have not only discouraged outside employment, but have also reduced a family's means for the educational investment per child. This situation is exacerbated still further by the fact that in traditional extended Muslim families it is the senior members who enjoy preference in terms of consumption.

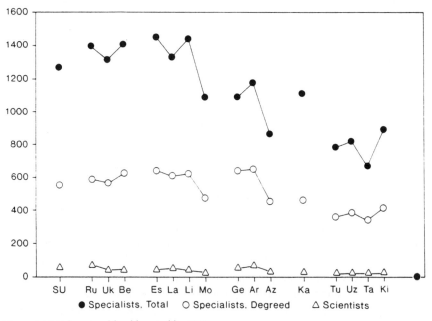

Figure 14.3 Educational level by republic 1989

---

8   The Soviets had been unable to establish birth control or planned parenthood programmes in
     the Central Asian republics, although Soviet experts had long been advocating the
     establishment of a differential demographic policy in the country (Kozlov 1982).

Recently published Soviet data corroborate the above concerns of the republican authorities in the area of skilled labour. In terms of the national composition of workers and employees, the 1989 Census data indicate that the proportion of the titular nationality in all the union republics (except the RSFSR) was higher among those employed in agriculture than in industry (Goskomstat SSSR 1990c). The exception of the RSFSR can be explained by the presence of a number of sizeable rural-oriented ethnic minorities within its territory (Goskomstat SSSR 1990b, Goskomstat Rossii 1992a). Furthermore, the data indicate pronounced variations across the republics in the proportion of non-titular nationalities among workers and employees in such sectors as industry, transportation/communication and construction. These proportions were persistently lower in the Slavic and Transcaucasian republics than in Estonia, Latvia, Kazakhstan and Central Asia.

Inter-Republican Allocation of Investment

The evidence presented in the preceding section suggests, therefore, that the Soviet strategy of unbalanced growth failed not only in equalising development among the republics, but also in developing diversified and balanced structures for the national and republican economies.[9] If the central government had been determined both to equalize levels of development among the republics and to rectify distortions in economic structures, that policy would have been most evident in the dynamics of capital formation and in the allocation of investment. Even if these goals had not been the only ones, their systematic implementation – given the sizeable development disparities and structural differences already existing – would have required a heavy and persistent emphasis on the less developed and most structurally imbalanced republican economies.

While Table 14.1 provides data on the 1989 republican shares of fixed productive assets, Figure 14.4 presents average annual growth rates of capital formation (total and per capita) during the years 1971–1985 and 1986–1989. Fixed assets employed in the goods-producing (so-called material) sphere of production are concentrated in absolute terms in the RSFSR, the Ukraine and Kazakhstan, which together account for 83% of the total. During the 1971–1985 period, five out of the eight republics of the southern belt had above-average growth rates of productive fixed assets, while between 1986 and 1989 the corresponding figures in five southern republics fell below the national average. By 1989, in terms of the national average, the indices of fixed assets per capita

---

9   As Western studies demonstrate, structural distortions in an economy are shown through a
     higher share of industrial-cum-construction employment and a lower share of services, when
     compared with countries at a similar level of development. For example, distorted structures
     are found even in the most developed constituent economies of the USSR, such as the Baltic
     ones, when the latter are compared with the economies of Northern European countries
     (Ozornoy 1991b).

were among the highest in the Baltic republics (111–126), the RSFSR (120), and Kazakhstan (102), and lowest in Central Asia (38–48), except Turkmenistan (76) (Goskomstat SSSR 1990d, 57–59). Moreover, the statistics show that on a per capita basis, the gaps have been widening since 1970, with a marked acceleration after 1985. Thus, between 1986 and 1989, annual growth rates in republican productive fixed assets per capita exceeded the national average rate in the RSFSR, Belorussia, Lithuania, Armenia and Kazakhstan, that is, only in two republics of the less-developed southern tier of the USSR (Figure 14.4).

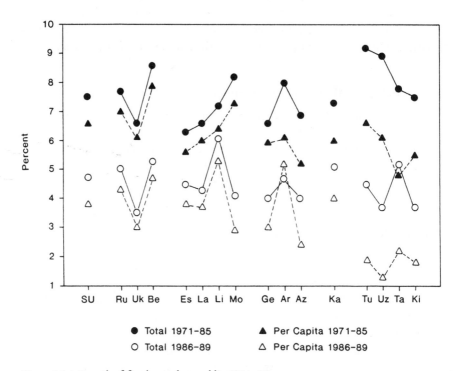

Figure 14.4 Growth of fixed assets by republic 1971–89

These outcomes obviously manifest a lack of persistent emphasis by the central authorities on resolving the economic problems of the less developed and more structurally imbalanced republics. Such outcomes spring from Soviet official policies, which tended to stress high rates of capital formation for, and to place top investment priorities on, the development of selected economic sectors and projects. Since the mid-1970s, Soviet investment priorities have largely been dictated by resource and energy development strategies (with their attendant high costs) and have been implemented by central economic agencies.[10]

The central authorities' efforts to deal with the energy 'crisis amid plenty' have made such a heavy demand for resources that energy policy must be recognised as the single most overall disruptive factor in the Soviet Union and regional economic development and one of the leading proximate causes of the stagnation or downturn of the Soviet economy as a whole and economies of all the energy-importing constituent republics. In the periods of 1971–1975 and 1986–1989, the share of the energy sector in total investment in the USSR rose from 10.1% to 20.7%, thereby confirming the leading place accorded to the sector in Soviet investment priorities (Goskomstat SSSR 1990a, pp.533–34). Furthermore, analysis of the 1976–1988 data on shares of investment and on energy exports/imports for the union republics reveals that, over that period, a substantial increase occurred only in the investment shares of the republics with net exports of fuel and energy, that is, in the RSFSR, Azerbaijan and Belorussia, while the shares of the Baltic republics, Georgia, Armenia and Kazakhstan remained stable or fluctuated only moderately. The overall investment share given to Central Asia also fluctuated during the period 1976–1988 and dropped slightly, while the Uzbekistan share fell markedly (Ozornoy 1991a).

The recent patterns of capital formation and investment growth among the union republics, thus, do not reveal any systematic effort to use the allocation of investment as a policy tool for reducing development disparities. Rather, the patterns suggest that the union government, while providing an increment in investment to ensure some development in all republics, based its spatial investment allocation decisions on an assortment of general political, geographical and economic considerations, such as geopolitical (strategic) factors, resource and energy development in Asiatic RSFSR, accessibility to market and return on capital (Hamilton 1973, Pallott and Shaw 1981).

Inter-Republican Economic Relations and Trade Balances

The Soviet economy long benefited from a substantial inter-republican division of labour arising in part from varying comparative advantages and a common economic union. The division of labour was reinforced by two factors peculiar to the Soviet economic system. The first is an organisation of economic ministries along branch (sectoral) lines, which has often favoured inter-republican trade *within* a ministry over inter-republican trade *across* ministries. The second is an emphasis

---

10 The Soviets have been in the throes of an energy crisis since the mid-1970s. Paradoxically, it is not a crisis of penury (i.e. the Soviets are not about to run out of their energy resources) but one of runaway costs, abysmal inefficiency and repeated shocks and surprises. For a thorough discussion of the energy crisis in the Soviet Union, see Gustafson (1989) and Dienes (1985).

Table 14.4 USSR: Republican trade in relation
to value added, 1988[1] (in domestic prices)

	Exports			Trade balance		
	Inter-republican	Abroad	Total	Inter-republican	Aboard	Total
(As percentage of GDP)[2]						
USSR	21.1	5.4	26.5	–	-5.8	-5.8
(As percentage of NMP)						
USSR	29.3	7.5	36.8	–	-8.0	-8.0
RSFSR	18.0	8.6	26.6	0.1	-8.7	-8.6
Ukraine	39.1	6.7	45.8	3.5	-6.4	-2.9
Belorussia	69.9	6.5	76.1	15.5	-7.5	8.0
Estonia	66.5	7.4	73.9	-8.2	-10.2	-18.4
Latvia	64.1	5.7	69.8	-1.7	-8.2	-9.9
Lithuania	60.9	5.9	66.8	-9.1	-8.1	-17.2
Moldavia	62.1	3.4	65.5	-2.4	-10.8	-13.2
Georgia	53.7	3.9	57.6	2.8	-8.6	-5.8
Armenia	63.7	1.4	65.1	-5.8	-13.4	-19.2
Azerbaijan	58.7	3.7	62.4	19.2	-9.1	10.1
Kazakhstan	30.9	3.0	33.9	-19.9	-7.1	-27.0
Turkmenistan	50.7	4.2	54.9	-2.0	-3.9	-6.0
Uzbekistan	43.2	7.4	50.6	-8.0	-0.8	-8.8
Tadzhikistan	41.8	6.9	48.7	-20.8	-2.8	-23.6
Kirgizia	50.2	1.2	51.4	-8.7	-14.3	-23.0

Source: Goskomstat SSSR (1990d, p.4, pp.34–9, pp.43–44)
Goskomstat SSSR (1990a, p.634)

[1] Trade figures exclude 'non-productive' services

[2] GDP figures are not available on a republican basis

on economies of scale, so that sometimes only one or two enterprises supply the entire union.[11]

Generally, in order to get a clear picture of inter-regional economic interactions, time series in current and constant prices should be used (Richardson 1978). In the former USSR, however, the information on exports and imports was compiled only once every five years (when republican input–output tables were constructed),

---

11 For instance, the shutdown (because of the unrest in Azerbaijan) of the only Soviet plant turning out oil drilling equipment has far-reaching nation-wide economic effects. This question of the monopolistic structure of Soviet industry figures prominently in current economic discussions in the USSR, and a number of Soviet economists assign the top priority among the aims of economic reform to the transition from the existing monopolistic market structures to competitive ones (Lavrovsky 1990).

and even then they were usually suppressed (Treml 1989). These data were published for the first time for 1988 (Goskomstat SSSR 1990a).[12] Data on republican trade flows and balances for 1988 in both domestic and world market prices are presented in Tables 14.4 and 14.5.

In domestic prices, inter-republican trade in the USSR amounted to 21% of GDP in 1988, about four times the size of exports abroad.[13] For comparison, in the European Community (EC) both trade in goods and services among its members and trade with the rest of the world are about 14% of GDP (Commission of the European Communities 1990). Prior to its dissolution, the Soviet economy appeared, therefore, to be more integrated internally than the EC but relatively less open to foreign markets.[14]

The ratio of inter-republican exports to republican NMP was lowest in the RSFSR (18%), Kazakhstan (31%) and the Ukraine (39%). Belorussia stood out as the republic most oriented to inter-republican trade, with an inter-republican export to NMP ratio of almost 70%, while the ratio exceeded 60% in the Baltic republics, Moldavia and Armenia. As for exports abroad relative to NMP, the RSFSR had the highest share (almost 9%), while Kirgizia and Armenia have barely 1% (Table 14.4).

In domestic prices, Azerbaijan and Belorussia tended to run total trade surpluses (respectively 10.2% and 7.9% of NMP in 1988), while the other republics ran trade deficits ranging in 1988 from 2.9% of NMP in the Ukraine to 27% in Kazakhstan. All the republics ran deficits in trade with the outside world in domestic prices. Whereas these deficits were relatively small for Uzbekistan, Tadzhikistan, and Turkmenistan (0.8% to 3.9% of NMP), they exceeded 10% in Armenia, Estonia, Kirgizia and Moldavia. In inter-republican trade, the RSFSR

---

12 Information on exports and imports of the republics was collected using current prices. The Soviet pricing system among the commodities, therefore, made the magnitude of trade flows and balances highly dependent upon the branch structure of each republic and region. For example, in the case of a republic specialising mainly in primary and/or capital-good industries, which have low relative prices, its exports would be low. At the same time, this republic would tend to import consumer goods, which are priced relatively high due to turnover taxes and distribution mark-ups, and thus would accrue a large trade deficit. The established domestic prices also distort the evaluation of foreign exports and imports. The reason is that most Soviet exports are primary goods with low domestic prices, while most imports are finished goods with high domestic prices. Therefore a republic's exports (to other republics and abroad) are valued in domestic prices much less than they would be in world market prices. On the other hand, a republic's foreign import figures expressed in domestic prices are grossly overstated because of the high conversion coefficients (the ratio between domestic and foreign prices) set by the state trade monopoly on imported goods.

13 For the union as a whole, GDP, inter-republican trade and export in 1988 equalled, respectively, 875, 185, and 47 billion roubles in current domestic prices (Goskomstat SSSR 1990a, p.6, p.634).

14 At the same time, certain Russian economists admitted that the USSR has noticeably trailed behind the European Economic Community in terms of the tempos and forms of economic integration over the past 20 years (Granberg 1990).

Table 14.5 USSR: Adjustments to trade balance of the republics, 1998[1]

	(As percentage of NMP)				Adjusted balance	World prices	Balance adjusted for foreign prices $\{(1) + (6)\}$
	Unadjusted balance	Turnover tax	Consumer subsidies	Trade by visitors	$\{(1) + (2) +(3) + (4)\}$		
	(1)	(2)	(3)	(4)	(5)	(6)	(7)
USSR	-8.0	–	–	–	-8.1	0.3	0.3
RSFSR	-8.6	-0.9	-1.3	–	-10.8	16.6	8.0
Ukraine	-2.3	-1.2	1.6	-0.4	-2.9	–	-2.8
Belorussia	7.9	-4.2	6.5	2.3	0.5	-16.0	-8.0
Estonia	-18.4	-2.5	4.9	7.4	-8.6	-14.8	-33.2
Latvia	-9.9	-2.8	5.7	7.1	0.1	-8.5	-18.4
Lithuania	-17.2	-4.5	9.0	5.6	-7.1	-24.3	-41.5
Moldavia	-13.2	0.7	3.9	7.8	0.1	-20.2	-33.4
Georgia	-5.8	5.9	-2.9	-6.8	-9.7	-12.8	-18.6
Armenia	-19.2	3.5	-5.2	-3.5	-24.4	-4.8	-24.0
Azerbaijan	10.2	0.5	-3.7	-3.7	19.3	-14.7	-4.5
Kazakhstan	-27.0	0.7	3.7	-1.9	-24.4	0.6	-24.4
Trukmenistan	-6.0	0.6	2.1	-4.2	2.5	0.3	0.3
Uzbekistan	-8.9	7.2	0	-1.9	-3.6	-3.2	-12.1
Tadzhikistan	-23.7	8.4	-2.1	4.2	-13.2	0.3	-22.4
Kirgizia	-23.1	6.0	2.0	0.1	-15.0	0.2	-20.9

Source: *Vestnik Statistiki.* No, 3, 1990, p.38; No. 4, 1990, p.49
Explanation of columns:
   (1) Net trade balance in existing domestic prices.
   (2) Change in trade balance if turnover tax were reallocated in proportion to labour expenditures incurred in production.
   (3) Change in trade balance if consumer subsidies were charged to consuming republic.
   (4) Change in trade balance if adjusted for sales and purchases by visitors to republic.
   (6) Change in trade balance if revalued at world market prices.

[1] Combined trade balance with other republics and in foreign trade

tended to be roughly in balance, while Belorussia and Azerbaijan ran substantial trade surpluses as a percentage of NMP (15.5% and 19.2%, respectively, in 1988). Seven republics (including Kazakhstan, Lithuania and Uzbekistan) ran substantial trade deficits, ranging in 1988 from 5.8% of NMP in Armenia to 20.8% in Tadzhikistan (Table 14.4).

These figures are significantly distorted by the uneven allocation of turnover taxes and consumer subsidies across republics, however, and by purchases and sales by visitors from other republics.[15] When turnover taxes are allocated in proportion to labour expenditures incurred in production, subsidies for consumer goods charged to the consuming republics, and transactions by visitors assigned to the republics of permanent residence, total trade balances deteriorate for the RSFSR, Armenia, and Georgia, remain unchanged for the Ukraine and improve for all other republics. The most significant improvements are registered by Moldavia, Latvia and Turkmenia, in all of which the total trade balances shift from negative to positive (Table 14.5).

Since 1988, inter-republican deliveries have declined significantly. The adverse economic impact was magnified by the high degree of monopolisation in Soviet industry and the limited flexibility of the transportation network, which causes bottlenecks at one stage of production to be transmitted to the next. Some of this contraction in inter-republican trade can be ascribed to political conflict, such as the blockade of Armenia by Azerbaijan in the winter of 1988–89 and the central authorities' blockade of Lithuania in the spring and summer of 1990. In general, however, the decline in trade reflects the difficulty of securing an exchange of comparable values without resort to barter, under the conditions of worsening shortages.

At issue here are the principles of fair pricing and equivalent exchange. In the absence of a market, the centrally-planned system failed to adjust gross price distortions in raw materials, agricultural products and consumer goods and to stabilise the supply and demand relationships. Also, the inflexibility of these prices set by the central planners makes the effects of shortages and planning errors, however caused, more visible. The economy of both the Union as a whole and of the union republics, therefore, seems less 'efficient' than would otherwise have been the case (Nove 1986, Ch. 7). As a result, mutual complaints over the value

---

15 Turnover (excise) tax constitutes one of the principal sources of revenue for the state budget in the USSR. In 1988, this source accounted for 21.5% of revenues for the state budget (Goskomstat SSSR 1989a, p.624). Turnover tax is primarily levied on processed food products and consumer goods; it is not applied equally across all products. Even though the amount of turnover tax actually collected in the republic is available from the republican ministries of finance, it is usually estimated by allocating all turnover tax collected across the USSR according to the geographic distribution of goods which are subject to this levy. However, the amount of turnover tax collected in the republic is not equal to the amount of levy actually retained in the republic budget. An extensive redistribution among the all-union and republican budgets occurs regularly, with a percentage of retention for each republic set each year in the annual budget law (see Shermenev 1987). Subsidies comprise another major aspect of the inter-republican trade balances, as well as the national income balances. Subsidies are paid out of the all-union budget on selected commodities to maintain low retail prices, while at the same time allowing producers to cover production costs. Though these mainly pertain to food products, they also apply to housing, utilities and farm machinery. As with turnover taxes, the distribution of subsidies among the republics for the purposes of adjusting trade balances (and national income used within a republic) is estimated by the centre, based upon the location of subsidised production.

of services and deliveries were multiplied (Granberg 1990, Mirsaidov 1990). The RSFSR spokesmen, for instance, often stated that other republics were taking advantage of the artificially low prices of energy, fuel and raw materials imports from that republic, turning these into finished products and selling at artificially high prices (Granberg 1990).

By the autumn of 1991, it became evident that the 'bill' for intra-union trade would not be settled to mutual satisfaction within the centre. At the same time, the virtual collapse of the command-type supply system in the USSR, resulted in a *de facto* regionalisation of the Soviet economy and a rise of protectionism, whereby each republic and region strove to protect its relative advantages and privileges. Numerous attempts to protect local markets were reported in the Soviet media over the years 1988–1991, including the ban of exports, the prohibition of sales of scarce items to 'outsiders', the setup of local customs and transit taxes, organised hoarding and the introduction of local currencies and surrogate monies in the form of vouchers and coupons (Bronshtein 1990, Granberg 1990). The most common motive behind these attempts was the protection of local supplies against shoppers from the more deprived areas.

These hectic efforts to protect 'local' economic prosperity provide eloquent evidence of the disintegrating of the 'national–economic complex' into what one Soviet economist called, 'closed economic systems at the republican level' (Bronshtein 1989). However, as convincingly shown by both the theory and practice of international economic relations, what makes sense at 'local' (in the case of the former USSR, at republican) level, can result in extensively detrimental welfare effects for an economic union as a whole (Corden 1984). Recent experience with *de facto* regionalization and economic protectionism in Gorbachev's USSR appears to confirm these predictable consequences. While net material product (NMP) and gross domestic product (GDP) had declined in 1990 by about 4% and 2%, respectively (in comparable prices), in 1991 real NMP fell by 15% and real GDP by 17% (IMF 1992, 4).[16]

Spatial Inequality, Nationalism, and the Exit from Communism

By the autumn of 1991, it became increasingly likely that the collapse of the national–economic complex would be followed by the dissolution of the Soviet Federation in terms of its existing composition and administrative arrangements. The economic reforms undertaken in the second half of the 1980s did little to address pronounced spatial inequality and other deep-seated economic problems of the USSR. Indeed, as discussed in the 1991 joint study (IMF *et al.* 1991), the

---

16 There were reports that, after the attempted coup in August 1991, the quality of statistical information passed on to the centre by the republics decreased markedly. At the same time, a growing share of output was distributed through unofficial channels. As a result, it is possible that the officially recorded fall in output (and exports) was exaggerated.

partial nature of the reforms introduced new distortions as the increasing economic freedoms tended to undermine the central planning mechanism. By 1990, the economic disarray became critical with the emergence of a steepening decline in activity and growing financial imbalances. At the same time, in the wake of similar developments in Eastern Europe, the republics were calling for greater political and economic independence. As the various nationalities reasserted themselves, Gorbachev tried to hold them back, avoiding the resolution of these issues, but his delaying tactics caused only a severe aggravation of all the nationality issues. In the event, however, because of these pressures, both constitutional and economic reforms accelerated in 1991.

In the first half of 1991, the central and republican authorities adopted an 'anti-crisis programme' which called for stabilisation measures and proposed a progressive – but not radical – shift towards privatization and a market economy. The programme was to be implemented in the context of a new union treaty which was intended to formalise constitutional and policy responsibilities between the centre and the republics. Before agreement was reached on the treaty, however, the attempted *coup d'etat* of August caused a shift in the political ground. The coup, organised by the leaders of the military–industrial complex and supported by the upper echelons of the army and the Party, demonstrated that these all-Union institutions had remained bastions of resistance to reforms throughout the years of perestroika.

Following the coup attempt, the transfer of power to the republics accelerated. A new decentralised structure was put forward which would give republics full responsibility for their internal affairs and a state council of republican presidents would retain responsibility for union-wide issues. In the economic area, during the autumn of 1991, attempts were made to establish an Economic Treaty that would establish various federal institutions for coordinating economic policies. In the event, however, these attempts were again overtaken by political events as the republics moved to disband the central structure altogether. The disintegration of the USSR into a host of smaller, ethnically more homogenous and more cohesive nation-states destroyed the institutions and forces of the old regime, thereby drastically undermining (though not completely eliminating) the institutional and social base for organised resistance to a radical transition to a market economy.

Looking back, one can now see the fallacy of Gorbachev's strategy to prevent the disintegration of the USSR. This, however, gives rise to a general theoretical question, namely: is it possible to conceive a feasible strategy that would reconcile democratisation and marketisation reform with the task of preserving the territorial integrity of the USSR? Given dramatic disparities in their economic, cultural and social development, and especially in the demographic behaviour, that the major territorially-based Soviet nationalities exhibited in Gorbachev's USSR, such a political and economic construct could hardly survive under conditions of market integration and a political pluralism. The demands and interests of major ethnic components of the USSR have become very different and, in the absence of a powerful redistributive centre, even irreconcilable. To keep such a society together, would require a heavy dose of coercion rather than forces of market integration. The destruction of the Soviet empire by forces of nationalism and separatism represents, therefore, a necessary pre-condition for a successful transition to political democracy and a market economy.

The unbiased analysis of the role of nationalism and separatism – arising from pronounced economic inequality and cultural differences among the major nation-alities groups in a multi-ethnic Soviet-type society – in the present great transfor-mation of the Soviet Union flies in the face of the traditional perception of nationalism as a largely divisive, xenophobic, and therefore anachronistic, move-ment. It reveals the liberal-democratic potential of the new post-communist nationalism which needs not only to be appreciated but, more importantly, constructively engaged in the reduction of pronounced socioeconomic disparities among the members of the Confederation of Independent States.

References

Bahry, D.L. and Nechemias, C. (1981) 'Half full or half empty: the debate over regional equality.' *Slavic Review 40*, 366–83.

Belkindas, M.V. (1989) *Soviet Regional Economic Autonomy: Baltics versus Moscow.* Falls Church, VA: Delphic Associates.

Bronshtein, M. (1989) 'Regional "nyj khozraschet: nuzhny trezvye dokazatel" stva.' *Kommunist 5*, 32–45.

Bronshtein, M. (1990) 'Al 'ternativa – nash obshchiy rynok.' *Izvestiia*, February 21, 3.

Commission of the European Communities (1990) *Stabilization, Liberalization, and Devolution: Assessment of the Economic Situation and Reform Process in the Soviet Union.* Luxembourg: Office for Official Publications of the European Communities.

Corden, W. Max (1984) Normative Theory of International Trade.' In R.W. Jones and P.B. Kenen (eds) *Handbook of International Trade 1.* New York: North-Holland.

Dienes, L. (1985) 'The energy system and economic imbalances in the USSR.' *Soviet Economy 1*, 340–72.

Gellner, E. (1983) *Nations and Nationalism.* Oxford: Basil Blackwell.

Gellner, E. (1990) 'Ethnicity and faith in Eastern Europe.' *Daedalus 119*, 1, 279–94.

Gibson, J.R. (1991) 'Interregional migration in the U.S.S.R.' *The Canadian Geographer 35*, 2, 143–56.

Goskomstat SSSR (1989a) *Narodnoe khoziaistvo SSSR v 1988 godu.* Moscow: Finansy i statistika.

Goskomstat SSSR (1989b) *Statisticheskie materialy ob ekonomicheskom i sotsial'nom razvitii soiuznykh i avtonomnykh respublik, avtonomnkh oblastei i okrugov.* Moscow: Informatsionno-izdatel'skii otdel.

Goskonstat SSSR (1990a) *Narodnoe khoziaistvo SSSR v 1989 godu.* Moscow: Finansy i statistika.

Goskomstat SSSR (1990b) *Demograficheskii ezhegodnik SSSR.* Moscow: Finansy i statistika.

Goskomstat SSSR (1990c) *Trud v SSSR.* Moscow: Finansy i statistika

Goskomstat SSSR (1990d) *Osnovnye pokasately balansa narodnogo khoziaistva SSSR i soiuznykh respublik.* Moscow: Informatsionno-izdatel'skii otdel.

Goskomstat SSSR (1999 la) *Narodnoe khoziaistvo SSSR v 1990 godu.* Moscow: Finansy i statistika.

Goskomstat SSSR (1991b) *Zhenshchiny v SSSR 1991.* Moscow: Finansy i statistika.

Goskomstat Rossii (1992) *Nekotoryie pokazateli kharakterizuiushchie natsional'nyj sostay naseleniia Rossiiskoi Federatssi: po dannym perepisi naseleniia 1989 goda.* Moscow: Tom II. Respublikanskii informatsionno – izdatel'skii tsentr

Granberg, A.G. (1990) 'Ekonomicheskii mekhanism mezhrespublikanskikh i mezhregional'nykh otnoshenii.' In V.I. Kuposov (ed) *Radikal'naia ekonomicheskaia reforma.* Moscow: Vysshaia Shkola.

Grossman, G. (1989) 'The sub-rosa privatization and marketization in the USSR.' *Berkeley-Duke Occasional Papers on the Soviet Economy 17.*

Gustafson, T. (1989) *Crisis Amid Plenty.* Princeton: Princeton University Press.

Hamilton, F.E.I. (1973) 'Spatial dimensions of Soviet economic decision-making.' In V.N. Bandera and Z.L. Melnyk (eds) *The Soviet Economy in Regional Perspective.* New York: Praeger.

Hobsbaum, E. (1990) *Nations and Nation-States.* Cambridge: Cambridge University Press.

IMF *et al.* (1991) *A Study of Soviet Economy.* 3 vols. Washington, DC: IMF.

IMF (1992) *The Economy of the Former U.S.S.R. in 1991: Economic Survey.* Washington, DC: IMF.

Kozlov, V.I. (1982) *Natsional'nosti SSSR.* Moscow: Mysl'.

Krumin'sh, Iu. (1990) 'Latviia: novye flagi.' In V. Mukomel *SSSR: Demograficheskii Diagnoz.* Moscow: Progress.

Lavrovsky, I. (1990) 'A new conception of the enterprise.' *International Quarterly of Business and Management 1*, 41–46.

Lubin, N. (1984) *Labour and Nationality in Soviet Central Asia.* Princeton: Princeton University Press.

McAuley, A. (1979) *Economic Welfare in the Soviet Union.* Wisconsin: Wisconsion University Press.

Mirsaidov, Sh. (1990) 'Sotsial'no-ekonomicheskoe razvitie soiuznoi respubliki.' *Planovoe Khozyaistvo 1*, 381–393.

Mukomel' V. (1990) 'Sredniaia Asia: bremia peremen.' In V. Mukomel *SSSR: Demograficheskii Diagnoz*, 535–46. Moscow: Progress.

Nove, A. (1986) *The Soviet Economic System.* London: George Allen and Unwin.

Ozornoy, G.I. (1985) 'The role of equalization and efficiency goals in Soviet regional development: an empirical analysis.' Unpublished PhD thesis, Department of Geography, University of Toronto.

Ozornoy, G.I. (1991a) 'Some Issues of Spatial Inequality in Gorbachev's USSR.' *Regional Studies 25*, 5, 381–393.

Ozornoy, G.I. (1991b) 'Regional economic issues and republican independence.' In A.L. Kagedan (ed) *Ethnicity and the Soviet Future.* Ottawa: Carleton University Press.

Pallott, J. and Shaw, D.J.B. (1981) *Planning in the Soviet Union.* London: Croom Helm.

Pankratova, M.G. (1990) *Sel'skaia zhenshchina v SSSR.* Moscow: Mysl'.

Richardson, H.W. (1978) *Regional and Urban Economics.* Chicago: University of Chicago Press.

Schiffer, J.R. (1989) *Soviet Regional Economic Policies.* New York: St. Martin's Press.

Shermenev, M.K. (ed) (1987) *Finansy SSSR*. Moscow: Finansy i Statistika.

Treml, V.G. (1989) 'The most recent input–output table: a milestone in Soviet statistics.' *Soviet Economy 5*, 4, 342–59.

Whitehouse, D.F. (1972) 'Soviet regional development in the 1960s – trends and implications.' Paper presented to AAASS convention in Dallas, Texas.

CHAPTER 15

Regional Policy and Regional Structure in the Former Soviet Union
From Unity to Disintegration

Oksana Dmitrieva

Introduction

During the last four years the world has been surprised by the disintegration of the USSR and the former unified state is now disrupted by constant inter-ethnic conflicts in different parts of the country which have the potential to transform themselves into international wars. The situation developing in the former USSR is not unique. The same tendencies – that is the disintegration followed by inter-ethnic conflicts – can also be observed in former Yugoslavia and Czechoslovakia.

What are the reasons for such phenomena? Was it an inevitable consequence of the administrative command system or rather an outcome of the failure of a regional policy? This chapter seeks to address the second part of this question and analyse the reasons for the disintegration of regional policy and the mechanisms of regional development.

The regional regulation in the USSR for the last 70 years has been an example of a highly paternalistic form of regional policy and of unprecedented expansion of central government interference in the location of production, migration flows and the distribution of finance. The USSR experience is unique from the point of view that, both in absolute and relative terms, the volume of finance directed annually into regional policy for many years was several times higher than similar expenditures in other countries. Nevertheless, this policy has resulted in a level of regional disparity which is greater than any in the market economies. Furthermore, of great importance is that these disparities have tended to diverge over time. The spatial consequences of the large-scale expenditures on regional policy were very significant both for the backward regions, towards which the help was directed, and the more developed regions, which supplied this help. It resulted in a high degree of dissatisfaction with the structure of inter-regional relations within all types of regions. This was one of the factors which contributed to the disintegration of the Union.

Analysis of regional trends raises a number of questions. What is the response of the different republics' economies to disintegration? Which republics will gain from the transition to a new order and which will lose? Have new tendencies in regional development appeared and which should be treated as the impact of disintegration?

It should be pointed out that it is very difficult to assess the impacts of disintegration in isolation because the process of disintegration coincided with the transition to a market economy and also a general economic crisis. However, in this chapter we will try to dwell upon the immediate impacts of disintegration with respect to the comparative economic behaviour of the former union republics in the context of a new political and economic framework.

Regional Structure and the Process of Regional Development in the USSR: A Model

The present-day regional structure in the USSR is the result of the mechanism of regional development and the system of objectives and impact of the pursued regional policy. Due to the considerable inertia of the regional structure its peculiarities, inequalities and trends are likely to dominate the pattern of regional development in the country in the short-term.

The process of regional development in the USSR was characterised by the domination of those rules and procedures of economic behaviour, systems of financial distribution and consumption that were appropriate for the administrative command economy and have little to do with the paradigms of economic behaviour and management found in the rest of the world. What are the particular features of this model of regional development and the resultant regional patterns? The main features of the former USSR regional development and regional structure can be summarised.

The principal feature of the realised regional policy is the *immense scale of budget transfers*. It must be noted that about 70% of national income in the USSR used to be redistributed through the budget. Therefore, the revenue–expenditure ratio of all the budgets on the territory is fairly representative of the financial flows.

The withdrawal of financial resources through budgets from a number of Povolzhie regions (i.e. regions situated along the Volga river) accounted for 57% of the total budget expenditures in the regions. In the Urals region budget transfers accounted for 37% of total budget expenditures and in other European regions of Russia (except the North) about 24%. However, the share of donations into republican and local budgets of Central Asian republics accounted for 50%. In the Far East regions and the Northern ones (e.g. Murmansk region) and several Siberian regions, up to 40% of budget expenditures were donated (Dmitrieva 1990).

The budget transfers were dominated by the principle of equity utilised in its primitive sense. USSR regional policy has never touched old industrial regions, as can be illustrated by an examination of the pattern of financial redistribution between the regions. In 1988, 40 billion roubles were redistributed through budget transfers: 18 billion roubles being redistributed between Russian regions, with the rest going to other republics and countries. Out of this 18 billion roubles just over half (51%) went to the social and economic development of Moscow which is not surprising in such a totalitarian state. Financing of the Northern, Siberian and Far East regions required 36% of the intra-republican redistribution. Donations of investments and budgets to autonomous republics, where the national minorities live, took a further 8%. The rest, less than 4%, went to the depressed regions of European Russia. Thus, the question of regional inequality was not considered and no purposeful measures were undertaken to address them.

The USSR regional structure can be distinctly divided into donor and recipient regions. Furthermore, 'buffer zones' can also be distinguished, that is, regions with an equal balance between donations and receipts, although this group is not as extensive as the first two. The distribution of the former union republics according to this classification is shown in Table 15.1.

Another peculiarity of the mechanism of regional development on the territory of the former USSR is the *inverse direction of capital flows*. Capital did not flow into those regions where it could earn the largest profits – in fact the opposite occurred. This was caused by the permanent shift of productive forces into the underdeveloped regions.

The movement of productive forces from the developed to the undeveloped regions was carried out in two distinct directions, with two groups of aims being pursued:

- the opening up of new regions by the shift of productive forces and population into the regions of Siberia, the North and Far East which had a very low population and economic activity density

- the shift of productive forces to the Caucasus and Central Asian regions which was designed to primarily redress the social and economic disparities.

The main mechanism used to achieve these aims was the construction of enterprises with the construction being financed from the federal budget sources.

Correlation analysis of the dynamics of investments and capital productivity ratios in the 87 regions showed a small negative correlation between investments and capital productivity ratio, that is, there were capital flows into those regions with the lowest productivity (sample correlation coefficient is 0.2270).

Table 15.1 Direct and indirect subsidies to Republican Budgets

Republic	The share of direct subsidy in republican budget revenues (%)			The share of direct and indrect subsidies in republican budget revenues (%)		
	1988	1989	1990	1988	1989	1990
Recipients						
Uzbekistan	21	19.5	27	28.6	29.8	
Kazahstan	20	18.9	26	28.6	29.3	No
Kirghistan	23	18.9	20.2	31.2	29.6	
Tadgikistan	19.9	13.5	16	28.2	23.8	data
Turkmenia	20.5	20.8	31	28.0	31.3	
Buffer group						
Georgia				10.2	12.5	
Lethjuania	Do not have direct subsidies			8.6	3.9	
Estonia				9.3	–	
Donors						
Russia						
Ukrania						
Bielorussia						
Azervajdzan			Do not have subsidies			
Moldova						
Latvia						
Armenia						

Source: Gosydarstvennij budget SSSR (1991) Krat. stat, sb. Moscow, Finansi i statisika, 1991; O gosydarstvennom budgete SSSR na 1989 god i ob ispolnendii gosydarstvennogo budgeta za 1987. Moscow, Politizdat, 1988

However, the regional policy created *obstacles to the operating of regional multipliers* for the following reasons. On the one hand, as the capital does not flow into the regions with the most developed industrial and social infrastructure, but rather the reverse, good infrastructural complexes have not been a major factor in the location decision of firms. On the other hand, the possibilities of structural change and the transition from primary kinds of employment to secondary, tertiary and quaternary ones in the old industrial regions are badly curtailed because of the continuous outflow of financial, material and labour resources. Therefore, the primitive kinds of employment which have underlain the process of town foundation are preserved and the diversification processes are not induced.

Obstacles which prevent regional multipliers functioning and lead to financial withdrawals encourage *forced, artificial depression*. Unlike regional problems in Western economies which are caused by the exhaustion of natural resources or by changes in the market, regional problems in the former USSR result from investment cycle distortions which were created by continuous budget transfers.

One of the main features of the USSR regional structure was the fact that *the level of economic development in a region does not in the least determine the living standards* in that region. Regions with high levels of economic development and high production efficiency can have an underdeveloped social infrastructure and relatively low living standards and vice versa.

To some extent this paradox can be explained by the system of financing social infrastructure and housing. The major part of allocations for this purpose was covered not by the direct payments of consumers (households) but rather was provided by the state. The peculiarity of the system lies in the fact that allocations were not given directly but were included with allocations for social purposes and housing in the total estimates of constructing industrial corporations which were funded by the federal budget. So far, as a result of this practice two-thirds of the total private and state capital expenditures for housing and social facilities were financed by corporations along with one-third of direct maintenance costs. One of the consequences of such a system of financing was the escalation of the number of industrial constructions to the detriment of social facilities and housing. This is one of the main reasons for the constant imbalance between levels of economic development and social welfare. Another effect of these practices is the escalation of new industrial construction in pursuit of a solution to the social and housing problems. In order to get state allocations for social facilities and housing, municipal authorities were forced to influence state decisions on new industrial constructions in their regions. As soon as a decision on the construction of any industrial enterprise was agreed the allocations for the different aspects of social infrastructure were included into the total construction estimate. This manner of decision-making resulted in a number of grave structural imbalances which are described in detail in Dmitrieva (1990). One of these imbalances was the deterioration of infrastructural complexes in old regions, the violation of resource constraints and the hypertrophia of industrial density in a number of regions.

The lack of correlation between the level of economic development and the standard of living in a region can be confirmed by the comparison of two typological classifications. The first typological classification of regions was made according to the level of life quality and the second one according to the level of economic development. Both classifications include six typological groups (clusters) which were listed in descending order. Eighty-seven data points (i.e. the total number of regions in the former USSR) were classified. All the union republics, except Russia, were treated as individual entries; Russia for this purpose was divided into 73 regions, territories and autonomous republics, with the cities of Moscow and St Petersburg being included as separate entries.

Regions with the highest living standards are included in the first cluster, while those with the lowest were allocated to the sixth cluster (Table 15.2, column 2; Figure 15.1). Those regions with the highest level of economic development were included in the first cluster, while those with the lowest went into the sixth one. For each region the ordinal number of the economic development cluster was compared with the ordinal number of the life quality cluster. For example, the Urals region is included in the first cluster according to the level of economic development and in the fifth cluster in terms of life quality. Hence, the displacement of the ordinal number of the economic development cluster relative to the life quality typology is -4 which indicates a worsening of life quality relative to economic performance of the region. The most striking fact to emerge from Table 15.2 is that the majority of the regions ranking first in the economic development level found themselves in the last and next to last clusters in terms of life quality. Thus, the Urals, Kemerovo, Omsk, Irkutsk regions, Tatars republic, while leading in terms of economic development, rank only in the sixth and fifth clusters with respect to life quality. There can be no doubt that the main social unrest, i.e. strikes, and riots, will take place first of all in these regions and this has already begun to occur.

Table 15.2 Generalised typological classification of the former USSR regions according to the socioeconomic development level

Republic/Region	The ordinal number of the cluster to which a region belongs in the economic development level classification	The ordinal number of the cluster to which a region belongs in the level of living classification	The displacement of an ordinal number of the cluster in the economic development level classification relative to an ordinal number of cluster in the level of living classification
Vladimir obl.	1	2	-1
Ivanovo obl.	1	2	-1
Rjazan obl.	1	4	-3
Jaroslavi obl.,	1	2	-1
Nidznij Novgorod obl.	1	2	-1
Tula obl.	1	3	-2
Russian Federation Republic	1	5	-4
Urals economic region (Kurgan obl. excluded)	1	5	-4
Arhangelsk obl.	1	4	-3
Tjumen obl. (Jamalo-Neetsk autonomous region excluded)	1	4	-3
Vologda obl.	1	5	-4
Tartarstan	1	5	-4
Karelian autonomous republic	1	4	-3
Leningrad obl.	1	4	-3
Tver obl.	1	4	-3
Kirov obl.	1	2	-1
Samara obl.	1	2	-1
Kemerovo obl.	1	6	-5
Omsk obl.	1	6	-5
Irkutsk obl.	1	6	-5
Krasnojarsk kraj (Evenk and Dolgano-Nentsk autonomous region excluded)	1	6	-5
Bielorussian republic	1	1	0
Lithuanian republic	1	1	0
Latvian republic	1	1	0
Estonian republic	1	1	0
Central Black-zone	2	3	-1

Table 15.2 Generalised typological classification of the former USSR regions according to the socioeconomic development level (continued)

Republic/Region	The ordinal number of the cluster to which a region belongs in the economic development level classification	The ordinal number of the cluster to which a region belongs in the level of living classification	The displacement of an ordinal number of the cluster in the economic development level classification relative to an ordinal number of cluster in the level of living classification
Orlov obl.	2	3	-1
Brjansk obl.	2	3	-1
Ulianovsk obl.	2	3	-1
Volgograd obl.	2	3	-1
Kostroma obl.	2	4	-2
Moscow obl.	3	5	-1
Moscow city	3	1	2
St Petersburg	3	2	1
Rostov obl.	3	2	1
Kaluga obl.	3	3	0
Tomsk obl.	3	3	0
Novosibirstk obl.	3	6	-3
Ukranian republic	4	2	2
Saratov obl.	4	2	2
Smolensk obl.	4	3	1
Novgorod obl.	4	4	0
Pskvo obl.	4	4	0
Krasnodar kraj	5	2	3
Stavropol kraj	5	2	3
Kabardino-Balkar autonomous republic	5	5	0
Severo-Osetin autonomous republic	5	5	0
Moldova republic	5	2	3
Georgian republic	5	2	3
Armenian republic	5	2	3
Mordovian autonomous republic	5	4	1
Chuvashian autonomous republic	5	4	1
Marl EL autonomous republic	5	5	0
Altaj kraj	5	5	0
Kurgan obl.	5	5	0
Kazah republic	5	5	0
Astrahan obl.	5	6	-1
Pensa obl.	5	3	2
Kalmukian autonomous republic	6	6	0
Dagestan autonomous republic	6	6	0
Checheno-Ingush autonomous republic	6	6	0
Chita obl.	6	6	0
Burjat obl.	6	6	0
Jamalo-Nenetsk autonomous region	6	6	0
Evenk autonomous region	6	6	0
Touvinian autonomous republic	6	6	0
Uzbek republic	6	6	0
Turkmenia republic	6	6	0
Kirghiz republic	6	6	0
Tadzik republic	6	6	0
Azerbajdzan republic	6	6	0

Special Far East economic region (Amur obl. excluded)
Murmansk obl.
Komi autonomous republic

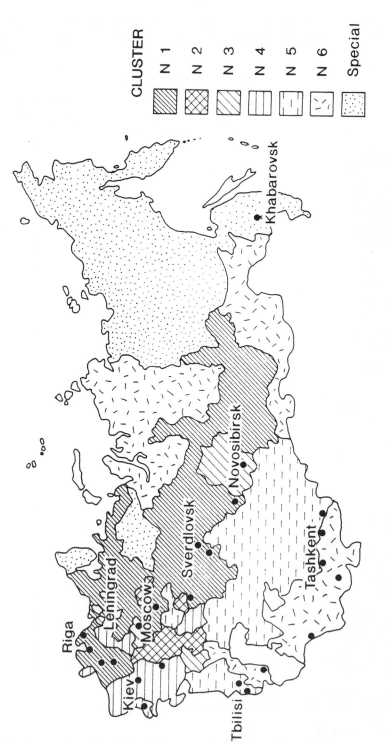

Figure 15.1 Generalised typological classification of the former USSR regions according to the socioeconomic development level

At the same time there were selected regions where the level of life quality is higher than the level of economic development. They are Moldova, Georgia, Krasnodar and Stavropol regions. This tendency is observed in the regions with favourable agricultural conditions and with effective agricultural production on personal land holdings.

Hence, one of the characteristic features of the pattern of regional inequality in the USSR is the *sharp social discrimination of the more economically developed regions*. The above analysis also shows that the kind of industrialisation developed in the USSR does not automatically lead to an improvement in the quality of life.

Costs and Results of Regional Policy

The costs of regional policy at its peak in Western Europe amounted to an average of 0.04–0.08% of the gross national product (GNP), with the United Kingdom being the only exception spending 0.5% of GNP (Weaver 1984, Deacon 1982, Gritsaya 1988).

In the USSR the aggregate costs of regional programmes and donations to backward regions amounted to 40–50 billion roubles in the 1970–80s: nearly 6% of gross national product. Consequently, the relative share of assignments for the USSR regional policy was 10–20 times higher than in any of the market economies (compared with the maximum level).

What have been the results? As stated above, there were two main aims of regional policy: reducing the scale of regional disparities and opening up new pioneer regions. The chapter first examines the dynamics of regional differences.

Regional differences in the USSR, besides being greater than in any of the advanced countries, have a consistent tendency to divergence over time. Thus, the discrepancy of the per capita industrial production levels (between the most and the least developed regions) was 3.6 at the beginning of the 1960s, and had grown to 4.25 by 1988. Furthermore, the discrepancy in per capita production of GNP, according to our calculations, is 5–5.5 times. Therefore, we could say that 'parturient montes nascetur ridiculus mus': the expensive policy of seeking to reduce regional disparities gave minimal results. Moreover, the continuous financial injections into backward regions favoured the preservation of backward economic structures and pre-industrial employment structures. These processes are analysed in detail in Dmitrieva (1990). These donations did not increase the rate of economic development either. On the contrary, they were accompanied by economic stagnation in the subsidised regions. In the last decade the growth rates in the total volume of industrial production in the majority of the subsidised Central Asian republics were lower than the USSR average. The lack of results in stimulating growth in the backward regions is but one side of the coin. The most regrettable results of this policy were the exhaustion of the most developed regions and the appearance of a general economic decline in the USSR.

As regards the efficiency of the development of the regions of Siberia, the North and Far East, a more disaggregated analysis is required, which focuses on individual regions or investment projects. In general, the economic expansion of pioneer regions failed to generate the stable indigenous sources for economic growth and diversified structure. To date the efficiency of investments in Siberia and the Far East has been at a lower level relative to investments in the European regions. The volume of capital investment per person employed in Siberia and the Far East in the 1970s exceeded the Russian republican average by nearly one and a half times. As to the efficiency of capital investments, one rouble invested in the Urals region was 45% more productive than one rouble invested in West Siberia and 215% more productive than one rouble invested in East Siberia. The efficiency of investments for the last 15 years in Povolzhie was 18% higher than in West Siberia and 158% higher than in East Siberia.

Winners and Losers from Disintegration?

The analysis of the existing regional structure allows for some speculation regarding the future prospects of the regions. The analysis in this section is divided into two parts. First, a comparative analysis of the economic dynamics of the different republics. Second, an analysis of the main trends in regional development within the Russian Federation.

The differences in the economic performance of different republics are affected by a number of factors. It might be expected beforehand that the major impacts would be experienced from the reduction in budget transfers and from a transition to a pattern of world prices. If the major factor influencing the economic situation was the great reduction of donations then the lagging recipient republics (Ubzbekistan, Turkmenia, Tadjikistan, Kirghizia; see Table 15.1) and the republics having negative trade balances with Russia (all republics except Bielorussia, Ukrainia and Latvia; Table 15.3) should find themselves in the most unfavourable position. However, these factors were not as influential as the differences in economic policy and the strategies of economic reform adopted in the different republics.

To confirm this statement it is useful to examine the growth rates in 1991 – the first year after disintegration. The comparative assessment of the growth rates in 1991 presents a certain difficulty due to the lack of comprehensive statistics and the incompatibility of estimations carried out by the different republics. However, the analysis in Table 15.4 shows that the impulses of decline originated in Russia and were then transferred to the other republics. However, the rates of decline differed from one republic to the other. The lowest rates of decline can be observed in Uzbekistan (- 0.9%), Turkmenia (- 0.6%) and Bielorussia (- 3%). Thus, republics with a more patriarchal economy and which are less involved in an all-union market (e.g. Uzbekistan, Turkmenia) have turned out to be less vulnerable to the effects of disintegration. Also, more successful were those republics who have chosen a cautious and conservative way of reforming without breaking

Table 15.3. Trade balance of Russia with former USSR republics
(Millions of roubles at prices on 2 April 1991)

Union republics	Export (+), Import (-)
Ukrania	-989.4
Bielorussia	-4551.9
Kazahstan	8636.6
Uzbekistan	1927.1
Azerbajdzan	-3944.2
Turkmenia	-208.0
Tadzikistan	833.3
Kirgistan	920.0
Latvia	-81.8
Lethjuania	567.5
Estonia	-527.0
Moldova	-2533.3
Georgia	-2169.0
Armenia	-1907.1

Source: Economica i djisn, N 20, 1991

Table 15.4. Indexes of national income growth rates

Republic	1986/ 1985	1987/ 1986	1988/ 1987	1989/ 1988	1990/ 1989	1991/ 1990
USSR	2.3	1.5	4.4	2.5	-4.0	
Russia	2.4	0.7	4.5	1.9	-5.1	-11
Ukraine	1.6	5.3	2.5	4.1	-1.6	-11
Beilorussia	4.3	3.5	2.4	7.9	-1.5	-3
Uzbekistan	-0.2	0.2	9.5	2.6	1.0	-0.9
Kazahstan	1.4	0.1	5.8	-0.5	-1.7	-10.0
Georgia	-1.1	-2.0	7.0	-3.5	2.0	
Azerbajdjan	1.6	3.9	0.7	-6.1	-8.0	-0.4
Lethuania	6.3	4.8	10.7	1.6	-12.8	
Moldova	7.2	1.8	2.0	8.6	-6.7	
Latvia	4.6	1.5	6.2	7.4	-3.2	
Kirghizstan	0.9	2.7	12.6	4.3	-1.0	-5.0
Tadjikistan	3.5	-1.4	12.2	-7.7	-10.0	-9.0
Armenia	1.7	-0.6	-2.3	7.4	-10.0	-11.0
Turkmenia	4.3	3.8	10.1	-6.7	10.4	-0.6
Estonia	2.9	1.2	5.2	6.7	1.1	

Source: Narodnoje hosajstvo SSSR sa 1990 god. Moscow: Finansi i statistika 1991, pp 12; Ekonomica stan-Chlenov SNG v 1991 gody. Ekonomica i djisn, N 6, 1992

existing supply networks and motivation systems (e.g. Bielorussia, Uzbekistan, Turkmenia). One of the decisive factors inducing recession was the degree of political instability. This is best illustrated by the cases of Armenia and Tadjikistan.

The collapse of the economic network has had such a crucial impact on the economic situation that republics with a greater dependency on a system of patriarchal agricultural (that is, less developed) turned out to be in a more favourable position due to their lack of elasticity towards endogenous demands and inputs. Another important factor was the choice of mechanism for economic reform. The radical means of market transition appears to have resulted in a heightening of economic problems. Consequently, those republics which were more conservative in their choice of a method of economic reform seem to have prevented their economies from a rapid process of economic collapse.

As far as the evaluations of the regional structure within Russia itself are concerned, it should be pointed out that there has been an absence of new growth tendencies which were expected as a result of the transition to a market economy. It was pointed out at the beginning that sectoral and regional policies were tightly interwoven. Thus, the state-supported shift of productive forces from the West to the East was pre-determined by the existence of extractive industries. Nowadays if a sectoral shift to manufacturing industries were undertaken, then it would be accompanied by the appropriate flows of investments and business activities from the East to the West. But the peculiarity of the current recession in Russia is that it is taking place without sectoral shifts. According to the data obtained in the course of a field survey of firms carried out in different regions of Russia by the Laboratory of Regional Diagnostics of St Petersburg University of Economics and Finance in 1992, Russia is faced with more or less the same degree of decline in output (by 35%) in all sectors of industry and about 45% in agriculture. According to the same field survey data another factor which prevents new flows of investments from appearing is the general investment crisis and the general reduction in the level of investments by 70%.

Changes in the pattern of living standards in the Russian regions have also not emerged. Against the background of an absence of sectoral and investment flows, changes in the standard of living among the regions might be caused simply by changes in prices and profitability of different commodities. Taking into consideration the rapid fall in the value of the rouble, the most profitable commodities for production have turned out to be export goods. But high export efficiency did not have any impact on the situation in the regions specialising on export industries. Due to the great outflow of export revenues from the country, which were equal in 1991 to 20 billion or to one-third of the total, incomes from export have not been invested back in the region or channelled into increased levels of consumption in the region's industries. Thus, due to the 'flight of capital', export industries do not contribute to the infrastructural improvement of a region or to a considerable improvement in the standard of living.

The overall pattern in the standard of living among the Russian regions preserves the tendency described above. That is, a relatively higher level in agricultural regions compared with that in industrially developed ones. It should also be mentioned that markets for consumption commodities have rather distinct regional patterns. The consumption or availability of agricultural products or other goods for general consumption were higher than in the regions specialising in investment products or research and development activities. Against the general background of the collapse of trade and transport networks the tendency for regionalisation of commodity markets was intensified.

Conclusion

The short time period of the functioning of the former unitary state in its disintegrated form have not so far provided sufficient data for any assessment of the changes in the regional structure or in the mechanism of regional development. The only speculation which can be supported is that all regional factors were dominated, firstly, by the political choices of the different republics. Political choice simply indicates the preference given to the model of economic reform and the efforts directed to preserving political stability and the prevention of inter-ethnic conflicts. Secondly, the economic performance of the regions has been determined to a great extent by the level of elasticity of a region's or republic's economy to the collapse of trade, transport and financial networks.

References

Gritsaya, O.V. (1988) *Western Europe: Regional Contrasts at a New Stage of the Scientific and Technical Revolution.* Moscow: Nuka.

Dmitrieva, O.G. (1990a) *Central Asia: The Failure of the Policy of Paternalism.* Reprint of a report. Leningrad: LSEI.

Dmitrieva, O.G. (1990b) *Economic Influence of Local Councils and Regional Diagnostics.* EKO.

Deacon, D. (1982) 'Competition policy in the Common Market: its links with regional policy.' *Regional Studies 16*, 53–63.

Weaver, G. (1984) *Regional Development and the Local Community Planning, Politics and Social Context.* Chichester: John Wiley.

CHAPTER 16

The Regional Dimension in Hungary
Aspects of Transformation in 1991–92

Peter de Souza and Attila Korompai

Introduction

The regional dimension (that is, encompassing structure and structural problems, administration, policy and implementation) in the former Soviet Union and the countries that used to be defined as centrally administered[1] is characterised by the general framework of the transformation and reform processes. The scale of regional problems and the role of regional policy is different from country to country and although not a central priority in the policy-forming process, there are several indications of its increasing importance.

Though Hungary is one of the smallest countries in the Eastern and Central European area and the transformation process has many special features, it is an interesting country to study because the reform processes were already in motion in 1968. Although temporarily restricted in the first half of the eighties they gradually began to strengthen again. The transformation processes have clearly gone much further when compared with the situation in neighbouring countries.

The regional dimension has specific Hungarian characteristics determined by historical legacy and local resources, but at the same time it shows common features with other former centrally administered countries as well as similarities with earlier phases of development in highly developed economies. The purpose of this chapter is to describe the Hungarian regional dimension in terms of its historical

---

1 The term 'centrally administered' rather than 'centrally planned' has been consciously used in order to emphasise the primary regulation of the economy, not through a planned long- and medium-term control but through the constant, day-to-day intervention by central authorities.

legacy, regional differentiation and problems, policies and policy implications and implementation problems. The analysis is made within the setting of the transition period's chaotic economic pre-conditions.

The Regional Pattern 1:
Interaction of Past and Present in the Transformation

Throughout its history, Hungary has, like any other country, been divided by different administrative and other regional schemes and its spatial patterns have been formed by conscious policies and spontaneous forces. Prominent among the administrative elements has been the megye (county) system, which has a long history.

The present scheme of 19 counties plus the capital (Budapest) was formed in 1949–50. In this structure, the counties were the arms of the central government through which redistribution was enacted. The local councils were hierarchically subordinated to the county councils and its bureaucracy. This was to a certain degree modified in accordance with the economic reform of 1968 by the Act on Councils passed in the Hungarian Parliament in 1971 which defined the principle of 'local interests' represented by the local councils through their 'organisation of self-government'. (Enyedi 1990) The financial conditions did, however, limit the Act's potential. Central control and central influence was guaranteed. Despite the limits, the independence of local authorities began to grow, primarily based on horizontal cooperation and the initiation of voluntary works.

In 1984 further changes were enacted in the administrative framework. The system now encompassed two tiers. Budapest and the 19 counties formed the first one. The municipalities (103 towns, 6 cities of county rank, 2957 villages with 681 individual and 700 common councils organised into urban influence zones around 139 towns and large villages) formed the lower tier. The aim was to reduce the status of the five regional cities and the other higher-order centres, thus implying that their claim on the central development funds was to be accorded a lower priority in future, while conversely the right of smaller settlements to assistance was enhanced. It was important that the settlements in the zones of influence were given equal rights with regard to their common affairs. All these historical events are reflected in the present structure and attitude.

From 1971 until 1985 there was a parallel administrative system of economic planning regions. They were used primarily for planning and statistical purposes and did not function in a wider sense due to their lack of authorisation and resistance of the counties.

The 1984 system has been modified by the Act on Local Self-Government in 1990, which acknowledged the right of local communities to autonomous self-government. In connection with the economic funds it recognises the right of a local government to local public property. There are, however, ongoing political debates about its realisation within the framework of privatisation and decentralisation of public (central state) property.

According to the new Act the counties have lost their redistributive role. There is no legal hierarchical dependency between the county and the settlements. The counties are responsible for regional affairs not belonging to individual municipalities in the area. Their bodies are elected by the delegates of the assemblies of local governments. The administration by branches preserved, however, its regional arms in the form of county offices for individual ministries. Other elements under previous county control were centralised.

As part of the present administrative picture, Hungary also has a system of commissionaires with an accompanying system of 8 regions. From a regional point of view they have the burden of being composed from the existing system of counties, which are not geographical units in any economic or social sense.

In summary, it can be stated that the role of regional policy or the emphasis on regional aspects was growing after the periods of democratic change in macro-level policy. The regional problems or the regular intervention into local affairs and interests were an integral part of the factors leading to the changes, but this was not always a conscious step. Sometimes only the support of different local forces were necessary. Thus the position of regional policy began to strengthen. Because it was attached especially to decentralisation processes its realisation was slowed down or modified in periods of centralisation. Based on this and on the sector-orientated industrial development, regional policy became gradually directed towards the social supply, and eventually began to function as a short-term social security valve. Because of its short-sightedness, sectoral administrative limits and financial shortages, it could not be effective in the long term.

Post-war planning had to, and present policy development has to, contend with severe imbalances in the spatial structure of Hungary. Among the historical roots for these can be identified the special, localised character of the impressive general economic development between 1867 and the First World War. Based on the market of the Austro-Hungarian Monarchy and on the extensively growing agricultural production all food industry amounted to 44% of the country's industrial production (Kóródi 1970). Owing to the railway construction boom, mining and metallurgy developed at a high rate. The development was based on raw material resources located in the peripheries of the country inhabited by national minorities. But engineering industry could not develop because of the more advanced Austrian and Bohemian industry. Possibilities opened only in newly emerging industries like electric appliances. In this field the new factories (e.g. Ganz, Tungsram) were the most advanced in the world. Spatially they were concentrated primarily in Budapest. Unfortunately, they could not preserve their high technological status and today they are among those factories which are facing radical transformation.

Regional development and regional problems in Hungary also emanate from a multitude of sources amongst which the agglomeration of Budapest, in itself, is one of the more prominent. Budapest was in 1949 more than ten times the size of the second city, Debrecen. Though there were definite efforts to decrease its dominance, the difference between the first and second city remained the same but in 1991 the second city had become Miskolc. The share of its population grew from 17.3% to 19.5% between 1949 and 1991. At the end of the post-war reconstruction period it contained 47% of the urbanized population (Compton 1987). Fifty per cent of all industry was concentrated here and 54% of industrial employment. The historical background for this phenomenon lay in the territorial losses after the First World War. Hungary lost 68% of its territory and 58% of its population. The arbitrary boundaries drawn by the French and British military commissions played havoc with the economic structures and relations as cities of second-rank importance suddenly were located outside the new Hungarian borders. The new boundaries made their impact by cutting off, in general terms, manufacturing from sources of raw materials, as well as agriculture and food industry from traditional markets. Changes at the turn of 1990s are similar in their economic impact, and as a consequence, Hungary and her neighbouring countries have had to face three radical cut-offs (1918, 1945, 1990) within 75 years.

Owing to the territorial changes the ratio of Budapest in the total population increased from 4.25% to 11.6% and in industrial employment from 27% to 54%. Budapest came to exert an overdominant position in the remaining national area. It could be said to dominate to such an extent that it acted as a brake on inter-regional economic ties. This situation formed the starting-point for one of the basic principles of regional policy: to transform the radial structure of the country to a more flexible and integrated system. These measures did have an effect and the relative importance of Budapest decreased in industrial production. Employment in industrial activity fell from 54% in 1949 to one-third by 1970, and to a quarter by 1980. In 1989 the figure was 21.2%. However, the figures for 1990 and 1991 (21.7% and over 22% respectively) show a possible break in this process.

The only other area of significant industrial activity lay along the Middle Mountains, stretching from the Borsod County in the north-east of the country to Zala county in the south-west, where Hungary's basic industries were located, and where a substantial manufacturing sector had grown up. The area forms a discontinuous 'densely settled zone' to the north-east and south-west of Budapest. The centre of the north-eastern part is Miskolc (the second largest city with 208,000 inhabitants) and the highly industrialized agglomeration in the Sajó valley with heavy industries. In the south-west part there are industrial centres of small and medium size and several of them have shown considerable growth in recent decades. Other urban settlements of importance include Györ, the manufacturing and commercial centre of the Little Plains, Pécs, with its neighbouring coalfield in the South-Transdanubia, while Szeged and Debrecen are typical centres in the agricultural region of the Great Plains.

Apart from Budapest's role in the regional structure, and in spite of a rather homogenous spatial distribution of natural and human resources, there exist in Hungary regional differences of such a magnitude that they deserve special attention.

The regional convergence (sectoral–structural change) induced automatically a territorial change which affected industrialisation and other socioeconomic indicators. This was produced by an extensive industrialization in large areas and was, during several decades and almost until the beginning of the 1980s, part of the most characteristic regional process. It even encouraged, for a time, the realisation of goals of the regional development policy. Today the structural outcome of these processes faces a reversal. It can be divided into two basic areas: export- and nationally-induced production. The structural impact in its general effect was caused by the heavy orientation towards the former CMEA countries and especially the former Soviet Union and the simultaneous continuance of central administration. The advantage of the stable East European market made the productive structure technologically lagging behind Western standards and badly prepared for the nearly total disappearance of its former export partners. The factor of international adaptability had been lacking for a long time. Accordingly this made the Hungarian economy extremely vulnerable to a market-orientated change and not at all prepared to form a basis for a smooth or at least not too complicated transition process. Switching-over to the market management system, crisis phenomena burst out in the form of large-scale sectoral and regional problems.

Changes in international economic relations had always very strong effects on the regional structure. For example, before the war the western part of Hungary had close connections with German and English firms. This significantly strengthened the higher level of development in this region. After the war the orientation of policy had been changed from the West to the East, and the western part was cut off from its previous relations. As a result, the development was stopped, especially in the border areas. On the other side, in the most backward eastern part of the country, only timber industry and railway transfer was developed on the basis of the raw material connection with the USSR and several branches of agriculture for the Soviet market. During 40 years these were not able to generate a developing economy for the region. Nowadays the whole process is reversing.

The centrally instigated priority maintained in the early years of Communist rule emphasised sectoral aspects of industrialisation, especially for the development of heavy industry. This priority accentuated a development along the Middle Mountains and the Pécs regions and drained the agricultural sector of investment resources and the agriculturally dominated regions of manpower with known effects on population age structures and the accompanying reduced economic potential. Although a diminished emphasis on heavy industry appeared in 1954, resources were still orientated towards industry, thus widening the regional differences. Efficient industrial development was possible primarily where industry was already located and a great part of the objectives (e.g. the industrialisation of the Great Plain) remained, for a long time only a policy declaration. Even natural gas and oil discovered in the Great Plain were used and processed in the already industrialised regions. (Lackó 1984).

In the 1960s, as a result of the changes in agriculture (collectivisation between 1959 and 1961 with the introduction of large-scale farming) and industrialisation programmes, there was a great migration from rural areas toward industrial centres. The population of Budapest grew by 200,000 inhabitants and that of the other cities by 700,000. In the early 1960s the largest regional centres (Budapest and the above mentioned five cities) and the traditional industrial cities accelerated their growth. In the second half the middle-sized towns (especially the county seats) showed a growing relative advantage together with the newly established or developed 'socialist cities'.

An important regional objective of the 1960s was the supply of infrastructure for the population. In all, this effort yielded fewer results than industrial locational policy because the proportion of the infrastructural investments (although its volume continuously increased) remained below that of production capacity investments throughout the whole decade. Partly because of housing shortages (especially in the cities), partly for preserving the food production possibilities as a second economy, the daily and weekly commuting has increased throughout the country and particularly around Budapest and the large cities.

In connection with the radical changes in agriculture the problem of backward agrarian provinces was brought sharply into focus. The instrument used to handle this priority was industrial development. Rural industry developed more rapidly in these backward areas and new industrial centres came into being in an island-like manner alongside, and within, traditional rural industrial centres. The policy, with its priorities had an impact as it decreased inequalities on a macro-regional level, and had by 1968 created 200,000 new industrial jobs in the priority areas. However, the impact did not change inter-regional or urban–regional proportions in any significant way.[2] Though a levelling had occurred between regions and counties in terms of economic development, differences in standard of living between towns and villages had increased. (Bauko and Korhonen 1991).

The process did also introduce other aspects with spatial implications and importance for present-day problems. The new priorities channelled through the centralised administrative system (read ministries) deformed the investment struc-tures in many ways. For instance, a large share of the decentralised or new production units was based on out-of-date technological processes or products, and as such were not given a sound financial and operational basis. Consequently they were finding themselves, from the start, in severe economic difficulties and

---

2   The reason is apparent as these backward regions still did not receive more than a quarter of the total investment.

allied to this the choice of technology and location did not take into consideration the severe impact on the environment. A traditional division of labour had appeared where research, development and management activities remained in the cities, especially Budapest.

The reform of 1968 set the framework for the future and even though the first stage soon saw implementational problems, regional policy and development yielded much more important results in the 1970s than earlier. The transformation of industry is indicated by the fact that while in 1949 the number of industrial employees per 1000 inhabitants was 90 to 130 in the three most industrialised counties, in 1981 the same figures were only comparable to the four least developed counties. It is characteristic of the rate of levelling that the difference between the most industrialised and least industrialised counties was fourfold in 1970 and only twofold in 1981 (Lackó 1984).

The fundamental change in the international oil market with rapidly increasing oil prices (1973–74) made Hungary, with its oil-dependent economy, face the new situation with a substantial change in economic policy. The policy chosen could, with hindsight, be identified as badly suited for long-term economic perspectives. It included an extension of subsidies in the consumer and in the foreign trade sectors, which cushioned the economy and necessary structural adjustments were not made. Budget-financing of these subsidies was made possible through heavy external borrowing which plays an important role in present-day structural problems. Financing the new economic situation through borrowing, without necessary adaptation to the new prerequisites, could not be sustained for very long, as Hungary's credibility as a debtor nation soon became questioned by the international financial institutions and new loans became increasingly expensive. Still not really adapting, the government turned to import reduction and export promotion. The balance-of-payment problem was mastered but the long-term structural economic problems were not. This is an important lesson. In the beginning of the 1980s a new wave of reform was on its way including a price reform, a new bankruptcy law for all types of enterprises, a two-level banking system, and a new company law. In general, however, these changes did not touch upon the basic characteristics of the old system.

The typical attributes of this period affecting the regional consequences of transformation were the expansion of structural–territorial problems of full employment, the decrease in functions of small and larger villages, their basically residential function with population loss in most cases, the liquidation of small villages and the forming of contiguous areas of depression and a further erosion of former backward ones (mainly along the national borders and in the frontier regions of the counties).

Since the end of the 1980s, with the successive introduction of market evaluation for different products simultaneously with diminishing or disappearing subsidies[3] and decreasing standard of living, physical production has decreased on a national level. The regional impact of these reductions and their consequences are uneven. Based on internal political tensions and through the change in the international environment (that is, perestroika and the new foreign policy in the former Soviet Union) there appeared time, will and space to question the fundamentals of the former economic-administrative and one-party systems.

Hungary's financial situation deteriorated in 1989 because the government was unable to stem the flow of funds from the country. This flow took the form of large and uncompensated CMEA exports and services and convertible currency allocation to tourists travelling to the West. The precarious financial situation made the IMF a major political factor in Hungary in 1989, as it had earlier in Poland and the former Yugoslavia. The new political situation formed the basis for a new political structure. The process of change has been extremely fast and programmes and policies formed under this process have been characterised by being incomplete and ad hoc in both their presentation and implementation. The call from foreign lenders and governments – the most prominent being the IMF and the German government – for concerted action on the economic front is an example. By the end of 1990 the Ministry of Finance announced its three-year economic programme. It envisaged a decline of 4% in Hungary's GDP in 1991 (the outcome was about 8%), a drop of 4–5% in consumption (7–8%), and an inflation rate of 35%. It was not a strict austerity plan and contained nothing that could have been termed 'shock therapy', comparable to the Polish model. The regional dimension appeared in this programme only in connection with unemployment. 1989 saw the start of privatisation and the beginning of the largest direct Western capital inflow into Hungary since World War II.

The foreign debt is approximately 23 billion dollars. The debt service in 1990 was 3.5 billion dollars. The total debt is the highest per capita in Eastern Europe and appears in a leading position even on a global scale (IMF Survey 1991). During 1991 and in the first half of 1992 the debt began to decrease (to 15 billion and 13.4 billion dollars respectively) due to export successes and gains in the exchange rate.

The traditionally high importance of food industry and agriculture within the Hungarian economy has been substantially changed as the traditional Soviet and East European markets have disappeared. The EC, due to its import restrictions in the agricultural sector, is not a realistic alternative and the domestic consumption potential is not big enough. In addition, substantial price increases have made the Hungarian consumer reduce consumption. Difficulties have emerged for meat, milk and wine production and for fruits and in 1991 even for wheat. This should

---

3   The ratio of consumer price subsidies in the central budget was 8.4% in 1987, 4.9% in 1988 and 2.4% in 1991. The ratio of all subsidies to gross value added at the enterprises on a national level was 17.5% in 1987, 14% in 1988 and 2.8% in 1991.

be considered in the face of the fact that 20% of the Hungarian population is dependent upon agricultural production. The heavy impact on the Alföld region and other areas where agriculture plays a prominent role is evident.

The previously hidden unemployment became visible and exacerbated by local crisis phenomena. The rate of unemployment has grown from 1.7% in December 1990 to 10.9% in July 1992. Today there is an openly recognized problem of poverty. The Central Statistical Office estimates that, at least, 3 million of Hungary's 10.6 million citizens fall into the poverty category. An estimated 1 million people live below the officially defined 'social minimum'.

The Regional Pattern 2:
The Conflict of Present and Future in the Transition

The strategy declared by the Hungarian government is an orientation towards a modern market economy called by several economists a 'social market economy'. The fundamental problem for the future is a general one. How to combine a strategic reorientation with short-term responses to a range of problems. There is also another question of fundamental importance and that is the speed of transformation set within the context of short-term economic necessities.

One of the most pressing problems is that of national debt. This is crucial as the debt service will continue to drain Hungary of its growth potential and sources for structural change. So far the government has not been willing to renegotiate. There are different approaches to the problem. The most widely accepted solution would be to attach Hungary's debt to the international agreement about the problem. But until that time it is in Hungary's interest to safeguard the country's solvency by continuing to fulfil its obligations.

For economic growth and increased efficiency in the Hungarian economy, liberalisation and privatisation are regarded as crucial mechanisms. Thirty-five per cent of the state-owned and controlled sector has already been privatised. The objective is defined as somewhere in the vicinity of 80–90% (Privatizacios Leltar Nepszabadsag July 8th 1992, Ojabb Kamatcsokkentes As Mnb-nel Nepszabadsag August 10th 1992). The process of privatisation has accelerated since the middle of 1991. Until that time there were 162 transformations of enterprises and yet by the end of the year there were around 600. There is, however, a tense debate on the nature of this process as exemplified by one or two dubious privatisation cases. Substantial legal and institutional frameworks were lacking as well as professional experience. One of the main drawbacks in this area was also the fact that a financial market was not functioning properly and was further handicapped by high interest rates (around 35%). In 1991 the Budapest Stock Exchange began its activity, although at present only a small section of the economy is involved. Based on a strict financial policy and the evolution of the banking system as well as the operation of a financial market, the interest rate began to decrease. In the middle of 1992 it had been reduced to around 25%.

The inflow of foreign capital is another potential source of economic growth. However, that in itself raises other problems. Three general problems, which also have a spatial impact, can be identified:

1. The interests of international finance do not necessarily coincide with national and local interests. The first inflow has been orientated towards the service sector where the incomes in convertible currency and high profits are most easily obtainable. As to the regional impact, detailed empirical information is still lacking. Initial major investments (e.g. General Motors in Szentgotthárd and Suzuki in Esztergom) indicate that the dominance of Budapest is in its indirect effects, not prominent and evident. This problem requires further study.

2. There is a possible tendency that international collaboration will buy out their Hungarian partners.

3. There is a growing suspicion and hostility, especially within the industrial workers community, towards the selling-out of 'Hungarian' property.

However, the growing role of international capital in the process of privatisation is an important one. Lately its share is 35–40% (Vannak Az Orszagban tokeeros Beruhazsok, Magyar Nemzet, July 30th 1992). There are already about 11,000 joint-stock companies and about 4 billion dollars of active capital has already been invested.

In connection with privatisation, the number of limited companies established during 1990 grew from 5978 (1989) to 21,303 and in 1991 there were already more than 40,000. The ratio of small and medium size enterprises (under 800 employees) is 80% by the number of organisations and 22% by the number of employees. This figure is still half of that in the developed market economies (Kiss 1991). This process has been stimulated by the government in order to reduce the problem of unemployment. Though the emergence of small enterprises may be observed all over the country it has been concentrated in Budapest and other urban agglomerations.

Concerning liberalisation a treasury reform is urged by almost everyone but neither 'monetarists' nor 'institutionalists' include it in their programmes. The 'Westernisation' of the accounting system uses serious taxation interests and the treasury reform would have catastrophic effects on the structure of real wages. This also points out the lack of a social protection network (Mandel and Veress 1991). The proposed liberalisation of wages in 1992 without this social security system, together with the growing rate of privatisation and other measures for market orientation will hardly achieve the desired objective of a 'social market economy' from the social side. At the same time a moderated decrease of the redistributive role of the state budget is planned for the next four years to avoid greater shocks. However, this will again weaken the objectives formulated for a 'social market economy'.

The inheritance of regional differences and inequalities appears in a very obvious way. The old two-tier system has been revoked and the authority of local communities strengthened. The counties' authority has been downgraded to a negligible level as they were closely linked with the previous system of redistribution, that is the regional organisation of the HSWP (Hungarian Socialist Workers Party) and with strong county-level party secretaries. Between the local self-government bodies and the central administration one can find the new dimension of eight regions with regional commissioners. They were the product of compromises made in the process of forming the first post-communist government and their authority and jurisdictions are still under formation.

In this situation a spontaneous organisation is possible and there is evidence that it is already appearing. First, the organisation of local communities with special-purpose integrative agreements. Second, the appearance of local branches of central administrative organisations. Third a strengthening of the eight-region system and the commissioners' roles. Fourth, the possible strengthening of some aspects of the old county organisation. Fifth, centrally instigated local regional development agencies working in the form of enterprises or foundations which will assist adaptation to a market and fill the gap between local and central development.

The situation would not be so problematic if there were a clear-cut strategy and organisational authority at governmental level, responsible for regional considerations and the development of a regional policy. The situation is, at present, characterised by the direct involvement of several ministries (i.e. Ministry of Finance, Ministry of Environment and Regional Development, Ministry of Transport, Communication and Water Management). The regional dimension is at present the focus of interdepartmental haggling and it is still at a relative standstill on the surface. Budgetary allocation is clearly the most important aspect of this debate but it has not been resolved.

By the autumn of 1992 the outline of a new Regional Development Act was due to be submitted to the government by the Minister of Environmental and Regional Development Affairs. The former was approved in 1985 and does not function under present circumstances. One of the most critical points was to construct a system in which the independence of local governments would be preserved and the regional interests represented and realised in an effective way. Another point was the involvement of regional policy aspects in the newly established framework of central government policy, because at the time of its elaboration the regional approach, owing to its weaknesses, was pushed into the background. Furthermore, it is also doubtful if the idea of planning or intervention, as such, will be well received by the present coalition government and the majority of the opposition with its highly liberal orientation. Still, the new law could, and should, define the organisation of the regional dimension and the authority and jurisdiction pertaining to different administrative units in order to reach some minimum level of efficiency and order.

The trouble with the new territorial and settlement development framework is that the increasing role of local resources and decision-making aimed at micro-economic progress is declared at the same time as central sources of funding are closed down. On the local level the possibility of resource mobilisation, although in general limited, varies from community to community. Local incomes (which will be increased in the future with a transfer of ownership of land, communal services, etc.), local negotiation skills and willingness to subsidise will make the future economic scenario a most complex and varied one. This may not necessarily lead to a positive outcome for the general pattern of regional development. It is evident that the concept of regional settlement systems and regional equality cannot function when the lack of economic growth or even reduction of the national income will be the trends for the foreseeable future. As at the present, regional policy is not part of the central economic strategy for the country. However, there are a number of ad hoc policies which do have a regional impact.

The final outcome of transformation will have markedly different effects on each region. Regions that were earlier defined as backward or potentially de-pressed, were finding themselves in an even worse situation both absolutely and relatively. Especially pronounced is where the sectoral crisis is closely connected with a regional concentration. The most important sectors in this respect are mining, metallurgy and the production and processing of foodstuffs. The areas most dependent are the Borsod and the North in general, the area around Pécs and the Alföld region (Bauko and Korhonen 1991). The magnitude of the problem becomes more pronounced when set in the framework of demographic tendencies and infrastructural potential. This is not a one-way process. The demographic tendencies affect the development through the high correlation between back-wardness and high rates of natural increase. In spite of the former constitutional recognition of the right-of-work, these regions have seen a continuous level of unemployment. With the current increase in unemployment the tendency to migrate will therefore increase. The problem of a lack of educational and craft skills and the lack of absorption capacity in other areas of the country for unskilled labour will exacerbate the problem.

The infrastructural potential is also a necessary part of any spatially orientated development programme. The lack of an infrastructural basis for modern economic development will also be an obstacle to the relocation of economic activities to these areas. The Borsod county with a production orientation towards low-grade brown coal, iron and steelworks registered 12,505 (3.5%) out of work at the end of 1990. The prognosis for 1992 was estimated at about 40,000 unemployed or around 15% of the labour force (Barta and Poszmik 1992). The situation is most critical within the region of Ozd (a city with 45,000 inhabitants) where the dominant employer is the steel-works which has become insolvent. Hidden industrial crises can also be detected in other parts of the North Hungarian region (Bartke 1991). In the Baranya and Komárom counties the impact of the orientation towards mining place them in an unfavourable position. In the Pécs area, where coal and uranium mining has been an important part of the picture, the production costs are substantially above world market price. Consequently, the coal mining industry will be phased out: by 1994 in Pécs and by the year 2000 in Komló where the dominant employer is the mining industry.

A traditional hard currency earning sector has been the armament industry. The best customers, over the years, have been the Soviet Union and several Middle Eastern countries. Both, for different reasons, are dropping out of the picture. This is behind the bankruptcy of Videoton Electronic Company, the largest manufacturer of electronic goods in Hungary, located in Székesfehérvár (the county seat of Fejér county with 110,000 inhabitants at about 65 km from Budapest). In 1991 the company had 138,000 employees but only 30% to 40% were effectively working. Other large factories in this city (Ikarus,[4] Aluminium Mill-Works) are also facing serious difficulties. It is slightly paradoxical that the enterprises of the modern electronics industry are operating at a loss whilst metallurgy established in the 1950s in Dunaújváros produces a profit within the same county (Juhász 1991)

The consistent realisation of the reform of economic management and the accomplishment of a market environment will, in all probability, cause a further impetus to the detachment process of less developed regions, since the relative backwardness and the extreme underdevelopment of the infrastructure, as a component of it, will exert a repulsive influence on profit-oriented undertakings. Within the process of market orientation this deterioration in the pattern of regional inequality should be recognised and addressed by policy-makers.

The status among some of the most backward and depressed regions is such that regional programmes have had to be launched. Verbal information reveals the availability of 1.5 billion forints for 1991 which was allocated specifically for problem regions. Foreign consultants have been employed and local development offices set up. They are, however, highly dependent upon local activity and there is no central regulation as to the utilisation of these resources. Large-scale foreign entrepreneurs are given large concessions. However, they do not necessarily turn to the regions where the problems are most acute.

The competition of regions within Hungary is highly orientated towards identifying and obtaining the resources for transformation. The important issue in the present process is not the conflict between state involvement and the market. Rather, in the context of regional inequalities it is the recognition by both the state and the market of the severe levels of backwardness and depression which currently exist in Hungary. The state must play a lead role in addressing these problems.

---

4   In 1989 over 5000 buses were delivered to the Soviet Union, or about 42% of Ikarus's total
    production. Without the Soviet, or today FIS, market, Ikarus would be hard hit.

References

Barta, G. and Poszmik, P. (1992) 'A gazdasági alkalmazkodás elsö jelei a borsodi válságtérségben.' *Közgazdasági Szemle 29*, 4.

Bartke (1991) *Reform of the Regional Management in Hungary*. Budapest: Institute for Economic Planning.

Bauko, T. and Korhonen, J. (1991) 'Post-war regional development in Hungary with special reference to the Alföld region.' *Occasional Papers*, 4. University of Gothenburg: Department of Human and Economic Geography.

Compton, P. (1987) 'Hungary.' In A.H. Dawson *Planning in Eastern Europe*. London: Croom Helm.

Enyedi, G. (1990) 'New basis for regional and urban policies in East-Central Europe.' *Discussion papers No 9*. Pécs: Centre for Regional Studies.

IMF Survey (1991) *IMF Survey 20*, 16. August 12.

Kiss, J.S. (1991) 'A nagy bukások és újrakezdések éve következik?' *Magyar Hírlap*, July 22.

Juhász, G. (1991) 'Hadiárva.' *Heti Világgazdaság*, July 12.

Kóródi J. (1970) *Változások Magyarország gazdaságitérképén*. Budapest: Kossuth Könyvkiadó.

Lackó, L. (1984) 'An assessment of regional policies and programs in Eastern Europe.' In G. Demko (ed) *Regional development problems and policies in Eastern and Western Europe*. London: Croom Helm.

Mandel, M. and Veress, J. (1991) 'Dilemmas of economic change – in crisis.' Working Paper, Budapest University of Economics, Economic Policy Department, Center for Independent Policy Studies, Budapest.

CHAPTER 17

Labour Mobility Between Western and Eastern European Countries[1]

Christos Nikas

Introduction

The revival of economic relationships between two previously segmented economies or groups of economies raises a series of questions concerning the nature and
pattern of their potential economic relations. Economic relations between countries or groups of countries refer to a wide spectrum of factors including the trading
of goods and services (which is sometimes surprisingly seen as the main if not the
only aspect to be taken into account) and factors of production (which attract less
attention).

The relatively recent developments in Europe seem to suggest that the above
points are applicable to the relations between Eastern Europe and the EC countries.
In fact the recent rapprochement between 'the two Europes' after a 45-year period
of relative political and economic isolation raises a series of questions concerning
the perspectives of economic relations between them, among which labour
mobility could be seen as one of the main areas of investigation.

It should be kept in mind that during the long period of isolation between
Western and Eastern Europe movements of labour were very limited; in fact
progress in trade and capital movements outweighed in importance movements of
labour despite the emergence of refugee flows.

In this chapter an examination of the perspectives of labour migration between
Western and Eastern European countries is placed within a background of

---

1   An earlier version of this chapter was published in *European Research*, Nov. 1991.

intra-European labour mobility in the post-war period and is followed by an analysis of the present situation in the European continent as far as this particular subject is concerned.

The main difficulty for the analysis arises from the lack of reliable and comparable data on the labour markets of the Eastern European countries, especially as far as unemployment is concerned; this is mainly due to the fact that the economic system in operation until recently in these countries provided for extremely low unemployment rates (12%) (Wiles 1977, p.378).

Background

The economic theory

The theory on the causes of movements of labour provides a series of factors which may affect the size and the pattern of migratory flows. Although no school of economic thought has really provided a complete theory on the causes of international migration, there is a clear distinction between neoclassical and Keynesian oriented approaches. The former stress the importance of wage differentials as the main driving force for migration to occur, while the latter stress the importance of availability of jobs (for a more comprehensive literature review on the theory of migration see Nikas 1992).

More recent approaches distinguish the factors causing migratory flows and determining their size into 'push' and 'pull' ones (Nikas 1989, 1992). The 'push' factors refer to the forces generated in the emigration countries and which induce people to leave, such as unemployment, limited job vacancies, low income, etc. The 'pull' factors refer to the attraction of labour by countries which possess many employment opportunities, high wages and good working and living conditions. In most cases, the operation of both sets of factors is necessary for migration to occur; the question, though, is which set of factors is the decisive one or, in other words, which factors influence the size and the pattern of migratory flows the most. On various occasions (Glitsos 1987, Vanhove and Klaassen 1983) empirical investigations on the determining factors of post-war migratory flows in Europe were mainly determined by the 'pull' factors. In fact, these flows seem to have been mainly determined by the availability of jobs in the immigration EC countries, although nobody could deny the existence of 'push' factors such as vast labour surpluses in the emigration countries.

The facts

The post-war intra-European movements of people can be divided into three distinct phases. The first refers to the period 1945–1961 and is characterised by the massive inflow of refugees from Eastern Europe; the second refers to the massive inflow of labour from Mediterranean European countries in the period

1961–1974 and the deceleration of immigration (followed by an acceleration of repatriation) since 1975. The third is the present situation.

Immigration from Eastern Europe

The early post-war period was marked by a massive flow of refugees from Eastern to Western Europe. In addition to the movements that followed agreements for population exchange just after the war, refugee movements accelerated after 1945. In the period 1945–1950 West Germany received 7.8 million refugees (mainly ethnic Germans from East Germany, Poland, Czechoslovakia and Hungary) (Salt and Clout 1976, p.22). By 1955 the number had increased by a million, rising to 17.4% of total population. Three million more, mainly from East Germany, came in via Berlin until the erection of the wall in 1961. To these numbers one should add 200,000 Hungarians after the uprising in 1956 and 200,000–300,000 Poles who moved until the 1960s (Salt and Glout 1976, pp.222–3).

Although in the beginning of this period fears were expressed about whether refugees could be absorbed in productive employment, the unprecedented increases in the demand for labour in many EC countries (mainly West Germany) following the reconstruction boom provided employment for them very quickly. In fact refugee labour proved to be one of the main sources of labour supply in that period (Kindleberger 1967, p.303). Furthermore, the increases in demand for labour in most EC countries in that period were of such an intensity that when the inflow of refugees ceased by 1961 they had to 'import' labour from other countries – mainly the Mediterranean ones.

It is not at all clear whether these movements of refugees should be treated as migratory ones in the economic sense of the term. Although they had an impact on the labour markets of the receiving countries these movements were mainly due to political rather than economic events. For example, a large number of the Hungarians who left their country in 1956 repatriated soon after (Salt and Clout 1976, p.210). Generally speaking, international migration does not seem to have been important in size even among Eastern European countries. Most of the labour mobility in these countries referred to internal (from rural to urban areas) rather than external migration – Yugoslavia being the main exception after the schism in its relations with the USSR. Even within the framework of CMEA (Comecon), intra-Eastern European migrations were very limited in extent.

These observations on international labour mobility in Eastern Europe are consistent with the barriers to entry and exit these countries erected. Besides which, the extremely high growth of employment (mainly due to political rather than economic factors) coupled with a negligible unemployment in these countries 'protected' them from undesirable population pressures.

Immigration from the Mediterranean countries

Unlike the case of refugee flows from Eastern Europe, movements from the Mediterranean emigration countries (Greece, Spain, Portugal, Turkey, Yugoslavia and Italy until the mid-1960s) were caused by economic factors.

The inflow of immigrants to several EC countries (especially West Germany) in the period 1961–1974 reached unprecedented levels. In the 1960s immigrant labour was the main source of labour supply for most EC countries (Bernabe 1982). Unlike the refugee flows of the 1950s, emigration from the Mediterranean countries was of a temporary nature and varied according to the demand for labour in the host countries. Furthermore, these movements were highly regulated in the sense that immigrants were usually moving to a certain area or job and, more generally, in the sense that these labour flows followed bilateral agreements between the emigration and the immigration countries.

The outbreak of the economic crisis in the 1970s clearly affected migration in Western Europe; the bilateral agreements were suspended, the inflow of new immigrants was minimised and the repatriation of the existing ones was encouraged. As a result, the stock of immigrant labour in the EC countries has drastically fallen ever since, although non-European immigrants have proved to be 'tougher' during the recession. The developments since 1974 clearly suggest the predominance of the 'pull' factors in determining migratory flows; by the time the 'pull' forces were no longer in operation immigration came to an end, although the 'push' factors never really ceased to exist.

The present situation

There is a series of factors which need to be taken into consideration in order to analyse labour mobility in Europe in the 1990s. These factors could be divided into purely economic and political ones, although the latter could have a clear effect on economic variables.

THE RECENT POLITICAL DEVELOPMENTS IN EUROPE RELATIVE TO LABOUR MOBILITY

Three main issues will be included in this analysis, namely the relationships between the EC and the Eastern and Western European countries after the political change in Eastern Europe, the unification of Germany and the progress of economic integration in the EC.

It is quite obvious that the relatively recent political changes in Eastern Europe have broadened the scope for closer economic relations in the future. Could this mean free labour mobility, especially from Eastern to Western countries? The answer will probably depend on how far these relations will go and on a series of economic aspects relative to the labour markets involved, which will be examined in the following sections. The point to be made here is that, under normal circumstances, one will hardly be able speak of political refugee flows from Eastern Europe in the future. If there are to be movements of people, they could only be of a migratory nature, that is, determined and administered by the same factors which apply to all emigration countries. More simply, Western European immigration countries are no longer committed to allow the entrance of people from Eastern Europe, the way they were in the past, since it will clearly be employment rather than asylum these people will be after.

The second issue is related to the reunification of the two Germanies. Unification means a reintegration of the two (previously separate) labour markets into one. As far as immigration to the unified Germany is concerned, this could simply mean that any surpluses of labour emerging in the Eastern part of the country will have to be dealt with before even considering any additional immigration. Taking into account that the former West Germany has been the main 'labour importer' in the post-war period, it is possible to see the reunification as a factor making the admission of immigrants from other Eastern European countries to Germany quite unlikely.

The third issue refers to the progress of economic integration in the Western part of the continent, which has accelerated in the last few years after the adoption of the Single European Act by EC members and the completion of the Single European Market at the end of 1992. One of the main changes to be expected, as far as migrations are concerned, is the perfect liberalisation of labour mobility between the Community Members. This of course does not necessarily imply massive intra-Community movements of labour, although the present EC includes several past immigration countries as full members. What it really means is that, administratively speaking, unless Eastern European workers acquire somehow the same privileges as the Community ones, they will always be 'less competitive' in the Community labour markets. The same, more or less, applies to the contents of the Maastricht Treaty decisions.

THE RECENT ECONOMIC DEVELOPMENTS

Although the economic transformation of the Eastern European economies to market ones is very recent, it is possible to distinguish some of the apparent implications, particularly as far as the labour markets are concerned.

The post-war performance of the Eastern European economies, especially as far as their labour markets are concerned, was characterised by a very rapid growth of employment and, in particular, employment in manufacturing. Although Eastern Europe witnessed relatively low population growth in the post-war period (Berelson 1974, p.152), employment growth was facilitated by the impressively high (by Western standards) female participation rates (ILO 1974, p.5) and the absorption of underemployed labour mainly from agriculture (ILO 1976, pp.747–9). As we can see in Tables 17.1 and 17.2, the growth rates of total and industrial employment in Eastern Europe were far higher than the Western European ones, at least until 1986. This could, of course, be attributed to the fact that under the system in operation in Eastern Europe everybody was guaranteed employment irrespective of productivity. It is quite indicative that employment in Eastern

Europe was increasing at impressive rates even during periods of recession for Western Europe (e.g. the mid-1970s). In fact the Eastern European industry in the 1970s appeared to be faced with a problem of shortage of skilled labour (ILO 1976, p.71).

Table 17.1 The growth of employment in Eastern and Western Europe, 1965–1989 (annual growth rates)

	1960–1970	1971–1975	1976–1980	1981	1982	1983	1984	1985	1986	1987	1988	1989
Eastern Europe[1]	1.83	2.58	1.98	1.60	0.20	0.50	0.40	0.60	0.70	0.40	0.10	0.60
Western Europe[2]	0.03	0.10	0.46	1.40	0.70	0.60	0.10	0.20	0.90	1.40	1.90	1.60

[1] Including Bulgaria, Czechoslovakia, Eastern Germany, Hungary, Poland and Yugoslavia.
[2] Including Belgium, Spain, France, W. Germany, Italy and the U.K.
Sources: 1. ILO, International labour statistics, various issues.
         2. Own calculations.

Things started to change during the early 1980s for two main reasons. First, the symptoms of de-industrialisation (mainly the inability of manufacturing to absorb labour at the same rate as before) started to appear in Eastern Europe in the same way they had earlier in Western Europe. Second, there was the beginning of a transformation of these economies to market ones. In fact, the case of Hungary, where transformation had started earlier than in the other countries, is quite indicative in the sense that the deceleration in employment coincides with the economic changes.

At this point it should be explained why the transformation of planned economies to market ones influences employment in a negative way, at least in the short run. First of all, the deregulation of the economy implies that firms are no longer forced to hire labour simply because this labour exists. Secondly, releasing labour that is not needed becomes possible since employment is no longer protected by laws in the way it used to be (Wiles 1977, pp.377–8).

In the particular case of Eastern Europe, transformation coincided with (or arguably caused) the outbreak of an unprecedented economic crisis; inflation rates in 1990 climbed to levels varying from 30% in Hungary (The Economist 30 September 1990) to 60% in Poland and the USSR (The Economist 17 November 1990, 22 December 1990). Industrial output and investment have fallen by up to a third in Poland (The Economist 26 January 1991) and the forecasts for the first half of the 1990s leave little room for optimism. In a few months, unemployment increased from zero to 1.2 million people in Poland (although one could argue that a large number of those declaring themselves as unemployed were simply seeking unemployment benefits).

Given the state the economies of most of these countries are in, the sizes of their external debts and the fact that their transformation will be a long and painful

Table 17.2 Employment growth in manufacturing in Eastern and Western Europe, 1965–88 (annual growth rates)

	1965–1970	1971–1975	1976–1980	1981	1982	1983	1984	1985	1986	1987	1988
Eastern Europe[1]	2.23	2.21	1.05	2.10	0.70	0.10	0.30	0.60	1.10	1.10	1.40
W. Europe[2]	0.69	0.80	2.19	4.40	2.00	3.70	1.30	0.80	0.80	0.20	0.80

[1] Including Bulgaria, Czechoslovakia, Eastern Germany, Hungary, Poland and Yugoslavia.
[2] Including Belgium, Spain, France, W. Germany, Italy and the U.K.
Sources: 1. ILO, International labour statistics, various issues.
　　　　　2. Own calculations.

Table 17.3 Unemployed (U), job vacancies (V) and vacancies per unemployed (V/U) in the main EC host countries, 1975–1989 (in thousands)

Year	UK U	UK V	UK V/U	FRG U	FRG V	FRG V/U	France U	France V	France V/U	Belgium U	Belgium V	Belgium V/U	Holland U	Holland V	Holland V/U
1975	1179	122	0.10	1074	236	0.21	839	–	–	208	4	0.02	195	47	0.24
1976	12	15	0.	10	23	0.	93	12	0.	26	4	0.	21	47	0.
	51	5	12	60	5	22	3	2	13	6		01	1		22
1977	12	21	0.	10	23	0.	10	10	0.	30	0.	20	55	0.	
	26	0	17	30	1	22	71	3	09	7		01	3		27
1978	11	24	0.	99	24	0.	11		0.	33	4	0.	20	63	0.
	40	1	21	3	6	24	67	86	07	3		01	5		30
1979	14	21	0.	87	30	0.	13		0.	35	5	0.	21	68	0.
	52	0	14	6	4	34	50	88	06	1		01	0		32
1980	22	24	0.	88	30	0.	14		0.	38	6	0.	24	54	0.
	70	1	10	9	8	34	67	89	06	2		01	8		21
1981	26		0.	12	20	0.	17		0.	45	4	0	28	20	0.
	26	91	03	72	8	16	50	69	03	4		01	5		07
1982	27	11	0.	18	10	0.	19		0.	53	4	0.	54	11	0.
	90	4	04	33	5	05	23	83	5		01	1		02	
1983	29	13	0.	22	76	0.	19		0.	58	6	0.	80	10	0.
	21	7	04	58		03	74	79	04	9		01	0		01
1984	30	15	0.	22		0.	23		0.	59	8	0.	82	15	0.
	36	0	05	66	88	03	23	46	01	5		01	2		01
1985	31	16	0.	23	11	0.	24		0.	55	18	0.	76	24	0.
	07	2	05	04	0	04	42	46	01	8		03	1		03
1986	28	18	0.	22	15	0.	24	49	0.	51	17	0.	71	27	0.
	22	8	06	28	4	06	89		01	6		03	0		03
1987	22	23	0.	22	17	0.	25	54	0.	50	–	–	68	26	0.
	95	4	10	29	1	07	32		02	0		5			03
1988	17	24	0.	22	18	0.	24	63	0.	45	–	–	43	–	–
	96	9	13	42	9	08	10		02	9			3		
1989	19	21	0.	20	25	0.	23	–	–	41	–	–	39	–	–
	53	9	11	38	1	12	12			9			3		

Source: ILO, International labour statistics, various issues; OECD, County surveys, various issues

process, one could say that the developments in Eastern Europe will probably lead to surpluses of labour, which are very unlikely to be domestically absorbed for a period of time. In other words, it seems that the 'push' factors for emigration (to Western Europe) to occur will be present. However, they will have to coincide with 'pull' factors.

Generally speaking (that is, referring to the labour markets in total rather than particular professions or groups of the labour force) the Western European host countries do not seem likely to need new immigrants in the near future. According to the information presented in Tables 17.3 and 17.4, the deterioration in the labour markets of the traditionally host EC countries (West Germany in particular) is such that only after a long-lasting and employment-creating boom could extra labour be needed. Even in such a case, though, one has to take into account that the Western European economies are more able now to substitute labour for high technology capital than they were in the 1960s. Furthermore, Western European countries may be unwilling to allow massive immigration because of the possible social and political implications it may have.

Table 17.4 Unemployed and job vacancies unfilled in (in thousands) in West Germany (1961–89)

YEAR	Unemployed (thousands)	Vacancies (thousands)	Ratio Vacancies Unemployed
1961	181	522	3.04
1965	148	644	4.35
1970	149	795	5.33
1975	1074	236	0.21
1980	889	308	0.34
1985	2304	110	0.04
1989	2038	251	0.12

Source: ILO, International labour statistics, various issues

Conclusion

The conclusions from the analysis presented in this chapter can be summarised as follows. The relatively recent developments in Eastern European countries, and the worsening economic environment there, could be seen as stimulating 'push' forces that will lead to major migrant flows to Western Europe. The present situation in the labour markets of the traditional host Western European countries, on the other hand, does not seem to suggest that 'pull' factors are in operation at present, nor are they very likely to reappear in the near future. Even if some immigrant labour is needed in Western Europe in the future, potential immigrants from Eastern Europe will have to 'compete' with those from Community members (including those from the Eastern part of Germany) who have the advantage of the free labour mobility within the EC. Taking these points into account, one could conclude that massive movements of labour from Eastern to Western Europe (similar to the ones from the Mediterranean countries in the 1960s and early 1970s) should not be expected in the near future, if existing labour market conditions continue.

What applies in general, though, may simply not apply for particular professions. One should not, therefore, exclude the possibility of migration of highly skilled labour, provided of course that the demand for such labour in Western Europe will substantially increase and that people possessing these skills could be found in Eastern Europe.

Furthermore, an in-flow of people, albeit limited in size, willing to accept jobs which are not attractive to the indigenous labour force (such as employment in domestic services for example) at relatively low wages, does not also seem to be entirely out of the question. These two points, though, do not really alter the basic conclusion of this chapter that there is unlikely to be significant (in size and importance) migration from Eastern to Western Europe.

References

Berelson, B. (ed) (1974) *Population Policy in Developed Countries.* Maidenhead: McGrawHill Book Company.

Bernabe (1982) In A, Boltho (ed) *The European Economy Growth and Crisis.* Oxford: Oxford University Press.

Boltho, A. (ed) (1982) *The European Economy Growth and Crisis.* Oxford: Oxford University Press.

The Economist (1990) 30th Spectember.

The Economist (1990) 17th November.

The Economist (1990) 22nd December.

The Economist (1991) 26th January.

Glitsos, N. (1987) *A Theoretical and An Empirical Analysis of the Migratory Movements and the Flows of Remittances Between Greece and Germany.* Unpublished manuscript, in Greek. Athens: KEPE.

Kindleberger, C.P. (1967) *Europe's Post-War Growth-The Role of Labour Supply.* Cambridge, MA: Harvard University Press.

ILO (1974) *Some Growing Employment Problems in Europe.* Geneva: ILO.

ILO (1976) *Employment Growth and Basic Needs.* Geneva: ILO.

Nikas, C. (1989) 'The causes and effects of migration: A survey.' *Discussion paper.* York: IRISS.

Nikas, C. (1992) 'Movements of labour and their effects: the case of movements between Greece and the other E.C. countries.' DPhil Thesis, University of York.

Salt, J. and Clout, H. (eds) (1976) *Migration in Post-War Europe.* Oxford: Oxford University Press.

Vanhove, N. and Klaassen, L.H. (1983) *Regional Policy: A European Approach.* Aldershot: Gower Publishing.

Wiles, P.J.D. (1977) *Economic Institutions Compared.* Oxford: Basil Blackwell.

Part Four

The Process of Adjustment
in Peripheral Regions

CHAPTER 18

Urban and Regional Restructuring in Northern Greece and the Single European Market

Lefteris Tsoulouvis

Introduction

This chapter examines patterns of development and restructuring in Northern Greece in relationship to nation-wide processes of socioeconomic and spatial change, and tentatively discusses the expected effect of the Single European Market (SEM) on this region.

Development Patterns and Industrial Restructuring

Northern Greece, which essentially is the hinterland of Thessaloniki, has 16 prefectures belonging to 3 planning regions (NUTS II: East Macedonia and Thrace, Central Macedonia and West Macedonia) and is one of the poorest EC areas. In 1985, per capita GDP – as a ratio to the EC average – was 0.43 for Thrace (ranking at the bottom of the EC regions); 0.56 for Central and West Macedonia; and 0.57 for East Macedonia. Since then trends have been negative and these per capita GDP ratios have decreased (Commission of the EC 1987, 1991).

With respect to intra-regional inequalities, the coastal strip of Central Macedonia belongs to the country's most developed S-shaped corridor. Another part (the coastal region of East Macedonia and Thrace), after a long period of stagnation in the 1950s and 1960s, grew (in the 1970s and 1980s) at rates higher than the national average. The rest of Northern Greece is underdeveloped.

Urban and regional growth and development in Northern Greece, as in the country as a whole, has happened 'spontaneously', that is, without the implementation of coherent plans, despite the very prolific plan-preparation process and omnipresent (ad hoc, casual) state interventionism. However, 'spontaneity' does not accurately describe this development process, since behind it there are lying very significant long-established characteristics of Greece's peculiar urban and regional political economy, involving informal economy practices and the use of the state as the 'par excellence' apparatus for the distribution of the social surplus (Tsoulouvis 1987). Put another way, there is a specific political power structure and balance between politics and the economy, that account for the weaknesses of the planning practice, the lack of implementation of land development and environment protection legislation, illegal building activities, the trespassing of public land and the illegal operation of several hundred thousand tourist rooms.

Since the 1950s, Greece's development path led to the depopulation of Northern Greece's countryside, to the loss of a significant number of workers to Europe (about 500,000, mostly to Germany) and the swelling of Thessaloniki, the population of which doubled in the period 1951–1971. Other smaller urban centres, if not decaying, were stagnating. Migration is mainly due to the willingness of the population to be at the places where decision-making power is concentrated. Other factors were the fragmentation of land in rural areas and employment opportunities in industrial centres, though it is the 'agglomeration factor' rather than the availability of jobs itself that has attracted rural population to the cities. Political intimidation and oppression (in the 1950s and 1960s) pushed also a considerable number of peasants to flee from the countryside. This migration flow has gradually dwindled since the mid-1970s, basically because of the unwillingness of the European countries to accept more foreign workers and Greece's ageing rural population. Another reason is the rising employment opportunities in small urban centres, especially in places with strong tourism and significant residential development prospects.

Thus, the common characteristic of most of Greece's prefectures, with population change ratios higher than the national average in the 1980s, is their tourism. The strength of the relationship between population change and manufacturing employment change in the 1980s, compared to the previous decades, has weakened. This is generally true in Northern Greece as well and implies a significant change in the logic of population growth.

Figure 18.1 shows the basic aspects of Greece's spatial structure with the help of principal component analysis. The data used by the analysis refers to the last decade and concerns demographic characteristics of the population (gender and age); hospital beds; electricity consumption; basic land uses (agricultural land, irrigated land, built-up land, pasture land); urbanisation aspects (population living in demises and in very small municipalities, density of the settlement system); age and structure of the building stock and house-building activity; tourism (beds, Greek and foreign visitors); manufacturing establishments by industry; and popu-

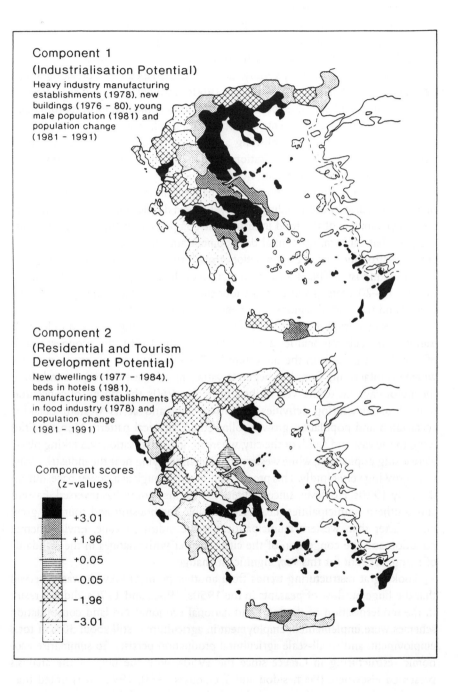

**Component 1
(Industrialisation Potential)**

Heavy industry manufacturing
establishments (1978), new
buildings (1976 – 80), young
male population (1981) and
population change
(1981 – 1991)

**Component 2
(Residential and Tourism
Development Potential)**

New dwellings (1977 – 1984),
beds in hotels (1981),
manufacturing establishments
in food industry (1978) and
population change
(1981 – 1991)

Component scores
(z-values)

+3.01
+1.96
+0.05
-0.05
-1.96
-3.01

Figure 18.1 Principal components analysis of Greece's spatial structure

lation change in the 1980s. Variables are expressed in the form of location quotients for tackling the normality problem. After eliminating variables not contributing significantly to the spatial patterns produced, 18 variables were used in the final test – the two components of which are presented here.

Component 1 shows very vividly that the old S-shaped corridor, along which development took place in the 1950s and 1960s, is still the dominant characteristic of spatial inequalities in the country. The variables contributing to its formation are manufacturing establishments of rubber, plastic, oil, coal, machinery, electrical, electronic, paper, printing, publishing and transport equipment industries; construction activity; level of urbanisation; male population aged 25–50; and population change, whose contribution however is not very significant. Component 2, in which the contribution of population change is more pronounced than in the first, includes also house-building activity; tourism development; and manufacturing establishments of the food industry. The comparison of the two components suggests that tourism, residential development and production for consumption are more strongly related to population growth than production of capital goods and heavy industry. This is a clear suggestion of the change that has happened in the last 15–20 years, given that fast tourism and residential development in the islands and the coastal regions is a phenomenon of this period.

For a long period during the last forty years restructuring followed industrialisation at the sub-regional level. For instance, in the 1950s, the strongest trends of population growth in the prefecture of Thessaloniki were observed in places where manufacturing firms had begun to gather, mostly near the seaport and along the motorways, i.e. to the west of the city. In the 1960s, the process of concentration of manufacturing activities within the city and at its western outskirts accelerated and population growth followed an identical pattern. Municipalities lying to the east and south of the city, where no industrialisation was taking place, were losing population, while western municipalities lying near the industrial zone were growing very rapidly. This process continued, though at a slower pace, during the early 1970s. However, since the mid-1970s this pattern has reversed. Eastern and southern municipalities, i.e. places suitable for housing and tourism, grew much faster than western municipalities by the industrial zone. Environmental pollution and the congestion of the city, together with changes in the standards of living, account for this very significant change.

Looking at restructuring trends from another point of view, it was observed that the huge outflow of peasants in the 1950s, 1960s and 1970s, did not result in the modernisation of the local and national economy. No land consolidation schemes were implemented; employment in agriculture is still about 30% of total employment; and small-scale agricultural production persists. To summarise economic restructuring in Greece since the 1950s, with the help of the analysis presented elsewhere (Petmesidou and Tsoulouvis 1990, 1992), it is noted that, apart from the fact that Greek capital (with the exception of shipping capital) never internationalised, the industrial basis of the country has remained thin. The inflow of foreign capital diminished, with the exception of the early 1990s, where several firms merged with foreign companies. However, foreign capital is not interested in establishing production plants; its policy is to get access into efficient networks of product distribution. This is why its main interest is in food and drink processing firms.

In addition, inter-sector connections have not become much stronger than in the past, so that forward and backward linkages between firms in the production process have remained weak. Also, value added to manufacturing products is still very low; the scale of production has stayed small, while the average number of workers per plant increased very slightly (3.9 in 1963; 5 in 1973; 5.2 in 1978 and 4.9 in 1988); and technological dependence on developed countries is strong.

Further, Greece's manufacturing sector has resisted changes that could potentially be brought about by restructuring processes operating on the international scale. It has never passed through a stage of full Fordist organisation. Neither has it restructured during the period of crisis to the extent it happened in other countries. In contrast to the jobless pattern of growth generally observed, manufacturing employment in Greece grew at an accelerated rate; and, in spite of the crisis, opportunities for entrepreneurs to establish new firms have been plentiful. In addition, small firms are not cooperating with one another to open new markets and expand the already existing ones, to invent new products or to learn how to use informatics in the production process and in running their business. They are afraid that cooperation will being to them not only benefits but also a clarification and fixation of the rules of competition, which they consider detrimental to them. Thus, they adopt a 'defensive' policy and prefer competing with one another on informal grounds (Lyberaki 1991).

Moreover, since diversification is limited and each good is provided by a huge number of small firms, there is hardly any possibility of production clusters with dense networking and collaboration developing. This is further inhibited by the family basis of firm-ownership, the poor level of management and the dominance of cultural values which breed suspicion among firms and between managers and workers. On the other hand, although networking and collaboration are absent, spatial concentration of industrial plants and regional specialisation do exist. However, it is only the very few big and medium-size plants, which can freely choose a favourable location on the basis of the transportation facilities available, the characteristics of the local labour market, the distance to consumers and financial incentives. Their choice determines the place of location of a great number of small firms of the same industry, sometimes gathering together at astonishing densities. Each industry has a different area of concentration, depending on its specific requirements. However, the overall pattern resembles the example of the two ice-cream sellers, described by textbooks on industrial location, who choose the centre of the market to locate; heavy concentration has basically to do with the competition between extremely small firms, producing very similar goods mainly for local consumption, with no power to influence the market and an

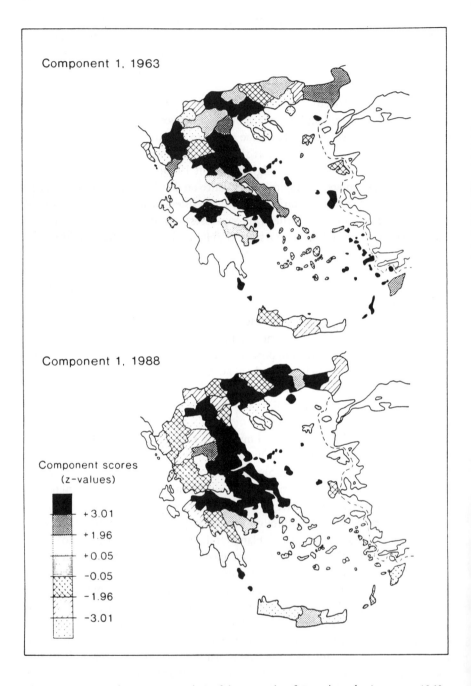

Figure 18.2 Principal components analysis of the geography of Greece's production system, 1963 and 1988

unstable position within it. In addition, given the significance of political processes in Greek society, because of which planned solutions for industrial location and competition problems have so far been impossible, the only choice for these firms has been centralisation and gathering together. Thus, there are many examples of concentration of several apparel manufacturing units in a single multistorey building at the centre of Thessaloniki; of several dozens of them in the same building block or along a very short street; and of several hundreds of them in the CBD.

Strongly related to these processes is the fact that the geography of the production system, and more specifically the heavy concentration of economic activities in Greater Athens and Thessaloniki, has not changed very much during the last thirty years. Figure 18.2 presents the maps of the first component derived by principal components analysis of location quotients of manufacturing statistics (establishments, employment and horsepower) for census years 1963 and 1988, by prefecture. These maps do not differ much from one another and roughly resemble component 1 of Figure 18.1 by emphasising again the S-shaped corridor. The analysis is based on a grouping of the 20-industry statistical data provided by official statistics into 10 industries, which are: (1) food, beverages, tobacco; (2) textile, footwear, apparel, leather and fur products; (3) wood and cork products, furniture; (4) paper products, publishing and printing; (5)rubber, plastic and chemicals; (6) mineral (non-metallic) products, petroleum and coal products; (7) metallurgy and metal products; (8) non-electric, electric and electronic machinery, and telecommunication equipment and supplies; (9) transport equipment; and (10) miscellaneous products.

Figure 18.2 indicates that in both 1963 and 1988 the same variables contribute to the formation of the first, most significant, component (accounting for about 22% of the variance). This is the share of Greece's prefectures in employment, establishments and horsepower in industries 6 and 8 (positive contribution). Space restrictions do not permit expansion on this analysis but, concisely, its meaning is that, first, for about three decades now the spatial structure of Greece's production system has been under the influence of a concentration process of chemicals, plastics, machinery and telecommunication equipment and supplies plants along the S-shaped corridor and dispersion of food and drink processing units in the rest of the country; and, second, amidst a world-wide spatial restructuring Greece's structure has remained almost intact, certainly not influenced by the emergence and growth of new industries. The results of a further analysis, with data arranged in different groups of industries and spatial units, lead to the same conclusion. They also suggest that Northern Greece shows a high degree of diversity, basically due to her recent industrialisation.

In Northern Greece, while there are several sub-regions concentrating large and modern food processing plants, units producing chemicals, plastics, machinery and transport equipment are almost exclusively located in Thessaloniki. Overall, despite the incentives offered, very little capital has been invested in Northern

Greece's peripheral places. Thus the prefecture of Thessaloniki concentrates, within Northern Greece, a very high percentage of plants and employment in any industry (44% of plants in the manufacturing sector as a whole and almost 50% of employment, in 1988), although there is some spatial specialisation in the rest of Northern Greece (food and drink processing plants and textiles in Emathia and Pella; fur and leather products in Kastoria; a recent expansion of garment industry in East Macedonia and Thrace; food processing plants in Serres and Kilkis).

Northern Greece and European Integration

There are four major themes in which the Greek literature concerning the SEM has been interested. The first, revealing Greece's strong interest in rules, legislation, directives and politics, concerns the legal, institutional, administrative and political aspects of the European integration and the procedures followed for its completion (Stefanou 1990, Ioakeimidis 1990, Kazakos 1991a, b). The second, as expected from the large size of Greece's primary sector, refers to the difficulties that peasants will be facing in the near future; the pressing requirement of reorganisation and introduction of new production methods; and the strong competition with other South-European Member States (Maraveyas 1990, Papageorgiou 1991). The third theme concerns the likely (negative) repercussions of the intensifying competition within the SEM on Greek exporters; and new opportunities and difficulties for the manufacturing sector (Mardas and Varsakelis 1990, Kioulafas and Zaragas 1990, Kazakos and Ioannou 1990, Eumiridis 1990, Karabinis 1990). Finally, the fourth is related to Greece's deep economic crisis and the structural problems that will act as restrictive factors to the process of integration of the country into the European Monetary System (Stournaras 1990, Alexakis 1991); and the expected change of her position in the international division of labour (Argyris 1989).

Other themes, like regional inequalities and EC policies to counterbalance them (Maraveyas 1991) and the impact of the SEM on cities and regions of the country (University of Liverpool *et al.* 1991, Petmesidou and Tsoulouvis 1992) have received less attention. This mirrors the weaknesses of Greece's regional planning institutions and policies. A more serious defect concerns the absence of substantial discussion about the future of services. Obviously this has to with the underdevelopment of Greece's service sector (producer services, banking and stock exchange, telecommunications). However, the poverty in reports, research projects and papers on tourism is astonishing. Ironically, although tourism is a sector crucial for Greece's economy which influences patterns of growth and can become the starting point for major projects concerning housing, environmental protection and the development of remote islands, the still dominant ideology dictates that the problems of the country have to be solved through an extensive and fast industrialisation process. Finally, very few of the studies mentioned so far are truly evaluative of the SEM, a fact that can be accounted for on the basis of the deficiencies of Greek planning procedures, which almost never reach the stages of monitoring and evaluation.

As to the whole country, pessimistic opinions about the impact of the SEM underline mainly the fear that Greeks may lose the control of their businesses; services of high quality will be provided by foreign companies; Greek agriculture may be ruined completely by competition, once state support is withdrawn; and the negative characteristics of the manufacturing sector (see above) will not permit Greek firms to become competitive.

A more optimistic view is that, because of her participation in the EC, Greece will be in a better position than the newly industrialising counties, despite the fact that during the recent years several of the latter have been growing faster then Greece. Demand for Greece's products will not decrease, because of her trade with North African and Middle-East countries. Further, Greece may significantly benefit from a proper use of high technology and new production methods. The small size of Greek firms may even be considered advantageous, given the global restructuring towards flexibility and subcontracting.

Finally, according to a very optimistic approach, from the moment the Greek economy opens completely and is integrated into the SEM while state protectionism is withdrawn, pressures exercised by harsh competition will compel firm-owners to modernise and adopt new production methods. Other optimistic versions add that integration of the Greek economy into the SEM means new opportunities and support from international bodies and Funds.

These views apply to Northern Greece in a very specific sense. Given that positive changes usually favour most of all Athens, Thessaloniki and a few other urban centres, optimistic scenarios do not necessarily apply to Northern Greece as a whole, if at all. On the other hand, since negative developments always hit underdeveloped areas first, pessimistic scenarios for Greece may underestimate the negative impact of the SEM on Northern Greece.

A central concept underlining pessimist scenarios is the peripherality of Greece in the EC or the world as a whole (depending on the approach) which imposes on her a specific economic structure or, at least, sets limits within which she can grow and develop. Sometimes the awkward expression 'semi-peripherality' of Greece is used to distinguish her from peripheral countries in a worse position. Given the absence of analytical assessments of the impact of the SEM on Northern Greece, in order to make such an assessment on the basis of Northern Greece's peripherality one should consider the additional fact that studies for peripheral, but more developed, EC regions (Ireland, Scotland) found that there is a big change for a negative impact on them (Bachtler and Clement 1990, Walsh 1990). Also, views about the SEM stress its probably negative repercussions on regions outside the core of Europe, at least in the short run (e.g. Clark 1990, Jensen-Butler 1987).

Other significant concepts are dependence, unequal exchange and the inequalities inevitably produced by the operation of the free market. However, these concepts raise more questions than they answer and, in fact, during the last two decades in Greece there has been a remarkable shift in the paradigm used to account for the weaknesses of the country, away from crude versions of dependence theory and unequal exchange, sometimes combined with international conspiracy theory, to more subtle and pragmatic analyses of the complex international conspiracy theory, to more subtle and pragmatic analyses of the complex international economic and political relationships. These involve Europe, the USA, the former Soviet Union, Japan and other parts of the world; supranational bodies; and Greece as a member of the EC, with her own bilateral relations with various countries, her participation in decision-making bodies at the international level and her association with overlapping groups of various countries (or regions) based on common interests (e.g. South European agricultural regions), geographical coexistence (e.g. the Balkans) and historical contingencies (e.g. ties with the Middle-East).

Nonetheless, a clear view about internal problems and how these relate to external factors is still missing, especially in government policy, which relies heavily on external factors and support for solving internal problems and dealing with the SEM and the complex situation in the Balkans. It also makes use of imported recipes for getting the economy out of the crisis, curbing inflation and decreasing the external debt while overlooking a great many of Greece's peculiarities. After all, it is these peculiarities which have permitted her to be a dependent economy and still differ substantially from the newly industrialising countries; to enter the EC, face harsh competition, receive financial support for reorganising the primary sector and still have surpluses of products not demanded by the EC; to see projects concerning modernisation almost fail without her economy totally collapsing; and to be an open economy and still have a state bureaucratic system controlling the everyday functioning of the market.

If this sounds very pessimistic, optimism can be added by observing that policy decisions in the EC, especially those concerning the use of funds, have up to now been highly influenced by broad political rather than strict economic principles. This is why, despite the fact that the Maastricht Agreement had to be endorsed by the Greek Parliament when heavy taxes and other austerity measures were imposed (August 1992), the government acted as if they wanted to defame Maastricht by blaming it for their measures. Greek politicians and the public are in favour of European integration. Everyone hopes that if the project of integration proceeds, Greece can get some help from the EC structural policies 1993–1997 ('Delors II package') to overcome her severe problems.

However, there is another significant factor that will decisively influence Northern Greece's future. This concerns her position in the Balkans. Cities of Northern Greece used to depend on and influence a vast hinterland extending far into the Balkans, from which they were cut off when they were integrated into the modern Greek state. Thessaloniki used to be an exceptional cosmopolitan city, but since Wold War I the situation has changed dramatically.

Studies of Northern Greece's economy and history have always been under-lining the fact that her present bad economic performance and deficient production structure, as shown in the foregoing discussion, is due to the loss of her hinterland. Thus Northern Greece's future depends heavily on developments in the rest of the Balkans and the acquisition of more independence from Athens in terms of decision-making power (University of Liverpool *et al.* 1991). In that case her position within the EC would improve. On the other hand, if the rest of the Balkan peninsula stays inaccessible to direct market exchange with Northern Greece, this region's access to and communication with the rest of the EC will continue to be strongly conditioned by central state decisions.

Thus the recent emergence of new Balkan states and the future integration of the formerly eastern countries to the EC might lead to a redefinition of urban regions and new functional relationships between cities and their hinterland in Northern Greece and the surrounding area; to the assignment of new roles for these urban centres at the national and international level; and, consequently, to the mitigation of the negative impact that the SEM might have on Northern Greece and Greece as a whole. Rising tourism in Halkidiki, Katerini, Thassos and other places; demand for housing and land for tourism development by EC citizens, could push in this direction. River valleys could once more become meeting places for different ethnicities and cultures, while rivers could even add to the transpor-tation infrastructure. All Northern Greek cities by the coast would flourish and grow since Bulgaria and the new states that have emerged from the dissolution of Yugoslavia need access to the Aegean. Further, foreign capital may find it profitable to invest in Northern Greece, first, because of a higher market demand and, second, because of the existence of a labour force cheaper than the Greek one. Indicative of such a prospect is the present inflow of Albanians, who, however, cannot find work in Northern Greece and are subject to frequent measures by the government to forcibly expel them.

Nonetheless, one should not be over-optimistic. First, leaving aside the present ongoing political crisis and war conditions, it has to be remembered that Albania, Bulgaria and some regions of the former Yugoslavia are very poor and, therefore, market demand is not going to rise spectacularly if these countries are integrated into the EC. Second, several places in the Balkans are significant tourist resorts; others have already formed significant industrial centres; while their distance from Central Europe is shorter than that of Northern Greece. These places will be competitive to cities and sub-regions of Northern Greece. Third, it will take a long time before mobility and ethnicity mixing in the area ceases to be considered a threat to the existence of the Balkan countries. Finally, Turkey is another significant competitor whose future integration into the EC will change dramatically North-ern Greece's position.

Another source of change for Northern Greece are the industrial restructuring processes taking place in Europe, which favour medium-sized cities, like Thessa-loniki, that can play a significant role at their regional level. They also favour smaller cities which can receive new service-sector activities and land development of a high standard. EC programmes and the way they are financed put a priority on these cities. Nonetheless, for this prospect to take place, both Thessaloniki and the smaller urban centres have to acquire a modern industrial base. They have also to provide their residents with a better urban environment and all the high standard services required which urban and regional restructuring in the last decades did not produce. Further, urban and inter-city transport as well as telecommunications have to be improved. Infrastructure projects, like the Trans-European Motorway from Gdansk to Thessaloniki and Volos, that the EC, in cooperation with the formerly eastern countries is ready to undertake, will certainly be decisive.

Finally, as suggested earlier, socioeconomic change and industrial restructuring in Northern Greece, at least in the short and medium term, cannot happen autonomously from changes in the country as a whole. Thus, Northern Greece's changing position in the EC has to be considered in close relationship to Greece's position.

Conclusion

The foregoing discussion suggests that for Northern Greece, apart from processes and factors internal to this region, there are three significant sources of change: Greece's economy and state policies; socioeconomic and political change in the Balkan peninsula; and economic change and policies in the EC.

No matter what the source of change the outcome heavily depends on the planning system of the country which, if reformed, could overcome its enduring weaknesses; become capable of dealing with regional inequalities originating in the new European framework; and create new opportunities for the cities. This means, for example, that local and regional government must be strengthened. Under the present system local government cannot exercise any policy whatsoever, while the thirteen planning regions, established in 1987, have become central state administrative units, headed by secretaries who are political personalities appointed by the government, without much decision-making power and not even a budget of their own (Andrikopoulou 1992). Furthermore, it also means that regional policies and development programmes have to expand in scope and become orientated towards the EC, while new local and regional planning agents have to be established. Community programmes (e.g. IMPs, LEADER, INTER-REG) have already pushed the country in this direction and several local development corporations have recently been established in Northern Greece. Finally, if regions and localities acquire political power they can use it to directly intervene in EC matters and influence the formulation of policy objectives and the distribution of resources.

This argument is generally accepted in the country. However, since Greece's accession to the EC, policy-makers have left a lot of the reforms to happen spontaneously, through the unplanned everyday pressures of the European market on the Greek economy. Reality proved that this was merely wishful thinking and that restructuring must actively and positively be sought for by all those involved in the development process. Without this, the impact of the European integration will be negative.

References

Alexakis, P. (1991) 'European Monetary Union.' In N. Maraveyas and M. Tsinisizelis (eds) *European Integration: Theory and Practice.* Athens: Themelio.

Andrikopoulou, E. (1992) 'Whither regional policy? Local development and state in Greece.' In M. Dunford and G. Kafkalas (eds) *Cities and Regions in the New Europe.* London: Belhaven.

Argyris, T. (1989) 'Prospects for Greek firms in the international division of labour.' In *1992 and Greece.* Conference Proceedings. The Greek Centre for Productivity, Thessaloniki (in Greek).

Bachtler, J. and Clement, K. (1990) *Regional Peripherality in the Single European Market, with Particular Reference to Ireland and Scotland.* University of Strathclyde, Glasgow: European Policies Research Centre.

Clark, M. (1990) 'The Single European Market – the regions beware?' *Town and Country Planning 59,* 170–172.

Commission of the EC (1987) *The Regions of the Enlarged Community: Third Periodic Report on the Social and Economic Situation and Development of the Regions of the Community.* Luxembourg: Office for Official Publications of the EC.

Commission of the EC (1991) *The Regions in the 1990s: Fourth Periodic Report on the Social and Economic Situation and Development of the Regions of the Community.* Luxembourg: Office for Official Publications of the EC.

Eumiridis, A. (1990) *European Integration and the Textiles Industry.* Athens: Institute for Economic and Industrial Research (IOBE) (in Greek).

Ioakeimidies, P.K. (1990) 'European Community of 'subsidiarity' or 'solidarity'?' *Economicos Tahydromos 43,* (1903); *52* (in Greek).

Jensen-Butler, C. (1987) 'The regional economic effects of European integration.' *Geoforum 18,* 213–227.

Kazakos, I. and Ioannou, I. (1990) *European Integration and the Food Processing Industry.* Athens: IOBE (in Greek).

Kazakos, P. (1991a) *Greece between Adjustment and Marginalization.* Athens: Diatton (in Greek).

Kazakos, P. (1991b) 'The project of the internal market.' In N. Maraveyas and M. Tsinisizelis (eds) *European Integration: Theory and Policy.* Athens: Themelio (in Greek).

Karabinis, D. (1990) *European Integration and the Greek Footwear Industry.* Athens: IOBE (in Greek).

Kioulafas, K. and Zaragas, L. (1990) *European integration and labour market.* Athens: IOBE (in Greek).

Lyberaki, A. (1991) 'Flexible restructuring and networking in the small firms of the industry of plastic products.' *Topos 2,* 89–117 (in Greek).

Maraveyas, N. (1990) 'Greece's agriculture in anticipation of the economic and currency integration in the EC.' *Review of the European Communities 8,* 8–9, 143–167 (in Greek).

Maraveyas, N. (1991) 'Regional policy.' In N. Maraveyas and M. Tsinisizelis (eds) *European Integration: Theory and Policy.* Athens: Themelio (in Greek).

Mardas, D. and Varsakelis, N. (1990) 'Report on Greece.' In *The Impact of the Internal Market by Industrial Sector: The Challenge for the Member States*. Luxembourg: Office for Official Publications of the European Communities, 175–202.

Papageorgiou, K. (1991) 'Agricultural policy.' In N. Maraveyas and M. Tsinisizelis (eds) *European Integration: Theory and Policy*. Athens: Themelio (in Greek).

Petmesidou, M. and Tsoulouvis, L. (1990) 'Planning technological change and economic development in Greece: high technology and the microelectronics industry.' *Progress in Planning 33*, 3, 175–262.

Petmesidou, M. and Tsoulouvis, L. (1992) *Spatial Clustering and Industry Networks in Northern Greece*. FAST-FINE-IAT Programme, Institute Artbeit and Technik, Gelsenkirchen (mimeo).

Stefanou, A. (1990) 'Towards a federal Europe, II.' *Review of the European Communities 8*, 8–9, 57–94 (in Greek).

Stournaras, I. (1990) 'Macro-economic imbalance, cost of adjustment, low productivity: three restrictive factors in Greece's integration to the EMU.' *Review of the European Communities 8*, 8–9, 169–180 (in Greek).

Tsoulouvis, L. (1987) 'Aspects of statism and planning in Greece.' *International Journal of Urban and Regional Research 11*, 500–521.

University of Liverpool (Centre for Urban Studies), ELLCONSULT and EKEM (1991) *Urbanisation and the Functions of Cities in the European Community: Case Study of Thessaloniki*. Athens (mimeo).

Walsh, J.A. (1990) 'Regional implications of a single market European Community.' *Geographical Viewpoint 18*, 43–58.

CHAPTER 19

Local Economic Development in Peripheral Rural Areas
The Case of Portugal

Stephen Syrett

Introduction

Since the early 1980s, the discourse surrounding areal development has become increasingly oriented towards strategies promoting local-level economic development (Commission of the EC 1983, OECD 1985, 1990, Harloe, Pickvance and Urry 1990). Concepts of endogenous development are particularly influential in Southern Europe where processes of small firm industrialisation in intermediate rural areas have become the focus of considerable attention (Garofoli 1992). However, there remain doubts, both conceptual and practical, regarding the appropriateness of this new policy orthodoxy to the needs of many regions in Southern Europe (Ferrao 1990, Hadjimichalis and Papamichos 1990). Excessive concentration on particular forms of small firm industrialisation in specific contexts (i.e. the case of the 'Third Italy') has resulted in little attention to the important differences between localities and between local growth dynamics.

This situation is well exemplified by the case of peripheral rural areas in Southern Europe. These areas comprise many of the least-developed regions of the European Union (EU) and consequently are high priority regions within EU regional policy. Yet, these peripheral rural societies, dominated by small agricultural producers producing primarily for their own consumption on marginal agricultural lands, possess few indigenous resources for local development strategies. Furthermore, peripheral rural areas in Southern Europe have historically only been weakly integrated into wider capitalist and state structures and have therefore been excluded from social sources of power and domination. Consequently, it is important to examine the basis for local-level development in these types of areas and their ability to compete with other European regions, as well as to analyse conceptions of endogenous development which equate it only with a narrow enterprise ideology.

Current restructuring processes are increasing the economic and political integration of these peripheral rural regions and producing new roles and relationships with political and economic structures. The question remains whether these ongoing processes of economic and political integration provide new possibilities for local economic development strategies, or whether they reproduce social networks which maintain the structural powerlessness of these local populations in their relations with wider economic and political structures. Furthermore, it is not sufficient to merely identify the operation of wider restructuring processes. Critically, it is the interrelationship between these processes and local differences which provides the potentialities and constraints for local economic development. Changes in local social processes and cultural practice in these rural regions cannot be read-off from broader economic changes. Instead, localities are actively involved in the production and reproduction of these restructuring processes (Urry 1987, Cooke 1989). Consequently, local economic development strategies in these rural areas both attempt to draw upon these changes and partly constitute their development.

Peripheral Rural Areas in Transition: The Southern European Context

The role of peripheral rural areas within Southern Europe is currently undergoing substantial change. This is related to a series of changes both in relations of production and exchange, and in the role of state organisations. This transition is related to fundamental changes in the nature of global processes of accumulation (Lipietz 1987, Harvey 1989). However, although analysis of the global transition beyond Fordism provides some limited insights into changes in the internal mode of accumulation and regime of regulation within Southern Europe, it is necessary to specify more clearly the nature of restructuring issues within Southern Europe. In past rounds of investment, marginal rural regions in Southern Europe have been integrated into the wider capitalist production system principally through their role as suppliers of cheap labour, as well as through commodity and financial flows. Although this role as a source of labour continues, the changes in the international economy towards a flexible, decentralised mode of production mark out new, and more complex, roles for such areas through rural industrialisation, home-working and tourism (Hadjimichalis 1987). Consequently, capitalist relations of production and exchange have become increasingly significant within these regions of traditional peasant production.

In terms of labour demand, the move towards increased flexibility in national and international labour markets has led to a growth in short-term and temporary migration. Economic organisation around the small farm household permits a high degree of flexibility as production for self-consumption is combined with sources of income from formal and informal working. Although traditional peasant production continues, greater economic integration and state subsidies have led to increases in agricultural specialisation and commercial production. A degree of commercialisation of traditional craft production has led to a limited development of small-scale enterprises, whilst processes of rural industrialisation have increased possibilities of paid employment within the region. The decentralisation of state services has led to a growth in some areas of public sector employment, whilst the growth of tourism also provides additional sources of income.

This changing integration into relations of production is intimately associated with these regions' changed integration with the state apparatus. Under previous authoritarian regimes in Portugal, Spain and Greece, rural areas were largely ignored by the central state, as these regimes discouraged changes in the structures of traditional rural life. Consequently, the transition to liberal-democratic state structures has had a dramatic impact on these formerly isolated rural communities. Since the 1970s, the development of local and regional government structures and increased public investment, stimulated by the availability of EC resources, has permitted rapid improvement of basic infrastructures. Accession to the EC has provided the finance and necessity for substantive changes to the policy environment. EC-backed agricultural and training policies providing subsidies and training have, often for the first time, attempted to stimulate changes in agricultural production processes through large-scale state intervention. In addition to the arrival of agricultural compensatory payments, the availability of a range of EC subsidies has led to some development of state clientelism.

This changed economic and political integration has led to significant changes in traditional cultural practice. The most obvious changes have been at the level of exchange relations and cultural practices, with the increase of monetisation and consumerism within the population. The direct impact of this on the local production system has been the reduction of home craft activity and the increase of bought equipment for agricultural production. Though this has stimulated changes in relations of market exchange it has seemingly had much less effect on agricultural practice, which has often remained largely unchanged. The improvement of road links, the migration process, and the arrival of television and the mass media, has greatly reduced the traditional isolation of these regions. Given that this isolation has been central to the development of past cultural practices, this has produced pressure for changes to traditional local culture and values.

The limits and potentialities of local economic development in marginal rural regions results from the interrelationship between wider restructuring processes and specific local social and cultural relations. Changes in the nature of economic integration for these regions does provide limited opportunities for local economic development strategies based around the commercialisation of agricultural and craft products and the development of tourism. However, these localities are weakly positioned to develop a local economic development strategy given the asymmetrical power relations between local peasant society and capitalist and state structures. These areas possess limited endogenous resources and contain few attractions for inward investment compared with other regions. They lose the most able section of their population through emigration and often have conservative, individualist cultures which run counter to local-level cooperation and proactivity.

Given these material constraints, the principal stimuli to local economic development in these regions has originated from changing state roles and policies. New state policies and a decentralisation of state structures suggest new possibilities for local economic development policy in these regions. However, the nature of the integration of these peripheral rural areas with state structures and policies also provides considerable constraints. The rest of this chapter will explore the character of political restructuring and its relation to local economic development in remote rural regions in Southern Europe through consideration of the case of Portugal and a specific rural locality in the Portuguese Interior.

Political Restructuring in Portugal

In Portugal, the transition to liberal-democratic state structures commenced following the 1974 revolution which ended fifty years of rule by a conservative-authoritarian regime. This transition has involved the democratisation of state structures and some decentralisation of state power, most notably through the development of local government (Gaspar 1985). Since the 1980s, accession to the EC has sponsored the emergence of a new policy framework in Portugal. This policy framework is better resourced financially and far broader in scope than past Portuguese public policy, and has involved changes to existing policies, and the development of whole new policy areas. It provides potential resources for local economic development both through sectoral policies, in areas such as industry, training, agriculture and tourism, as well as through policies specifically aimed at promoting regional/local development.

Given these changes, the major problem facing the development of local level strategies in the 1990s is the continuing imbalance between political and administrative structures which is an enduring legacy of the pre-1974 Estado Novo (New State) (Opello 1985, Graham 1983). This has two components. Firstly, the continuation of a powerful centralised bureaucracy which is unable to effectively deliver the new policies and respond to local differences. Secondly, the weakness of political infrastructures, notably the absence of strong participatory party politics and the existence of authoritarian party structures, which act to maintain a passive political culture (Gallagher 1985).

These legacies of the Estado Novo are particularly evident in peripheral rural regions. In these regions the central state attempted to retain traditional rural social relations principally through a policy of neglect. Consequently, there is no history of effective national state policies operating in these regions nor state structures capable of implementing policies or responding to local needs. However, significant changes are occurring. The strengthening of local government has provided some resources for reversing this situation, and despite only slow changes in the central state bureaucracies, the policy framework which emerged during the 1980s has had a significant impact on all aspects of rural life. These policies provide a range of resources suitable for local economic development strategies, particularly in the areas of basic infrastructure provision, agriculture and education and training.

Local Economic Development on the Serra do Montemuro

Given the material constraints on economic development and the existence of conservative-individualist cultures, across Portugal there are relatively few examples of local economic development strategies in marginal rural areas. However, since the late 1980s, the availability of EC resources has sponsored an increase in rural development projects across Portugal. In the cases where initiatives have developed, they generally reflect the involvement of an outside organisation, usually from the church or voluntary sector, who have acted as the stimulus for activity. For the Serra do Montemuro, a mountainous region in the Interior of North-East Portugal, a local development project has been underway since the early 1980s, initiated by a self-supporting international development organisation, the Institute for Cultural Affairs (ICA), which has attempted to mobilise the local population and external resources.

The Serra do Montemuro is characterised by peasant economic practice and culture. Economic organisation is based around small-scale, highly fragmented and privately owned peasant farms. Agricultural production is primarily for self-consumption and limited by poor soils and a harsh climate. Within the primary economic unit of the household, a variety of economic strategies are pursued in addition to farming. These include migration, double job-holding and part-time and seasonal work. The high degree of self-sufficiency based on the family unit means producers are highly individualistic with little tradition of communal or cooperative practice. Migration continues to be particularly important to the economic and social development of the Montemuro, removing the most able members of the population and contributing to the concretising of land structures. Migrant remittances are primarily utilised for household consumption rather than productive investment (see also Lewis and Williams 1986).

Historically, the population of the Montemuro has been marginalised from state structures. It has only been from the 1970s, and particularly the 1980s, that state resources have had a significant impact on the traditional peasant culture. As a result of improved state provision, since the 1970s the Serra do Montemuro has experienced a dramatic increase in the level of physical infrastructure provision, most notably in roads, electricity, water supply and sanitation.[1] However, other social infrastructures are less well developed, and the weak national social security system means that dependence on state transfers, prevalent in poor rural communities in the richer countries of Southern Europe, has not yet occurred on the Montemuro. Yet the arrival of EC subsidies and agricultural compensatory payments indicates the beginning of state resources becoming a significant additional source of income to peasant households.

Politically, peasant society in this region remains strongly conservative. This tradition has roots in a historic corporatist tradition which strongly supports the individual family, the village community, the Church and the monarchy (Wiarda 1979),[2] and has been maintained by the physical isolation of the Montemuran communities. The enduring legacy of this corporatist tradition is evident in a political culture which is individualist and non-participative, and which views state structures as external and non-responsive to local demands. Despite the introduction of democratic elections and the development of local government structures, much of the operation of local politics in the area reflects pre-revolutionary corporatist attitudes. However, higher educational levels, greater access to the mass-media and new political attitudes amongst the youth have begun to undermine the basis of this traditional political culture.

The historical political marginalisation of the Montemuran population, and the existing conservative and non-participative local political culture, has meant that the population is poorly placed to take advantage of resources which have become available under the reformulated policy environment. That local economic initiatives have developed on the Serra do Montemuro has been due to the presence of the international voluntary group, ICA,[3] who have critically increased local power in relation to state structures. As well as mobilising voluntary sector resources, ICA has extracted state sector resources from bureaucratic and largely non-responsive local, national and international state structures, on behalf of a powerless local population.

In response to the changing policy environment, ICA has altered the emphasis within its integrated development strategy. Since 1986, ICA have prioritised the

---

1   For example, with respect to the supply of electricity, between 1974 and 1986 the number of consumers in the local authority area of Castro Daire increased from 1546 to 7384. By 1986 the network covered all the local authority area aside from a small number of individual farms and small hamlets.

2   This places Montemuran political culture within a broad Portuguese corporatist tradition which invests authority in the central state or crown and various corporate units such as the Church, the nobility and the military. This tradition is rooted in a predominantly Catholic society which invests the State with a natural and moral power and within which hierarchy and stratification are considered to be the natural order of things (Wiarda 1979).

3   ICA is committed to a development philosophy which requires the full participation of the local community, and a comprehensive and integrated approach to all aspects of community life (ICA 1985).

development of economic initiatives as a means for restructuring the regions' income base and developing new employment opportunities, particularly for women. Given local indigenous resources, these economic initiatives have concentrated in three areas the commercialisation of craft products; changes to agricultural practice; and the development of rural tourism.[4] Actions have principally related to attempts to commercialise traditional craft practice. In particular, ICA has developed a number of women's village-based cooperatives which currently employ over 50 women on a predominantly part-time basis. These craft initiatives have proceeded through a number of common stages of development (Table 19.1), all originating in six-month state-subsidised training courses sponsored by the European Social Fund (ESF) and administered by the department for Employment and Training (IEFP).

Table 19.1. Stages in the development of craft initiatives on the Serra do Montemuro, 1986–91

Stage	Features	Problems	Aid/support
Training course (6–12 mths)	State-supported training course	Identification of suitable courses Location of teaching staff	IEFP (Employment and Training Dept)/ESF funding Organisation by ICA
Survival period (1–3 years)	Difficult transition period, progress via trial and error Survival requires strong group commitment, emergence of local leader and state/voluntary sector aid	Lack of capital Difficulties of adjustment to commercial operation (e.g. selecting goods, pricing, productivity, location of markets)	Assorted finance from voluntary and state (IEFP) sources mobilised by ICA Minimal state aid providing further support and training for progression to commercial enterprise
Self-supporting enterprise (+3 years)	Economically fragile enterprise Sales mainly via craft fairs Reduced/minimal reliance on subsidies	Low wages and only viable as part of household income Continuing reliance on grants for capital investment	ICA support role Mutual support between cooperatives for sales and marketing Grants for capital investment

4   See Syrett (1991) for a fuller discussion of local economic initiatives undertaken on the Serra do Montemuro.

Local Economic Development and Political Restructuring

Despite the achievements of ICA in developing craft initiatives on the Montemuro, the majority of initiatives remain reliant on state and voluntary sector subsidies, and all are economically precarious. Fundamental constraints on local action in a peasant-based society result from their highly marginalised position with respect to the wider economic structures. Integration of the Montemuro into capitalist structures remains principally through the Montemuro's role as a source for the reproduction of cheap and flexible labour supply via the peasant farm. This remains the case with respect to the commercialisation of Montemuran agricultural and craft goods where competitiveness is underlain by low labour costs. Within the locality, aside from the environmental conditions of the mountain, there are basic constraints on local economic development strategies which emerge out of the interrelationship between economic change and traditional peasant practice (Syrett 1992). Resources for local economic development are still drawn primarily from the traditional peasant sector and are consequently limited by the material conditions of peasant economy, knowledge and technology (Iturra 1987).

Given these considerable economic constraints on local initiatives the impact of changing state roles and policies in sponsoring and sustaining these initiatives is critical. This interrelationship of local actions to processes of political restructuring can be analysed with respect to changes both in the state apparatus and the policy framework.

The state apparatus

Although local government elsewhere in Portugal has become increasingly involved in local economic policy since the mid-1980s (Henriques 1987, Campos, Jacinto and Syrett 1987, Mozzicafreddo, Guerra, Fernandes and Quintela 1988), on the Montemuro there continues a tradition of a strongly administrative local government. Local economic policy pursued by the two main local authorities on the Montemuro, Lamego and Castro Daire, is conceived principally in terms of basic infrastructure provision, with minor initiatives promoting tourism and local culture. Local government in the region has generally remained distant and disinterested in ICA's development project. A critical factor in the role of local authorities is the attitude of the local authority President. Given the powerful position of the President within the relatively small local authorities, the relationship with this key actor is crucial. Recent years have seen evidence of improved relations between ICA and the local authorities; partly a result of new elected officials, and partly due to the expansion, in the 1990s, of local authority planning departments staffed by non-elected professionals.

Much of the national state apparatus continues to be characterised by centralisation, bureaucracy and lack of coordination (e.g. see Cunha 1982). These problems are aggravated on the Montemuro by the region consistently falling between two or more administrative divisions.[5] The department for Employment and Training (IEFP), which has been the most important state department relating to the development of local economic initiatives on the Montemuro, has made some limited progress in decentralising operations and changing its bureaucratic culture; although decision-making is still slow and concentrated in Lisbon and the regional centres. There is also evidence of change elsewhere, with ICA developing positive relationships with smaller and more recent state departments such as the Commission on the Status of Women (CCF) and the Ministry for Youth (FAOJ).

Despite the difficulties, ICA continues to utilise state structures wherever possible with the aim of making these effective rather than by-passing them by utilising external resources.[6] This has contributed to a gradual change in the relationship between ICA and some state departments and local authorities in the 1990s. As pressure for policy performance has increased upon state structures, their lack of grassroots orientation has been exposed. State departments, such as the IEFP and the Ministry of Education, have begun to recognise their need for reliable social partners at the grassroots level to legitimate their role. As a result, ICA has found that the former one-way relationship, whereby they attempted to extract resources from non-responsive state departments, has begun to change.

The policy framework

The principal origin of state resources for local economic initiatives on the Montemuro has been via the IEFP in the form of training courses, temporary employment schemes and employment creation policies. EC resources and objectives have underwritten all of these policies, and in addition, certain resources for the women's cooperatives have been obtained directly from Brussels. The availability of state financial support has not only been fundamental to the whole local economic development strategy, but the types of initiatives pursued have been strongly influenced by policy criteria. However, despite the positive aspects of a new policy framework and the availability of significant new resources, the local economic development strategy has been weakened through substantive problems

---

5   This is a significant problem with respect to all state departments but is particularly harmful with respect to the Regional Planning Commissions (CCRs). The CCRs are responsible for elaborating regional development programmes and the Montemuro's cross-boundary location has isolated this region from this process.

6   In this respect the actions of ICA can be contrasted with a larger rural development project in Trancoso in the Interior of Central Portugal. In this instance, a returned migrant priest has made use of substantial contacts in the EC and Germany to build up a largely self-supporting project. Consequently, in this region the project employs more agronomists than the agricultural ministry MAPA.

relating to policy delivery, the incomplete and uncoordinated nature of the policy framework, and its poor adjustment to local conditions.

Policy delivery

Bureaucratic and inflexible state departments lacking in technical staff have meant that many policies have never been effective in practice. Firstly, applications for support are time-consuming. Delays in receiving financial resources can be critical in development initiatives where there is little financial capital available. Partially as a result of these factors, from 1987, ICA drastically cut the numbers of ESF/IEFP sponsored training courses they were running as it was judged that these courses presented administrative problems beyond the value of the resources they provided. Secondly, the profusion of policies, particularly from the IEFP, has confused both deliverers and clients alike. Following the suspension of applications and rationalisation of its policies in 1990, the IEFP has reduced the policy range and applications should be simpler and quicker in the future. Finally, the lack of technical personnel is widespread throughout state departments in the Interior which are not equipped with sufficient numbers of adequately trained personnel to effectively deliver policy.

Incomplete and uncoordinated policy

The new policy framework is characterised by significant gaps and a lack of coordination both within and between state departments. The most serious policy gap evident in the local economic development strategy pursued on the Montemuro has been the absence of state policies to support follow-on actions to training courses. Similarly, despite the encouragement from state policies to start up local initiatives, there is a complete lack of second-tier support organisations. In a peasant-based society such as the Montemuro, where basic management, administrative and commercial skills are entirely lacking, this has meant that economic initiatives have proceeded at a slow pace, largely by a process of trial and error. The one positive exception to this has been the Women's Commission (CCF), which has attempted to provide a series of training courses related to the ongoing development of women's craft-based enterprises.

Coordination between state departments is almost completely absent. For example, overlap between state departments is currently evident with respect to developing education and training for students who have completed compulsory schooling, with both the IEFP and the Ministry of Education pursuing parallel policy initiatives. Although state/EC financial resources are for the first time reaching interior regions, this lack of coordination greatly reduces their effectiveness. Although current EC policy directions are keen to promote greater integration between structural funds, there must remain doubts about the ability of state departments to respond positively to this.

Policy adjustment to local conditions

Local economic development on the Montemuro raises questions about the adequacy of criteria for policy eligibility and how well adjusted national/EC policies are to local conditions. Policy criteria stipulating initiatives pay minimum wages or become economically self-supporting within a short period of time, take no account of the construction of the local economy and the hostile economic environment, or of the rationale for their development. Enterprises on the Montemuro draw on the resources of both peasant culture and modern capitalist society and must make sense within the practices of the family unit and the local community.[7] This is not the same as them being profitable capitalist enterprises, hence it is inappropriate to assess initiatives only in terms of conventional economic criteria.

In terms of orientation of policy to local needs, a critical constraint to the development of local economic initiatives in a peasant-based rural economy is lack of capital. However, in all the enterprises developed on the Montemuro, the amounts of capital made available under state policies have been insufficient, with external finance from voluntary groups being critical to their survival. Similarly, the lack of policies promoting management and commercial skills again reflects a lack of adjustment to local need. Success in developing local leaders for initiatives has only been achieved on the Montemuro through massive inputs of time, training and support from ICA. This contrasts with the poorly conceived and implemented state policies aimed at stimulating the emergence of 'local development agents', which have had few positive results. The situation is further aggravated by heavy reliance on external/EC funding whereby the development of local actions is dictated by external priorities. In the past, the availability of funding has encouraged groups with limited financial resources to run training courses often without prior assessment of local needs. As a CCF official pointed out, whilst the CCF could easily obtain ESF finance for a women's information and technology course, it is more difficult to get funding for courses teaching traditional female activities, despite the inappropriate nature of IT courses to the needs of women from Interior rural districts.

Conclusion

In marginal rural economies throughout Southern Europe the structure of local economies and the nature of their integration into the wider European economy constrains their ability to compete with other regions of Europe. The limited

---

7   For example, although the local population are willing to accept grants from state organisations, they are reluctant to take out state loans as these obligate the peasant household to a body outside of traditional social relations. Consequently, producers are suspicious of such arrangements and prefer to resolve this problem within the household and community spheres.

options available on the Montemuro in the development of any endogenous development strategy are far from unique. In the peripheral rural areas of Southern Europe, local economic strategies are largely reduced to a similar basic recipe: tourism, craft goods, and a limited commercialisation of agriculture, all reliant on the availability of cheap and flexible labour. When the craft cooperatives of the Montemuro attempt to market their products they enter into competition not only with other rural economies of Southern Europe but also beyond, to developing countries. Whilst the markets for traditional rural tourist dwellings, goats' cheese and hand-knitted jumpers have expanded in recent years, these are now highly competitive and reliant on continued consumer preference for craft goods within the advanced economies.

For the Southern European members of the EC, the new EC-sponsored policy context does provide new possibilities for local action, but peripheral rural localities, traditionally marginalised from state structures, are poorly positioned to take advantage. Given external and internal constraints, spontaneous processes of local economic development are unlikely to occur. Both the local and national state often appear disinterested in local actions, lacking the structures, policies and desire to respond to local demands. Consequently, in addition to further decentralisation of state power, local bases are required to empower the local population in relation to state and economic structures. Where such local power bases do exist there is evidence that local participation in political structures has begun to modify traditional political cultures. Furthermore, increased pressure on state structures, both internally and externally, for improved responsiveness to local differentiation is broadening awareness that grassroots groups can operate in the interests of the state and legitimate state roles.

In policy terms, whilst the free flow of international experiences can provide benefits if utilised to inform policy formulation, there is a danger that external policies can dictate policy development. In the case of Portugal, the significance of Brussels has not just been through the provision of financial resources, but perhaps more critically through its dominance of the terms of reference for policy development. Financially, this dependence on Brussels is potentially problematic, as competition for resources from the EC's Structural Funds increases. It appears unlikely that the priority afforded to peripheral rural regions in Southern Europe during the late 1980s and early 1990s can be sustained. Currently, the EC is being forced to confront new demands for regional development funding, not least because of the potential consequences of enlargement and the necessity to aid the development of Eastern European economies.

Since the mid-1980s, Portugal, like other countries of Southern Europe, has rapidly produced a policy framework compatible with the EC's liberal-capitalist ideology. The historical weakness of internal policy-making and the existence of severe policy deficiencies, has seen Portugal's political elite enthusiastically embrace external policy initiatives. The result is a fundamental difficulty with the new policy framework, in that the conceptual basis for policies is largely imported from advanced industrial economies, with little analysis of local realities. Consequently, the dangers of poorly defined and ill-adjusted policies are considerable, whilst such ideological effects act to enforce existing asymmetrical power relations between Northern and Southern Europe.

Changes in the development strategy pursued on the Montemuro reflect wider changes in the evolution of the development discourse. National and international orientation of policy towards enterprise creation and training during the 1980s led ICA to readjust its priorities within their integrated development programme. However, in rural societies, the strong integration of rural life and the limited possibilities for effective local economic ventures means the resulting emphasis on economic actions remains problematic in both practical and conceptual terms. In practical terms, health, education and culture are all spheres where initiatives might represent more manageable objectives. Furthermore, local economic development cannot be effective without basic physical and social infrastructures (i.e. education) which are prerequisites for the successful development of enterprises. Conceptually, meaningful endogenous development in these regions must emerge out of local cultural formations and promote grassroots participation and mobilisation of the local population; something which a narrow focus on enterprise creation fails to achieve.

It is somewhat ironic that current EC initiatives are attempting to stimulate the very type of integrated rural approach to which ICA on the Montemuro has always been committed. The objectives of the LEADER initiative (Links between Actions for the Development of the Rural Economy) stress not only the need for the integration of development activities, but also aim to stimulate local rural development groups. This renewed policy interest in integrated development and locally based groups is undoubtedly to be welcomed. However, it remains to be seen how effective this policy will be, given that it requires the prior existence of local groups and continues to rely on effective action from existing state structures.

References

Campos, B., Jacinto, R. and Syrett, S.J. (1987) 'Desenvolvimento local: política da administraçao central e envolvimento autárquico – o caso da Regiao Centro.' In *Desenvolvimento Regional* 24/25, 29–56.

Cooke, P. (ed) (1989) *Localities.* London: Unwin Hyman.

Commission of the European Communities (1983) *Community Action to Combat Unemployment – The Contribution of Local Employment Initiatives* COM (83) 662 Final/2. Brussels: Commission of the European Communities.

Acknowledgements
This article is based upon research supported by the Economic and Social Research Council. I would like to thank the Comissão de Coordenação da Região Centro and the members of ICA for their help with fieldwork in Portugal.

Cunha, A.M. (1982) 'Some considerations about the Portuguese experience in the implementation and management of rural development policies.' *Economia 6*, 1, 55–70.

Ferrão, J. (1990) 'Da diversidade de situações à multiplicidade de políticas.' In Comissão de Coordenação da Região Centro (ed) *Industrialização em Meios Rurais e Competitividade Internacional*. Coimbra: Comissão de Coordenação da Região Centro.

Gallagher, T. (1985) 'Democracy in Portugal since the 1974 revolution.' In E. de Sousa Ferreira and W.C. Opello (eds) *Conflitos e Mudanças em Portugal 1974–84*. Lisboa: Teorema.

Garofoli, G. (ed) (1992) *Endogenous Development and Southern Europe*. Aldershot: Avebury.

Gaspar, J. (1985) '10 anos de democracia: reflexos na geografia politica.' In E. Ferreira and W.C. Opello (eds) *Conflict and change in Portugal, 1974–84*. Lisboa: Teorema.

Graham, L.S. (1983) 'Bureaucratic politics and the problems of reform in the state apparatus.' In L.S. Graham and D.L. Wheeler (eds) *In Search of Modern Portugal*. Wisconsin: University of Wisconsin Press.

Hadjimichalis, C. (1987) *Uneven Development and Regionalism: State Territory and Class in Southern Europe*. Beckenham: Croom Helm.

Hadjimichalis, C. and Papamichos, N. (1990) '"Local" development in Southern Europe: towards a new mythology.' *Antipode 22*, 3, 181–210.

Harloe, M., Pickvance, C. and Urry, J. (eds) (1990) *Place Policy and Politics*. London: Unwin Hyman.

Harvey, D. (1989) *The Condition of Postmodernity*. Oxford: Basil Blackwell.

Henriques, J.M. (1987) 'Os municípios e a promoçao do desenvolvimento: reforço da integraçao "funcional ou 'territorial"?' Unpublished MSc Thesis, Instituto Superior de Economia, Universidade Técnica de Lisboa, Lisbon.

Institute for Cultural Affairs (1985) *Annual Report*. Brussels: ICA.

Iturra, R. (1987) 'Continuity and change: peasant transition in a Galician parish.' *International Social Science Journal 114*, 481–504.

Lewis, J.R. and Williams, A.M. (1986) 'The economic impact of return migrants in Central Portugal.' In R. King (ed) *Return Migration and Regional Economic Problems*. London: Croom Helm.

Lipietz, A. (1987) *Mirages and Miracles: the Crisis of Global Fordism*. London: Verso.

Mozzicafreddo, J., Guerra, I., Fernandes, M.A. and Quintela, J. (1988) 'Poder autárquico e desenvolvimento local.' *Revista Crítica de Ciências Sociais 25/26*, 79–114.

Opello, W.C. (1985) *Portugal's Political Development*. Boulder and London: Westview Press.

Organisation for Economic Cooperation and Development (1985) *Creating Jobs at the Local Level*. Paris: OECD.

Organisation for Economic Cooperation and Development (1990) *Implementing Change: Entrepreneurship and Local Initiative*. Paris: OECD.

Syrett, S.J. (1991) 'Capital, state and local action: the emergence of local economic initiatives in Central Portugal.' Unpublished PhD Thesis, Department of Geography, University of Exeter.

Syrett, S.J. (1992) 'Culture and community economic initiatives: the case of Portugal.' *World Futures 33*, 67–85.

Urry, J. (1987) 'Society, space and locality.' *Environment and Planning D, Society and Space 5*, 4, 435–444.

Wiarda, H.J. (1979) 'The corporatist tradition and the corporative system in Portugal: structured, evolving, transcended, persistent.' In L.S. Graham and H.M. Makler (eds) *Contemporary Portugal*. Austin and London: University of Texas Press.

CHAPTER 20

Economic Restructuring within the European Periphery
The Experience of Ireland

Michael R. Murray, John V. Greer and James A. Walsh

Introduction

It is frequently the case that discussion of economic issues within the island of Ireland deals separately with Northern Ireland (as part of the United Kingdom) and the Republic of Ireland (as an independent state). Important differences between the economies of each territory do exist comprising, for example, the financing of shortfalls between public expenditure and revenue, the tax system and the exchange rate (Bradley 1990). Nevertheless, recent years have witnessed significant and common adjustments for most sectors of these economies prompted by factors operating at a variety of scales. The phenomenon of economic restructuring *per se* is well documented (see, for example, Allen and Massey 1988, Albrechts and Swyngedouw 1989, Martin 1989, Stöhr 1990). It remains the agreed case that outcomes associated with the reorganisation of capital and production are expressed spatially at regional and local levels.

Thus it is that the European Commission (1991a) has reconfirmed that on a range of economic indices both the Republic of Ireland and Northern Ireland remain most seriously disadvantaged. An analysis of 171 Level 2 regions within the Community found each respectively to have the 14th and 16th highest unemployment rates for the period 1988–1990. In both territories per capita GDP remains significantly less than the Community average. However, the island of Ireland is located not only on the economic periphery of Europe but also on the geographical margin. It suffers from the double disadvantage of distance from major markets and isolation by sea, the associated effects of which can be expressed in terms of higher transport costs for local business, additional organisational and administrative costs and potential production dislocation (Keeble, Owens and Thompson 1982, Keeble, Offord and Walker 1988, Peida 1984). Yet it is this European dimension which increasingly seeks to shape the economic environment of Ireland. The passage of the Single European Act in 1986 and the adoption of measures towards closer market integration have added impetus to the urgency of structural adjustment. In this context Ireland as a whole enjoys Objective 1 status for the reformed operation of the Community Structural Funds, while the Maastricht Treaty holds out the promise of additional transfers to the Republic of Ireland from a newly established Cohesion Fund. But the extent to which this intervention is capable of countering any tendency towards over-concentration of capital in the core regions of Europe remains uncertain.

It is against this background of circumstance and change that the experience of Ireland can make a useful contribution to the wider debate about regional and local dimensions of economic restructuring within the Europe of the 1990s. Stated briefly this chapter has the following aims:

1. To outline important dimensions of the scope and impact of economic development policy in Ireland during recent decades

2. To review aspects of the contemporary context which have a bearing upon regional and local development in Ireland during the 1990s

3. To identify some key issues that need to be addressed as an input into future policy formulation and implementation.

For purposes of clarity the term 'Ireland' is used in this chapter to refer to the island of Ireland as a whole. 'Northern Ireland' and the 'Republic of Ireland' refer to the two jurisdictions which make up the island. Each constitutes a Level 2 region within the current European Community regional framework.[1]

Economic Development Since the 1960s

The evolution and impact of economic development policies in Ireland since the 1960s have generated a substantial literature drawn from a variety of disciplines (see, for example, Bull and Hart 1987, Brunt 1988, Kennedy, Giblin and McHugh 1988, Rowthorn and Wayne 1988, Drudy 1989, Walsh 1989, Gaffikin and Morrissey 1990). Close reading of these commentaries allows for three broad and related themes to be identified: agricultural restructuring, industrialisation and economic development and physical planning. Each may be briefly considered.

---

1   See Roberts, L. (1992) 'Doing it our Way – The County Councils' Role in a Europe of Regions.' Conference Presentation at Regional Studies Association Annual Conference 'Regionalism: Defining a New Agenda?'.

Agricultural restructuring

A basic division of problem regions within the European Community into agricultural and industrial has placed the Republic of Ireland and Northern Ireland in the former category (Klein 1981). The prosperity of the agricultural sector has long had a major bearing on the prosperity of the economies of Ireland, not least because of the role of agriculture-related industries. Thus within Northern Ireland primary agriculture production accounts for 4% of GDP and 7% of civil employment making the industry three times as important than at the United Kingdom level. When the agri-business sector is viewed as a whole the estimated shares of GDP and employment rise to 7% and 10% respectively (Department of Agriculture for Northern Ireland 1992). Within the Republic of Ireland the economic contribution of agriculture is even more marked; during the 1980s, it was accounting for some 11% of GDP and 15% of total employment (Brunt 1988). In both jurisdictions production agriculture is essentially similar, comprising livestock husbandry in medium and small owner-occupied farms in the main. As noted by Gillmor (1989) this resemblance is to be expected given a shared island location, a largely common land heritage and similar physical conditions.

During recent decades the re-structuring of agriculture is evident in increased use of technology, the replacement of labour by capital, specialisation in production, the enlargement of the scale of production units, and the concentration of production on larger farms and in particular regions (Walsh 1991, 1992, Commins, Greer and Murray, in preparation). With the long-term tendency for the cost of purchased inputs to rise more rapidly than product prices there has been a sustained downward pressure on farm incomes. Significant inequalities have emerged between farmers and farming regions so that a large proportion of farm households have become marginalised rather than modernised (Kelleher and O'Mahony 1984, Walsh 1986). The behavioural responses of farmers in Ireland have varied from becoming even more commercialised in conventional agriculture to opting for part-time farming. Thus in Northern Ireland some 17% of farmers under the age of 65 are engaged in other gainful activity (Moss *et al.* 1991); in the Republic of Ireland income from farming is not the main source of livelihood in 42% of households where the head of household has farming as a principal occupation. Latterly farmers under pressure from reform of the Common Agricultural Policy have been urged to diversify into non-conventional forms of production, though recent research in Northern Ireland (Magee 1990) points to little enthusiasm for take-up; only 8% of farms are engaged in some form of alternative enterprise. In short the agricultural imperative is changing to that of sustaining incomes and retaining a presence on the land. The difficulties created by these restructuring tendencies are most directly experienced in the less favoured areas of Ireland, which extend over more than 60% of the land area.

At a wider level farming has increasingly become incorporated into transnational food chains through the globalisation of agri-business both in sourcing inputs and marketing outputs. A much greater emphasis on quality food production has put pressure on farmers to invest in upgraded production facilities. The net result of this change has been keenly felt in the food and drink industries within which employment has fallen markedly in an effort to facilitate competitive processing on an international basis. In the Republic of Ireland the number of dairy cooperatives, for example, declined over the period 1973–1990 as small farmer-owned enterprises were absorbed by large integrated companies (Agriculture and Food Policy Review Group 1990). In Northern Ireland about a quarter of total milk output is now grouped under the control of one operator. It may well be the case that even greater increases in scale are necessary to maintain European competitiveness in milk assembly and processing costs (Northern Ireland Economic Council 1992).

Industrialisation

The agricultural personality of Ireland, while perhaps true on a general scale, does serve, however, to mask other significant internal characteristics. Industrialisation has long been a feature of economic development policy, and over the period since the 1960s state-sponsored multinational investment has formed an important element of government economic strategy in both Northern Ireland and the Republic. Research by Harrison (1986) has demonstrated that between 1946 and 1970 over 110,000 manufacturing jobs were promoted in Northern Ireland with just over 50% of these falling into the category of new inward investment. But problems of large-scale labour shedding in the traditional industries of ship-building, engineering and textiles did considerably offset this success. By 1960 in the Republic of Ireland, new outward-oriented policies of attracting foreign enterprise and producing for the export market had replaced an earlier preference for trade protection and a dependency on indigenous industry. This resulted in an immediate improvement in economic performance with GDP increasing at an annual rate of 4.4% over the period 1960–1973 (Kennedy *et al.* 1988). The effect on the labour force was dramatic in that the decline of some 200,000 in the number at work in the previous decade was replaced by an increase of just over 30,000 between 1961 and 1971.

During the late 1970s and 1980s high rates of new inward investment proved difficult to maintain, though there was some difference in the experience of Northern Ireland and the Republic of Ireland in this regard. Over the period 1973–1990 there was an increase from 31% to 45% in the proportion of industrial employment accounted for by externally owned companies in the Republic of Ireland. As noted by the Northern Ireland Economic Council (1992), this contrasts with a falling dependence on employment in externally owned plants in Northern Ireland from 53% in 1973 to 39% by 1990. The international impact of the 'Troubles' in Northern Ireland would seem to account for this poor performance. But also significant has been global economic stagnation and the restructuring of the capitalist space economy. Previously dominant industries, technologies, production methods and skills were being increasingly superseded by alternative systems (Martin 1989). These new arrangements involved greater mobility of different components of capital in search of more profitable sites and inevitably in Ireland the implications of these restructuring processes lay in the vulnerability of a small island economy to international movements of investment. In Ireland throughout most of the 1980s there were significant losses in overseas industry employment as some plants were either closed as part of international rationalisation programmes by their parent corporations or subjected to automation.

Government has responded to these shifts with reviews of industrial policy. In the Republic of Ireland several weaknesses were identified including the degree of dependence on foreign controlled firms, the low skill content of much of the employment, the high cost and short duration of much of the assisted employment, the low level of commitment to research and development, the very limited amount of independent marketing capacity, the poor performance of the indigenous sector and the limited linkages with the rest of the economy (National Economic and Social Council 1982). A corresponding assessment of the need for structural change was undertaken within Northern Ireland (Department of Economic Development 1987). The key problems in the face of difficulties attached to maintaining an inward investment strategy were identified as the lack of an entrepreneurial culture, an over-dependence on external funds, the predominance of service sector activity and in particular a disproportionately large public sector based service economy. Key proposals included the stimulation of a more positive local attitude to enterprise, changing attitudes to competitiveness, encouraging export activity, exploiting the strengths of the public sector and the better targeting of public funds. While the Pathfinder process, as it was known, generated a measure of debate on its vision and prescription (see, for example Teague 1989a, b, Hitchins and Birnie 1989), the fact remains that with the unemployment rate at that time running at about 18% (comparable with the Republic of Ireland) it represented an important milestone in establishing the direction of economic development policy for the outset of the 1990s.

Economic development and physical planning

The outward-oriented economic policies pursued in Ireland during the 1960s were paralleled by an intense interest in the contribution which physical planning could make to spatial restructuring. Within Northern Ireland the publication of the Belfast Regional Survey and Plan in 1963 advanced a strategy of demagnetising the Belfast Urban Area while simultaneously expanding several of the larger towns within the immediate sphere of influence of the city. These de facto growth centres were not only to receive population from Belfast but were also to act as holding points for people migrating from the rural heartland of Northern Ireland in search of jobs and houses. The distinct urban bias of physical and economic planning at that time was echoed in the Republic of Ireland with the preparation of a national planning strategy by Colin Buchanan and Partners. This report, published in 1968, proposed that regional planning policy should be based on a hierarchy of growth centres involving, in addition to Dublin, two national and six regional centres. Essentially this prescription sought to inform local physical planning, while at the same time match efficiency with equity in the distribution of economic opportunity.

However, political considerations played a major part in modifying these blueprints. In Northern Ireland the number of selected growth centres was repeatedly increased by the 1970–1975 Development Programme and the 1975–1995 Regional Physical Development Strategy. This reflected a somewhat belated recognition of the important economic and social role played by more peripheral parts of the region. Within the Republic of Ireland the abandonment of the concept of promoting growth in a small number of centres was underscored by manufacturing employment targets set in 1972 by the Industrial Development Authority for some 137 towns. This action effectively sounded the death-knell for the Government's brief flirtation with regionalism (Breathnach 1982). The mid-1970s recession further diverted interest from regional issues to national concerns, while membership of the European Community created the imperative of having the Republic of Ireland declared as a single region for drawing down resources from the European Regional Development Fund. As noted by Bannon (1989) the emphasis was to shift from internal regional disparities to a priority on bringing the Republic of Ireland as a whole into line with the rest of Europe.

The 1980s, in contrast, have evidenced a profound change of emphasis to more local levels of concern. Ireland is marked by highly centralised public administration systems and under their auspices a number of initiatives have been promulgated by each government, occasionally in partnership with the European Commission, which can appropriately be dubbed central government localism (after Martin 1989). In Northern Ireland the implementation of an Integrated Operations Programme for the Belfast Urban Area, a Making Belfast Work Programme, the designation of Enterprise Zones, and the regeneration of Belfast's waterfront by Laganside Development Corporation have been matched by a number of Designated Area revitalisation schemes in key cities within the Republic of Ireland. The operational hallmarks of this planning style are marketing, negotiation and leverage in order to capture an even greater private sector investment within these urban cores. This mode of intervention at the local scale continues to embed itself ever more deeply in urban and *rural* Ireland during the 1990s and is helping to forge new relationships between place, society and economy, whose characteristics include forceful expressions of rooted identity, self-help, voluntarism, networking and partnership.

In concluding this review of some regional and local dimensions of economic restructuring during the past three decades in Ireland, it would seem that the dominant large-scale development paradigm conceived and directed by central government has begun to break down. A great diversity of macro- and micro-level factors has successively adjusted to this top-down focus. There are issues herein which need to be addressed in order to meet the ongoing restructuring challenge at the regional and local scale; but before doing so, it is appropriate to review certain aspects of the contemporary context.

The Context of the 1990s

There is currently emerging within Europe a technical consensus that development models should emphasise broad-based strategies involving mobilisation of indige-nous regional and local resources through a multi-annual programme approach which is facilitated by formalised partnerships between individuals, institutions and agencies at different geographical scales. In working towards this policy framework in Ireland much is owed to the direction given by the European Commission, in consultation with Member States, in devising the regulations for the allocation of the reformed structural funds for the period to 1993. Indeed, it would not be overstating the case to adapt the observation offered by Stöhr (1989) that the 1990s will largely witness the substitution of national regional strategies by European Community programmes for regional development. The policy context for regions and local areas is thus itself being restructured and for purposes of this chapter there are two matters which deserve consideration: the experience of Ireland in drawing down funds support and the emergence of rural development policy as an alternative paradigm for regional and local change.

Ireland and the Structural Funds

To assist with the preparations for enhanced economic integration and to help reduce regional disparities within the European Community, the Council of Ministers agreed in 1988 to reform the operation of the Structural Funds comprising the European Regional Development Fund, the European Social Fund and the guidance section of the European Agricultural Guidance and Guarantee Fund. Total resources have been increased from 7.7bn ecu in 1988 to 14.5bn ecu in 1993 (at 1988 prices). Their allocation has been marked by a promise of much greater coordination than previously and a greater regional concentration, with some 60% being targeted on Objective 1 regions whose development is lagging behind. These cover 40% of the Community, account for some 21% of its population and are primarily rural in character. The areas include both Northern Ireland and the Republic of Ireland.

Within the Republic the government prepared a National Development Plan 1989–1993 which it submitted to the European Commission in support of its bid for aid. The process of plan preparation generated considerable controversy, most of which was centred on the principle of partnership. Despite formal consultative procedures designed to facilitate local and regional inputs to the plan preparation process, the final document appeared to give little recognition to these detailed submissions. In Northern Ireland, by way of contrast, the regional development plan and operational programmes were hastily drafted by government with only minimal consultation between it and interested parties, a reflection perhaps of the limited appreciation at that time of the potential significance of the structural funds by these other interests.

The Commission subsequently responded with agreed Community support frameworks which in the case of the Republic of Ireland provided for aid of some £2550m spread across four specific priorities: (1) agriculture, fisheries, forestry, tourism and rural development; (2) industry and services; (3) measures to offset the effects of peripherality; and (4) human resource measures. In Northern Ireland the allocation of some £551m related principally to: (1) agriculture; (2) transport; (3) tourism; (4) physical and social environment; (5) industrial development; (6) unemployed young people; and (7) long-term unemployed. A notable absentee from this latter inventory of operational programmes is rural development, with that for agriculture comprising mainly measures offered by the existing Northern Ireland Agricultural Development Programme.

While it may be premature to assess the impact of these expenditure commitments a useful insight into potential benefits is offered by an *ex ante* analysis of the role of the structural funds in the Republic of Ireland (Economic and Social Research Institute 1992). No comparable assessment has yet been published for Northern Ireland. Within the Republic it is anticipated that the investment programme will provide a major stimulus to the economy with demand effects, particularly in the building industry, being felt within the 1989–1993 period. Infrastructure accounts for some 27% of the cumulative expenditure up to 1993. The supply-side impact will take longer to work through and, while initially the effects may be modest, it is expected that the benefits will persist in the long run and have a major impact at that stage on economic development. Of fundamental importance in this regard is not only the infrastructure commitment but more particularly the expenditure on human resources, which accounts for almost 42% of the Community Support Framework budget. Improvements in human capital through education and training will increase labour market participation with an anticipated gain in total employment of 31,000 by the year 2000. However, the envisaged reduction of unemployment by that date is less significant – at just under 1% of the labour force – because of the combined effects of reduced emigration levels and a larger labour pool. The overall conclusion to emerge from this analysis is that the Structural Funds expenditure has the potential to increase the productive capacity of the Republic of Ireland in a permanent way and in a manner which the alternative of straight income transfers from the European Community could not achieve. There are clear implications here for restructuring in Northern Ireland which traditionally has been very dependent on this latter mechanism within the context of the United Kingdom to help reduce disparities in living conditions. In short, it has been suggested elsewhere (Cuddy and Keane 1990) that the Community's Structural Funds will help to ameliorate the relative deterioration of the

Republic of Ireland's position in Europe, but any expectation of regional convergence may still remain illusory.

Rural development

Economic and social change within rural areas of Ireland may be viewed as but one element of a much wider process of restructuring within the island as a whole and which in turn is conditioned by changing relationships in the international economy. Commins (1991) has cogently argued that many rural socioeconomic issues can no longer be usefully analysed separately from mainstream national or regional trends and that there are common sets of forces impacting on local areas in modern advanced economies. Previous sections of this chapter have identified key dimensions of the transformation of production, capital and labour. It is within this complexity of organising forces that a new agenda for rural development has emerged of late. Interest in this matter within Ireland is currently unprecedented and extends from central government agencies and local authorities to a wide network of voluntary and local community groups. Much is owed to the stimulus given by the European Commission in its seminal publication *The Future of Rural Society* (Commission of the European Communities 1988). This expressed deep concern about the human dimension of rural areas and commended the role of rural development programmes as a preferred mode of intervention.

In the Republic of Ireland an important initiative has been the Pilot Programme for Integrated Rural Development 1988–1990 (O'Malley 1992). At its most basic this sought to improve the employment opportunities, earning potential, quality of life and sense of community identity among people in rural areas. Local people were to be mobilised to work for the development of their own area, decide priorities and bring aspirations to reality. The bottom-up style programme operated in twelve rural areas and involved the appointment of a full-time coordinator or animateur to each. Much emphasis was placed on the concept of shared learning between individuals and groups. Almost 400 projects were brought forward for purposes of securing local economic and social development, thus demonstrating the potential of this type of approach in promoting positive change. One of the most important conclusions from the evaluation of the programme was that while it was able to stimulate and encourage local initiatives the process was not spontaneous but instead relied heavily on clearly focused and carefully directed interventions. In other words, while the initiatives taken on projects were genuinely local there had to be systematic central guidance of the whole process. On the basis of this success the government announced in 1991 a nationwide extension of the Integrated Rural Development Programme. The experience gained is also helping to inform the European Commission LEADER programme involving 16 local and development groups.

Within Northern Ireland, by way of contrast, much of the recent effort directed at rural development has concerned the setting up of appropriate structures for policy delivery.

Rural development requires close links between central government agencies and local level implementation and can be assisted by having formal mechanisms in place whereby obstacles encountered can be quickly addressed. It is paradoxical that Northern Ireland, coming from a dominant urban policy tradition and not the Republic of Ireland with its long-standing empathy with rural life, should have established an apparatus which meets that requirement. This comprises the creation of a ministerial portfolio of responsibility for rural development, the establishment of a resourced agency outside government known as the Rural Development Council, the appointment of rural area coordinators and community animateurs and the launch of an umbrella organisation for community groups – Rural Community Network. The future transformation of rural society and economy in Northern Ireland will depend much on the effectiveness of this innovative framework (Murray and Greer 1992).

Key Issues

The previous section of this chapter has identified a number of matters which are central to the current phase of approaches to regional and local development. The emphasis is on partnerships, programmes and integration. However, the adoption and application of these concepts may pose serious challenges to conventional thinking and modes of policy operation in Ireland and beyond. It is appropriate therefore to consider some of the key issues which are likely to influence policy formulation and implementation.

The local dimension

It may be passé to suggest greater coordination by state agencies so that the bureaucratic delays which frustrate and retard local development can be overcome. The challenge, nevertheless, remains valid; for partnership and integration to be effective traditional sectional interests must be overcome. A necessary requirement here is for a shared vision of a desirable future and which in the case of rural society in Ireland is only noticeable by its absence. As Cuddy and O'Cinneide (1990) suggest, there would seem to be very little evidence that any serious thinking has been devoted to considering what might constitute a desirable future and what the regional and local dimensions of this might be.

The sole attempt to outline a vision of the future for rural Ireland has come from the Conference of Major Religious Superiors which has to a large degree endorsed the integrated and interdisciplinary approach to rural development that is favoured by the European Commission (Healy and Reynolds 1991). More specifically, with regard to local development in rural areas, recent research by

O'Cinneide (1991) points to some useful conclusions. First, the widespread apathy and sense of powerlessness that exists in many localities needs to be addressed through programmes of social animation involving education and training. Second, the commitment to rural development does not generate quick-fix results. This fact is not always appreciated by those who seek rapid solutions to problems that have developed over a long time. Third, it would seem that localities do vary in their capacity to successfully promote economic development. There is therefore a need for more realistic expectations of what can be achieved through small-scale local development efforts. An approach which over-emphasises the role of bottom-up initiatives is unlikely to succeed if it involves shifting too much responsibility and too little assistance from state to inadequately equipped local communities.

The sub-national dimension

Both Northern Ireland and the Republic of Ireland are marked by highly centralised systems of bureaucratic control. In the former, policy-making and administration are inextricably linked to a legacy of political division regarding the relationship of the region with the remainder of the United Kingdom. But in acting as a bridge between central government departments and communities local authorities do occupy a pivotal position. During the past two decades their executive functions have been restricted. However recent policy innovation now allows for even greater expenditure on local economic development initiatives: concepts such as partnership, programmes and integration are now very much on the local development agenda. In the Autumn of 1992 the government in the Republic announced plans to establish County Enterprise Partnership Boards in both urban and rural areas. Following a recent report on local government reorganisation and reform (Barrington 1991), government has also accepted the prescription that local authorities must be able to stimulate and harness local initiative. The effectiveness of this new direction in both jurisdictions will ultimately depend on the degree of political will and maturity at both central and local levels to adapt to the new roles envisaged for local government.

The cross-border dimension

The peripherality of the island of Ireland within the European Community demands that full use is made of its locational advantages if it is to effectively compete against the prospect of ever greater concentration of investment in core regions during the 1990s and beyond. A key issue here is how to more effectively shift towards closer economic partnership between Northern Ireland and the Republic of Ireland so as to give Ireland a new competitive edge as a single *economic* entity. At present Ireland is included with the EC initiatives on Border Areas Programme (INTERREG) and investment plans relating to transport and communications, tourism, environmental protection and waste disposal have been prepared. Cooperation, however, is still regarded as being more inter-state rather than truly inter-regional and, while structures for cross-border discussion and information exchange are quite well developed, there is – as suggested by the Commission of the European Communities (1991b) – a need to move towards a more committed expression of regional and sectoral planning which can generate integrated cross-border action programmes.

The European dimension

The regional and local dimensions of economic restructuring in Ireland are increasingly located within an international framework which not only forces change but also through the intervention of the European Community seeks to mitigate the most negative effects. The pioneering application of rural development initiatives within peripheral regions of Europe under the EC LEADER programme is illustrative of the need for devising new structures, processes and products at regional and local levels which can meet that challenge. But this raises the issue of the sheer necessity for a much greater external perspective by those whose brief is economic development in Ireland. It is the case that an understanding of policy formulation and delivery fixed in different socioeconomic, cultural, political and institutional contexts can be a contributing influence on domestic policy succession. In Ireland a key concern must be how to more effectively build this international network of shared learning which can embrace the sectoral and spatial dimensions of continued regional and local economic restructuring.

Conclusion

This chapter has identified a number of regional and local dimensions related to economic restructuring in Ireland. In tracing the scope and impact of policy over time the suggestion was made that perhaps the dominant large-scale/top-down paradigm is increasingly being replaced by a more local/bottom-up approach to policy action. However, the complexity of global and local restructuring tendencies combined with the need to address the deep structural problems of Ireland, not least its high unemployment, warrant a more balanced approach to future change. Each perspective has a useful contribution to make. It is this search for and delivery of balance in economic development policy which represents an important challenge for Ireland and its European partners during the 1990s.

References

Agriculture and Food Policy Review Group (1990) *Agriculture and Food Policy Review*. Dublin: Stationery Office.

Albrechts, L. and Swyngedouw, E. (1989) 'The challenges for regional policy under a flexible regime of accumulation.' In L. Albrechts, F. Moulaert, P. Roberts and E. Swyngedouw (eds) *Regional Policy at the Crossroads: European Perspectives*. London: Jessica Kingsley Publishers.

Allen, J. and Massey, D. (eds) (1988) *Restructuring Britain: The Economy in Question*. London: Sage Publications.

Bannon, M. (1989) 'Development planning and the neglect of the critical regional dimension.' In M. Bannon (ed) *Planning – The Irish Experience 1920–1988*. Dublin: Wolfhound Press.

Barrington, T.J. (1991) 'Local Government Reform: problems to resolve.' In J.A. Walsh (ed) *Local Economic Development and Administrative Reform*. Dublin (Irish Branch): Regional Studies Association.

Bradley, J.F. (1990) 'The Irish economies: some comparisons and contrasts.' In R.I.D. Harris, C.W. Jefferson and J.E. Spencer (eds) *The Northern Ireland Economy: A Comparative Study in the Economic Development of a Peripheral Region*. London: Longman.

Breathnach, P. (1982) 'The demise of growth-centre policy: the case of the Republic of Ireland.' In R. Hudson and J. Lewis (eds) *Regional Planning in Europe*. London: Pion.

Brunt, B. (1988) *The Republic of Ireland*. London: Paul Chapman Publishing.

Bull, P.J. and Hart, M. (1987) 'Northern Ireland.' In P. Damesick and P. Wood (eds) *Regional Problems, Problem Regions and Public Policy in the United Kingdom*. Oxford: Clarendon Press.

Commins, P. (1991) *Rural Change and Development in the Republic of Ireland: Global Forces and Local Responses*. Dublin: Mimeograph, Teagasc.

Commins, P., Greer, J.V. and Murray, M.R. (in preparation) 'Rural development – a common challenge.' In P. Teague and B. Walker (eds) *Comparing the Irish Economies*. Oxford: Basil Blackwell.

Commission of the European Communities (1988) *The Future of Rural Society*. Luxembourg: Office for Official Publications of the EC.

Commission of the European Communities (1991a) *The Regions in the 1990s*. Luxembourg: Office for Official Publications of the EC.

Commission of the European Communities (1991b) *Europe 2000: Outlook for the Development of the Community's Territory*. Luxembourg: Office for Official Publications of the EC.

Cuddy, M.J. and Keane, M.J. (1990) 'Ireland – a peripheral region.' In A. Foley and M. Mulreany (eds) *The Single European Market and the Irish economy*. Dublin: Institute of Public Administration.

Cuddy, M.J. and O'Cinneide, M. (1990) 'Critical issues in rural development.' In M.J. Cuddy, M. O'Cinneide and M. Owens (eds) *Revitalising the Rural Economy – How Can it be Done*. Galway: University College.

Department of Agriculture for Northern Ireland (1992) *Annual Report 1991/1992*. Belfast: HMSO.

Department of Economic Development (1987) *The Pathfinder Initiative: An Interim Report*. Belfast: HMSO.

Drudy, P.J. (1989) 'Problems and priorities in the development of rural regions.' In L. Albrechts *et al.* (eds) *Regional Policy at the Crossroads: European Perspectives*. London: Jessica Kingsley Publishers.

Economic and Social Research Institute (1992) *The role of the Structural Funds: Analysis of the Consequences for Ireland in the Context of 1992*. Policy Research Series Paper No. 13. Dublin: The Economic and Social Research Institute.

Gaffikin, F. and Morrissey, M. (1990) *Northern Ireland – The Thatcher Years*. London: Zed Books.

Gillmor, D. (1989) 'Agricultural development.' In R.W.G. Carter and A.J. Parker (eds) *Ireland – Contemporary Perspectives on a Land and its People*. London: Routledge.

Harrison, R.T. (1986) 'Industrial development policy and the restructuring of the Northern Ireland economy.' *Environment and Planning 4*, 53–70.

Healy, S. and Reynolds, B. (1991) 'Towards an integrated vision of rural Ireland.' In B. Reynolds and S.J. Healy (eds) *Rural Development Policy: What Future for Rural Ireland?* Dublin: Conference of Major Religious Superiors.

Hitchins, D. and Birnie, J.E. (1989) 'Economic development in Northern Ireland: has Pathfinder lost its way? A Reply.' *Regional Studies 23*, 5, 477–483.

Keeble, D., Offord, J. and Walker, S. (1988) *Peripheral Regions in a Community of Twelve Member States.* Brussels: Commission of the European Communities.

Keeble, D., Owens, P. and Thompson, C. (1982) *Centrality, Peripherality and EEC Regional Development.* London: HMSO.

Kelleher, C. and O'Mahony, A. (1984) *Marginalisation in Irish Agriculture.* Dublin: An Foras Taluntais.

Kennedy, K.A., Giblin, T. and McHugh, D. (1988) *The Economic Development of Ireland in the Twentieth Century.* London: Routledge.

Klein, L. (1981) 'The European Community's regional policy.' *Built Environment 7*, 3, 4.

Magee, S.A.E. (1990) *Diversification in Northern Ireland Farms 1989.* Belfast: Studies in Agricultural and Food Economics, Department of Agriculture for Northern Ireland.

Martin, R. (1989) 'The new economics and politics of regional restructuring: the British experience.' In L. Albrechts, F. Moulaert, P. Roberts and E. Swynagedouw (eds) *Regional Perspectives: European Perspectives.* London: Jessica Kingsley Publishers.

Moss, J., McHenry, H., Cuskie, D.P., Markey, A.P. and Phelan, J.F. (1991) *Study of Farm Incomes in Northern Ireland and the Republic of Ireland.* Third Study Series: Report No. 1. Belfast: Co-operation North.

Murray, M.R., and Greer, J.V. (1992) 'Rural development in Northern Ireland: policy formulation in a peripheral region of the European Community.' *Journal of Rural Studies 8*, 2, 173–184.

National Economic and Social Council (1982) *A Review of Industrial Policy.* No. 64. Dublin: Stationery Office.

Northern Ireland Economic Council (1992) *The Food Processing Industry in Northern Ireland.* Report 92, Belfast.

Northern Ireland Economic Council (1992) *Inward Investment in Northern Ireland.* Report 99, Belfast.

O'Cinneide, M. (1991) 'An innovative approach to local economic development in Inishowen, Republic of Ireland.' Paper presented to conference on Marginal Regions, Littlehammer, Norway.

O'Malley, E. (1992) *The Pilot Programme for Integrated Rural Development 1988–1990.* Broadsheet Series Paper No. 27. Dublin: The Economic and Social Research Institute.

Peida (1984) *Transport Costs in Peripheral Regions.* Report to the European Commission, Industry Department for Scotland and Department of Economic Development for Northern Ireland.

Rowthorn, B. and Wayne, N. (1988) *Northern Ireland – The Political Economy of Conflict.* Cambridge: Polity Press.

Stöhr, W. (1989) 'Regional Policy at the Crossroads: An Overview.' In L. Albrechts, F. Moulaert, P. Roberts and E. Swynagedouw (eds) *Regional Policy at the Crossroads: European Perspectives.* London: Jessica Kingsley Publishers.

Stöhr, W. ed. (1990) *Global Challenge and Local Response.* London: Mansell Publishing.

Teague, P. (1989a) 'Economic development in Northern Ireland: has Pathfinder lost its way?' *Regional Studies 23*, 1, 63–69.

Teague, P. (1989b) 'Pathfinder: a reply to Hitchins and Birnie.' *Regional Studies 23*, 5, 483–485.

Walsh, J.A. (1986) 'Uneven Development of Agriculture in Ireland.' *Geographical Viewpoint 14*, 37–65.

Walsh, J.A. (1989) 'Regional development strategies.' In R.W.G. Carter and A.J. Parker (eds) *Ireland – Contemporary Perspectives on a Land and its People.* London: Routledge.

Walsh, J.A. (1991) 'A regional analysis of enterprise substitution in Irish agriculture in the context of a changing Common Agriculture Policy.' *Irish Geography 24*, 1, 10–23.

Walsh, J.A. (1992) 'Adoption and diffusion processes in the mechanisation of Irish agriculture.' *Irish Geography 25*, 1, 33–53.

Part Five

Conclusion

CHAPTER 21

Policy Agenda for the Decade

John Bachtler

Introduction

This book, under the appropriate title of *An Enlarged Europe: Regions in Competition?*, encompasses the twin challenges for future regional development in Europe. The political and economic geography of Europe is changing, as the European Union expands its boundaries to include Austria, Finland and Sweden and resumes a closer association with a Central and Eastern European region engaged in radical restructuring. Within the European Union, regions are engaged in both greater competition *and* increased cooperation as EU integration intensifies.

What do these challenges, and the many subsidiary issues raised throughout this book, mean for policy-makers? The purpose of this final chapter is to draw out the policy imperatives arising from the previous chapters and to place them in context. The following sections review the environment for regional policy across the EU and discuss the current trends and future developments in regional policy at three levels: the European Union, the Member States and Central and Eastern Europe.

Regional Problems and Disparities in the European Union

From the perspective of regional policy-makers, many of the previous chapters reinforce three themes: the rapidity and complexity of economic, social and political change; the challenge of economic and social cohesion; and the uncertain spatial implications of European integration.

First, the economies and societies of Europe are in a state of flux, part of the fundamental restructuring of the global economy. Louis Albrechts observes that the shift to a service society, with a freer movement of people, goods, capital, services and information, is associated with a quantitative and qualitative change in economic activity and employment. The internationalisation of economic activity and associated geo-political developments are encouraging greater inter-dependency among regions, countries, markets and sectors. Changes in the organisation and structure of international finance and production, facilitated by advances in information technology and telecommunications, are reflected in new forms and spatial patterns of industrial location. In a context of greater regional integration and trade liberalisation – under NAFTA, the Single European Market and the GATT agreement – the issue of competitiveness has become a central policy concern, especially in peripheral or lagging regions. Almost all regions have been engaged in a process of local restructuring, whether driven by decline in traditional or more modern industrial sectors, overcapacity in agriculture or fishing, or defence industry conversion.

Second, regional disparities across the EC remain very wide. According to the latest (fifth) EU Periodic Report (CEC 1994), regional income variation across the EU continues to be characterised by major core–periphery contrasts. In 1991, the top 10 EU regions had average GDP per head levels approximately 3.6 times higher than the bottom 10 regions; incorporating data for the new German Länder widens the difference to 4.5 times. Regional unemployment disparities are more complex, with high unemployment rates in traditional industrial areas as well as lagging regions. However, the core–periphery differences are again striking: in 1993, unemployment rates ranged from an average of 25.3% in the 10 worst-placed regions, in Spain and southern Italy, to a 3.6% average in the 10 least-af-fected regions, primarily in western Germany.

The picture is not all negative. Looking back over the past decade, there have been some notable improvements in the differences between EU regions. As Hall and van der Wee point out: 'the recent statistical evidence on the performance of the weakest parts of the Community is relatively encouraging'. There has indeed been significant economic convergence at Member State level over the past decade, and there is some evidence to suggest that the position of many industrial problem regions has been improving. But the major income disparities between the richest and poorest regions remain extremely wide – and are widening.

The causal factors underlying these trends are less clear. Hall and van der Wee acknowledge our lack of understanding of the reasons for differences in perform-ance between regions: 'we know a great deal about the necessary conditions for economic development in the regions, but we seem to know less about the sufficient conditions'. One contributory factor is the lack of comparable data, although the periodic reports of the EU (and the regional quantification exercise currently being conducted by DG XVI) are steadily improving the database for EU-wide regional analysis. A more important issue is perhaps the need to develop better analytical techniques. The suggestion of Hall and van der Wee for a multi-disciplinary approach – incorporating the insights of economics as well as other social sciences – is worth highlighting. The relevance of such an approach is evident in the research conducted in Ireland by Lars Mjøset which analysed economic development in the context of socio-cultural trends and institutional arrangements (Mjøset 1992).

Third, there is still considerable uncertainty about the spatial impact of European integration. At the Member State level, it has been argued that there will be few benefits for northern EU countries from the completion of the Single European Market (SEM), the main beneficiaries of 1992 being southern European Member States which have much greater potential to exploit comparative advantage and scale economies (Neven 1990). For the regions, Ross MacKay foresees divergence and a widening of regional disparities: the SEM involves a reallocation of market areas and redistribution of production in favour of the core regions of the Community, fostered by internal and external economies of scale which protect those locations obtaining an initial advantage. This appears to be especially true for the financial sector. According to Iain Begg: 'the benefits of completion of the internal market for financial services will accrue disproportionately to existing financial centres which tend to be in the more prosperous and rapidly growing regions of the European Community'.

Taking into account the effects of techno-industrial changes in conjunction with the SEM, Michel Quévit foresees a differential impact on the problem regions. While traditional industrial regions are vulnerable to the indirect effects of the SEM by virtue of their relatively low R&D capacities, 'these regions will be likely to position themselves more positively than the less-favoured regions towards the SEM insofar as they comprise industrial sectors where scale economies can still be achieved'. Objective 1 regions, by contrast, have far fewer opportunities for generating technical economies of scale in industry owing, *inter alia*, to the small size of many SMEs, structural weaknesses in the service sector and peripherality.

Following a faltering of the drive towards European integration, leading EU politicians are again pressing the case for economic and monetary union before the end of the century. Although the degree and direction of future economic and monetary union in the EU is still unclear, there has been some speculation (though little thorough research) as to the effect of EMU on regional disparities, mostly concerning the macroeconomic costs and benefits.

It is arguable that the economic stringency required by the EMU convergence conditions will promote effective structural change in less developed countries such as Portugal; notably greater labour market efficiency and improved productivity (Torres 1992). However, the benefits from EMU may materialise only in the long term and will be spread widely. During the transitional phase, the deflationary costs of reducing inflation (e.g. curbing public expenditure) may slow down economic growth, enhancing regional disparities in regions which already have below-average GDP levels. These costs are likely to be most evident in the form of unemployment, borne by specific individuals and groups (and incurred almost immediately), especially those in high-inflation and low productivity countries and regions which are dependent on international cost competitiveness (Boltho 1992, O'Donnell and Van den Bempt 1991, Begg and Mayes 1991).

The European Commission's view is that the regional effects of economic and monetary integration are highly uncertain: simple predictions, for example, that the core will benefit at the expense of the periphery, are inhibited by conflicting paradigms and require the adoption of 'a rather agnostic view' (Delors 1989). In a major review of economic theory and empirical evidence undertaken in 1990, the Commission concluded that the consequences of EMU for the less-favoured regions of the Community were ambiguous, the region-specific effects depending on 'initial conditions' and the implementation of appropriate policies (CEC 1990). However, Andrew Leyshon and Nigel Thrift find that the prospect of EMU raises serious questions for regional development: 'EMU as currently envisaged may well introduce a new destabilising dynamic into development processes within the EC. As German unification has plainly illustrated, monetary integration in itself is no panacea for uneven development'. Furthermore, 'the creation of an independent central bank the remit of which will be to achieve price stability across Europe begs the question as to how the EC will tackle such problems of uneven development'.

Regional Policy Responses: The Structural Funds

The EU's main response to regional disparities is through the Structural Funds – the ERDF, ESF and EAGGF Guidance Section – which have been transformed radically over the past decade. The reforms began in 1988 with a view to achieving greater economic impact, to use a multi-annual approach for expenditure planning with greater stability and predicability, and to implement the Funds in partnership with all relevant parties, especially regional authorities. The 1988 reform involved a shift from individual project support to programme financing, a commitment to greater coordination between the three Structural Funds, and an increased budget (annual expenditure rising from 6.3 billion ecu in 1987 to 14.1 billion ecu by 1993) concentrated on the poorest, most structurally backward regions. Five objectives were specified, three of which were spatially targeted – on lagging regions (Objective 1), declining industrial regions (Objective 2) and rural areas (Objective 5b).

The Maastricht Treaty on European Union upgraded significantly the importance of EC regional policy. Article 2 of the Treaty established economic and social cohesion as one of the 'pillars of the Community structure' and agreed to set up an additional new Cohesion Fund for the poorer Member States. Subsequently a Structural Funds budget rising to 27.4 billion ecu by 1999 was agreed (with an additional 15.15 billion ecu for the Cohesion Fund over 1993–1999). Regulations passed in 1993 introduced new financial measures to promote cohesion, new assisted areas were designated, and a new spatially-targeted Objective 6 was created for the sparsely populated regions of the Nordic countries.

In political terms, the reforms of the Structural Funds represented a necessary commitment to economic and social cohesion in the context of the accession of Spain and Portugal in 1986, the ratification of the Single European Act in 1987 and agreement on the Maastricht Treaty in 1991. The Funds also continue to serve as a means for ensuring a 'juste retour' for major contributors to the EU budget such as the UK. The haggling over the designation of Objective 1 regions in 1993, and over the designation criteria for Objective 2 and 5b, underscores how EU regional policy can be (ab)used for political purposes by the Member States.

In the context of widening regional disparities, the reforms recognised the need for more effective concentration on regions in greatest need. From an operational perspective, the reform of the Structural Funds in 1988 was a major improvement on the project-based approach that preceded it. Multi-annual planning and the focus on programmes provided greater coherence and integration to Community support.

The economic impact is more difficult to assess. Commission-sponsored research in the early 1990s attempted to quantify the effect of the Structural Funds on Objective 1 regions. It estimated that Structural Fund assistance may have increased the GDP of Objective 1 regions by between 1.5% and 3.5% over the period 1989–93. In these areas, EC grants account for shares of total investment ranging from 7.5% (Ireland) to 12% (Greece); a combination of EC and national expenditure yields Structural Fund programme participation rates of almost 25% of total investment in Greece and Portugal. Moreover, the Structural Funds were associated with the creation of 500,000 new jobs, mostly in Spain (120,000), Italy (85,000) and Portugal (70,000) (CEC 1992).

Apart from this quantitative research, much of the Commission's assessment of the impact of the Structural Funds is subjective. The Fifth Periodic Report is therefore cautious about the effect of EU regional policy on the problem regions: 'it is possible to conclude that the weaker regions have made some progress towards convergence in real terms with the rest of the Community. There are encouraging signs that this may have accelerated after the reform of the Structural Funds in 1989' (CEC 1994). In the context of a 'mixed picture' of regional performance, the progress of Objective 2 regions is considered to be particularly positive – over the 1989–93 period, the average rate of job creation was approximately double the Community average – even allowing for a falling labour supply in these areas.

This lack of certainty about the impact of the Funds underlines the importance of improving evaluation if the contribution of EU regional policy is to be fully understood – an issue emphasised in the 1993 Regulations. There are, though, major conceptual and methodological obstacles to better evaluation, including insufficiently precise objectives, inadequate data and difficulties in establishing causality and the counterfactual. The very breadth of EU regional policy, covering a growing mix of measures (productive investment, infrastructure, research and technology activities, education, healthcare, tourism and environmental improvement), militates strongly against detailed evaluation.

A related issue concerns the additionality of EC spending in the Member States. Under the 1988 reform, Member States were legally required to ensure that increases in Fund expenditure would be matched by an equivalent increase in domestic structural aid spending, that is EC expenditure should encourage spending *additional* to what would have taken place otherwise. Much of the debate in recent years has focused critically on the United Kingdom's differences with the Commission in the interpretation of additionality – illustrated by the contribution of Stephen Fothergill. More significant, however, is the conclusion of Richard Barnett and Vidya Borooah that the Commission's new procedures for assessing whether expenditure is additional will not actually provide a satisfactory test of additionality. Apart from the considerable problems of obtaining data in the required form, it is argued that the additionality test only relates to the *increase* in spending since 1988, not the original expenditure, and the procedures do not allow for national policy trends in the absence of EC spending.

Apart from such technical issues, there are important questions to be resolved about the objectives of EU regional policy. The overriding aim of 'economic and social cohesion' lacks a clear definition and rationale, and may be in significant contradiction to the EU's objective of macroeconomic convergence in preparation for economic and monetary union. The pursuit of Community RTD or industrial policies to improve international competitiveness and technological advancement may also affect negatively EU regional policy goals. By assisting enterprises based primarily in the core regions of the Community, EC RTD and industrial policies may be reinforcing the regional disparities that EC regional policy is attempting to counteract.

Further, is it valid to expect a significant impact from the Structural Funds? EU regional policy is thinly spread (in parts) across almost 52% of the Community's population. As earlier contributors have noted, the Structural Funds, secondary to agricultural expenditure in the EC budget, represent a very small share of Community GDP and are minor relative to the size of domestic public expenditure. Thus, the level of EC regional aid can surely only be considered ameliorative rather than transformational.

Looking to the future, the 1996 Intergovernmental Conference will, *inter alia*, have to address the future of EU regional policy after 1999. One of the main internal pressures for change may come from several northern EU Member States keen on a 'repatriation' of responsibility for regional policy under the principle of subsidiarity. Some national governments believe that EU regional policy – with its matrix of areas, objectives and Funds – is excessively complex, administratively bureaucratic and implemented with insufficient flexibility to take account of specific national and regional conditions. Such criticisms were particularly evident during the 1989–93 programming period, compounded by hostility to many of the Community Initiatives. To some extent the criticisms were allayed by the 1993 revisions, but the degree of Commission intervention in the recent preparation of regional development programmes for the 1994–99 period – leading in some cases to unwanted measures and administrative arrangements – has engendered renewed frustration on the part of some Member States (Bachtler 1995 forthcoming). These criticisms are compounded by the perceived unilateralism of the European Commission in restricting the regional aid provided by national governments under the EC competition policy powers exercised by DGIV (Bachtler and Michie 1993, Wishlade 1993).

The external pressure on EU regional policy is future enlargement. Under the 1995 enlargement, Austria caused few problems given its limited regional problems; indeed it had difficulty meeting some qualifying criteria for Structural Fund aid. The Nordic regional problems of peripherality and sparsely populated regions required adaptation of both Structural Fund criteria (in the form of a new Objective 6) and the EU competition policy methodology for approving domestic assisted area maps. However, all three accessants could broadly be accommodated within the existing regional policy structure of the EU.

In extending the EU further east and south-east, the EU faces two challenges: creating workable institutional mechanisms and meeting the costs of enlargement. In an EU encompassing at least some of the Central and Eastern European countries, there is the question of how the major regional problems of the EU's eastern neighbours will be financed. Unless there is a massive increase in the Structural Funds' budget, this would mean a reorientation of EU regional policy to the detriment of current recipient areas, particularly those in Objective 2 and 5b regions.

In the light of these internal and external pressures, it is not implausible to foresee a situation where EU regional development programmes are restricted to the southern and eastern parts of an enlarged EU, perhaps on the basis of transfers to Member States rather than regions, an approach similar to the present Cohesion Fund. For northern Member States, EU involvement in regional development might be constrained to areas with extreme socioeconomic deprivation, to operations that are truly transnational, or to promoting experimental, innovative and best practice projects.

Regional Policy Responses: The Member States

The central feature of regional policy at the Member State level over the past decade has been the reformulation of policy objectives in the face of a significantly changed policy environment. Most EU countries have seen a shift – across the policy spectrum – towards more market-based solutions. This has led to a generally reduced emphasis on state control and intervention: less public sector ownership, fewer subsidies and deregulation. Increasingly, government support has been focused more on the business environment than on individual firms. The pressure to reduce the growth of public expenditure has eliminated many programmes and required more cost-effectiveness in others.

Regional development policies have not been immune from these trends. The challenge for regional policymakers has been to continue providing an effective response to regional restructuring in the face of competitive pressures while adapting to significantly reduced resources and greater emphasis on value-for-money in regional expenditure. During the 1980s regional policies became less orientated towards redistributing income and employment in favour of greater emphasis on encouraging structural change in less favoured regions to promote diversification and to enhance their contribution to national economic growth. A broader range of policy targets is evident: in addition to capital investment and job creation, regional policies increasingly address issues such as training, technology transfer, innovation and business services.

The mainstay of the regional policies of the EU Member States has long been the financial incentive, mainly in the form of a grant for capital investment or employment. Although they remain a favoured measure for promoting both inward investment and indigenous development in the problem regions (Yuill *et al.* 1994), the long-term trend seems likely to encompass a declining role for regional incentives. This is reflected in more focused aid areas, tighter eligibility conditions, greater administrative discretion and selectivity in expenditure. Over the past 10 years, the coverage of assisted areas has fallen by 20–25%, and the maximum rates of award have been reduced in almost all the northern Community countries (Bachtler 1992a, Bachtler and Michie 1993).

The next decade may see a further erosion of regional incentive support, if the European Commission – through its Competition Policy Directorate DGIV – continues to push the coverage of designated assisted areas downwards and to cut award rates. The last remaining large-scale automatic subsidies, such as those in Italy, may well disappear. Increasingly, the remaining incentives are likely to target small and medium-sized enterprises, and assistance for capital investment may be restricted in favour of greater support for human capital (Bachtler 1992a).

These trends focus attention on the approach to promoting inward investment. For many EU countries, one of the main arguments for retaining a major regional grant (such as Regional Selective Assistance in the UK) is the competition for foreign investment projects. Incentives may not be as important as market or skill factors, but they may still be a significant location determinant, especially at the margin. If DGIV is serious about eliminating large-scale subsidies, sooner or later it will have to address the issue of competitive outbidding for inward investment projects between countries and regions, with some form of regulation of the subsidy bidding process.

In terms of the overall strategy towards regional problems, the broader approach towards regional development exemplifies the maxim that regional development involves more than just regional policy. On the one hand, there have been several attempts, as in Germany, to interconnect regional policy with related policy areas – transport, education, labour market and RTD policies. On the other hand, a series of 'spatial' initiatives have emerged in several countries that (initially) were only marginally connected to 'regional' policy, such as the urban policy measures in the United Kingdom.

The broadening of regional development strategies is particularly evident at the regional level. The devolution and decentralisation of regional development responsibility to regional and local levels has been a feature of most West European countries over the past decade, often involving a wider range of economic actors in both public and private sectors. The trend emphasises the importance of regional and local initiatives being undertaken within an economic development framework that maximises the possibility for coordination and cooperation by different levels of government and different organisations. Prime examples of this approach are the future-oriented initiatives in support of structural change in North Rhine Westphalia, undertaken since the late 1980s, and the 'Contrats du Plan' system of state–region planning contracts in France. Both initiatives placed great emphasis on incorporating measures to promote education, training, research and technical development in regional development strategies.

Among other issues on the policy agenda, environmental factors are likely to be given a higher profile in regional policy. Regional development strategies are becoming more sensitive to, and attempting to assign an economic cost to, environmental protection and improvement – although with limited success to date (Clement, Bachtler, Karl and Downes 1994).

The social dimension of regional development is also significant. Mike Danson notes how disadvantaged communities in traditional industrial regions, already marginalised by past restructuring, face a 'new poverty' caused by 'low pay, secondary employment and self-perpetuating deprivation.' With the growing casualisation and peripheralisation of parts of the labour force as a result of flexible forms of production, significant social groups could be excluded from employment for substantial periods. Consequently, although there may be a potential conflict between social and regional objectives, in lagging regions in particular, regional policy cannot be seen as separate from social policy. There is also a need to view the promotion of human resources as more than vocational training and flexible attitudes to employment; it encompasses socio-cultural issues such as quality of life and amenity.

Last, approaches to regional policy over the coming decade are likely to contain more of an inter-regional and international dimension. Regional policy has been discussed extensively in terms of its role in improving regional competitiveness and assisting adaptation to the effect of 1992 on competition between the regions. However, the SEM also enhances the potential for greater *cooperation* between regions and enterprises. Inter-regional cooperation already extends far beyond the early 'twinning' arrangements to include trade and investment links, technology transfer, the promotion of joint ventures and the interchange of policy experiences. Indeed, strategic alliances and joint ventures between enterprises have become popular routes for market entry or expansion, developing new products or acquiring new technology. There does, though, appear to be a fundamental disconnection between inter-regional and inter-enterprise linkages; the strategic framework established by regional authorities is frequently unsuited or irrelevant to the operational needs of enterprises seeking partners or developing alliances (Raines et al. 1995).

Regional Policies in Central and Eastern Europe

In terms of regional disparities, there are enormous differences in socioeconomic development across the Central and East European (CEE) countries. All regions have been affected by the process of economic transformation: privatisation, the progressive reorientation of production and trade, massive falls in output, price liberalisation, high inflation rates and rising unemployment.

The more highly urbanised regions with a diversified industrial structure and well-developed infrastructure appear to have been less vulnerable. The recognised 'leaders' of economic transformation have been the capitals and major, diversified cities (Warsaw, Poznan, Krakow, Prague, Bratislava, Kosice, Budapest, Veszprem, etc.) with higher levels of new firm formation and foreign investment. Also, the western parts of individual countries and the CEE region as a whole have better development prospects, with higher growth rates and lower unemployment. Following liberalisation, regions close to the border with Western Europe have been able to reverse some former problems such as out-migration and inadequate infrastructure (Gorzelak et al. 1994, Bachtler and Downes 1993, Gorzelak and Kuklinski 1993, Bachtler 1992b).

The CEE countries face an enormous range of regional development problems and policy challenges. They include national, regional and local infrastructure provision, the management of privatisation, industrial conversion and diversification, the creation of a producer services sector, measures to contain the growth of unemployment, combating severe environmental degradation and reducing tension among territorial minorities.

In the past, regional development in Central and Eastern Europe was weak, equivalent to centrally determined regional planning and the regional dimensions of national, sectoral plans (Gorzelak 1993). In developing regional policies in Eastern Europe, there are several important obstacles to be overcome. As several contributors, such as Peter de Souza and Gyula Horváth, emphasise, free-market ideologies have been the guiding light for much of the early reform period, and there is the danger that any government intervention may be viewed unfavourably. For some countries, the regional dimension has been considered unnecessary or secondary during the early stages in the transformation process when priority needed to be given to national reform policies. Regional policy was also neglected because of the need to reform territorial structures and create new regional units, an expectation of significant changes in regional disparities and the emergence of new regional problems, inadequacies of statistical data at the regional level, lack of funds, and lack of knowledge of regional policy under market systems.

Currently, many of these factors continue to apply in the CEE countries. Although there is growing interest and awareness of regional policy, fostered by the EU (under programmes such as PHARE) and OECD, there have been few practical measures beyond the development of concepts and plans and the designation of various categories of problem regions.

The main 'regional' development measures are restricted to the allocation of local/regional authority grants from central government, for example the Fund for Regional Development in Hungary targeted on the north-eastern counties. In Poland, 16 development agencies have been established throughout the country by regional and local authorities, and a range of special employment or environmental measures (tax and depreciation allowances, infrastructure grants) are being applied in 'crisis' regions, although under the headings of employment or environmental policy rather than regional policy (Bachtler and Downes 1994).

Even if regional policies are initiated, there is little experience with market-based regional development strategies in Eastern Europe. By contrast, Western European countries have considerable experience and expertise in this field; this knowledge would be of great value for policymakers in Eastern Europe as they begin to address regional disparities. The EU as a whole can also provide guidance on implementing local and regional economic development strategies. Finally, professional and academic organisations have a role to play in developing structures, networks and for a to promote the continued transfer and exchange of information and ideas between the EU and Central and Eastern Europe.

References

Bachtler, J (1992a) 'The reshaping of regional policy in the European Community.' In A. Kuklinksi and G. Gorzelak (eds) *Dilemmas of Regional Policies in Eastern and Central Europe.* Warsaw: University of Warsaw.

Bachtler, J. (ed) (1992b) *Socio-Economic Situation and Development of the Regions in the Neighbouring Countries of the Community in Central and Eastern Europe.* Regional Development Studies 2. Brussels: Commission of the European Communities DGXVI.

Bachtler, J. (1995, forthcoming) 'Regional Development Planning in Objective 1 Regions.' *European Urban and Regional Studies.*

Bachtler, J. and Downes, R. (1993) *Regional Socio-Economic Development in Poland, Hungary, the Czech Republic and Slovakia.* Report to the Commission of the European Communities (DGXVI).

Bachtler, J. and Downes, R. (1994) *Developing a Regional Policy in Eastern Europe: The Case of Hungary.* Paper to the 5th British-Russian (Soviet) Seminar Economic Crisis and Regional Regeneration, 17–20 May 1994, Lucas House Conference Centre, University of Birmingham.

Bachtler, J. and Michie, R. (1993) 'The Restructuring of Regional Policy in the European Community.' *Regional Studies 27,* 8, 719–725.

Begg, I. and Mayes, D, (1991) *A New Strategy for Social and Economic Cohesion After 1992.* Research and Documentation Papers. Regional Policy and Transport Series, 19. Brussels: European Parliament.

Boltho, A. (1992) 'On Regional Differentials Between the United States and the EEC.' Paper to Centre for European Policy Studies Conference on Economic and Social Cohesion, Brussels, 22–23 June 1992.

CEC (1990) *One Market, One Money, European Economy.* Commission of the European Communities, October 1990.

CEC (1992) *Community Structural Policies – Assessment and Outlook.* COM (92) 84 Final, 18 March 1992, Commission of the European Communities, Brussels.

CEC (1994) *Competitiveness and Cohesion: Trends in the Regions. Fifth Periodic Report on the Social and Economic Situation and Development of the Regions in the Community.* Brussels: Commission of the European Communities.

Clement, K., Bachtler, J., Karl, K. and Downes, R. (1994) *Integration or Co-ordination? Regional Policy an Environmental Sensitivity in Germany and the United Kingdom.* Report to DATAR, Paris.

Delors, J. (1989) *Regional Implications of Economic and Monetary Integration.* Collection of Papers submitted to the Committee for the Study of Economic and Monetary Union, Brussels.

Gorzelak, G. (1993) 'Dilemmas of Polish regional policies during transition.' In G. Gorzelak and A. Kuklinski (eds) (1993) *Dilemmas of Regional Policies in Eastern and Central Europe*, European Institute for Regional and Local Development Series, 8, University of Warsaw.

Gorzelak, G. *et al.* (1994) *Eastern and Central Europe 2000.* Warsaw: Commission of the European Union, Institute for Human Sciences and European Institute for Regional and Local Development.

Gorzelak, G. and Kuklinski, A. (eds) (1993) *Dilemmas of Regional Policies in Eastern and Central Europe.* Warsaw: European Institute for Regional and Local Development. University of Warsaw.

Mjøset, L. (1992) *The Irish Economy in a Comparative Institutional Perspective.* National Economic and Social Council, 93, Dublin.

Neven, D. (1990) 'EEC integration towards 1992: some distributional aspects.' *Economic Policy 10,* 13–46.

O'Donnell, R. and Van Den Bempt, P. (1991) *Methods for Achieving Greater Economoc and Social Cohesion in the EC.* Report to DGXXII by the Trans-European Policy Studies Association, Dublin.

Raines, P., Bachtler, J. and McBride, M. (1994) *Interim Cooperation in Europe: A Scottish Perspective.* ESU Research Paper No 36. The Scottish Office Industry Department. Glasgow: HMSO. (94 120 124) 12/94.

Torres, J. (1992) *The Issue of Convergence and Portugal's ERM Membership.* Paper to Centre for European Policy Studies Conference on Economic and Social Cohesion, Brussels, 22–23 June 1992.

Wishlade, F. (1993) 'Competition Policy, Cohesion and Co-ordination of Regional Aids in the European Community.' *European Competition Law Review 14,* 4, 143–150.

Yuill, D., Allen, K., Bachtler, J., Clement, K. and Wishlade, F. (1994) *European Regional Incentives.* 14th Edition. London: Bowker-Saur.

List of Contributors

Louis Albrechts, Professor of Planning, Katholieke Universiteit Leuven.

John Bachtler, Deputy Director, European Planning Research Centre, University of Strathclyde.

Richard R. Barnett, Dean, Faculty of Business and Management, University of Ulster.

Iain Begg, Professor of Economics, South Bank University.

Vidya Borooah, Research Officer, University of Ulster.

Mike Danson, Senior Lecturer, University of Paisley.

Oksana Dmitrieva, Head of Research Laboratory, St Petersburg University.

Stephen Fothergill, Visiting Professor, Sheffield Hallam University.

John Greer, Senior Lecturer, Queen's University, Belfast.

Ronnie Hall, DG XVI, European Commission.

Sally Hardy, Director, Regional Studies Association.

Mark Hart, Senior Lecturer, University of Ulster.

Trevor Hart, CUDEM, Leeds Metropolitan University.

Gyula Horváth, Director, Transdanubian Research Institute, Hungarian Academy of Sciences.

Anastasios Katos, Professor of Informatics, University of Macedonia.

Attila Korompai, Lecturer, Budapest University of Economic Sciences.

Andrew Leyshon, Lecturer, University of Bristol.

R. Ross MacKay, Director, Institute of Economic Research, University College of North Wales.

Michael Murray, Lecturer, University of Ulster.

David Newlands, Senior Lecturer, University of Aberdeen.

Christos Nikas, Lecturer, University of York.

Gennady I. Ozornoy, Department of Geography, Carleton University.

Michel Quévit, RIDER, Université Catholique de Louvain.

Peter Roberts, Professor of Planning, University of Dundee.

Peter de Souza, School of Economics and Commercial Law, University of Gothenburg.

Stephen Syrett, Centre for Enterprise and Economic Development Research, University of Middlesex.

Nigel Thrift, Professor of Geography, University of Bristol.

Lefteris Tsoulouvis, Senior Lecturer, University of Thessaloniki.

James A. Walsh, Senior Lecturer, St Patrick's College, Maynooth.

Mik van der Wee, DG XVI, European Commission.

Subject Index

References in italic indicate figures or tables.

Author Index